MILLER
ANALOGIES TEST®

Test: Miller Analogies Test

Date: Tuesday, April 04, 2006

Examinee Name: Jeanna C Caputo

SSN/ID: 258-49-8386

Date of Birth: 6/17/1984

CTC ID: 08004017

Score:
Your preliminary scaled score is 403.

This is your preliminary scaled score. MAT scaled scores are based on the number of test items answered correctly and range from 200-600 with an average of 400. You will find more information about the meaning of this score in the MAT Candidate Information Booklet.

The score displayed above is not an official score. Your official scaled scores and percentile ranks will be mailed to you and the schools you have specified, pending verification that no irregularities have occurred that could have affected your performance.

Note: Harcourt Assessment adheres to test administration and security standards that require the review of all Miller Analogies Test (MAT) scores and administrative conditions. Harcourt Assessment reserves the right to cancel any score believed to be obtained in a questionable manner. In the event that a score is cancelled, the examinee will be notified in writing and given the opportunity to provide additional information about the situation. The examinee will also be given the option to either retest to verify the score at no additional charge or to cancel the score. Harcourt Assessment will make no reimbursements for any expenses incurred by an examinee whose score is canceled. All score cancellations are held in strict confidence, with the reason for the cancellation disclosed only to the examinee. Possible reasons for a score cancellation include the following:

1. The examinee did not submit the most recent Retest Admission Ticket to the Controlled Testing Center where the MAT was taken.
2. The examinee took the same form of the MAT more than once within a 12-month period.
3. The score seems questionable when compared to MAT scores obtained previously by the examinee.
4. An administrative irregularity occurred at the Controlled Testing Center where the MAT was taken.

🖨 Print Report   ✖ Close

W9-AZY-690

Date: Tue, 14 Mar 2006 16:51:00 -0600
From: RegisterBlast@PrepBlast.com
To: caput001@bama.ua.edu
Subject: PrepBlast Exam Registraion

2 unnamed text/html 1.96 KB

Dear Jeanna,

Thank you for registering for your exam with us today. We wish you the best success!

Best regards,
The Team at PrepBlast

INVOICE:
PrepBlast
PO Box 158517
Nashville, TN 37215
United States
Email: RegisterBlast@PrepBlast.com

Date: 3/14/2006 Time: 4:51:00 PM   Order Number: 14139
Terms: Visa   Contact: Jeanna Caputo

Address:
Jeanna Caputo
PO Box 865519
Tuscaloosa, AL 35486

Phone: (205)310-3452
caput001@bama.ua.edu

Exam Details:
Exam: MAT
Test Date: 4/4/2006 3:00:00 PM
Testing Center: The University of Alabama
ID Number: 14863
Test Location: 205 Student Services Center (A valid government-issued ID is required.)
Location:

INVOICE DETAILS:

Exam Registration	Price
Chauncey Exam Fee	$0
The University of Alabama Administration Fee	$73
TOTAL:	$73

Thank you! Please return when you need to register for another exam.
We appreciate your business.

If you have any questions about your order, please contact PrepBlast
by clicking on the link below.

RegisterBlast@PrepBlast.com

Print this invoice for your records.

McGraw-Hill's

MAT

MILLER ANALOGIES TEST

Kathy A. Zahler

McGraw-Hill
New York Chicago San Francisco
Lisbon London Madrid Mexico City
Milan New Delhi San Juan
Seoul Singapore Sydney Toronto

ISBN 0-07-145223-0

McGraw-Hill books are available at special quantity discounts to use as premiums and sales promotions, or for use in corporate training programs. For more information, please write to the Director of Special Sales, Professional Publishing, McGraw-Hill, Two Penn Plaza, New York, NY 10121-2298. Or contact your local bookstore.

 This book is printed on recycled, acid-free paper containing a minimum of 50% recycled, de-inked fiber.

Finally, for Paul.

CONTENTS

Part I

Introduction to the Miller Analogies Test

All about the Miller Analogies Test

MAT VS. GRE

Who takes the Miller Analogies Test?

The Miller Analogies Test (MAT) is used for admission to certain graduate programs. In some cases, it may be taken in lieu of the Graduate Record Exam (GRE). In other cases, it may be the only test required.

Unlike the GRE, which is a test of general knowledge, the MAT is an assessment of logical thinking skills. Instead of being broken into sections on writing, verbal skills, and quantitative skills, the MAT consists of a single 50-item section of 100 multiple-choice analogies.

How do I know whether I should take the Miller Analogies Test?

Review the admissions requirements of the graduate programs to which you wish to apply. Some will require the GRE instead of the MAT. Some will give you a choice. Some will require the MAT. If you have any questions, contact the appropriate admissions departments directly.

PLANNING TO TAKE THE MILLER ANALOGIES TEST

When is the Miller Analogies Test given, and how do I register for it?

The test is given at testing centers around the country, but the schedule and fees are set by the centers themselves. Your local college or university may well be the site of a testing center. To find the testing center nearest you, call (800) 622-3231 or go to www.milleranalogies.com and click on "MAT Controlled Testing Centers."

When should I take the Miller Analogies Test?

You have the option of designating recipients of your score report when you take the test. It takes about four weeks for scores to be sent out. Check with your chosen graduate programs to find out when they require score transcripts. Then work backward from that date to determine when you should take the test.

What do I need on the day of the test?

If you are taking a pencil-and-paper version of the test, you will need several sharpened number 2 pencils with erasers that work well and erase thoroughly. Mechanical pencils are not allowed.

If you are taking the MAT on computer, you will need two forms of identification, one of which contains a photograph. Passports, driver's licenses, or school IDs are fine; credit card photos or snapshots are not.

If you are retaking the MAT, you will need the Retest Admission Ticket you received the last time you took the test. You will also need one form of identification, preferably a photo ID.

You may not use any resources such as calculators or reference books. You may not carry a cell phone, pager, or other electronic device. You may not bring food or beverages into the testing site.

SCORING THE MILLER ANALOGIES TEST

How is the Miller Analogies Test scored?

You will receive a raw score, which is based on the total number of test items you answer correctly out of 100. This will be the first number on your score report.

You will also receive two percentile scores. The first is the percentile for your intended area of study. If, for example, you plan to enroll in an engineering program, you will see how you rank compared to other examinees enrolling in engineering programs. If you plan to attend graduate school in the social sciences, you will be compared to other students who plan to attend graduate school in the social sciences, and so on.

The second percentile score shows how you rank compared to the general population (all majors) of MAT examinees. These percentiles derive from normative data taken from the last few years of testing. It's worth remembering that your chosen graduate program may have very different conditions for admission than these percentiles suggest.

When will I receive my score?

You should receive your score within four weeks of taking the test. Your designated score recipients should receive it at about the same time.

How do I submit my score to graduate programs?

When you register to take the MAT, your fee includes free reporting of your scores to up to three universities or fellowship/scholarship programs you specify. To have additional transcripts sent, visit the MAT Web site: www.milleranalogies.com. You will need to pay an additional fee.

How to Use This Book

Because the Miller Analogies Test is different from any other test you are likely to take, preparing for it ahead of time is worth the effort. This book will help you:

- Familiarize yourself with the test format.

- Practice analogical thinking.

- Recognize the types of relationships tested on the MAT.

- Review some key concepts that often appear on the MAT.

- Practice your test-taking skills using sample MATs.

Here is a practical study program that will help you make the best use of this book. You may discover that you can change the steps around or move back and forth between two steps. Use whatever strategy makes the most sense for your needs.

STEP 1. LEARN HOW TO THINK ANALOGICALLY

Once you complete this chapter, turn to Part II. Read it carefully. It contains all the information you need to know to solve the kind of analogies used on the MAT. Once you see what kinds of relationships are tested and what kinds of concepts are included, you will have a better sense of what to expect, and you will be several steps ahead of any test-taker who has not read Part II.

STEP 2. LOCATE YOUR CULTURAL LITERACY GAPS

Why, you might ask, do I need to know any physics if I'm planning to major in English? Although the MAT purports to test only analogical thinking, it really requires a range of general background knowledge. The MAT does not focus on a particular subject area. You are expected to have a smattering of knowledge in many areas rather than specific expertise in one or two. The last section of Part II tells you about those content areas that show up again and again on the MAT. If you have gaps in your cultural literacy, this might be the time to bone up in those areas. At this point, you may skim the appendixes (Part IV) to review some areas where you have gaps, or you may proceed to step 3.

STEP 3. TAKE THE PRACTICE TESTS

There are 10 practice tests, and each one is designed to take 50 minutes, just as the real MAT does. Do not take more than one practice test a day. As you take each test, try to simulate actual test conditions. Sit in a quiet room, time yourself, and work through as much of the test as time allows. Stop when your 50 minutes are up. Take a break. Then check your answers against the explanatory answers that follow the test you took. Each answer is labeled with the type of relationship being tested. Watch for patterns. Do you, as an English major, do poorly on any question that involves a science concept? Do you do well on vocabulary questions involving synonyms and antonyms and terribly on questions about places, people, movements, or ideas? Do you ace all the Action/Object questions and fall short on the Classification questions?

Use the explanatory answers to figure out where you went wrong. Was it a failure of analogical thinking, or did you simply not recognize one or more elements of the analogy? Remember, this is a time for you to gather information on your abilities, not to worry about your score.

STEP 4. REVIEW AND IMPROVE

Each time you take a test, review the explanatory answers. Use the information you obtain to fill in your cultural literacy gaps. Use the appendixes (Part IV) to review concepts that were stumbling blocks. Use Part II to review analogical thinking. Take another test and see whether you do better. Look for patterns. Look for gaps. Continue to review, and you will continue to improve.

Strategies for Top Scores

As with any test, you can use certain strategies to improve your MAT score. The MAT is not an exam you can cram for; its lack of subject-matter focus makes cramming impossible. That being said, there are still several ways you can get a leg up on the competition.

STUDY STRATEGIES

- **Get to know the format of the exam.** The practice tests in this book will make solving analogies second nature by the time you arrive at your test site for the real thing.

- **Get to know the test directions.** Most high school students are familiar with the kind of analogy in which A is related to B, and C is similarly related to D. Understanding the way in which Miller Analogies differ from the standard high school analogy will help you face the test with confidence. Part II of this book reviews this difference in detail.

- **Get to know what topics are covered.** A few content areas turn up again and again in Miller Analogies. Studying molecular biology or Renaissance painting will not help you take the test, but reviewing generalities like the ones that appear in the appendixes (Part IV) of this book will move you toward success on the MAT. Here are the general content areas that are reviewed within the analogies on the MAT.

  - Vocabulary
  - Literature
  - Art
  - Music
  - Natural sciences
  - Social sciences
  - Mathematics and Numbers

- **Test and review.** If possible, give yourself time to take each of the practice tests in this book. Review the answers, look for patterns, and use the appendixes to fill in any gaps in your background knowledge.

TEST-TAKING STRATEGIES

- **Answer all the easy questions first; then tackle the harder ones.** You have only 50 minutes, so use your time wisely. If you are stumped completely, move on. If you have time at the end, go back and complete any questions you left blank.

- **Use the process of elimination.** Even if you have never seen two out of three words in the incomplete analogy in front of you, you will almost always be able to eliminate one or two of the answer choices. That changes your odds dramatically.

- **When in doubt, guess.** On the MAT, every question counts the same, and there are no points taken off for guessing. Use the process of elimination, but if you're baffled, go ahead and guess. You have a 25 percent chance of getting the answer right. If you leave the answer blank, your chance drops to zero.

- **Beware of answer choices that look reasonable but are not correct.** Because the choices on the MAT are multiple-choice, the test-makers have many chances to mislead you with tricky "distracters" (wrong answers). Focus, and remember your goal—to complete an analogy in a way that is logical and correct. There is more about this in Part II of this book.

TIPS FOR TEST DAY

- **Get a good night's sleep.** You need energy to face 100 analogies, and you won't have it if you're exhausted from worry or from excessive, unnecessary review. Remember, this is not a test for which you can cram, so last-minute hysteria will not improve your score. Arriving well rested and alert probably will.

- **Be careful as you indicate your answers.** If you take the pencil-and-paper MAT, your answer sheet will be machine-scored, so mark it carefully. Fill in answer ovals completely, erase thoroughly if necessary, and do not make any stray marks anywhere on the sheet. Be sure that the answer space you are marking matches the number of the question you are answering. If you skip a question, skip the corresponding space on the answer sheet. Use your finger to hold your place, if it helps. If you are taking the test on computer, the MAT allows you to move back and forth freely. Just take care not to skip any questions without going back to complete them later.

- **Watch the time.** Wear a watch and check yourself from time to time. Fifty minutes is not a long time. If you have timed yourself on the practice tests, you should be pretty good at estimating the amount of time you have left as you progress through the MAT.

- **Use any extra time to go back and fill in answers.** If you have skipped any questions, go back and complete them. Even if you need to guess, you're better off filling in the ovals than leaving them blank.

Part II

Introduction to Analogies

What Is an Analogy?

An **analogy** is a relationship between or among words or concepts. When you take a test of analogies, you are looking for parallel relationships among four words or phrases.

Analogies may be set up like mathematical ratios.

OSTRICH : BIRD :: BLUE WHALE : MAMMAL

You read the analogy above this way: "Ostrich is to bird as blue whale is to mammal." An ostrich is a bird, and a blue whale is a mammal. The relationships are parallel.

MILLER ANALOGIES

Solving any analogy requires understanding the relationship between pairs of words or phrases. Questions on the MAT may present that relationship in two different ways.

Combinations on the MAT

Most analogies you may have seen before have a simple correspondence:

A is to B as C is to D.

In other words, the first item in the analogy is related to the second item in the same way that the third item is related to the fourth item.

PANTHEON : ROME :: PARTHENON : ATHENS

In the analogy above, the Pantheon (A) is found in Rome (B). The Parthenon (C) is found in Athens (D). A is to B as C is to D.

The MAT mixes this up from time to time and presents analogies with a different combination:

A is to C as B is to D.

For example,

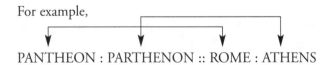

PANTHEON : PARTHENON :: ROME : ATHENS

In this analogy, you would most likely look first at A and B. Seeing no obvious relationship, other than the fact that both are buildings, you would then need to look at A and C: Pantheon is to Rome. That relationship is parallel to the one between B and D: Parthenon is to Athens.

Multiple-Choice on the MAT

On the MAT, you will not be given all four pieces of the analogy. You will be given three and asked to choose the fourth from a set of four options. MAT analogies look like this:

> UMBRELLA : PARASOL :: RAIN : (*a.* hail, *b.* sun, *c.* shade, *d.* snow)

To solve the analogy, you select the letter of the choice that fits. Here, since A and B have no clear relationship (except that they name objects that protect), you would look at A and C. An umbrella blocks the rain. Now look for a parallel relationship between B and D. A parasol blocks the sun, so the correct answer is (b).

The multiple-choice piece is not always in the D position. It may appear as A, B, or C as well. Try your hand at these simple analogies. The answers appear below.

Multiple-Choice in the A Position

> (*a.* well, *b.* lovely, *c.* sick, *d.* doctor) : ILL :: PRETTY : ATTRACTIVE

Multiple-Choice in the B Position

> ADMIRAL : (*a.* soldier, *b.* submarine, *c.* football, *d.* general) :: NAVY : ARMY

Multiple-Choice in the C Position

> HOUSE : WINDOW :: (*a.* ship, *b.* door, *c.* canoe, *d.* port) : PORTHOLE

Multiple-Choice in the D Position

> NEW YORK CITY : CHICAGO :: NEW YORK : (*a.* Albany, *b.* Miami, *c.* Michigan, *d.* Illinois)

EXPLANATORY ANSWERS

A position, (c): A is to B as C is to D. *Sick* and *ill* are synonyms. So are *pretty* and *attractive*.

B position, (d): A is to C as B is to D. An *admiral* holds a top position in the *navy*. A *general* holds a top position in the *army*.

C position, (a): A is to B as C is to D. *Windows* in a *house* are used the same way *portholes* are used in a *ship*.

D position, (d): A is to C as B is to D. *New York City* is the biggest city in *New York*. *Chicago* is the biggest city in *Illinois*.

Analogical Thinking

When you first see an analogy, sometimes you may immediately infer how the two pairs correspond. When the connection is not immediately obvious, you need to fill in the blanks between the words in each pair. Filling in the blanks accurately will help you solve the analogy. For example,

PARIS : FRANCE :: GENEVA : SWITZERLAND

You might think, "Paris is a city in France. Geneva is a city in Switzerland." Since A names a city in B and C names a city in D, the analogy works.

Now suppose the analogy looks like this:

PARIS : FRANCE :: (*a.* Geneva, *b.* Bern, *c.* Zurich, *d.* Gstaad) : SWITZERLAND

Suddenly, your "blank is a city in blank" correspondence does not work. All four of the answer choices name cities in Switzerland. You need to dig deeper to fill in the blanks. What special relationship does Paris have to France? Think: "Paris is the capital of France. Bern is the capital of Switzerland." Now you can choose (b) and have a valid analogy.

Try filling in the blanks between each pair of words below. In each case, you may find that there are several ways to do it, but one is the most likely and therefore the most logical.

CAR : AUDI

BANANA : PEEL

MERLIN : WIZARD

CANADA : NORTH AMERICA

REVEAL : CONCEAL

WHISKER : CAT

POTATO : EYE

MEASLES : RASH

FORTUNATE : LUCKY

KANSAS : TOPEKA

ARCH : FOOT

SALAMANDER : AMPHIBIAN

CZAR : RULER

BUCK : DOE

CITRUS : LEMON

PLUMBER : SNAKE

SALT : WHITE

EDISON : PHONOGRAPH

KILO- : THOUSAND

FOUGHT : FIGHT

STAY PARALLEL

The logic of an analogy has to do with its parallelism. You will often see answer choices on the MAT that are presented expressly to fool you. They may have a connection with one part of the analogy but not with the others. For the analogy to be valid, all four parts must connect.

Try this analogy:

ATTORNEY : CLIENT :: GUIDANCE COUNSELOR : (*a.* school, *b.* privilege, *c.* student, *d.* customer)

Here, the "distracters," or incorrect answer choices, are all designed to throw you off. A *guidance counselor* does work in a *school* (a). *Attorney-client privilege* is a matter of law (b). A *client* is synonymous with a *customer* (d).

To get the right answer, you need to recall the original connection. Fill in the blanks. Think: "An attorney gives advice to a client. A guidance counselor gives advice to a student." The only answer that maintains the logic of the analogy is (c).

MATCH PARTS OF SPEECH

The parallelism on the MAT is even more rigid than that. Part A will always be the same part of speech as B or C, or both. B will always be the same part of speech as A or D or both. C will always be the same part of speech as A or D or both. D will always be the same part of speech as B or C or both. Take these analogies:

FLY : SOAR :: CRASH : COLLIDE

FLY : SOAR :: CRASH : COLLISION

The word *crash* (C) may be either a verb or a noun. In the first analogy, D is *collide*, which is a verb like A *(fly)*, B *(soar)*, and C *(crash)*. In the second analogy, D is *collision*, which is a noun like C *(crash)*. Either analogy is valid, because A *(fly)* and B *(soar)* are synonyms, and so are C *(crash)* and D *(collide/collision)*.

What you would never see is this:

FLEW : SOARED :: CRASHED : COLLISION

Here, A *(flew)*, B *(soared)*, and C *(crashed)* are clearly verbs in the past tense, but D *(collision)* is a noun.

MAINTAIN ORDER

Remember that there are two possible relationships on MAT analogies.

A is to B as C is to D

A is to C as B is to D

Relationships between A and D or B and C are impossible on the MAT. You will never see:

LARK : FROG :: CROAK : SING

Not only that, but the MAT will never reverse a relationship. In other words, you will never see A is to B as D is to C or A is to C as D is to B. That doesn't mean that the test-maker won't throw in some distracters to fool you, as in this example:

TROUT : FISH :: DUCK : (*a.* mallard, *b.* swan, *c.* swim, *d.* bird)

If you weren't thinking, you might fill in the blanks this way: "A *trout* is a kind of *fish*. A *mallard* is a kind of *duck*. The answer is (a)." Wrong! A is to B as C is to D, not as D is to C. The right way to fill in the blanks is this: "A *trout* is a kind of *fish*. A *duck* is a kind of *bird*. The answer is (d)."

Types of Relationships on the MAT

There are as many possible relationships between words and concepts as there are words and concepts. However, the MAT tests only a select few.

SYNONYMS

If the correspondence is A is to B as C is to D, and A and B are synonyms, then C and D are synonyms. For example,

> RHYTHM : BEAT :: RHYME : VERSE

Rhythm means about the same thing as *beat*. *Rhyme* means about the same thing as *verse*.

If the correspondence is A is to C as B is to D, and A and C are synonyms, then B and D are synonyms. For example,

> STOUT : TALL :: FAT : LOFTY

Stout means about the same thing as *fat*. *Tall* means about the same thing as *lofty*.

Try these Synonym analogies. The answers appear at the end of this section.

SYNONYMS

1. CLUE : (*a.* suspect, *b.* hint, *c.* chimney, *d.* puzzle) :: FLUE : OUTLET

2. FIRST : ORIGINAL :: LAST : (*a.* ultimate, *b.* primary, *c.* next, *d.* tertiary)

3. (*a.* happy, *b.* sad, *c.* furious, *d.* kind) : SYMPATHETIC :: LIVID : CONSIDERATE

4. BROOK : POND :: (*a.* stream, *b.* lake, *c.* ocean, *d.* swimming) : POOL

5. (*a.* ancestor, *b.* child, *c.* descendant, *d.* gender) : FOREBEAR :: BABY : INFANT

ANTONYMS

If the correspondence is A is to B as C is to D, and A and B are antonyms, then C and D are antonyms. For example,

> HUNGRY : REPLETE :: SLEEPY : ALERT

Hungry means the opposite of *replete*. *Sleepy* means the opposite of *alert*.

If the correspondence is A is to C as B is to D, and A and C are antonyms, then B and D are antonyms. For example,

PLEASE : ASK :: OFFEND : REPLY

Please means the opposite of *offend. Ask* means the opposite of *reply.*

Try these Antonym analogies. The answers appear at the end of this section.

ANTONYMS

6. FEBRILE : COOL :: (*a.* heated, *b.* humid, *c.* chilly, *d.* stiff) : PARCHED

7. PEACEFUL : MINDFUL :: AGGRESSIVE : (*a.* loving, *b.* staunch, *c.* scatterbrained, *d.* clever)

8. JOCULAR : (*a.* morose, *b.* uncaring, *c.* jolly, *d.* laugh) :: FOND : INDIFFERENT

9. FORLORN : LOVELORN :: (*a.* sad, *b.* hated, *c.* aloof, *d.* jovial) : BELOVED

10. (*a.* cruelty, *b.* hallucination, *c.* treachery, *d.* truth) : REALITY :: DUPLICITY : HONESTY

DEGREE

Degree analogies are much like Synonym analogies. However, in a Degree analogy, one word in each pair is greater in some way than the other.

HUNGRY : RAVENOUS :: HAPPY : ECSTATIC

To be *ravenous* is to be very, very *hungry.* To be *ecstatic* is to be very, very *happy.*

Try these Degree analogies. The answers appear at the end of this section.

DEGREE

11. TRY : STRUGGLE :: SUCCEED : (*a.* fight, *b.* fail, *c.* thrive, *d.* manage)

12. INTERESTED : (*a.* interesting, *b.* insensible, *c.* drunk, *d.* rapt) :: TIPSY : SMASHED

13. CLEVER : INGENIOUS :: (*a.* brainy, *b.* irksome, *c.* terrible, *d.* furious) : INFURIATING

14. SMILE : FROWN :: (*a.* beam, *b.* grimace, *c.* funny, *d.* anger) : GLOWER

15. (*a.* admire, *b.* extol, *c.* fear, *d.* criticize) : CONDEMN :: PRAISE : EULOGIZE

AFFIX

An *affix* is a word part. The MAT tests prefixes, suffixes, and roots by expecting you to know what they mean.

UN- : NOT :: RE- : AGAIN

The prefix *un-*, as in *unhappy*, means "not." The prefix *re-*, as in *reheat*, means "again."

Try these Affix analogies. The answers appear at the end of this section.

AFFIX

16. PRO- : SUPPORTING :: A- : (*a.* after, *b.* under, *c.* without, *d.* having)

17. CARDIO : (*a.* toe, *b.* heart, *c.* hand, *d.* blood) :: DACTYL : FINGER

18. ANTI- : ANTE- :: (*a.* against, *b.* within, *c.* after, *d.* because) : BEFORE

19. -FUL : -IST :: (*a.* made from, *b.* full of, *c.* having no, *d.* up to) : ONE WHO

20. (*a.* macro-, *b.* acro-, *c.* iso-, *d.* hypo-) : LARGE SCALE :: MICRO- : SMALL SCALE

CLASSIFICATION

In this kind of analogy, one word in each pair is the category into which the other word falls. If A is to B as C is to D, and A is a category, then B is an example of something within that category, as here:

DOCTOR : SURGEON :: FISH : STURGEON

A *surgeon* is one kind of *doctor*. A *sturgeon* is one kind of *fish*.

This is a very common kind of analogy. What makes it tricky is that the relationship may appear in any of eight orders, as here:

DOCTOR : SURGEON :: FISH : STURGEON (A is to B as C is to D)

FISH : STURGEON :: DOCTOR : SURGEON (A is to B as C is to D)

SURGEON : DOCTOR :: STURGEON : FISH (A is to B as C is to D)

STURGEON : FISH :: SURGEON : DOCTOR (A is to B as C is to D)

SURGEON : STURGEON :: DOCTOR : FISH (A is to C as B is to D)

STURGEON : SURGEON :: FISH : DOCTOR (A is to C as B is to D)

DOCTOR : FISH :: SURGEON : STURGEON (A is to C as B is to D)

FISH : DOCTOR :: STURGEON : SURGEON (A is to C as B is to D)

You will need to use your best analogical thinking to determine which two parts of the analogy make up a pair and in what order they are related. Remember, the order in the second pair will be the same as the order in the first.

Try these Classification analogies. The answers appear at the end of this section.

CLASSIFICATION

21. ICE : (*a.* steam, *b.* frozen, *c.* water, *d.* liquid) :: SOLID : GAS

22. CAPITAL PUNISHMENT : CORPORAL PUNISHMENT :: HANGING : (*a.* crime, *b.* prison, *c.* spanking, *d.* court martial)

23. KID : GOAT :: LEVERET : (*a.* bear, *b.* shoat, *c.* hare, *d.* billy)

24. FROST: MILLER :: (*a.* artist, *b.* poet, *c.* novelist, *d.* drama) : PLAYWRIGHT

25. (*a.* comet, *b.* galaxy, *c.* asteroid, *d.* nova) : STAR :: JOVIAN : PLANET

PART/WHOLE

In a Part/Whole analogy, one word in each pair may be part of the other.

GENESIS : MATTHEW :: OLD TESTAMENT : NEW TESTAMENT

The book of *Genesis* is part of the *Old Testament.* The book of *Matthew* is part of the *New Testament.*

The trickier Part/Whole analogies are those in which each pair consists of parts of a whole, but the two wholes are unrelated.

WATTLE : BEAK :: SCALE : FIN

A *wattle* and a *beak* are parts of a turkey. A *scale* and a *fin* are parts of a fish.

Try these Part/Whole analogies. The answers appear at the end of this section.

PART/WHOLE

26. ERASER : GRAPHITE :: (*a.* ferrule, *b.* quill, *c.* painter, *d.* boar) : BRISTLE

27. SKATE : (*a.* ice, *b.* bearing, *c.* slide, *d.* fetter) :: BICYCLE : CHAIN

28. HORN : ANTLER :: RHINOCEROS : (*a.* elephant, *b.* unicorn, *c.* shed, *d.* elk)

29. STONE : WALL :: TILE : (*a.* window, *b.* brick, *c.* roof, *d.* grout)

30. (*a.* ball, *b.* hoop, *c.* web, *d.* tale) : NET :: CROSSBAR : UPRIGHTS

CONVERSION

Conversion is a weird one, but you are likely to run into a few of these on the MAT. Conversion analogies take many forms. A favorite is one in which one word in each pair is a name for another, especially a name no longer in use, or a name from a different culture.

> EROS : CUPID :: ODYSSEUS : ULYSSES

Cupid is the Roman name for the Greek god *Eros*. *Ulysses* is the Roman name for the Greek hero *Odysseus*.

In another kind of Conversion analogy, one word is a different grammatical form from another.

> BACTERIUM : BACTERIA :: VIRUS : VIRUSES

Bacterium is the singular form of *bacteria*. *Virus* is the singular form of *viruses*.

Rarely, one word is related to the other in a pair only by the letters in the word or by the fact that both words in the pair sound alike.

> FAR : OWL :: ARF : LOW

Both *far* and *arf* contain the same letters. Both *owl* and *low* contain the same letters.

Sometimes, one part of the analogy is a fraction of another. In these cases, the analogy is truly a mathematical ratio.

> 12 : 24 :: 36 : 72

Here, *12* is half of *24*, and *36* is half of *72*. You might also look at the relationship between A and C and B and D, in which case you could say that *12* is one-third of *36* and *24* is one-third of *72*.

Try these Conversion analogies. The answers appear at the end of this section.

CONVERSION

31. 121 : 11 :: (*a.* 124, *b.* 164, *c.* 166, *d.* 196) : 14

32. WAND : (*a.* sock, *b.* baton, *c.* wands, *d.* dawn) :: SHOE : HOSE

33. ABYSSINIA : ETHIOPIA :: SOUTH-WEST AFRICA : (*a.* South Africa, *b.* Namibia, *c.* Nigeria, *d.* Rwanda)

34. NICKEL : QUARTER :: DIME : (*a.* nickel, *b.* penny, *c.* half-dollar, *d.* dollar)

35. (*a.* indicate, *b.* index, *c.* indexes, *d.* indice) : INDICES :: CHAPTER : CHAPTERS

CHARACTERISTIC

Characteristic analogies are extremely common on the MAT. In this kind of analogy, one word in each pair may be a description of the other, as here:

MOURNER : SORROWFUL :: SCOUNDREL : WICKED

A *mourner* may be described as *sorrowful.* A *scoundrel* may be described as *wicked.*

One word in each pair may be either a feature of the other or a feature that the other lacks.

MOURNER : JOY :: SCOUNDREL : CONSCIENCE

A *mourner* lacks *joy.* A *scoundrel* lacks a *conscience.*

One word in each pair may name the location of the other.

MOURNER : CEMETERY :: SCOUNDREL : REFORMATORY

A *mourner* might be found in a *cemetery.* A *scoundrel* might be found in a *reformatory.*

Finally, one word in each pair might name the material from which the other is made. This kind of analogy is similar to a Part/Whole analogy.

BEET : BORSCHT :: TOMATO : SALSA

Borscht is a Russian soup made of *beets. Salsa* is a Spanish sauce usually made of *tomatoes.*

Try these Characteristic analogies. The answers appear at the end of this section.

CHARACTERISTIC

36. GOBI : KALAHARI :: MONGOLIA : (*a.* Botswana, *b.* Cambodia, *c.* Kenya, *d.* Argentina)

37. SEER : PRESCIENCE :: (*a.* phantom, *b.* ruler, *c.* author, *d.* grantee) : AUTHORITY

38. AMPHORA : (*a.* wine, *b.* grease, *c.* clay, *d.* mosaic) :: TEST TUBE : GLASS

39. VENEZUELA : CARACAS :: BRAZIL : (*a.* Amazon, *b.* La Paz, *c.* Brasilia, *d.* Buenos Aires)

40. (*a.* changeable, *b.* compliant, *c.* valuable, *d.* potable) : FLEXIBLE :: CHAMELEON : SNAKE

SEQUENCE

Some MAT analogies involve sequential arrangements of one sort or another. Some are clearly numerical, as shown here:

2 : 4 :: 1 : 3

The first pair is sequential even numbers. The second pair is sequential odd numbers.

Other sequences are verbal:

PREFIX : SUFFIX :: PRETEST : POSTTEST

A *prefix* comes before a base word, and a *suffix* follows it. A *pretest* comes before instruction, and a *posttest* follows it.

Other sequences are not so much sequential as familial. They may involve family or other human relationships:

FATHER : DAUGHTER :: ZEUS : APHRODITE

Zeus was the *father*, and *Aphrodite* was his *daughter*.

Try these Sequence analogies. The answers appear at the end of this section.

SEQUENCE

41. JIANG QING : MAO TSE-TUNG :: ALEXANDRA : (*a.* Rasputin, *b.* Nicholas II, *c.* Alexander the Great, *d.* Cleopatra)

42. (*a.* harbinger, *b.* antebellum, *c.* battle, *d.* posttraumatic) : POSTWAR :: SURGICAL PREP : RECOVERY

43. DUO : TRIO :: 2 : (*a.* 1, *b.* 3, *c.* 4, *d.* 6)

44. DIAMETER : RADIUS :: (*a.* 2, *b.* 5, *c.* 12, *d.* 20) : 10

45. IDEA : (*a.* brainstorm, *b.* formation, *c.* proposal, *d.* thought) :: APPROVAL : ENDORSEMENT

OBJECT/ACTION

This final type of relationship is quite common on the MAT. It involves an object or agent that causes or uses another. This relationship may involve invention or creation, as shown here:

PASCAL : ADDING MACHINE :: NEWTON : TELESCOPE

Blaise *Pascal* invented an *adding machine*. Isaac *Newton* invented a *telescope*.

The relationship may involve cause and effect.

VICTOR : DEFEAT :: INVADER : INCURSION

A *victor* causes the loser's *defeat*. An *invader* causes an *incursion*.

Sometimes, one word in the pair is a tool used by the other.

FENCER : FOIL :: SKIER : POLE

A *fencer* uses a *foil* to fence. A *skier* uses a *pole* to ski.

Often, one word has to do with the function of the other. This is often posed in the form of a measurement unit and whatever it measures.

CENTIMETER : CENTILITER :: LENGTH : CAPACITY

A *centimeter* measures *length*. A *centiliter* measures *capacity*.

Try these Object/Action analogies. The answers appear at the end of this section.

OBJECT/ACTION

46. TWAIN : JOYCE :: FINN : (*a.* Gatsby, *b.* Bennet, *c.* Flanders, *d.* Bloom)

47. WELDER : TORCH :: PAPERER : (*a.* glue, *b.* staples, *c.* wall, *d.* sponge)

48. DYNE : FORCE :: (*a.* amp, *b.* minute, *c.* sone, *d.* din) : LOUDNESS

49. DROUGHT : (*a.* water, *b.* hollow, *c.* implosion, *d.* famine) :: RAIN : EROSION

50. (*a.* Edison, *b.* Sikorsky, *c.* Lear, *d.* Apgar) : HELICOPTER :: DAIMLER : MOTORCYCLE

EXPLANATORY ANSWERS

SYNONYMS

1. CLUE : (*a.* suspect, ***b.* hint**, *c.* chimney, *d.* puzzle) :: FLUE : OUTLET
   (**b**) A *clue* is the same as a *hint*. A *flue* is an *outlet*, as in a chimney.

2. FIRST : ORIGINAL :: LAST : (***a.* ultimate**, *b.* primary, *c.* next, *d.* tertiary)
   (**a**) *First* and *original* are synonyms, as are *last* and *ultimate*.

3. (*a.* happy, *b.* sad, ***c.* furious**, *d.* kind) : SYMPATHETIC :: LIVID : CONSIDERATE
   (**c**) If you are *furious*, you are *livid*. If you are *sympathetic*, you are *considerate*. Notice the A is to C as B is to D correspondence here.

4. BROOK : POND :: (*a.* **stream**, *b.* lake, *c.* ocean, *d.* swimming) : POOL
   (a) A *brook* and a *stream* are similar, as are a *pond* and a *pool*. Again, the correspondence is A to C and B to D.

5. (*a.* **ancestor**, *b.* child, *c.* descendant, *d.* gender) : FOREBEAR :: BABY : INFANT
   (a) Your *ancestor* is your *forebear*. A *baby* is an *infant*.

ANTONYMS

6. FEBRILE : COOL :: (*a.* heated, *b.* **humid**, *c.* chilly, *d.* stiff) : PARCHED
   (b) If you are *febrile*, or feverish, you are not *cool*. A place that is *humid* is not *parched*.

7. PEACEFUL : MINDFUL :: AGGRESSIVE : (*a.* loving, *b.* staunch, *c.* **scatterbrained**,
   d. clever)
   (c) If you are *peaceful*, you are not *aggressive*. If you are *mindful*, you are not
   scatterbrained. Notice the A is to C as B is to D correspondence here.

8. JOCULAR : (*a.* **morose**, *b.* uncaring, *c.* jolly, *d.* laugh) :: FOND : INDIFFERENT
   (a) *Jocular* is the opposite of *morose*. *Fond* is the opposite of *indifferent*.

9. FORLORN : LOVELORN :: (*a.* sad, *b.* hated, *c.* aloof, *d.* **jovial**) : BELOVED
   (d) *Forlorn* is the opposite of *jovial*. *Lovelorn* is the opposite of *beloved*.
   This correspondence is A to C and B to D.

10. (*a.* cruelty, *b.* **hallucination**, *c.* treachery, *d.* truth) : REALITY :: DUPLICITY :
    HONESTY
    (b) A *hallucination* lacks *reality*. *Duplicity* lacks *honesty*.

DEGREE

11. TRY : STRUGGLE :: SUCCEED : (*a.* fight, *b.* fail, *c.* **thrive**, *d.* manage)
    (c) To *try* mightily is to *struggle*. To *succeed* greatly is to *thrive*.

12. INTERESTED : (*a.* interesting, *b.* insensible, *c.* drunk, *d.* **rapt**) :: TIPSY :
    SMASHED
    (d) If you are very *interested*, you are *rapt*. If you are very *tipsy*, you are *smashed*.

13. CLEVER : INGENIOUS :: (*a.* brainy, *b.* **irksome**, *c.* terrible, *d.* furious) :
    INFURIATING
    (b) If you are very *clever*, you are *ingenious*. If you are very *irksome*, you are *infuriating*.

14. SMILE : FROWN :: (*a.* **beam**, *b.* grimace, *c.* funny, *d.* anger) : GLOWER
    (a) To *smile* broadly is to *beam*. To *frown* hugely is to *glower*. Note the correspondence:
    A is to C as B is to D.

15. (*a.* admire, *b.* extol, *c.* fear, *d.* **criticize**) : CONDEMN :: PRAISE : EULOGIZE
    (d) To *criticize* greatly is to *condemn*. To *praise* greatly is to *eulogize*.

AFFIX

16. PRO- : SUPPORTING :: A- : (*a.* after, *b.* under, *c.* **without**, *d.* having)
    (**c**) The prefix *pro-*, as in *proponent*, means "supporting." The prefix *a-*, as in *asymptomatic*, means "without."

17. CARDIO : (*a.* toe, *b.* **heart**, *c.* hand, *d.* blood) :: DACTYL : FINGER
    (**b**) The root *cardio*, as in *cardiovascular*, means "*heart.*" The root *dactyl*, as in *pterodactyl*, means "*finger.*"

18. ANTI- : ANTE- :: (*a.* **against**, *b.* within, *c.* after, *d.* because) : BEFORE
    (**a**) The prefix *anti-*, as in *antiwar*, means "*against.*" The prefix *ante-*, as in *antebellum*, means "*before.*"

19. -FUL : -IST :: (*a.* made from, *b.* **full of**, *c.* having no, *d.* up to) : ONE WHO
    (**b**) The suffix *-ful*, as in *hopeful*, means "*full of.*" The suffix *-ist*, as in *stylist*, means "*one who.*"

20. (*a.* **macro-**, *b.* acro-, *c.* iso-, *d.* hypo-) : LARGE SCALE :: MICRO- : SMALL SCALE
    (**a**) *Macro-* means "*large scale,*" and *micro-* means "*small scale,*" as in *macroeconomics* vs. *microeconomics*.

CLASSIFICATION

21. ICE : (*a.* **steam**, *b.* frozen, *c.* water, *d.* liquid) :: SOLID : GAS
    (**a**) *Ice* is water as a *solid*. *Steam* is water as a *gas*. Notice the correspondence: A to C and B to D.

22. CAPITAL PUNISHMENT : CORPORAL PUNISHMENT :: HANGING :
    (*a.* crime, *b.* prison, *c.* **spanking**, *d.* court martial)
    (**c**) *Hanging* is one example of *capital punishment*. *Spanking* is one example of *corporal punishment*. Again, the correspondence is A to C and B to D.

23. KID : GOAT :: LEVERET : (*a.* bear, *b.* shoat, *c.* **hare**, *d.* billy)
    (**c**) A *kid* is a young *goat*. A *leveret* is a young *hare*.

24. FROST : MILLER :: (*a.* artist, *b.* **poet**, *c.* novelist, *d.* drama) : PLAYWRIGHT
    (**b**) Robert *Frost* was an American *poet*. Arthur *Miller* was an American *playwright*.

25. (*a.* comet, *b.* galaxy, *c.* asteroid, *d.* **nova**) : STAR :: JOVIAN : PLANET
    (**d**) *Nova* names one kind of *star*, and *Jovian* names one kind of *planet*.

PART/WHOLE

26. ERASER : GRAPHITE :: (*a.* **ferrule**, *b.* quill, *c.* painter, *d.* boar) : BRISTLE
    (**a**) An *eraser* and *graphite* are both parts of a pencil. A *ferrule* and *bristle* are both parts of a paintbrush.

27. SKATE : (*a.* ice, ***b.* bearing**, *c.* slide, *d.* fetter) :: BICYCLE : CHAIN
    (b) A *bearing* is part of a roller *skate*. A *chain* is part of a *bicycle*.

28. HORN : ANTLER :: RHINOCEROS : (*a.* elephant, *b.* unicorn, *c.* shed, ***d.* elk**)
    (d) A *rhinoceros* has a *horn*, but an *elk* has *antlers*. Here, the correspondence is A to C and B to D.

29. STONE : WALL :: TILE : (*a.* window, *b.* brick, ***c.* roof**, *d.* grout)
    (c) A *wall* may be made of *stones*. A *roof* may be made of *tiles*.

30. (*a.* ball, ***b.* hoop**, *c.* web, *d.* tale) : NET :: CROSSBAR : UPRIGHTS
    (b) A basketball hoop is made up of the *hoop* and the *net*. A football goalpost is made up of the *crossbar* and the *uprights*.

CONVERSION

31. 121 : 11 :: (*a.* 124, *b.* 164, *c.* 166, ***d.* 196**) : 14
    (d) *121* is *11* squared. *196* is *14* squared.

32. WAND : (*a.* sock, *b.* baton, *c.* wands, ***d.* dawn**) :: SHOE : HOSE
    (d) Mixing up letters makes *dawn* from *wand* and *hose* from *shoe*.

33. ABYSSINIA : ETHIOPIA :: SOUTH-WEST AFRICA : (*a.* South Africa, ***b.* Namibia**, *c.* Nigeria, *d.* Rwanda)
    (b) *Ethiopia* is the modern name for *Abyssinia*. *Namibia* is the modern name for *South-West Africa*.

34. NICKEL : QUARTER :: DIME : (*a.* nickel, *b.* penny, ***c.* half-dollar**, *d.* dollar)
    (c) Five *nickels* equal one *quarter*. Five *dimes* equal one *half-dollar*.

35. (*a.* indicate, ***b.* index**, *c.* indexes, *d.* indice) : INDICES :: CHAPTER : CHAPTERS
    (b) One plural of *index* is *indices* (the alternative is *indexes*). The plural of *chapter* is *chapters*.

CHARACTERISTIC

36. GOBI : KALAHARI :: MONGOLIA : (***a.* Botswana**, *b.* Cambodia, *c.* Kenya, *d.* Argentina)
    (a) The *Gobi* is a desert in *Mongolia*. The *Kalahari* is a desert in *Botswana*. Note the A to C and B to D correspondence here.

37. SEER : PRESCIENCE :: (*a.* phantom, ***b.* ruler**, *c.* author, *d.* grantee) : AUTHORITY
    (b) A key trait of a *seer* is *prescience*. A key trait of a *ruler* is *authority*.

38. AMPHORA : (*a.* wine, *b.* grease, ***c.* clay**, *d.* mosaic) :: TEST TUBE : GLASS
    (c) An *amphora* (wine jug) is made of *clay*. A *test tube* is made of *glass*.

39. VENEZUELA : CARACAS :: BRAZIL : (*a.* Amazon, *b.* La Paz, ***c.* Brasilia**, *d.* Buenos Aires)
    (c) *Venezuela's* capital is *Caracas*. *Brazil's* capital is *Brasilia*.

40. (*a.* **changeable**, *b.* compliant, *c.* valuable, *d.* potable) : FLEXIBLE :: CHAMELEON : SNAKE
    (a) A *chameleon* is typically *changeable*. A *snake* is typically *flexible*.

SEQUENCE

41. JIANG QING : MAO TSE-TUNG :: ALEXANDRA : (*a.* Rasputin, *b.* **Nicholas II**, *c.* Alexander the Great, *d.* Cleopatra)
    (b) *Jiang Qing* was the wife of *Mao Tse-Tung*. *Alexandra* was the wife of *Nicholas II*.

42. (*a.* harbinger, *b.* **antebellum**, *c.* battle, *d.* posttraumatic) : POSTWAR :: SURGICAL PREP : RECOVERY
    (b) *Antebellum* is before war, and *postwar* is after war. *Surgical prep* comes before an operation, and *recovery* comes after an operation.

43. DUO : TRIO :: 2 : (*a.* 1, *b.* **3**, *c.* 4, *d.* 6)
    (b) Adding one to a *duo* makes a *trio*. Adding 1 to *2* makes *3*.

44. DIAMETER : RADIUS :: (*a.* 2, *b.* 5, *c.* 12, *d.* **20**) : 10
    (d) A *diameter* is twice the length of a *radius*. *20* is twice *10*.

45. IDEA : (*a.* brainstorm, *b.* formation, *c.* **proposal**, *d.* thought) :: APPROVAL : ENDORSEMENT
    (c) An *idea* generally precedes a *proposal*, and *approval* generally precedes an *endorsement*.

OBJECT/ACTION

46. TWAIN : JOYCE :: FINN : (*a.* Gatsby, *b.* Bennet, *c.* Flanders, *d.* **Bloom**)
    (d) Author Mark *Twain* invented the character Huckleberry *Finn*. Author James *Joyce* invented the characters Leopold and Molly *Bloom*. The correspondence here is A to C and B to D.

47. WELDER : TORCH :: PAPERER : (*a.* **glue**, *b.* staples, *c.* wall, *d.* sponge)
    (a) A *welder* uses a *torch* to join things. A *paperer* uses *glue* to join things.

48. DYNE : FORCE :: (*a.* amp, *b.* minute, *c.* **sone**, *d.* din) : LOUDNESS
    (c) A *dyne* is a unit used to measure *force*. A *sone* is a unit used to measure *loudness*.

49. DROUGHT : (*a.* water, *b.* hollow, *c.* implosion, *d.* **famine**) :: RAIN : EROSION
    (d) A *drought* may cause *famine*. *Rain* may cause *erosion*.

50. (*a.* Edison, *b.* **Sikorsky**, *c.* Lear, *d.* Apgar) : HELICOPTER :: DAIMLER : MOTORCYCLE
    (b) Igor *Sikorsky* invented the *helicopter*. Gottlieb *Daimler* invented the gas-engined *motorcycle*.

Cultural Literacy and the MAT

Although the MAT purports to be a test of higher-level thinking skills, it is, at least secondarily, a test of your cultural literacy. Cultural literacy is the background knowledge everyone within a culture needs in order to read, write, and communicate efficiently and successfully. It's fair to say, for example, that a superficial awareness of Shakespeare's major works is part of our cultural literacy. Being able to name all the secondary characters in *Macbeth* is probably not. Identifying the parts of an atom is part of our cultural literacy; explaining the interactions of subatomic particles is not.

While testing your ability to complete an analogy, the MAT sneaks in content that assesses your general background knowledge in a number of areas. This section identifies those areas and shows how they might be tested.

VOCABULARY

Vocabulary plays a big role on the MAT. The biggest difficulty you are likely to have on the test as a whole will be your unfamiliarity with some of the words you see in the questions. Vocabulary may be tested in four ways: in Synonym analogies, in Antonym analogies, in Degree analogies, and in Affix analogies.

Try these Vocabulary analogies. Answers appear at the end of this section.

VOCABULARY

1. HELPLESS : DEPENDENT :: (*a.* guileless, *b.* genuine, *c.* stoic, *d.* independent) : INGENUOUS

2. (*a.* multi-, *b.* deca-, *c.* ovo-, *d.* peri-) : AROUND :: POLY- : MANY

3. PRANK : HOAX :: PEEK : (*a.* fool, *b.* hide, *c.* fraud, *d.* gaze)

4. (*a.* innocent, *b.* desolate, *c.* fecund, *d.* sullen) : BARREN :: GLUM : OPTIMISTIC

5. QUIESCENT : (*a.* nascent, *b.* intrusive, *c.* choleric, *d.* latent) :: DORMANT : INVASIVE

LITERATURE

You may be expected to know classics and their authors, whether from European, U.S., or (to a far lesser degree) South American or Asian cultures. You may be expected to match authors to genres and movements, to countries of origin, or to characters they have created. You may need to know the qualities or actions of some major characters, especially those from Greek mythology. Finally, you should be familiar with the books of the Bible, if only by name.

Literature questions usually fall into the categories of Classification, Characteristic, Conversion, Sequence, and Object/Action analogies.

Here are some Literature analogies from each of those categories. Answers appear at the end of this section.

LITERATURE

6. BAUDELAIRE : (*a.* Dante, *b.* Paz, *c.* Angelou, *d.* Breton) :: FRENCH : SPANISH

7. HERA : (*a.* Minerva, *b.* Venus, *c.* Juno, *d.* Vesta) :: ZEUS : JUPITER

8. DICKENS : PIP :: (*a.* Eliot, *b.* Thackeray, *c.* Austen, *d.* Hugo) : FANTINE

9. (*a.* neoclassicism, *b.* romanticism, *c.* fauvism, *d.* pre-Raphaelism) : NATURALISM :: BYRON : HARDY

10. TELEMACHUS : PENELOPE :: HECTOR : (*a.* Helen, *b.* Athena, *c.* Hecuba, *d.* Euterpe)

ART

You should know major artists and architects and their works, major museums of the world, basic media, and which artists typify which artistic movements.

Art questions are nearly always Classification, Characteristic, or Object/Action analogies.

Here are some typical Art analogies. Answers appear at the end of this section.

ART

11. EXPRESSIONISM : KANDINSKY :: SURREALISM : (*a.* Magritte, *b.* Delacroix, *c.* Pissaro, *d.* Matisse)

12. PITTI PALACE : (*a.* Rome, *b.* Madrid, *c.* Florence, *d.* Barcelona) :: NOTRE DAME : PARIS

13. (*a.* sculpture, *b.* film, *c.* portraiture, *d.* landscape) : PHOTOGRAPHY :: BERGMAN : STIEGLITZ

14. CLOISONNÉ : POINTILLISM :: (*a.* embroidery, *b.* mosaic, *c.* enamel, *d.* engraving) : PAINTING

15. (*a.* Hermitage, *b.* Odessa, *c.* Hirschhorn, *d.* Faaborg) : ST. PETERSBURG :: RIJKSMUSEUM : AMSTERDAM

MUSIC

You should know classics and their composers; famous singers, musicians, dancers, and choreographers; instruments of the orchestra; certain musical terms; and which composers typify which musical movements.

Like Art questions, Music questions are usually Classification, Characteristic, or Object/Action analogies. Certain terminology questions may fall under Synonym, Antonym, Degree, or even Sequence analogies.

Try your hand at these Music analogies. Answers appear at the end of this section.

MUSIC

16. STRINGS : PERCUSSION :: MANDOLIN : (*a.* guitar, *b.* xylophone, *c.* saxophone, *d.* bass)

17. TENOR : (*a.* baritone, *b.* Pavarotti, *c.* soprano, *d.* diva) :: CARUSO : CALLAS

18. (*a.* drum, *b.* pedal, *c.* allegro, *d.* forte) : PIANO :: LOUD : SOFT

19. *THE RITE OF SPRING* : (*a.* Tchaikovsky, *b.* Stravinsky, *c.* Rimsky-Korsakov, *d.* Rachmaninoff) :: *LES SYLPHIDES* : CHOPIN

20. RHYTHM : BEAT :: (*a.* cadence, *b.* intonation, *c.* tempo, *d.* pitch) : SPEED

NATURAL SCIENCES

The MAT barely scratches the surface of the sciences. The level of knowledge you are expected to have is no more than you might attain in a freshman biology, chemistry, or physics class. You might need to know basic taxonomy and some examples of animals that fit each category. You might want to review the elements and their properties. You might be asked about the location or function of familiar bones or other parts of the body. A question might ask you to classify rocks or to locate objects in the solar system. Often there is a question about animal groups or homes. Questions about scientists and their inventions or discoveries are common.

Most Natural Sciences questions are Classification, Characteristic, Part/Whole, or Object/Action analogies. All Vocabulary questions that involve the *-ology* suffix might be considered Natural Sciences questions as well.

Try these Natural Sciences analogies. Answers appear at the end of this section.

NATURAL SCIENCES

21. AVIAN : APIAN :: BIRDS : (*a.* reptiles, *b.* cattle, *c.* bees, *d.* monkeys)

22. ABDUCTOR MUSCLE : (*a.* intestine, *b.* arm, *c.* heart, *d.* skull) :: BALL-AND-SOCKET JOINT : HIP

23. MOSQUITO : TERMITE :: (*a.* flock, *b.* school, *c.* troop, *d.* swarm) : COLONY

24. H_2O : NaCl :: WATER : (*a.* gas, *b.* sugar, *c.* rock, *d.* salt)

25. (*a.* Planck, *b.* Avogadro, *c.* Priestly, *d.* Roentgen) : TESLA :: QUANTUM THEORY : ALTERNATING CURRENTS

SOCIAL SCIENCES

Social Sciences is an all-encompassing category on the MAT. It includes geography, history, philosophy, and psychology. You will need to match cities to countries and countries to continents. You might need to know the difference between a mountain and a butte or a province and a canton. You might need to identify the longest, tallest, or largest river, mountain, or continent.

In the area of history, you might benefit from a review of early explorers and their discoveries. You may be asked about kings or queens and their dynasties or eras, or about presidents and their cohorts and achievements. In the areas of philosophy and psychology, you might need to know major figures and the movements they represent.

Social Sciences questions tend to be Classification, Characteristic, Part/Whole, or Object/Action analogies.

Here are some Social Sciences analogies. Answers appear at the end of this section.

SOCIAL SCIENCES

26. NIXON : AGNEW :: EISENHOWER : (*a.* Kennedy, *b.* Truman, *c.* Dulles, *d.* Nixon)

27. DAMASCUS : (*a.* Syria, *b.* Jordan, *c.* Haifa, *d.* Armenia) :: BEIRUT : LEBANON

28. (*a.* ethics, *b.* sexuality, *c.* cognition, *d.* desires) : PIAGET :: NEEDS : MASLOW

29. CHINESE : GREEK :: (*a.* Confucius, *b.* Buddha, *c.* Pantheon, *d.* Tao) : LOGOS

30. (*a.* Niagara Falls, *b.* Angel Falls, *c.* Victoria Falls, *d.* Yosemite Falls) : MOUNT EVEREST :: WATERFALLS : MOUNTAINS

MATHEMATICS AND NUMBERS

There won't be many numerical analogies on the MAT, but there are likely to be a few. Most math questions deal with measurement, currency, geometric terms, and famous mathematicians from history. You may find one that requires you to decipher Roman numerals or complete a mathematical ratio.

Math questions are likely to be Part/Whole, Conversion, or Sequence analogies. Questions involving units of measure or mathematicians and their discoveries may be Object/Action analogies. You may even face an Affix analogy that asks you to determine the meaning of a mathematical prefix.

Try these Mathematics and Numbers analogies. Answers appear at the end of this section.

MATHEMATICS AND NUMBERS

31. RAY : (*a.* point, *b.* line, *c.* circle, *d.* arc) :: ANGLE : POLYGON

32. (*a.* dime, *b.* nickel, *c.* ha'penny, *d.* half-dollar) : PENNY :: QUARTER : NICKEL

33. 9/3 : 1/3 :: (*a.* 1/8, *b.* 4/3, *c.* 4/1, *d.* 12/2) : 1/4

34. BRAZIL : REAL :: (*a.* Guatemala, *b.* Portugal, *c.* Uruguay, *d.* Venezuela) : BOLIVAR

35. VII : (*a.* X, *b.* DCC, *c.* DL, *d.* LXX) :: 1 : 10

EXPLANATORY ANSWERS

VOCABULARY

1. HELPLESS : DEPENDENT :: (***a.* guileless**, *b.* genuine, *c.* stoic, *d.* independent) : INGENUOUS
   (**a**) To be *helpless* is to be *dependent*. To be *guileless* is to be *ingenuous*.

2. (*a.* multi-, *b.* deca-, *c.* ovo-, ***d.* peri-**) : AROUND :: POLY- : MANY
   (**d**) The prefix *peri-*, as in *perimeter*, means "*around.*" The prefix *poly-*, as in *polyglot*, means "*many.*"

3. PRANK : HOAX :: PEEK : (*a.* fool, *b.* hide, *c.* fraud, ***d.* gaze**)
   (**d**) An involved *prank* might be a *hoax*. A long *peek* might be a *gaze*.

4. (*a.* innocent, *b.* desolate, ***c.* fecund**, *d.* sullen) : BARREN :: GLUM : OPTIMISTIC
   (**c**) If you are *fecund*, you are not *barren*. If you are *glum*, you are not *optimistic*.

5. QUIESCENT : (*a.* nascent, ***b.* intrusive**, *c.* choleric, *d.* latent) :: DORMANT : INVASIVE
   (**b**) *Quiescent* is a synonym for *dormant*. *Intrusive* is a synonym for *invasive*.

LITERATURE

6. BAUDELAIRE : (*a.* Dante, ***b.* Paz**, *c.* Angelou, *d.* Breton) :: FRENCH : SPANISH
   (**b**) Poet Charles *Baudelaire* wrote in *French*. Poet Octavio *Paz* wrote in *Spanish*.

7. HERA : (*a.* Minerva, *b.* Venus, ***c.* Juno**, *d.* Vesta) :: ZEUS : JUPITER
   (**c**) *Juno* is the Roman name for the Greek goddess *Hera*. *Jupiter* is the Roman name for the Greek god *Zeus*.

8. DICKENS : PIP :: (*a.* Eliot, *b.* Thackeray, *c.* Austen, **d. Hugo**) : FANTINE
   (**d**) Charles *Dickens* created the orphan *Pip* for his novel *Great Expectations*. Victor *Hugo* created the fallen woman *Fantine* for his novel *Les Miserables*.

9. (*a.* neoclassicism, **b. romanticism**, *c.* fauvism, *d.* pre-Raphaelism) : NATURALISM :: BYRON : HARDY
   (**b**) Lord *Byron* is considered a writer in the *romantic* tradition. Thomas *Hardy* is a writer in the *naturalist* tradition.

10. TELEMACHUS : PENELOPE :: HECTOR : (*a.* Helen, *b.* Athena, **c. Hecuba**, *d.* Euterpe)
    (**c**) In *The Odyssey, Telemachus* was the son of *Penelope* (and Odysseus). In *The Iliad, Hector* was the son of *Hecuba* (and Priam).

ART

11. EXPRESSIONISM : KANDINSKY :: SURREALISM : (**a. Magritte**, *b.* Delacroix, *c.* Pissaro, *d.* Matisse)
    (**a**) Wassily *Kandinsky* was a major artist in the *expressionist* movement. René *Magritte* was a major artist in the *surrealist* movement.

12. PITTI PALACE : (*a.* Rome, *b.* Madrid, **c. Florence**, *d.* Barcelona) :: NOTRE DAME : PARIS
    (**c**) The *Pitti Palace* was built beginning in 1458 in *Florence. Notre Dame* was built beginning in 1163 in *Paris.*

13. (*a.* sculpture, **b. film**, *c.* portraiture, *d.* landscape) : PHOTOGRAPHY :: BERGMAN : STIEGLITZ
    (**b**) Ingmar *Bergman* is a famous *film* director. Alfred *Stieglitz* was a famous *photographer.*

14. CLOISONNÉ : POINTILLISM :: (*a.* embroidery, *b.* mosaic, **c. enamel**, *d.* engraving) : PAINTING
    (**c**) *Cloisonné* is one form of *enamel* work. *Pointillism* is one style of *painting.*

15. (**a. Hermitage**, *b.* Odessa, *c.* Hirschhorn, *d.* Faaborg) : ST. PETERSBURG :: RIJKSMUSEUM : AMSTERDAM
    (**a**) The *Hermitage* is a major art museum in *St. Petersburg,* Russia. The *Rijksmuseum* is a major art museum in *Amsterdam,* the Netherlands.

MUSIC

16. STRINGS : PERCUSSION :: MANDOLIN : (*a.* guitar, **b. xylophone**, *c.* saxophone, *d.* bass)
    (**b**) A *mandolin* is a *stringed* instrument. A *xylophone* is a *percussion* instrument.

17. TENOR : (*a.* baritone, *b.* Pavarotti, **c. soprano**, *d.* diva) :: CARUSO : CALLAS
    (**c**) Enrico *Caruso* was a famous Italian *tenor.* Maria *Callas* was a famous Greek-American *soprano.*

18. (*a.* drum, *b.* pedal, *c.* allegro, **d. forte**) : PIANO :: LOUD : SOFT
    (**d**) In musical notation, *forte* means "*loud*," and *piano* means "*soft*."

19. *THE RITE OF SPRING* : (*a.* Tchaikovsky, **b. Stravinsky**, *c.* Rimsky-Korsakov, *d.* Rachmaninoff) :: *LES SYLPHIDES* : CHOPIN
    (**b**) *The Rite of Spring* is a ballet with music by Igor *Stravinsky. Les Sylphides* is a ballet with music by Frédéric *Chopin.*

20. RHYTHM : BEAT :: (*a.* cadence, *b.* intonation, **c. tempo**, *d.* pitch) : SPEED
    (**c**) *Rhythm* refers to the *beat* of a musical work. *Tempo* refers to the *speed* of a musical work.

NATURAL SCIENCES

21. AVIAN : APIAN :: BIRDS : (*a.* reptiles, *b.* cattle, **c. bees**, *d.* monkeys)
    (**c**) In taxonomy, *birds* are known as *avian,* and *bees* are known as *apian.*

22. ABDUCTOR MUSCLE : (*a.* intestine, **b. arm**, *c.* heart, *d.* skull) :: BALL-AND-SOCKET JOINT : HIP
    (**b**) An *abductor muscle* may be found in the *arm* (or in other limbs as well). A *ball-and-socket joint* may be found in the *hip* (or in the shoulder).

23. MOSQUITO : TERMITE :: (*a.* flock, *b.* school, *c.* troop, **d. swarm**) : COLONY
    (**d**) A group of *mosquitoes* is called a *swarm.* A group of *termites* is called a *colony.*

24. H_2O : NaCl :: WATER : (*a.* gas, *b.* sugar, *c.* rock, **d. salt**)
    (**d**) In chemical notation, H_2O refers to a molecule formed of two atoms of hydrogen and one of oxygen, or *water.* NaCl refers to a molecule formed of one atom of sodium and one of chloride, or sodium chloride, commonly known as table *salt.*

25. (**a. Planck**, *b.* Avogadro, *c.* Priestly, *d.* Roentgen) : TESLA :: QUANTUM THEORY : ALTERNATING CURRENTS
    (**a**) Max *Planck* was the German scientist who first proposed what would become *quantum theory.* Nikola *Tesla* was the Serbian-American scientist who discovered *alternating currents.*

SOCIAL SCIENCES

26. NIXON : AGNEW :: EISENHOWER : (*a.* Kennedy, *b.* Truman, *c.* Dulles, **d. Nixon**)
    (**d**) Spiro *Agnew* was vice president under Richard *Nixon.* Richard *Nixon* was vice president under Dwight *Eisenhower.*

27. DAMASCUS : (**a. Syria**, *b.* Jordan, *c.* Haifa, *d.* Armenia) :: BEIRUT : LEBANON
    (**a**) *Damascus* is the capital of *Syria. Beirut* is the capital of *Lebanon.*

28. (*a.* ethics, *b.* sexuality, **c. cognition**, *d.* desires) : PIAGET :: NEEDS : MASLOW
    (**c**) Psychologist Jean *Piaget* specialized in early childhood *cognition.* Psychologist Abraham *Maslow* specialized in human motivation and *needs.*

29. CHINESE : GREEK :: (*a.* Confucius, *b.* Buddha, *c.* Pantheon, ***d.* Tao**) : LOGOS
    (**d**) *Tao, Chinese* for "the way," is a fundamental concept in several Eastern religions. *Logos, Greek* for "the word," is a fundamental concept in several Western religions.

30. (*a.* Niagara Falls, ***b.* Angel Falls**, *c.* Victoria Falls, *d.* Yosemite Falls) : MOUNT EVEREST :: WATERFALLS : MOUNTAINS
    (**b**) *Angel Falls* in Venezuela is the highest of the world's *waterfalls*. *Mount Everest* in Nepal is the tallest of the world's *mountains*.

MATHEMATICS AND NUMBERS

31. RAY : (*a.* point, ***b.* line**, *c.* circle, *d.* arc) :: ANGLE : POLYGON
    (**b**) A *ray* is part of a *line*. An *angle* is part of a *polygon*.

32. (*a.* dime, ***b.* nickel**, *c.* ha'penny, *d.* half-dollar) : PENNY :: QUARTER : NICKEL
    (**b**) A *nickel's* value is five times that of a *penny*. A *quarter's* value is five times that of a *nickel*.

33. 9/3 : 1/3 :: (*a.* 1/8, *b.* 4/3, ***c.* 4/1**, *d.* 12/2): 1/4
    (**c**) *9/3*, or 3/1, is the reciprocal of *1/3*. *4/1* is the reciprocal of *1/4*.

34. BRAZIL : REAL :: (*a.* Guatemala, *b.* Portugal, *c.* Uruguay, ***d.* Venezuela**) : BOLIVAR
    (**d**) The *real* is the basic currency of *Brazil*. The *bolivar* is the basic currency of *Venezuela*.

35. VII : (*a.* X, *b.* DCC, *c.* DL, ***d.* LXX**) :: 1 : 10
    (**d**) *VII* = 7, and *LXX* = 70. The ratio 7 to 70 is equivalent to the ratio *1 to 10*.

Part III

Full-Length Practice Exams

PRACTICE TEST 1
ANSWER SHEET

1. Ⓐ Ⓑ Ⓒ Ⓓ	26. Ⓐ Ⓑ Ⓒ Ⓓ	51. Ⓐ Ⓑ Ⓒ Ⓓ	76. Ⓐ Ⓑ Ⓒ Ⓓ
2. Ⓐ Ⓑ Ⓒ Ⓓ	27. Ⓐ Ⓑ Ⓒ Ⓓ	52. Ⓐ Ⓑ Ⓒ Ⓓ	77. Ⓐ Ⓑ Ⓒ Ⓓ
3. Ⓐ Ⓑ Ⓒ Ⓓ	28. Ⓐ Ⓑ Ⓒ Ⓓ	53. Ⓐ Ⓑ Ⓒ Ⓓ	78. Ⓐ Ⓑ Ⓒ Ⓓ
4. Ⓐ Ⓑ Ⓒ Ⓓ	29. Ⓐ Ⓑ Ⓒ Ⓓ	54. Ⓐ Ⓑ Ⓒ Ⓓ	79. Ⓐ Ⓑ Ⓒ Ⓓ
5. Ⓐ Ⓑ Ⓒ Ⓓ	30. Ⓐ Ⓑ Ⓒ Ⓓ	55. Ⓐ Ⓑ Ⓒ Ⓓ	80. Ⓐ Ⓑ Ⓒ Ⓓ
6. Ⓐ Ⓑ Ⓒ Ⓓ	31. Ⓐ Ⓑ Ⓒ Ⓓ	56. Ⓐ Ⓑ Ⓒ Ⓓ	81. Ⓐ Ⓑ Ⓒ Ⓓ
7. Ⓐ Ⓑ Ⓒ Ⓓ	32. Ⓐ Ⓑ Ⓒ Ⓓ	57. Ⓐ Ⓑ Ⓒ Ⓓ	82. Ⓐ Ⓑ Ⓒ Ⓓ
8. Ⓐ Ⓑ Ⓒ Ⓓ	33. Ⓐ Ⓑ Ⓒ Ⓓ	58. Ⓐ Ⓑ Ⓒ Ⓓ	83. Ⓐ Ⓑ Ⓒ Ⓓ
9. Ⓐ Ⓑ Ⓒ Ⓓ	34. Ⓐ Ⓑ Ⓒ Ⓓ	59. Ⓐ Ⓑ Ⓒ Ⓓ	84. Ⓐ Ⓑ Ⓒ Ⓓ
10. Ⓐ Ⓑ Ⓒ Ⓓ	35. Ⓐ Ⓑ Ⓒ Ⓓ	60. Ⓐ Ⓑ Ⓒ Ⓓ	85. Ⓐ Ⓑ Ⓒ Ⓓ
11. Ⓐ Ⓑ Ⓒ Ⓓ	36. Ⓐ Ⓑ Ⓒ Ⓓ	61. Ⓐ Ⓑ Ⓒ Ⓓ	86. Ⓐ Ⓑ Ⓒ Ⓓ
12. Ⓐ Ⓑ Ⓒ Ⓓ	37. Ⓐ Ⓑ Ⓒ Ⓓ	62. Ⓐ Ⓑ Ⓒ Ⓓ	87. Ⓐ Ⓑ Ⓒ Ⓓ
13. Ⓐ Ⓑ Ⓒ Ⓓ	38. Ⓐ Ⓑ Ⓒ Ⓓ	63. Ⓐ Ⓑ Ⓒ Ⓓ	88. Ⓐ Ⓑ Ⓒ Ⓓ
14. Ⓐ Ⓑ Ⓒ Ⓓ	39. Ⓐ Ⓑ Ⓒ Ⓓ	64. Ⓐ Ⓑ Ⓒ Ⓓ	89. Ⓐ Ⓑ Ⓒ Ⓓ
15. Ⓐ Ⓑ Ⓒ Ⓓ	40. Ⓐ Ⓑ Ⓒ Ⓓ	65. Ⓐ Ⓑ Ⓒ Ⓓ	90. Ⓐ Ⓑ Ⓒ Ⓓ
16. Ⓐ Ⓑ Ⓒ Ⓓ	41. Ⓐ Ⓑ Ⓒ Ⓓ	66. Ⓐ Ⓑ Ⓒ Ⓓ	91. Ⓐ Ⓑ Ⓒ Ⓓ
17. Ⓐ Ⓑ Ⓒ Ⓓ	42. Ⓐ Ⓑ Ⓒ Ⓓ	67. Ⓐ Ⓑ Ⓒ Ⓓ	92. Ⓐ Ⓑ Ⓒ Ⓓ
18. Ⓐ Ⓑ Ⓒ Ⓓ	43. Ⓐ Ⓑ Ⓒ Ⓓ	68. Ⓐ Ⓑ Ⓒ Ⓓ	93. Ⓐ Ⓑ Ⓒ Ⓓ
19. Ⓐ Ⓑ Ⓒ Ⓓ	44. Ⓐ Ⓑ Ⓒ Ⓓ	69. Ⓐ Ⓑ Ⓒ Ⓓ	94. Ⓐ Ⓑ Ⓒ Ⓓ
20. Ⓐ Ⓑ Ⓒ Ⓓ	45. Ⓐ Ⓑ Ⓒ Ⓓ	70. Ⓐ Ⓑ Ⓒ Ⓓ	95. Ⓐ Ⓑ Ⓒ Ⓓ
21. Ⓐ Ⓑ Ⓒ Ⓓ	46. Ⓐ Ⓑ Ⓒ Ⓓ	71. Ⓐ Ⓑ Ⓒ Ⓓ	96. Ⓐ Ⓑ Ⓒ Ⓓ
22. Ⓐ Ⓑ Ⓒ Ⓓ	47. Ⓐ Ⓑ Ⓒ Ⓓ	72. Ⓐ Ⓑ Ⓒ Ⓓ	97. Ⓐ Ⓑ Ⓒ Ⓓ
23. Ⓐ Ⓑ Ⓒ Ⓓ	48. Ⓐ Ⓑ Ⓒ Ⓓ	73. Ⓐ Ⓑ Ⓒ Ⓓ	98. Ⓐ Ⓑ Ⓒ Ⓓ
24. Ⓐ Ⓑ Ⓒ Ⓓ	49. Ⓐ Ⓑ Ⓒ Ⓓ	74. Ⓐ Ⓑ Ⓒ Ⓓ	99. Ⓐ Ⓑ Ⓒ Ⓓ
25. Ⓐ Ⓑ Ⓒ Ⓓ	50. Ⓐ Ⓑ Ⓒ Ⓓ	75. Ⓐ Ⓑ Ⓒ Ⓓ	100. Ⓐ Ⓑ Ⓒ Ⓓ

PRACTICE TEST I

Directions: For each question, you will see three capitalized words and four answer choices labeled *a, b, c,* and *d* in parentheses. Choose the answer that best completes the analogy posed by the three capitalized words. Use the answer sheet on page 41 to record your answers.

Time: 50 Minutes

1. REPULSIVE : VILE :: COMPLACENT : (*a.* smug, *b.* bilious, *c.* pleasant, *d.* anxious)

2. DEFOLIATE : DEFOREST :: (*a.* pages, *b.* skin, *c.* leaves, *d.* woods) : TREES

3. NORTH AMERICA : SOUTH AMERICA :: (*a.* Rockies, *b.* states, *c.* prairies, *d.* borders) : PAMPAS

4. EXPROPRIATE : (*a.* experts, *b.* appropriate, *c.* reinstate, *d.* possessions) :: EXPUNGE : ERRORS

5. APPLIQUÉ : STITCHERY :: (*a.* intaglio, *b.* computer, *c.* embroidery, *d.* Gutenberg) : PRINTMAKING

6. COUNTY : NEW YORK :: PARISH : (*a.* priest, *b.* Church, *c.* Louisiana, *d.* Colombia)

7. CHLORINE : HALOGEN :: NEON : (*a.* noble gas, *b.* light, *c.* plasma, *d.* nitrogen)

8. (*a.* Eartha Kitt, *b.* Dizzy Gillespie, *c.* New Orleans, *d.* John Coltrane) : CHARLIE PARKER :: TRUMPET : SAXOPHONE

9. x^2 : (*a.* x, *b.* $2x$, *c.* $4x$, *d.* x^3) :: AREA : PERIMETER

10. SINNER : ATONEMENT :: CRIMINAL : (*a.* crime, *b.* penalty, *c.* judge, *d.* theft)

11. LOUISIANA PURCHASE : GADSDEN PURCHASE :: (*a.* France, *b.* Jefferson, *c.* Louisiana, *d.* England) : MEXICO

12. -ER : (*a.* most, *b.* again, *c.* not, *d.* one who) :: -FUL : FULL OF

13. (*a.* garment, *b.* artwork, *c.* foundation, *d.* principle) : UNDERPINNING :: FRAMEWORK : SKELETON

14. OSMOSIS : (*a.* salt, *b.* membrane, *c.* water, *d.* dialysis) :: SOLVENT : SOLUTE

15. FRANTIC : UNRUFFLED :: BEWILDERED : (*a.* confused, *b.* enlightened, *c.* ruffled, *d.* stupefied)

16. IRS : OSHA :: TREASURY : (*a.* State, *b.* FDA, *c.* Labor, *d.* HUD)

17. BIBLE : (*a.* Bhagavad-Gita, *b.* Koran, *c.* Obadiah, *d.* Mahayana) :: JUDAISM : HINDUISM

18. 4 : 5 :: 64 : (*a.* 25, *b.* 50, *c.* 75, *d.* 125)

19. POLITE : OBSEQUIOUS :: LENIENT : (*a.* spineless, *b.* moderate, *c.* rude, *d.* strict)

20. RADAR : (*a.* light waves, *b.* telegraphy, *c.* electromagnetic waves, *d.* broadcasting) :: SONAR : SOUND WAVES

21. DAMAGED : SPOILED :: FIXED : (*a.* detached, *b.* refurbished, *c.* razed, *d.* varied)

22. (*a.* Grant Wood, *b.* Man Ray, *c.* Marc Chagall, *d.* Edward Hopper) : HENRI ROUSSEAU :: *NIGHTHAWKS* : *THE SLEEPING GYPSY*

23. OBESE : CHUBBY :: (*a.* uncontrollable, *b.* distracting, *c.* helpful, *d.* fretful) : DISRUPTIVE

24. SHIITE : IRAN :: SUNNI : (*a.* Muslim, *b.* Bahrain, *c.* Afghanistan, *d.* Sri Lanka)

25. CHRISTOPHER WREN : (*a.* Windsor Castle, *b.* St. Paul's Cathedral, *c.* Tower Bridge, *d.* Crystal Palace) :: INIGO JONES : THE QUEEN'S HOUSE

26. LIVER : BILE :: KIDNEY : (*a.* excrete, *b.* stone, *c.* ureter, *d.* urine)

27. CLIO : URANIA :: (*a.* advertising, *b.* history, *c.* literature, *d.* astrology) : ASTRONOMY

28. FEVERISH : CHILLY :: (*a.* slow, *b.* ill, *c.* frigid, *d.* animated) : SLUGGISH

29. QUASI- : (*a.* quarter, *b.* somewhat, *c.* more, *d.* verified) :: HEMI- : HALF

30. COACH : CONVEYANCE :: ROACH : (*a.* vehicle, *b.* filth, *c.* insect, *d.* repulsion)

31. CAMELOT : ENGLAND :: SHANGRI-LA : (*a.* Tibet, *b.* China, *c.* Mongolia, *d.* Bali)

32. (*a.* corporation, *b.* misdeed, *c.* paralegal, *d.* advice) : LAWYER :: TREATMENT : PSYCHIATRIST

33. ADA : ARF :: (*a.* sound, *b.* girl, *c.* palindrome, *d.* lawyer) : ONOMATOPOEIA

34. KEROUAC : BEAT :: POUND : (*a.* modernism, *b.* poetry, *c.* hammer, *d.* romanticism)

35. JEANETTE RANKIN : (*a.* table, *b.* Supreme Court, *c.* medicine, *d.* House of Representatives) :: FRANCES PERKINS : CABINET

36. (*a.* Renoir, *b.* Degas, *c.* van Gogh, *d.* Picasso) : PASTELS :: GAUGUIN : OILS

37. FRACTIOUS : (*a.* shattered, *b.* friendly, *c.* peevish, *d.* fearful) :: VOLUBLE : CHATTY

38. QUILT : BLOCKS :: PATIO : (*a.* veranda, *b.* al fresco, *c.* benches, *d.* pavers)

39. SCOTTO : (*a.* conductor, *b.* soprano, *c.* opera, *d.* bass) :: PAVAROTTI : TENOR

40. EUGENE DEBS : LYNDON LAROUCHE :: (*a.* socialists, *b.* labor unions, *c.* Freemasons, *d.* Know-Nothings) : LIBERTARIANS

41. SUTURES : SURGEON :: SINEW : (*a.* weightlifter, *b.* butcher, *c.* carpenter, *d.* leatherworker)

42. MOUSE : WOOFER :: (*a.* listener, *b.* computer, *c.* rodent, *d.* hairdresser) : SPEAKER

43. PANAMA : BAJA :: ISTHMUS : (*a.* island, *b.* bay, *c.* peninsula, *d.* bridge)

44. DEMANDING : FULFILLED :: (*a.* flowery, *b.* succinct, *c.* requesting, *d.* consoling) : FLORID

45. AXE : CHOP :: PLANE : (*a.* fire, *b.* wing, *c.* flap, *d.* smooth)

46. PENGUIN : (*a.* Antarctica, *b.* Aves, *c.* feathers, *d.* Mammalia) :: LOUSE : CRUSTACEA

47. MAJORCA : SPAIN :: CORSICA : (*a.* Sicily, *b.* France, *c.* Italy, *d.* Portugal)

48. (*a.* lavender, *b.* green, *c.* indigo, *d.* sky) : BLUE :: VIOLET : PURPLE

49. KANDINSKY : EXPRESSIONISM :: (*a.* Renoir, *b.* Rembrandt, *c.* Dalí, *d.* Klee) : IMPRESSIONISM

50. CACTUS : CACTI :: LEAF : (*a.* leave, *b.* lief, *c.* leaves, *d.* leafs)

51. MINOTAUR : (*a.* man, *b.* monster, *c.* harpy, *d.* eagle) :: BULL : BIRD

52. DYE : (*a.* bread, *b.* wry, *c.* hue, *d.* year) :: DIE : RYE

53. ENFRANCHISE : VOTE :: ENTHRONE : (*a.* act, *b.* rule, *c.* crown, *d.* king)

54. SAMUEL GOMPERS : JOHN L. LEWIS :: (*a.* NFL, *b.* ACLU, *c.* AFL, *d.* UAW) : CIO

55. 1/2 : (*a.* 1/5, *b.* 1/4, *c.* 1/10, *d.* 2/4) :: 5 : 1

56. DOMINANT : RECESSIVE :: (*a.* left-handedness, *b.* blue eyes, *c.* anemia, *d.* dimples) : ATTACHED EARLOBES

57. (*a.* Mercury, *b.* Mars, *c.* Jove, *d.* Hephaestus) : NEPTUNE :: HERMES : POSEIDON

58. VERSAILLES : WWI :: (*a.* Paris, *b.* Munich, *c.* Tripoli, *d.* Yalta) : WWII

59. CU : (*a.* Io, *b.* Rh, *c.* Fe, *d.* Ir) :: COPPER : IRON

60. GENEROUS : PARSIMONIOUS :: OBSTINATE : (*a.* stubborn, *b.* bountiful, *c.* accommodating, *d.* mulish)

61. CROSSBREED : (*a.* clone, *b.* hybrid, *c.* color, *d.* farming) :: CROSSHATCH : SHADING

62. FEZ : MOROCCO :: (*a.* London, *b.* Oxford, *c.* Derby, *d.* Bath) : ENGLAND

63. FLASHY : UNASSUMING :: QUIXOTIC : (*a.* mercurial, *b.* levelheaded, *c.* corrupt, *d.* daring)

64. GOSPELS : BIOGRAPHY :: REVELATIONS : (*a.* autobiography, *b.* covenant, *c.* fantasy, *d.* prophecy)

65. (*a.* firefighter, *b.* museum, *c.* conservator, *d.* sculptor) : PROTECTION :: CURATOR : EXHIBITION

66. HURRICANE : (*a.* flood, *b.* tornado, *c.* typhoon, *d.* cyclone) :: ATLANTIC : PACIFIC

67. MANDIBLE : JAW :: SCAPULA : (*a.* tool, *b.* elbow, *c.* shoulder, *d.* spine)

68. PETROLOGY : (*a.* speleology, *b.* archaeology, *c.* teleology, *d.* phrenology) :: ROCKS : CAVES

69. PICTS : (*a.* Wales, *b.* Scotland, *c.* France, *d.* Germany) :: CELTS : IRELAND

70. (*a.* reptile, *b.* constrictor, *c.* serpent, *d.* viper) : PYTHON :: POISON : SUFFOCATE

71. IRON : ANEMIC :: WATER : (*a.* caustic, *b.* dehydrated, *c.* humidified, *d.* flowing)

72. ROBERT FROST : NEW ENGLAND :: (*a.* William Carlos Willams, *b.* John Crowe Ransom, *c.* Carl Sandburg, *d.* Lucille Clifton): MIDWEST

73. SATIN : SMOOTHNESS :: (*a.* corduroy, *b.* rasp, *c.* silk, *d.* tulle) : ROUGHNESS

74. LOCKE : EMPIRICISM :: MILL : (*a.* Stoicism, *b.* dogma, *c.* rationalism, *d.* utilitarianism)

75. VIRUS : INFLUENZA :: (*a.* amoeba, *b.* plankton, *c.* mold, *d.* vermin) : DYSENTERY

76. WAG : HUMOR :: NAG : (*a.* absurdity, *b.* displeasure, *c.* human, *d.* harassment)

77. (*a.* prose, *b.* tall tale, *c.* fable, *d.* poesy) : HYPERBOLE :: POETRY : IMAGERY

78. WEBSTER : DICTIONARY :: (*a.* Diderot, *b.* Johnson, *c.* Barnes, *d.* Boswell) : ENCYCLOPEDIA

79. (*a.* sunlight, *b.* oak tree, *c.* fungus, *d.* fern) : PHOTOSYNTHESIZE :: ANAEROBE : RESPIRATE

80. ABRAHAM : (*a.* Ra, *b.* God, *c.* Moses, *d.* Isaac) :: ZEUS : APOLLO

81. (*a.* puberty, *b.* menses, *c.* menarche, *d.* month) : MENOPAUSE :: ONSET : CESSATION

82. COLANDER : (*a.* cook, *b.* drain, *c.* Dutch, *d.* vermin) :: BELT GRINDER : POLISH

83. CONTRALTO : MEZZO-SOPRANO :: (*a.* tenor, *b.* alto, *c.* bass, *d.* countertenor) : BARITONE

84. FCC : FDA :: TELEVISION : (*a.* radio, *b.* banking, *c.* computers, *d.* cosmetics)

85. EST : PST :: (*a.* 7:00, *b.* 3:00, *c.* 1:00, *d.* 10:00) : 4:00

86. (*a.* virus, *b.* blood, *c.* antibody, *d.* pathogen) : ANTIGEN :: SHIELD : INVADER

87. PSALTERY : (*a.* drum, *b.* hymnal, *c.* dulcimer, *d.* trumpet) :: MUSETTE : BAGPIPE

88. INCONCEIVABLE : COMPREHENSION :: INCORRIGIBLE : (*a.* pretension, *b.* incomprehension, *c.* apprehension, *d.* correction)

89. DELECTABLE : DELICIOUS :: (*a.* tasty, *b.* muffled, *c.* sonorous, *d.* sentient) : RESONANT

90. ELIAS HOWE : (*a.* tractor, *b.* sewing machine, *c.* textbook, *d.* harvester) :: ELI WHITNEY : COTTON GIN

91. SUICIDE : SELF :: PATRICIDE : (*a.* other, *b.* homicide, *c.* father, *d.* priest)

92. (*a.* papyrus, *b.* algebra, *c.* cuneiform, *d.* mosaic) : SUMERIANS :: HIEROGLYPHICS : EGYPT

93. PADEREWSKI : PIANO :: (*a.* Paganini, *b.* Puccini, *c.* Pachelbel, *d.* Piatagorsky) : VIOLIN

94. CANDOR : (*a.* insincerity, *b.* ruse, *c.* compassion, *d.* frankness) :: DANDER : TEMPER

95. STOPPLE : CLOSE :: THROTTLE : (*a.* open, *b.* drive, *c.* partition, *d.* regulate)

96. CROWBAR : (*a.* loosen, *b.* between, *c.* pry, *d.* elevate) :: WRENCH : TIGHTEN

97. FOOT : YARD :: SIDE : (*a.* top, *b.* triangle, *c.* vertex, *d.* polygon)

98. HUMBLE : HUMBUG :: (*a.* fumble, *b.* arrogant, *c.* modest, *d.* poster) : IMPOSTER

99. COLLAPSE : (*a.* appeal, *b.* tumble, *c.* implode, *d.* subside) :: REQUEST : IMPORTUNE

100. IMPERVIOUS : PENETRATION :: IMPLACABLE : (*a.* appeasement, *b.* generosity, *c.* confirmation, *d.* subdivision)

STOP

If there is any time remaining, go back and check your work.

PRACTICE TEST 1
ANSWER KEY

1. a	26. d	51. c	76. d
2. c	27. b	52. b	77. b
3. c	28. d	53. b	78. a
4. d	29. b	54. c	79. c
5. a	30. c	55. c	80. d
6. c	31. a	56. d	81. a
7. a	32. d	57. a	82. b
8. b	33. c	58. d	83. c
9. c	34. a	59. c	84. d
10. b	35. d	60. c	85. a
11. a	36. b	61. b	86. c
12. d	37. c	62. c	87. c
13. c	38. d	63. b	88. d
14. d	39. b	64. d	89. c
15. b	40. a	65. c	90. b
16. c	41. d	66. c	91. c
17. a	42. b	67. c	92. c
18. d	43. c	68. a	93. a
19. a	44. b	69. b	94. d
20. c	45. d	70. d	95. d
21. b	46. b	71. b	96. c
22. d	47. b	72. c	97. b
23. a	48. c	73. a	98. c
24. c	49. a	74. d	99. c
25. b	50. c	75. a	100. a

PRACTICE TEST 1 EXPLANATORY ANSWERS

1. REPULSIVE : VILE :: COMPLACENT : (*a.* **smug**, *b.* bilious, *c.* pleasant, *d.* anxious)
   (**a**) *Repulsive* and *vile* are synonymous, as are *complacent* and *smug*. **Synonym**

2. DEFOLIATE : DEFOREST :: (*a.* pages, *b.* skin, *c.* **leaves**, *d.* woods) : TREES
   (**c**) To *defoliate* is to rid of *leaves* in the same way that to *deforest* is to rid of *trees*.
   Object/Action

3. NORTH AMERICA : SOUTH AMERICA :: (*a.* Rockies, *b.* states, *c.* **prairies**,
   d. borders) : PAMPAS
   (**c**) The grasslands of *North America* are known as *prairies*, and those of *South America*
   are known as *pampas*. **Characteristic**

4. EXPROPRIATE : (*a.* experts, *b.* appropriate, *c.* reinstate, *d.* **possessions**) ::
   EXPUNGE : ERRORS
   (**d**) One can *expropriate*, or seize, someone's *possessions*, just as one can *expunge*, or
   erase, someone's *errors*. **Object/Action**

5. APPLIQUÉ : STITCHERY :: (*a.* **intaglio**, *b.* computer, *c.* embroidery, *d.* Gutenberg) :
   PRINTMAKING
   (**a**) Just as *appliqué* is a particular form of *stitchery*, *intaglio* is a particular form of
   printmaking. **Classification**

6. COUNTY : NEW YORK :: PARISH : (*a.* priest, *b.* Church, *c.* **Louisiana**,
   d. Colombia)
   (**c**) *New York* is subdivided into *counties*, but the same kind of governmental division is
   called a *parish* in *Louisiana*. **Part/Whole**

7. CHLORINE : HALOGEN :: NEON : (*a.* **noble gas**, *b.* light, *c.* plasma, *d.* nitrogen)
   (**a**) On the periodic table of elements, the element *chlorine* is classified as one of the
   halogens, and *neon* is classified as a *noble gas*. **Classification**

8. (*a.* Eartha Kitt, *b.* **Dizzy Gillespie**, *c.* New Orleans, *d.* John Coltrane) : CHARLIE
   PARKER :: TRUMPET : SAXOPHONE
   (**b**) *Dizzy Gillespie* was a *trumpet* player in the bebop tradition. *Charlie Parker* was a
   saxophone player in the bebop tradition. **Object/Action**

9. x^2 : (*a.* x, *b.* $2x$, *c.* **$4x$**, *d.* x^3) : AREA : PERIMETER
   (**c**) If x^2 is an example of *area* and x represents the length of a side, then the area must
   be that of a square. In that case, the only formula that shows that same square's
   perimeter is $4x$. **Classification**

10. SINNER : ATONEMENT :: CRIMINAL : (*a.* crime, *b.* **penalty**, *c.* judge, *d.* theft)
    (**b**) A *sinner's* payment for his or her sin is *atonement*; a *criminal's* payment for his or
    her crime is a *penalty*. **Object/Action**

11. LOUISIANA PURCHASE : GADSDEN PURCHASE :: (*a.* **France**, *b.* Jefferson, *c.* Louisiana, *d.* England) : MEXICO
(a) These purchases were part of American expansionism. The *Louisiana Purchase* was a transaction with *France*, and the *Gadsden Purchase* was a transaction with *Mexico*. **Object/Action**

12. -ER : (*a.* most, *b.* again, *c.* not, *d.* **one who**) :: -FUL : FULL OF
(d) The suffix *-er* means "*one who*," as in work**er** or danc**er**. The suffix *-ful* means "*full of*," as in beauti**ful** or joy**ful**. **Affix**

13. (*a.* garment, *b.* artwork, *c.* **foundation**, *d.* principle) : UNDERPINNING :: FRAMEWORK : SKELETON
(c) The *foundation* of something (a building, for example) may be considered its *underpinning*, just as the *framework* of something may be considered its *skeleton*. **Synonym**

14. OSMOSIS : (*a.* salt, *b.* membrane, *c.* water, *d.* **dialysis**) :: SOLVENT : SOLUTE
(d) Both *osmosis* and *dialysis* have to do with diffusion through a membrane. In the case of *osmosis,* the movement begins with a fluid, or *solvent;* in the case of *dialysis,* it involves the dissolution of a *solute.* **Object/Action**

15. FRANTIC : UNRUFFLED :: BEWILDERED : (*a.* confused, *b.* **enlightened**, *c.* ruffled, *d.* stupefied)
(b) To be *frantic* is the opposite of being *unruffled.* To be *bewildered* is the opposite of being *enlightened.* **Antonym**

16. IRS : OSHA :: TREASURY : (*a.* State, *b.* FDA, *c.* **Labor**, *d.* HUD)
(c) The *IRS* (Internal Revenue Service) and *OSHA* (Occupational Safety and Health Administration) are governmental departments within the departments of *Treasury* and *Labor,* respectively. **Part/Whole**

17. BIBLE : (*a.* **Bhagavad-Gita**, *b.* Koran, *c.* Obadiah, *d.* Mahayana) :: JUDAISM : HINDUISM
(a) The *Bible* (specifically the Old Testament) is a sacred text to followers of *Judaism,* and the *Bhagavad-Gita* is a sacred text to followers of *Hinduism.* **Characteristic**

18. 4 : 5 :: 64 : (*a.* 25, *b.* 50, *c.* 75, *d.* **125**)
(d) Although the two numbers *4* and *5* are sequential, that relationship does not hold in the analogy as presented. Looking at the relationship between *4* and *64,* you should notice that $64 = 4^3$. Similarly, $125 = 5^3$. **Conversion**

19. POLITE : OBSEQUIOUS :: LENIENT : (*a.* **spineless**, *b.* moderate, *c.* rude, *d.* strict)
(a) To be *obsequious* is to be extremely *polite,* to the point of a negative connotation. To be *spineless* is to be extremely *lenient,* again with a negative connotation. **Degree**

20. RADAR : (*a.* light waves, *b.* telegraphy, *c.* **electromagnetic waves**, *d.* broadcasting) :: SONAR : SOUND WAVES
(c) *Radar* functions via a form of *electromagnetic waves,* just as *sonar* functions based on *sound waves.* **Object/Action**

21. DAMAGED : SPOILED :: FIXED : (*a.* detached, ***b.* refurbished**, *c.* razed, *d.* varied)
    (**b**) If something is *damaged*, you might also say it is *spoiled*. If something is *fixed*, you might also say it is *refurbished*. **Synonym**

22. (*a.* Grant Wood, *b.* Man Ray, *c.* Marc Chagall, ***d.* Edward Hopper**) : HENRI ROUSSEAU :: *NIGHTHAWKS* : *THE SLEEPING GYPSY*
    (**d**) *Nighthawks*, which portrays a city diner late at night, is a famous painting by *Edward Hopper. The Sleeping Gypsy*, which is a dreamscape of a gypsy and a lion, is a famous painting by *Henri Rousseau*. **Object/Action**

23. OBESE : CHUBBY :: (***a.* uncontrollable**, *b.* distracting, *c.* helpful, *d.* fretful) : DISRUPTIVE
    (**a**) If you are *obese*, you are more than *chubby*. If you are *uncontrollable*, you are more than *disruptive*. **Degree**

24. SHIITE : IRAN :: SUNNI : (*a.* Muslim, *b.* Bahrain, ***c.* Afghanistan**, *d.* Sri Lanka)
    (**c**) *Shiite* Muslims are a majority in *Iran* (and in Bahrain), but *Sunni* Muslims are a majority in *Afghanistan*. **Characteristic**

25. CHRISTOPHER WREN : (*a.* Windsor Castle, ***b.* St. Paul's Cathedral**, *c.* Tower Bridge, *d.* Crystal Palace) :: INIGO JONES : THE QUEEN'S HOUSE
    (**b**) *Christopher Wren* was the architect of *St. Paul's Cathedral; Inigo Jones* designed *The Queen's House*. **Object/Action**

26. LIVER : BILE :: KIDNEY : (*a.* excrete, *b.* stone, *c.* ureter, ***d.* urine**)
    (**d**) Just as the *liver* produces *bile*, the *kidney* produces *urine*. **Object/Action**

27. CLIO : URANIA :: (*a.* advertising, ***b.* history**, *c.* literature, *d.* astrology) : ASTRONOMY
    (**b**) In Greek mythology, both *Clio* and *Urania* were Muses, and each had a special assignment. Clio's was *history*, and Urania's was *astronomy*. **Characteristic**

28. FEVERISH : CHILLY :: (*a.* slow, *b.* ill, *c.* frigid, ***d.* animated**) : SLUGGISH
    (**d**) If you are *feverish*, you are hot rather than *chilly*. If you are *animated*, you are lively rather than *sluggish*. **Antonym**

29. QUASI- : (*a.* quarter, ***b.* somewhat**, *c.* more, *d.* verified) :: HEMI- : HALF
    (**b**) The prefix *quasi-* means "*somewhat*," as in *quasiformal*. The prefix *hemi-* means "*half*," as in *hemisphere*. **Affix**

30. COACH : CONVEYANCE :: ROACH : (*a.* vehicle, *b.* filth, ***c.* insect**, *d.* repulsion)
    (**c**) A *coach* is one form of *conveyance*, or transport; a *roach* (cockroach) is one form of *insect*. **Classification**

31. CAMELOT : ENGLAND :: SHANGRI-LA : (***a.* Tibet**, *b.* China, *c.* Mongolia, *d.* Bali)
    (**a**) The mythical kingdom of *Camelot* was believed to have been in *England;* the mythical land of *Shangri-La* was believed to have been in *Tibet*. **Characteristic**

32. (*a.* corporation, *b.* misdeed, *c.* paralegal, ***d.* advice**) : LAWYER :: TREATMENT : PSYCHIATRIST

   (**d**) In much the same way that a *lawyer* dispenses *advice* on legal matters, a *psychiatrist* offers *treatment* to his or her patients. **Object/Action**

33. ADA : ARF :: (*a.* sound, *b.* girl, ***c.* palindrome**, *d.* lawyer) : ONOMATOPOEIA

   (**c**) The name *Ada* is a *palindrome* (a word that is spelled the same way backward and forward). The word *arf* is an example of *onomatopoeia*, a word that imitates the sound it names. **Classification**

34. KEROUAC : BEAT :: POUND : (***a.* modernism**, *b.* poetry, *c.* hammer, *d.* romanticism)

   (**a**) Jack *Kerouac* was an American writer in the *beat* tradition. Ezra *Pound* was an American poet in the *modernist* tradition. **Classification**

35. JEANETTE RANKIN : (*a.* table, *b.* Supreme Court, *c.* medicine, ***d.* House of Representatives**) :: FRANCES PERKINS : CABINET

   (**d**) In 1916, *Jeanette Rankin* (R-Montana) was the first woman elected to the U.S. *House of Representatives. Frances Perkins* was the first woman in the *Cabinet*, serving as Secretary of Labor under Franklin Roosevelt from 1933 to 1945. **Classification**

36. (*a.* Renoir, ***b.* Degas**, *c.* van Gogh, *d.* Picasso) : PASTELS :: GAUGUIN : OILS

   (**b**) The impressionist artist *Degas* was known for his work in *pastels*, whereas *Gauguin* worked almost entirely in *oils*. **Object/Action**

37. FRACTIOUS : (*a.* shattered, *b.* friendly, ***c.* peevish**, *d.* fearful) :: VOLUBLE : CHATTY

   (**c**) A *fractious* child is *peevish* or cranky; a *voluble* child is *chatty* or talkative. **Synonym**

38. QUILT : BLOCKS :: PATIO : (*a.* veranda, *b.* al fresco, *c.* benches, ***d.* pavers**)

   (**d**) A *quilt* is made up of quilting *blocks*, much as a *patio* is made of interconnected *pavers*, or paving stones. **Classification**

39. SCOTTO : (*a.* conductor, ***b.* soprano**, *c.* opera, *d.* bass) :: PAVAROTTI : TENOR

   (**b**) Both Scotto and Pavarotti are opera singers. Renata *Scotto* is a famous Italian *soprano*, and Luciano *Pavarotti* is a famous Italian *tenor*. **Classification**

40. EUGENE DEBS : LYNDON LAROUCHE :: (***a.* socialists**, *b.* labor unions, *c.* Freemasons, *d.* Know-Nothings) : LIBERTARIANS

   (**a**) *Eugene Debs* and *Lyndon Larouche* were frequent candidates for the presidency, Debs as a member of the *Socialist Party*, and Larouche as a *Libertarian*. **Part/Whole**

41. SUTURES : SURGEON :: SINEW : (*a.* weightlifter, *b.* butcher, *c.* carpenter, ***d.* leatherworker**)

   (**d**) A *surgeon* uses *sutures* in much the same way that a *leatherworker* uses *sinew*—to sew things together. **Object/Action**

42. MOUSE : WOOFER :: (*a.* listener, ***b.* computer**, *c.* rodent, *d.* hairdresser) : SPEAKER

   (**b**) A *mouse* is part of a *computer*, if a peripheral part, and a *woofer* is part of a *speaker*. **Part/Whole**

43. PANAMA : BAJA :: ISTHMUS : (*a.* island, *b.* bay, *c.* **peninsula**, *d.* bridge)
(**c**) *Panama* is an *isthmus*, a narrow piece of land that connects two larger landmasses. *Baja* is a *peninsula* that extends into the Pacific south of California. **Classification**

44. DEMANDING : FULFILLED :: (*a.* flowery, *b.* **succinct**, *c.* requesting, *d.* consoling) : FLORID
(**b**) If people are *demanding*, they are clearly not *fulfilled*, which implies that their wishes have not been met. If a speech is *succinct*, or to the point, it is not *florid*, or overblown. **Antonym**

45. AXE : CHOP :: PLANE : (*a.* fire, *b.* wing, *c.* flap, *d.* **smooth**)
(**d**) The multiple-meaning word *plane* is used here to denote a tool. You use an *axe* to *chop* wood; you use a *plane* to *smooth* wood. **Object/Action**

46. PENGUIN : (*a.* Antarctica, *b.* **Aves**, *c.* feathers, *d.* Mammalia) :: LOUSE : CRUSTACEA
(**b**) A *penguin* is a bird, or a member of the *Aves* class. A *louse* is a crustacean, or a member of the *Crustacea* class. **Classification**

47. MAJORCA : SPAIN :: CORSICA : (*a.* Sicily, *b.* **France**, *c.* Italy, *d.* Portugal)
(**b**) *Majorca* is a Mediterranean island owned by *Spain*. *Corsica* is a Mediterranean island owned by *France*. **Part/Whole**

48. (*a.* lavender, *b.* green, *c.* **indigo**, *d.* sky) : BLUE :: VIOLET : PURPLE
(**c**) The color *indigo* is a dark shade of *blue*. The color *violet* is a dark shade of *purple*. **Degree**

49. KANDINSKY : EXPRESSIONISM :: (*a.* **Renoir**, *b.* Rembrandt, *c.* Dalí, *d.* Klee) : IMPRESSIONISM
(**a**) All the people named are painters. Wassily *Kandinsky* was a member of the school known as *expressionism*. Auguste *Renoir* was a member of the school known as *impressionism*. **Part/Whole**

50. CACTUS : CACTI :: LEAF : (*a.* leave, *b.* lief, *c.* **leaves**, *d.* leafs)
(**c**) This analogy involves singular and plural nouns. *Cacti* is the plural form of *cactus*, and *leaves* is the plural form of *leaf.* **Conversion**

51. MINOTAUR : (*a.* man, *b.* monster, *c.* **harpy**, *d.* eagle) :: BULL : BIRD
(**c**) Both the Minotaur and the harpy are creatures from Greek mythology. The *Minotaur* had the body of a man and the head of a *bull*. A *harpy* had the body of a *bird* and the head of a woman. **Characteristic**

52. DYE : (*a.* bread, *b.* **wry**, *c.* hue, *d.* year) :: DIE : RYE
(**b**) The word pairs in this analogy are homophones. *Dye* and *die* sound alike, as do *wry* and *rye*. **Conversion**

53. ENFRANCHISE : VOTE :: ENTHRONE : (*a.* act, *b.* **rule**, *c.* crown, *d.* king)
(**b**) The effect of *enfranchisement* is *voting*, and the effect of *enthroning* is *ruling*. **Object/Action**

54. SAMUEL GOMPERS : JOHN L. LEWIS :: (*a.* NFL, *b.* ACLU, *c.* **AFL**, *d.* UAW) : CIO

    (**c**) *Samuel Gompers* was a founding member of the American Federation of Labor (*AFL*), and *John L. Lewis* was a founding member of the Congress of Industrial Organizations (*CIO*). Both were labor organizations. **Part/Whole**

55. 1/2 : (*a.* 1/5, *b.* 1/4, *c.* **1/10**, *d.* 2/4) :: 5 : 1

    (**c**) It's useful to look at mathematical analogies as ratios. Here, the only correct choice to complete the ratio is *1/10*, which has the same relationship to *1/2* as *1* does to *5*. In other words, 1/2 is 5 multiplied by 1/10, as 5 is 5 multiplied by 1. **Conversion**

56. DOMINANT : RECESSIVE :: (*a.* left-handedness, *b.* blue eyes, *c.* anemia, *d.* **dimples**) : ATTACHED EARLOBES

    (**d**) Of the characteristics listed, only *dimples* are a *dominant* trait in humans. All the other traits are *recessive*. **Classification**

57. (*a.* **Mercury**, *b.* Mars, *c.* Jove, *d.* Hephaestus) : NEPTUNE :: HERMES : POSEIDON

    (**a**) *Mercury* is the Roman name for the Greek god *Hermes*, and *Neptune* is the Roman name for the Greek god *Poseidon*. **Conversion**

58. VERSAILLES : WWI :: (*a.* Paris, *b.* Munich, *c.* Tripoli, *d.* **Yalta**) : WWII

    (**d**) A treaty signed at *Versailles* marked the end of *World War I*. A treaty signed at *Yalta* marked the end of *World War II*. **Object/Action**

59. CU : (*a.* Io, *b.* Rh, *c.* **Fe**, *d.* Ir) :: COPPER : IRON

    (**c**) *Cu* is the atomic symbol for the element known as *copper*. *Fe* (from the Latin word *ferrum*) is the atomic symbol for the element known as *iron*. **Conversion**

60. GENEROUS : PARSIMONIOUS :: OBSTINATE : (*a.* stubborn, *b.* bountiful, *c.* **accommodating**, *d.* mulish)

    (**c**) *Generous* is the opposite of *parsimonious*, or stingy. *Obstinate* is the opposite of *accommodating*, or cooperative. **Antonym**

61. CROSSBREED : (*a.* clone, *b.* **hybrid**, *c.* color, *d.* farming) :: CROSSHATCH : SHADING

    (**b**) The act of *crossbreeding* in plant or animal husbandry leads to a *hybrid* plant or animal. The act of *crosshatching* in charcoal or pencil drawing leads to *shading*. **Object/Action**

62. FEZ : MOROCCO :: (*a.* London, *b.* Oxford, *c.* **Derby**, *d.* Bath) : ENGLAND

    (**c**) Although *Fez* is a city in *Morocco* and all four of the answer choices are cities in *England*, only *Derby* has the corresponding quality of naming a hat as well as a city. **Characteristic**

63. FLASHY : UNASSUMING :: QUIXOTIC : (*a.* mercurial, *b.* **levelheaded**, *c.* corrupt, *d.* daring)

    (**b**) A *flashy* person is the opposite of *unassuming* or modest; a *quixotic* (unrealistic) person is the opposite of *levelheaded*. **Antonym**

64. GOSPELS : BIOGRAPHY :: REVELATIONS : (*a.* autobiography, *b.* covenant, *c.* fantasy, *d.* **prophecy**)
(**d**) Whereas the *Gospels* of Mark, Matthew, Luke, and John are all *biographies* of Jesus, the book of *Revelations* is a *prophecy* of the future. **Characteristic**

65. (*a.* firefighter, *b.* museum, *c.* **conservator**, *d.* sculptor) : PROTECTION :: CURATOR : EXHIBITION
(**c**) Both a *conservator* and a *curator* work in a museum, but a conservator's job is to *protect* old documents and artwork, while a curator's job is to put together *exhibitions*. **Object/Action**

66. HURRICANE : (*a.* flood, *b.* tornado, *c.* **typhoon**, *d.* cyclone) :: ATLANTIC : PACIFIC
(**c**) Hurricanes and typhoons are similar storms, but *hurricanes* form in the *Atlantic* Ocean, and *typhoons* form in the *Pacific* Ocean. Both may be referred to as tropical cyclones. **Characteristic**

67. MANDIBLE : JAW :: SCAPULA : (*a.* tool, *b.* elbow, *c.* **shoulder**, *d.* spine)
(**c**) The *mandible* is the bone in the *jaw*, and the *scapula* is the bone in the *shoulder*. **Characteristic**

68. PETROLOGY : (*a.* **speleology**, *b.* archaeology, *c.* teleology, *d.* phrenology) :: ROCKS : CAVES
(**a**) *Petrology* (think "petrify") is the study of *rocks*. *Speleology* (think "spelunking") is the study of *caves*. **Object/Action**

69. PICTS : (*a.* Wales, *b.* **Scotland**, *c.* France, *d.* Germany) :: CELTS : IRELAND
(**b**) The *Picts* were ancient inhabitants of what is now *Scotland*, just as the *Celts* were ancient inhabitants of what is now *Ireland*. **Characteristic**

70. (*a.* reptile, *b.* constrictor, *c.* serpent, *d.* **viper**) : PYTHON :: POISON : SUFFOCATE
(**d**) A *viper* is a venomous snake that uses *poison* to kill its prey. A *python* is a nonvenomous snake that uses constriction, or *suffocation*, to kill its prey. **Object/Action**

71. IRON : ANEMIC :: WATER : (*a.* caustic, *b.* **dehydrated**, *c.* humidified, *d.* flowing)
(**b**) Lack of *iron* can make you *anemic*. Lack of *water* can make you *dehydrated*. **Characteristic**

72. ROBERT FROST : NEW ENGLAND :: (*a.* William Carlos Willams, *b.* John Crowe Ransom, *c.* **Carl Sandburg**, *d.* Lucille Clifton): MIDWEST
(**c**) Certain American writers are associated with the region about which or from which they write. As *Robert Frost* is associated with *New England*, so *Carl Sandburg*, who wrote about Chicago and the Great Plains, is associated with the *Midwest*. **Characteristic**

73. SATIN : SMOOTHNESS :: (*a.* **corduroy**, *b.* rasp, *c.* silk, *d.* tulle) : ROUGHNESS
(**a**) *Satin* is a fabric known for its *smoothness*. *Corduroy* is a fabric known for its raised wales, which lead to *roughness*. **Characteristic**

74. LOCKE : EMPIRICISM :: MILL : (*a.* Stoicism, *b.* dogma, *c.* rationalism, *d.* **utilitarianism**)

(**d**) John *Locke* was a philosopher who espoused *empiricism*, the notion that all knowledge derives from experience. John Stuart *Mill* was a philosopher and economist who espoused *utilitarianism*, the notion that the goal should be the greatest happiness for the greatest number. **Object/Action**

75. VIRUS : INFLUENZA :: (*a.* **amoeba**, *b.* plankton, *c.* mold, *d.* vermin) : DYSENTERY

(**a**) *Influenza* is a disease caused by a *virus*. *Dysentery* is a disease often caused by an *amoeba*. **Object/Action**

76. WAG : HUMOR :: NAG : (*a.* absurdity, *b.* displeasure, *c.* human, *d.* **harassment**)

(**d**) A *wag*, or comical person, is typified by *humor*. A *nag*, or shrewish person, is typified by *harassment*. **Object/Action**

77. (*a.* prose, *b.* **tall tale**, *c.* fable, *d.* poesy) : HYPERBOLE :: POETRY : IMAGERY

(**b**) *Hyperbole*, or exaggeration, is typical of a *tall tale*. *Imagery*, or descriptive language, is typical of *poetry*. **Characteristic**

78. WEBSTER : DICTIONARY :: (*a.* **Diderot**, *b.* Johnson, *c.* Barnes, *d.* Boswell) : ENCYCLOPEDIA

(**a**) Noah *Webster* created an early *dictionary*. Jacques *Diderot* created an early *encyclopedia*. **Object/Action**

79. (*a.* sunlight, *b.* oak tree, *c.* **fungus**, *d.* fern) : PHOTOSYNTHESIZE :: ANAEROBE : RESPIRATE

(**c**) A *fungus* such as a mushroom is unable to *photosynthesize*—use sunlight to create energy. An *anaerobe*, such as certain bacteria, cannot *respirate*—use oxygen to create energy. **Characteristic**

80. ABRAHAM : (*a.* Ra, *b.* God, *c.* Moses, *d.* **Isaac**) :: ZEUS : APOLLO

(**d**) In the Bible, *Abraham* was the father of *Isaac*. In Greek mythology, *Zeus* was the father of *Apollo*. **Sequence**

81. (*a.* **puberty**, *b.* menses, *c.* menarche, *d.* month) : MENOPAUSE :: ONSET : CESSATION

(**a**) In women, the *onset* of menstruation is the time of life called *puberty*. The *cessation* of menstruation is the time of life called *menopause*. **Sequence**

82. COLANDER : (*a.* cook, *b.* **drain**, *c.* Dutch, *d.* vermin) :: BELT GRINDER : POLISH

(**b**) A *colander* is a strainer that is used to *drain* cooking water from pasta or vegetables. A *belt grinder* is a tool that is used to *polish* metal. **Object/Action**

83. CONTRALTO : MEZZO-SOPRANO :: (*a.* tenor, *b.* alto, *c.* **bass**, *d.* countertenor) : BARITONE

(**c**) In singing voices, *contralto* is one step down in range from *mezzo-soprano*, and *bass* is one step down in range from *baritone*. **Sequence**

84. FCC : FDA :: TELEVISION : (*a.* radio, *b.* banking, *c.* computers, ***d.* cosmetics**)
    (**d**) The Federal Communications Commission *(FCC)* is involved in the regulation of *television*. The Food and Drug Administration *(FDA)* is involved in the regulation of *cosmetics* as well as food and pharmaceuticals. **Object/Action**

85. EST : PST :: (***a.* 7:00**, *b.* 3:00, *c.* 1:00, *d.* 10:00) : 4:00
    (**a**) When it is *7:00* Eastern Standard Time (*EST*), it is *4:00* Pacific Standard Time (*PST*). **Sequence**

86. (*a.* virus, *b.* blood, ***c.* antibody**, *d.* pathogen) : ANTIGEN :: SHIELD : INVADER
    (**c**) In fighting disease, an *antibody* plays the part of a *shield* to the *invading antigen*, which is defined as any substance that activates an immune response. **Object/Action**

87. PSALTERY : (*a.* drum, *b.* hymnal, ***c.* dulcimer**, *d.* trumpet) :: MUSETTE : BAGPIPE
    (**c**) A *psaltery* was an early form of the musical instrument we now know as the *dulcimer*. A *musette* was an early form of the musical instrument we now know as the *bagpipe*. **Conversion**

88. INCONCEIVABLE : COMPREHENSION :: INCORRIGIBLE :
    (*a.* pretension, *b.* incomprehension, *c.* apprehension, ***d.* correction**)
    (**d**) Something that is *inconceivable*, or unbelievable, resists *comprehension*. Something that is *incorrigible*, or incurable, resists *correction*. **Object/Action**

89. DELECTABLE : DELICIOUS :: (*a.* tasty, *b.* muffled, ***c.* sonorous**, *d.* sentient) : RESONANT
    (**c**) A food that is *delectable* might also be called *delicious*. A sound that is *sonorous* might also be called *resonant*. **Synonym**

90. ELIAS HOWE : (*a.* tractor, ***b.* sewing machine**, *c.* textbook, *d.* harvester) :: ELI WHITNEY : COTTON GIN
    (**b**) Elias Howe and Eli Whitney were American inventors. *Howe* was one of the inventors of the *sewing machine*, and *Whitney* was one of the inventors of the *cotton gin*. **Object/Action**

91. SUICIDE : SELF :: PATRICIDE : (*a.* other, *b.* homicide, ***c.* father**, *d.* priest)
    (**c**) Someone guilty of *suicide* kills him*self* or her*self*. Someone guilty of *patricide* kills his or her *father*. **Object/Action**

92. (*a.* papyrus, *b.* algebra, ***c.* cuneiform**, *d.* mosaic) : SUMERIANS :: HIEROGLYPHICS : EGYPTIANS
    (**c**) *Cuneiform* and *hieroglyphics* both name early forms of writing, the former created by the *Sumerians*, and the latter created by the *Egyptians*. **Object/Action**

93. PADEREWSKI : PIANO :: (***a.* Paganini**, *b.* Puccini, *c.* Pachelbel, *d.* Piatagorsky) : VIOLIN
    (**a**) Ignace *Paderewski* was a master of the *piano*, and Nicolò *Paganini* was a master of the *violin*. **Object/Action**

94. CANDOR : (*a.* insincerity, *b.* ruse, *c.* compassion, *d.* **frankness**) :: DANDER : TEMPER

    (**d**) A synonym for *candor* is *frankness*, and a synonym for *dander* is *temper*. **Synonym**

95. STOPPLE : CLOSE :: THROTTLE : (*a.* open, *b.* drive, *c.* partition, *d.* **regulate**)

    (**d**) You would use a *stopple* to *close* something (for example, a bottle). You would use a *throttle* to *regulate* something (for example, power produced by an engine). **Object/Action**

96. CROWBAR : (*a.* loosen, *b.* between, *c.* **pry**, *d.* elevate) :: WRENCH : TIGHTEN

    (**c**) You would use a *crowbar* to *pry*, or force open, something, and you would use a *wrench* to *tighten* something. **Object/Action**

97. FOOT : YARD :: SIDE : (*a.* top, *b.* **triangle**, *c.* vertex, *d.* polygon)

    (**b**) There are three *feet* in a *yard*, and there are three *sides* in a *triangle*. **Part/Whole**

98. HUMBLE : HUMBUG :: (*a.* fumble, *b.* arrogant, *c.* **modest**, *d.* poster) : IMPOSTER

    (**c**) Someone who is *humble* is *modest*. Someone who is a *humbug* is an *imposter*, or a fake. **Synonym**

99. COLLAPSE : (*a.* appeal, *b.* tumble, *c.* **implode**, *d.* subside) :: REQUEST : IMPORTUNE

    (**c**) If something *implodes*, it *collapses* violently. In a similar vein, to *importune* is to make a *request* in the most dramatic of ways. **Degree**

100. IMPERVIOUS : PENETRATION :: IMPLACABLE :
    (*a.* **appeasement**, *b.* generosity, *c.* confirmation, *d.* subdivision)

    (**a**) A substance that is *impervious* is resistant to *penetration*. A person who is *implacable* is resistant to *appeasement*, or conciliation. **Object/Action**

PRACTICE TEST 2
ANSWER SHEET

1. Ⓐ Ⓑ Ⓒ Ⓓ	26. Ⓐ Ⓑ Ⓒ Ⓓ	51. Ⓐ Ⓑ Ⓒ Ⓓ	76. Ⓐ Ⓑ Ⓒ Ⓓ
2. Ⓐ Ⓑ Ⓒ Ⓓ	27. Ⓐ Ⓑ Ⓒ Ⓓ	52. Ⓐ Ⓑ Ⓒ Ⓓ	77. Ⓐ Ⓑ Ⓒ Ⓓ
3. Ⓐ Ⓑ Ⓒ Ⓓ	28. Ⓐ Ⓑ Ⓒ Ⓓ	53. Ⓐ Ⓑ Ⓒ Ⓓ	78. Ⓐ Ⓑ Ⓒ Ⓓ
4. Ⓐ Ⓑ Ⓒ Ⓓ	29. Ⓐ Ⓑ Ⓒ Ⓓ	54. Ⓐ Ⓑ Ⓒ Ⓓ	79. Ⓐ Ⓑ Ⓒ Ⓓ
5. Ⓐ Ⓑ Ⓒ Ⓓ	30. Ⓐ Ⓑ Ⓒ Ⓓ	55. Ⓐ Ⓑ Ⓒ Ⓓ	80. Ⓐ Ⓑ Ⓒ Ⓓ
6. Ⓐ Ⓑ Ⓒ Ⓓ	31. Ⓐ Ⓑ Ⓒ Ⓓ	56. Ⓐ Ⓑ Ⓒ Ⓓ	81. Ⓐ Ⓑ Ⓒ Ⓓ
7. Ⓐ Ⓑ Ⓒ Ⓓ	32. Ⓐ Ⓑ Ⓒ Ⓓ	57. Ⓐ Ⓑ Ⓒ Ⓓ	82. Ⓐ Ⓑ Ⓒ Ⓓ
8. Ⓐ Ⓑ Ⓒ Ⓓ	33. Ⓐ Ⓑ Ⓒ Ⓓ	58. Ⓐ Ⓑ Ⓒ Ⓓ	83. Ⓐ Ⓑ Ⓒ Ⓓ
9. Ⓐ Ⓑ Ⓒ Ⓓ	34. Ⓐ Ⓑ Ⓒ Ⓓ	59. Ⓐ Ⓑ Ⓒ Ⓓ	84. Ⓐ Ⓑ Ⓒ Ⓓ
10. Ⓐ Ⓑ Ⓒ Ⓓ	35. Ⓐ Ⓑ Ⓒ Ⓓ	60. Ⓐ Ⓑ Ⓒ Ⓓ	85. Ⓐ Ⓑ Ⓒ Ⓓ
11. Ⓐ Ⓑ Ⓒ Ⓓ	36. Ⓐ Ⓑ Ⓒ Ⓓ	61. Ⓐ Ⓑ Ⓒ Ⓓ	86. Ⓐ Ⓑ Ⓒ Ⓓ
12. Ⓐ Ⓑ Ⓒ Ⓓ	37. Ⓐ Ⓑ Ⓒ Ⓓ	62. Ⓐ Ⓑ Ⓒ Ⓓ	87. Ⓐ Ⓑ Ⓒ Ⓓ
13. Ⓐ Ⓑ Ⓒ Ⓓ	38. Ⓐ Ⓑ Ⓒ Ⓓ	63. Ⓐ Ⓑ Ⓒ Ⓓ	88. Ⓐ Ⓑ Ⓒ Ⓓ
14. Ⓐ Ⓑ Ⓒ Ⓓ	39. Ⓐ Ⓑ Ⓒ Ⓓ	64. Ⓐ Ⓑ Ⓒ Ⓓ	89. Ⓐ Ⓑ Ⓒ Ⓓ
15. Ⓐ Ⓑ Ⓒ Ⓓ	40. Ⓐ Ⓑ Ⓒ Ⓓ	65. Ⓐ Ⓑ Ⓒ Ⓓ	90. Ⓐ Ⓑ Ⓒ Ⓓ
16. Ⓐ Ⓑ Ⓒ Ⓓ	41. Ⓐ Ⓑ Ⓒ Ⓓ	66. Ⓐ Ⓑ Ⓒ Ⓓ	91. Ⓐ Ⓑ Ⓒ Ⓓ
17. Ⓐ Ⓑ Ⓒ Ⓓ	42. Ⓐ Ⓑ Ⓒ Ⓓ	67. Ⓐ Ⓑ Ⓒ Ⓓ	92. Ⓐ Ⓑ Ⓒ Ⓓ
18. Ⓐ Ⓑ Ⓒ Ⓓ	43. Ⓐ Ⓑ Ⓒ Ⓓ	68. Ⓐ Ⓑ Ⓒ Ⓓ	93. Ⓐ Ⓑ Ⓒ Ⓓ
19. Ⓐ Ⓑ Ⓒ Ⓓ	44. Ⓐ Ⓑ Ⓒ Ⓓ	69. Ⓐ Ⓑ Ⓒ Ⓓ	94. Ⓐ Ⓑ Ⓒ Ⓓ
20. Ⓐ Ⓑ Ⓒ Ⓓ	45. Ⓐ Ⓑ Ⓒ Ⓓ	70. Ⓐ Ⓑ Ⓒ Ⓓ	95. Ⓐ Ⓑ Ⓒ Ⓓ
21. Ⓐ Ⓑ Ⓒ Ⓓ	46. Ⓐ Ⓑ Ⓒ Ⓓ	71. Ⓐ Ⓑ Ⓒ Ⓓ	96. Ⓐ Ⓑ Ⓒ Ⓓ
22. Ⓐ Ⓑ Ⓒ Ⓓ	47. Ⓐ Ⓑ Ⓒ Ⓓ	72. Ⓐ Ⓑ Ⓒ Ⓓ	97. Ⓐ Ⓑ Ⓒ Ⓓ
23. Ⓐ Ⓑ Ⓒ Ⓓ	48. Ⓐ Ⓑ Ⓒ Ⓓ	73. Ⓐ Ⓑ Ⓒ Ⓓ	98. Ⓐ Ⓑ Ⓒ Ⓓ
24. Ⓐ Ⓑ Ⓒ Ⓓ	49. Ⓐ Ⓑ Ⓒ Ⓓ	74. Ⓐ Ⓑ Ⓒ Ⓓ	99. Ⓐ Ⓑ Ⓒ Ⓓ
25. Ⓐ Ⓑ Ⓒ Ⓓ	50. Ⓐ Ⓑ Ⓒ Ⓓ	75. Ⓐ Ⓑ Ⓒ Ⓓ	100. Ⓐ Ⓑ Ⓒ Ⓓ

PRACTICE TEST 2

> **Directions**: For each question, you will see three capitalized words and four answer choices labeled *a*, *b*, *c*, and *d* in parentheses. Choose the answer that best completes the analogy posed by the three capitalized words. Use the answer sheet on page 61 to record your answers.

Time: 50 Minutes

1. (*a*. Gauguin, *b*. Picasso, *c*. Monet, *d*. Cezanne) : BLUE BOY :: RODIN : THE THINKER

2. GERBIL : RODENT :: (*a*. hare, *b*. cat, *c*. fox, *d*. bear) : LAGOMORPH

3. DECADE : YEAR :: CENTURY : (*a*. millennium, *b*. decade, *c*. biannual, *d*. month)

4. (*a*. trapezoid, *b*. equilateral, *c*. prism, *d*. heptagon) : QUADRILATERAL :: SQUARE : RECTANGLE

5. RONALD REAGAN : (*a*. Alexander Haig, *b*. George H. W. Bush, *c*. Jimmy Carter, *d*. William Rehnquist) :: JOHN ADAMS : JOHN MARSHALL

6. PUFFIN : PUFFBALL :: BIRD : (*a*. birdhouse, *b*. reptile, *c*. fern, *d*. fungus)

7. (*a*. evolve, *b*. surround, *c*. rotate, *d*. alternate) : REVOLVE :: DIVE : PLUMMET

8. DEMOSTHENES : (*a*. medicine, *b*. oratory, *c*. drama, *d*. government) :: LYSANDER : WARFARE

9. TWO : FOUR :: (*a*. vice president, *b*. governor, *c*. prime minister, *d*. representative) : PRESIDENT

10. (*a*. anchor, *b*. gunwale, *c*. hull, *d*. cabin) : STRUCTURE :: KEEL : STABILITY

11. BOW : VALVE :: CELLIST : (*a*. engineer, *b*. mechanic, *c*. trumpeter, *d*. scientist)

12. OMNI- : (*a*. poly-, *b*. ambi-, *c*. meta-, *d*. ante-) :: ALL : MANY

13. JAIL : STIR :: OFFICE : (*a.* work, *b.* storeroom, *c.* building, *d.* HQ)

14. BIG BANG : UNIVERSE :: (*a.* quantum, *b.* conservation, *c.* thermal, *d.* gravitational) : ENERGY

15. (*a.* action, *b.* scene, *c.* monologue, *d.* drama) : ACTOR :: SOLO : SINGER

16. SPANISH : CUBA :: FRENCH : (*a.* Grenada, *b.* Haiti, *c.* Brazil, *d.* St. Thomas)

17. REMINISCE : (*a.* consider, *b.* acquiesce, *c.* discuss, *d.* recall) :: CHAT : CONVERSE

18. 2/5 : 3/7 :: (*a.* 4/5, *b.* 7/5, *c.* 5/2, *d.* 1/5) : 7/3

19. PERIDOT : (*a.* green, *b.* orange, *c.* blue, *d.* silver) :: GARNET : RED

20. (*a.* Gl, *b.* Mu, *c.* Si, *d.* Ag) : AU :: SILVER : GOLD

21. HYPOTHALAMUS : EMOTIONS :: (*a.* cerebellum, *b.* cerebrum, *c.* pancreas, *d.* medulla) : BALANCE

22. (*a.* whole milk, *b.* vitamins, *c.* distilled water, *d.* soybeans) : MINERALS :: SOY MILK : LACTOSE

23. REQUIRED : ESSENTIAL :: REDUNDANT : (*a.* again, *b.* pointless, *c.* vital, *d.* ongoing)

24. PHANTASM : (*a.* reality, *b.* mystery, *c.* dread, *d.* buoyancy) :: INMATE : FREEDOM

25. (*a.* Edmund Quincy, *b.* John Deere, *c.* Cyrus McCormick, *d.* Jethro Tull) : SEED DRILL :: EDMOND HALLEY : DIVING BELL

26. LOW : (*a.* high, *b.* felines, *c.* cattle, *d.* gloomy) :: CROW : ROOSTERS

27. (*a.* Parliament, *b.* Duma, *c.* KGB, *d.* Mir) : KNESSET :: RUSSIA : ISRAEL

28. DOTE : DOTAGE :: (*a.* neglect, *b.* young, *c.* teenager, *d.* adore) : YOUTH

29. DALI : PAINTING :: GAUDI : (*a.* sculpture, *b.* architecture, *c.* poetry, *d.* drama)

30. (*a.* scuttle, *b.* stagger, *c.* swoop, *d.* shamble) : SHUFFLE :: HUSTLE : AMBLE

31. OPERA : ACT :: SYMPHONY : (*a.* instrument, *b.* bar, *c.* prelude, *d.* movement)

32. (*a.* equilateral triangle, *b.* hexagon, *c.* polygon, *d.* quadrilateral) : 360 :: PENTAGON : 540

33. IRAN : PERSIA :: (*a.* Turkey, *b.* Jordan, *c.* Iraq, *d.* Yemen) : MESOPOTAMIA

34. FEARFUL : TERRIFIED :: (*a.* petrified, *b.* surprised, *c.* miraculous, *d.* unconcerned) : ASTOUNDED

35. TRADE DEFICIT : EXPORTS :: FEDERAL DEFICIT : (*a.* imports, *b.* tariffs, *c.* revenue, *d.* trade)

36. KILO- : (*a.* milli-, *b.* hecto-, *c.* deci-, *d.* multi-) :: THOUSAND : HUNDRED

37. (*a.* Hinduism, *b.* meditation, *c.* metaphysics, *d.* sociology) : PHILOSOPHY :: BUDDHISM : RELIGION

38. FREETOWN : SIERRA LEONE :: (*a.* Monrovia, *b.* Georgetown, *c.* Washington, *d.* Liberty) : LIBERIA

39. TEST PILOT : (*a.* volt, *b.* rpm, *c.* mach, *d.* anemometer) :: ELECTRICIAN : OHM

40. CROWBAR : LEVER :: AUGER : (*a.* tool, *b.* screw, *c.* drill bit, *d.* motor)

41. (*a.* brine shrimp, *b.* lobster, *c.* flea, *d.* octopus) : MOLLUSK :: CRAB : CRUSTACEAN

42. FIBULA : TIBIA :: RADIUS : (*a.* scapula, *b.* phalange, *c.* clavicle, *d.* ulna)

43. HALE : (*a.* muscular, *b.* ailing, *c.* chaotic, *d.* vigorous) :: NEAT : DISORDERLY

44. MERLIN : ARTHUR :: (*a.* Dr. Pangloss, *b.* Voltaire, *c.* Siddhartha, *d.* Cunegonde) : CANDIDE

45. TARANTULA : TARANTELLA :: SPIDER : (*a.* dance, *b.* fabric, *c.* weasel, *d.* automobile)

46. (*a.* viruses, *b.* monerans, *c.* E. coli, *d.* spirochete) : BACTERIA :: PLANTS : MOSSES

47. SOLID : LIQUID :: GAS : (*a.* air, *b.* hydrogen, *c.* plasma, *d.* matter)

48. AUBERGINE : PURPLE :: (*a.* berry, *b.* spectrum, *c.* chartreuse, *d.* cobalt) : BLUE

49. CALIPER : WEIR :: THICKNESS : (*a.* dam, *b.* river, *c.* flow, *d.* distance)

50. CAESURA : PAUSE :: (*a.* metonymy, *b.* elision, *c.* anaphora, *d.* apostrophe) : REPETITION

51. RED DELICIOUS : APPLE :: (*a.* yellow, *b.* Bosc, *c.* poire, *d.* cultivar) : PEAR

52. FIRST WORLD : THIRD WORLD :: (*a.* capitalist, *b.* Old World, *c.* discovered, *d.* monarchy) : UNDERDEVELOPED

53. SUPERIOR : (*a.* anterior, *b.* Atlantic, *c.* Erie, *d.* Native American) :: PACIFIC : INDIAN

54. ROOSEVELT : NEW DEAL :: (*a.* Hoover, *b.* Kennedy, *c.* Truman, *d.* Johnson) : FAIR DEAL

55. (*a.* pleasure, *b.* concern, *c.* dream, *d.* health) : RAPTURE :: WORRY : AFFLICTION

56. PRESBYTERIAN : (*a.* Baptist, *b.* Protestant, *c.* Mennonite, *d.* Calvinism) :: MAHAYANA : BUDDHIST

57. (*a.* volt, *b.* electricity, *c.* map, *d.* dampness) : AMP :: DIET : TIDE

58. RACECOURSE : HORSERACE :: HIPPODROME : (*a.* zoo, *b.* battle, *c.* dressage, *d.* footrace)

59. TILDE : (*a.* cedilla, *b.* accent, *c.* inflection, *d.* circumflex) :: ˜ : ˆ

60. 1919 : 1984 :: (*a.* Hemingway, *b.* O'Connor, *c.* Faulkner, *d.* Dos Passos) : ORWELL

61. (*a.* CPU, *b.* television, *c.* radio, *d.* supervisor) : MONITOR :: ANTENNA : DIAL

62. DIONYSUS : (*a.* Apollo, *b.* Ulysses, *c.* Bacchus, *d.* Ceres) :: EROS : CUPID

63. ADULT : JUVENILE :: SHAM : (*a.* bogus, *b.* bona fide, *c.* sage, *d.* quack)

64. (*a.* Hart, *b.* Evans, *c.* Bernstein, *d.* Newman) : RODGERS :: LYRICS : MUSIC

65. ST. PAUL'S : ST. PETER'S :: (*a.* New York, *b.* Florence, *c.* London, *d.* Paris) : ROME

66. PORTENTOUS : PORTABLE :: MODEST : (*a.* permanent, *b.* unassuming, *c.* convenient, *d.* arrogant)

67. DOCTOR : PROCTOR :: CLINIC : (*a.* church, *b.* school, *c.* hospital, *d.* alleyway)

68. NAST : STUART :: (*a.* landscape, *b.* sketch, *c.* watercolor, *d.* cartoon) : PORTRAIT

69. (*a.* Kilimanjaro, *b.* Mount Everest , *c.* K2, *d.* Makalu) : KORAKARAM :: MONT BLANC : ALPS

70. GREECE : EGYPT :: APOLLO : (*a.* Amun, *b.* Ra, *c.* Osiris, *d.* Pharaoh)

71. (*a.* pituitary, *b.* adrenal, *c.* oxytocin, *d.* endocrine) : ADH :: PANCREAS : INSULIN

72. FLAMENCO : SPAIN :: (*a.* troika, *b.* mazurka, *c.* polka, *d.* schottische) : POLAND

73. WALKING STICK : CAMOUFLAGE :: HAWK MOTH : (*a.* mimicry, *b.* prey, *c.* coloration, *d.* distraction)

74. MILLARD FILLMORE : (*a.* Democrat, *b.* Tory, *c.* Federalist, *d.* Whig) :: ABRAHAM LINCOLN : REPUBLICAN

75. ID : SUPEREGO :: INSTINCT : (*a.* impulse, *b.* morality, *c.* personality, *d.* heroism)

76. PATENT : (*a.* contract, *b.* inventor, *c.* device, *d.* application) :: COPYRIGHT : DOCUMENT

77. TANKARD : FLUTE :: PEWTER : (*a.* tin, *b.* ale, *c.* goblet, *d.* crystal)

78. FISSION : (*a.* missile, *b.* A-bomb, *c.* automatic weapon, *d.* nuclear energy) :: FUSION : H-BOMB

79. (*a.* quarter, *b.* dime, *c.* nickel, *d.* penny) : HALF-DOLLAR :: WASHINGTON : KENNEDY

80. NOVEMBER : OCTOBER :: WEDNESDAY : (*a.* Thursday, *b.* weekend, *c.* Tuesday, *d.* Sunday)

81. (*a.* rings, *b.* moon, *c.* Venus, *d.* planet) : 2 :: SATURN : 6

82. ATAXIA : (*a.* hearing, *b.* oration, *c.* movement, *d.* sight) :: APHASIA : SPEECH

83. ERIC THE RED : LEIF ERICCSON :: HENRY VIII : (*a.* Henry VII, *b.* Elizabeth I, *c.* Anne Boleyn, *d.* James I)

84. ANTONY AND CLEOPATRA : CAESAR AND CLEOPATRA :: SHAKESPEARE : (*a.* Wilde, *b.* Jonson, *c.* Marlowe, *d.* Shaw)

85. TOPSOIL : (*a.* agrarianism, *b.* subsoil, *c.* loess, *d.* clay) :: SUBSOIL : BEDROCK

86. ANTIQUARIAN : STATIONER :: (*a.* jeroboam, *b.* merlot, *c.* grape, *d.* wine cellar) : VINTNER

87. FLUTE : FLUGELHORN :: (*a.* silver, *b.* woodwind, *c.* tuba, *d.* sharp) : BRASS

88. CLARENCE BIRDSEYE : FROZEN FOOD :: LADISLO BIRO : (*a.* fast food, *b.* freezer, *c.* ballpoint pen, *d.* electric shaver)

89. JUG : (*a.* flagon, *b.* vat, *c.* container, *d.* beaker) :: MUG : TANKARD

90. WANT : LIKE :: (*a.* need, *b.* venerate, *c.* crave, *d.* loathe) : WORSHIP

91. KING JOHN : MAGNA CARTA :: KING HENRY VIII : (*a.* Church of England, *b.* Synod of Whitby, *c.* Petition of Right, *d.* Atlantic Charter)

92. AUGUST : MARCH :: (*a.* dance, *b.* vagabond, *c.* harvest, *d.* impressive) : TRAMP

93. (*a.* exist, *b.* lift, *c.* exorcise, *d.* hail) : SPIRIT :: EXCISE : TUMOR

94. FDIC : (*a.* stockbrokers, *b.* consumers, *c.* bank depositors, *d.* petitioners) :: FEMA : DISASTER VICTIMS

95. PHOBOS : MARS :: IO : (*a.* satellite, *b.* Saturn, *c.* sun, *d.* Jupiter)

96. WAVE : FAREWELL :: HANDSHAKE : (*a.* exit, *b.* summons, *c.* agreement, *d.* businessperson)

97. (*a.* luscious, *b.* pungent, *c.* diminutive, *d.* corpulent) : MINUSCULE :: AROMATIC : FRAGRANT

98. INDELIBLE : ERASURE :: (*a.* inexorable, *b.* indisputable, *c.* inaccurate, *d.* indirect) : ARGUMENT

99. EINE KLEINE NACHTMUSIC : A LITTLE NIGHT MUSIC :: MOZART : (*a.* Sondheim, *b.* Hammerstein, *c.* Copland, *d.* Ives)

100. ALGAE : (*a.* spruce, *b.* lichen, *c.* bean, *d.* petunia) :: CACTUS : PALM

STOP

If there is any time remaining, go back and check your work.

PRACTICE TEST 2
ANSWER KEY

1. b	26. c	51. b	76. c
2. a	27. b	52. a	77. d
3. b	28. a	53. c	78. b
4. a	29. b	54. c	79. a
5. d	30. a	55. a	80. c
6. d	31. d	56. b	81. c
7. c	32. d	57. c	82. c
8. b	33. c	58. c	83. b
9. d	34. b	59. d	84. d
10. c	35. c	60. d	85. b
11. c	36. b	61. a	86. a
12. a	37. c	62. c	87. b
13. d	38. a	63. b	88. c
14. a	39. c	64. a	89. a
15. c	40. b	65. c	90. c
16. b	41. d	66. a	91. a
17. d	42. d	67. b	92. d
18. c	43. b	68. d	93. c
19. a	44. a	69. c	94. c
20. d	45. a	70. b	95. d
21. a	46. b	71. a	96. c
22. c	47. c	72. b	97. c
23. b	48. d	73. a	98. b
24. a	49. c	74. d	99. a
25. d	50. c	75. b	100. b

PRACTICE TEST 2
EXPLANATORY ANSWERS

1. (*a.* Gauguin, ***b.* Picasso**, *c.* Monet, *d.* Cezanne) : BLUE BOY :: RODIN : THE THINKER
   (**b**) *Blue Boy* is a painting from Pablo *Picasso's* blue period, and *The Thinker* is a statue by Auguste *Rodin*. **Object/Action**

2. GERBIL : RODENT :: (***a.* hare**, *b.* cat, *c.* fox, *d.* bear) : LAGOMORPH
   (**a**) *Gerbils* belong to the order *Rodentia*, and *hares* belong to the order *Lagomorpha*. **Classification**

3. DECADE : YEAR :: CENTURY : (*a.* millennium, ***b.* decade**, *c.* biannual, *d.* month)
   (**b**) Just as a *year* is part of a *decade*, a *decade* is part of a *century*. There are 10 years in a decade and 10 decades in a century. **Part/Whole**

4. (***a.* trapezoid**, *b.* equilateral, *c.* prism, *d.* heptagon) : QUADRILATERAL :: SQUARE : RECTANGLE
   (**a**) A *trapezoid* is one kind of *quadrilateral*, or a four-sided figure. A *square* is one kind of *rectangle*, or four-sided figure with four right angles. **Classification**

5. RONALD REAGAN : (*a.* Alexander Haig, *b.* George H. W. Bush, *c.* Jimmy Carter, ***d.* William Rehnquist**) :: JOHN ADAMS : JOHN MARSHALL
   (**d**) *Ronald Reagan* appointed *William Rehnquist* to the Supreme Court, and Rehnquist became chief justice. *John Adams* appointed *John Marshall* to the Supreme Court, where Marshall achieved the same position. **Object/Action**

6. PUFFIN : PUFFBALL :: BIRD : (*a.* birdhouse, *b.* reptile, *c.* fern, ***d.* fungus**)
   (**d**) A *puffin* is a northern sea*bird*. A *puffball* is a ball-shaped *fungus*. **Classification**

7. (*a.* evolve, *b.* surround, ***c.* rotate**, *d.* alternate) : REVOLVE :: DIVE : PLUMMET
   (**c**) To *rotate* is to *revolve*, or turn around. To *dive* is to *plummet*, or drop downward. **Synonym**

8. DEMOSTHENES : (*a.* medicine, ***b.* oratory**, *c.* drama, *d.* government) :: LYSANDER : WARFARE
   (**b**) *Demosthenes* (384–322 B.C.) was an Athenian statesman known for his grand *oratory*. *Lysander* (d. 395 B.C.) was the Spartan commander who helped win the Peloponnesian *War*. **Object/Action**

9. TWO : FOUR :: (*a.* vice president, *b.* governor, *c.* prime minister, ***d.* representative**) : PRESIDENT
   (**d**) A *representative* in the House of Representatives serves a *two*-year term. The *president* serves a *four*-year term. **Characteristic**

10. (*a.* anchor, *b.* gunwale, ***c.* hull**, *d.* cabin) : STRUCTURE :: KEEL : STABILITY
    (**c**) A boat's *hull* gives the boat its shape, or *structure*. A boat's *keel* exists to give it *stability* in the water. **Object/Action**

11. BOW : VALVE :: CELLIST : (*a.* engineer, *b.* mechanic, **c. trumpeter**, *d.* scientist)
(**c**) Although a valve may appear on a number of machines, look for the answer choice that matches most closely to *cellist*. A *cellist* makes music using a *bow*. A *trumpeter* makes music using the *valves* on the trumpet. **Object/Action**

12. OMNI- : (**a. poly-**, *b.* ambi-, *c.* meta-, *d.* ante-) :: ALL : MANY
(**a**) *Omni-* is a prefix that means "*all*," as in *omnivorous*. *Poly-* is a prefix that means "*many*," as in *polygamous*. **Affix**

13. JAIL : STIR :: OFFICE : (*a.* work, *b.* storeroom, *c.* building, **d. HQ**)
(**d**) A slang term for *jail* is *stir;* a slang term for an *office* is *HQ* (headquarters). **Synonym**

14. BIG BANG : UNIVERSE :: (**a. quantum**, *b.* conservation, *c.* thermal, *d.* gravitational) : ENERGY
(**a**) The *big bang* theory is a theory about the inception of the *universe*, and *quantum* theory is a theory about the creation of *energy*. **Characteristic**

15. (*a.* action, *b.* scene, **c. monologue**, *d.* drama) : ACTOR :: SOLO : SINGER
(**c**) An *actor* performs a *monologue* unaccompanied by other actors; a *singer* performs a *solo* unaccompanied by other singers. **Object/Action**

16. SPANISH : CUBA :: FRENCH : (*a.* Grenada, **b. Haiti**, *c.* Brazil, *d.* St. Thomas)
(**b**) *Spanish* is the principal language of *Cuba*, and *French* is the principal language of *Haiti*. **Characteristic**

17. REMINISCE : (*a.* consider, *b.* acquiesce, *c.* discuss, **d. recall**) :: CHAT : CONVERSE
(**d**) When you *reminisce* about something, you *recall*, or remember it. When you *chat*, you *converse*, or make conversation. **Synonym**

18. 2/5 : 3/7 :: (*a.* 4/5, *b.* 7/5, **c. 5/2**, *d.* 1/5) : 7/3
(**c**) The fractions *2/5* and *5/2* are reciprocals; in other words, 2/5 × 5/2 = 1. The fractions *3/7* and *7/3* are also reciprocals. **Conversion**

19. PERIDOT : (**a. green**, *b.* orange, *c.* blue, *d.* silver) :: GARNET : RED
(**a**) A *peridot* is a pale *green* gemstone. A *garnet* is a deep *red* gemstone. **Characteristic**

20. (*a.* Gl, *b.* Mu, *c.* Si, **d. Ag**) : AU :: SILVER : GOLD
(**d**) *Ag* (from Latin *argentum*) is the atomic symbol for *silver*, and *Au* (from Latin *aurum*) is the atomic symbol for *gold*. **Conversion**

21. HYPOTHALAMUS : EMOTIONS :: (**a. cerebellum**, *b.* cerebrum, *c.* pancreas, *d.* medulla) : BALANCE
(**a**) Brain studies indicate that the small part of the brain called the *hypothalamus* is responsible for our *emotions*, whereas the *cerebellum* is responsible for our ability to *balance*. **Object/Action**

22. (*a.* whole milk, *b.* vitamins, **c. distilled water**, *d.* soybeans) : MINERALS :: SOY MILK : LACTOSE

(c) *Distilled water* is water from which *minerals* have been removed. *Soy milk*, which is made from soy rather than cow's milk or goat's milk, lacks the milk sugar known as *lactose*. **Characteristic**

23. REQUIRED : ESSENTIAL :: REDUNDANT : (*a.* again, ***b.* pointless**, *c.* vital, *d.* ongoing)

    (**b**) If something is absolutely *required*, it is *essential.* If something is very much *redundant*, or superfluous, it might be considered *pointless.* **Degree**

24. PHANTASM : (***a.* reality**, *b.* mystery, *c.* dread, *d.* buoyancy) :: INMATE : FREEDOM

    (**a**) A *phantasm*, or phantom, lacks *reality*. An *inmate*, or prisoner, lacks *freedom.* **Characteristic**

25. (*a.* Edmund Quincy, *b.* John Deere, *c.* Cyrus McCormick, ***d.* Jethro Tull**) : SEED DRILL :: EDMOND HALLEY : DIVING BELL

    (**d**) *Jethro Tull* was a real person, not just a rock band, and his invention of the *seed drill* in 1701 revolutionized farming. *Edmond Halley*, better known for his discovery of the comet that bears his name, invented the *diving bell* in 1690. **Object/Action**

26. LOW : (*a.* high, *b.* felines, ***c.* cattle**, *d.* gloomy) :: CROW : ROOSTERS

    (**c**) The sound *cattle* make is called *lowing*, and the sound *roosters* make is called *crowing.* **Object/Action**

27. (*a.* Parliament, ***b.* Duma**, *c.* KGB, *d.* Mir) : KNESSET :: RUSSIA : ISRAEL

    (**b**) The *Duma* is the *Russian* parliament, and the *Knesset* is the *Israeli* parliament. **Characteristic**

28. DOTE : DOTAGE :: (***a.* neglect**, *b.* young, *c.* teenager, *d.* adore) : YOUTH

    (**a**) The opposite of *dote*, or adore, is *neglect.* The opposite of *dotage*, or old age, is *youth.* **Antonym**

29. DALI : PAINTING :: GAUDÍ : (*a.* sculpture, ***b.* architecture**, *c.* poetry, *d.* drama)

    (**b**) Salvador *Dali* was a Spanish *painter* in the surrealist tradition. Antonio *Gaudí* was a Spanish *architect* in the Spanish art nouveau tradition. **Object/Action**

30. (***a.* scuttle**, *b.* stagger, *c.* swoop, *d.* shamble) : SHUFFLE :: HUSTLE : AMBLE

    (**a**) To *scuttle* is to move quickly; to *shuffle* is to move slowly. To *hustle* is to move quickly; to *amble* is to move slowly. **Antonym**

31. OPERA : ACT :: SYMPHONY : (*a.* instrument, *b.* bar, *c.* prelude, ***d.* movement**)

    (**d**) An *opera* is divided into *acts*, and a *symphony* is divided into *movements.* **Part/Whole**

32. (*a.* equilateral triangle, *b.* hexagon, *c.* polygon, ***d.* quadrilateral**) : 360 :: PENTAGON : 540

    (**d**) The sum of the angles in a *quadrilateral* (four-sided figure) is *360.* The sum of the angles in a *pentagon* (five-sided figure) is *540.* **Characteristic**

33. IRAN : PERSIA :: (*a.* Turkey, *b.* Jordan, *c.* **Iraq**, *d.* Yemen) : MESOPOTAMIA
    (c) The country we call *Iran* encompasses what was once ancient *Persia*. The countries of *Iraq* and part of Syria encompass what was once ancient *Mesopotamia*. **Conversion**

34. FEARFUL : TERRIFIED :: (*a.* petrified, *b.* **surprised**, *c.* miraculous, *d.* unconcerned) : ASTOUNDED
    (b) If you are very *fearful*, you are *terrified*. If you are very *surprised*, you are *astounded*. **Degree**

35. TRADE DEFICIT : EXPORTS :: FEDERAL DEFICIT : (*a.* imports, *b.* tariffs, *c.* **revenue**, *d.* trade)
    (c) A *trade deficit* arises when *exports* lag behind imports. A *federal deficit* arises when *revenue* (money taken in, as through taxes) lags behind spending. **Object/Action**

36. KILO- : (*a.* milli-, *b.* **hecto-**, *c.* deci-, *d.* multi-) :: THOUSAND : HUNDRED
    (b) The prefix *kilo-*, as in *kilogram*, means "*thousand.*" The prefix *hecto-*, as in *hectare*, means "*hundred.*" **Affix**

37. (*a.* Hinduism, *b.* meditation, *c.* **metaphysics**, *d.* sociology) : PHILOSOPHY :: BUDDHISM : RELIGION
    (c) *Metaphysics* is one branch of *philosophy*, just as *Buddhism* is one kind of *religion*. **Classification**

38. FREETOWN : SIERRA LEONE :: (*a.* **Monrovia**, *b.* Georgetown, *c.* Washington, *d.* Liberty) : LIBERIA
    (a) *Freetown* is the capital of *Sierra Leone*, and *Monrovia* (named after James Monroe) is the capital of *Liberia*. Freed slaves first settled both African countries; ergo, the names of the capitals refer to past history. **Characteristic**

39. TEST PILOT : (*a.* volt, *b.* rpm, *c.* **mach**, *d.* anemometer) :: ELECTRICIAN : OHM
    (c) The *mach* is a unit of measure used by *test pilots* to measure speed. The *ohm* is a unit of measure used by *electricians* to measure resistance. **Object/Action**

40. CROWBAR : LEVER :: AUGER : (*a.* tool, *b.* **screw**, *c.* drill bit, *d.* motor)
    (b) The *crowbar* is a classic example of the kind of tool known as the *lever*.
    The *auger*, a kind of drill, is a classic example of the class of tool known as the *screw*. **Classification**

41. (*a.* brine shrimp, *b.* lobster, *c.* flea, *d.* **octopus**) : MOLLUSK :: CRAB : CRUSTACEAN
    (d) An *octopus* is a member of the phylum known as *Mollusca*. *Crabs* and all of the other answer choices are members of the *Crustacea* phylum. **Classification**

42. FIBULA : TIBIA :: RADIUS : (*a.* scapula, *b.* phalange, *c.* clavicle, *d.* **ulna**)
    (d) The *fibula* and *tibia* are the outer and inner leg bones. The *radius* and *ulna* are the outer and inner arm bones. **Part/Whole**

43. HALE : (*a.* muscular, *b.* **ailing**, *c.* chaotic, *d.* vigorous) :: NEAT : DISORDERLY
    (b) *Hale*, or healthy, is the opposite of *ailing*. *Neat* is the opposite of *disorderly*. **Antonym**

44. MERLIN : ARTHUR :: (***a*. Dr. Pangloss**, *b*. Voltaire, *c*. Siddhartha, *d*. Cunegonde) : CANDIDE

    (**a**) In the legend of King *Arthur*, *Merlin* is Arthur's teacher. In Voltaire's *Candide*, *Dr. Pangloss* instructs *Candide*. **Object/Action**

45. TARANTULA : TARANTELLA :: SPIDER : (***a*. dance**, *b*. fabric, *c*. weasel, *d*. automobile)

    (**a**) A *tarantula* is a type of *spider*, and the *tarantella* is a lively Italian *dance*. **Classification**

46. (*a*. viruses, ***b*. monerans**, *c*. E. coli, *d*. spirochete) : BACTERIA :: PLANTS : MOSSES

    (**b**) *Bacteria* are members of the kingdom *Monera*, and *mosses* are members of the kingdom *Plantae*. **Classification**

47. SOLID : LIQUID :: GAS : (*a*. air, *b*. hydrogen, ***c*. plasma**, *d*. matter)

    (**c**) The four parts of this analogy name the four states of matter: *solid, liquid, gas,* and *plasma*. **Part/Whole**

48. AUBERGINE : PURPLE :: (*a*. berry, *b*. spectrum, *c*. chartreuse, ***d*. cobalt**) : BLUE

    (**d**) *Aubergine*, or eggplant, is a shade of *purple*. *Cobalt* is a shade of *blue*. **Classification**

49. CALIPER : WEIR :: THICKNESS : (*a*. dam, *b*. river, ***c*. flow**, *d*. distance)

    (**c**) A *caliper* is a tool used to measure *thickness*. A *weir* is a low dam that may be used to divert or to measure a river's *flow*. **Object/Action**

50. CAESURA : PAUSE :: (*a*. metonymy, *b*. elision, ***c*. anaphora**, *d*. apostrophe) : REPETITION

    (**c**) In poetry or prose, a *caesura* is a break or *pause* in a line. An *anaphora* is the *repetition* of a word or a phrase. **Synonym**

51. RED DELICIOUS : APPLE :: (*a*. yellow, ***b*. Bosc**, *c*. poire, *d*. cultivar) : PEAR

    (**b**) A popular variety of *apple* is the *red delicious*; a popular variety of *pear* is the *Bosc*. **Classification**

52. FIRST WORLD : THIRD WORLD :: (***a*. capitalist**, *b*. Old World, *c*. discovered, *d*. monarchy) : UNDERDEVELOPED

    (**a**) These are terms left over from the Cold War. When we speak of the *third world*, we refer to *underdeveloped* nations, which are differentiated from *first world* nations, which are *capitalist*, and second world nations, which are communist. **Classification**

53. SUPERIOR : (*a*. anterior, *b*. Atlantic, ***c*. Erie**, *d*. Native American) :: PACIFIC : INDIAN

    (**c**) *Superior* and *Erie* are the names of two of the Great Lakes. *Pacific* and *Indian* are the names of two oceans. **Part/Whole**

54. ROOSEVELT : NEW DEAL :: (*a*. Hoover, *b*. Kennedy, ***c*. Truman**, *d*. Johnson) : FAIR DEAL

    (**c**) *Roosevelt's New Deal* was a series of social programs meant to counter the Great Depression. *Truman's Fair Deal* was a series of postwar social programs. **Object/Action**

55. (*a.* **pleasure**, *b.* concern, *c.* dream, *d.* health) : RAPTURE :: WORRY : AFFLICTION
    (a) Intense *pleasure* may be called *rapture*; intense *worry* may be called *affliction*.
    Degree

56. PRESBYTERIAN : (*a.* Baptist, *b.* **Protestant**, *c.* Mennonite, *d.* Calvinism) ::
    MAHAYANA : BUDDHIST
    (b) *Presbyterianism* is a sect within *Protestantism*, and *Mahayana* is a sect within
    Buddhism. **Part/Whole**

57. (*a.* volt, *b.* electricity, *c.* **map**, *d.* dampness) : AMP :: DIET : TIDE
    (c) The words *map* and *amp* contain the same letters in mixed order, as do the words
    diet and *tide*. **Conversion**

58. RACECOURSE : HORSERACE :: HIPPODROME : (*a.* zoo, *b.* battle, *c.* **dressage**,
    d. footrace)
    (c) You might go to a *racecourse* to see a *horserace*, and you might go to a *hippodrome*
    (the Greek root *hippos* means "horse") to see *dressage*, or fancy horseback riding.
    Characteristic

59. TILDE : (*a.* cedilla, *b.* accent, *c.* inflection, *d.* **circumflex**) :: ˜ : ^
    (d) The two symbols shown are a *tilde*, used especially in Spanish words such as *niño*,
    and a *circumflex*, used frequently in dictionary entries as a diacritical mark. **Conversion**

60. 1919 : 1984 :: (*a.* Hemingway, *b.* O'Connor, *c.* Faulkner, *d.* **Dos Passos**) : ORWELL
    (d) John *Dos Passos* wrote a book called *1919* as part of his *U.S.A.* trilogy. George
    Orwell wrote the futuristic novel *1984*. **Object/Action**

61. (*a.* **CPU**, *b.* television, *c.* radio, *d.* supervisor) : MONITOR :: ANTENNA : DIAL
    (a) A *CPU* (central processing unit) and a *monitor* are both parts of a computer. An
    antenna and a *dial* are both parts of a radio. **Part/Whole**

62. DIONYSUS : (*a.* Apollo, *b.* Ulysses, *c.* **Bacchus**, *d.* Ceres) :: EROS : CUPID
    (c) *Bacchus* is the Roman name for the Greek god of wine, *Dionysus*. *Cupid* is the
    Roman name for the Greek god of love, *Eros*. **Conversion**

63. ADULT : JUVENILE :: SHAM : (*a.* bogus, *b.* **bona fide**, *c.* sage, *d.* quack)
    (b) *Adult* and *juvenile* are opposites. The same is true of *sham* (fake) and *bona fide*
    (real). **Antonym**

64. (*a.* **Hart**, *b.* Evans, *c.* Bernstein, *d.* Newman) : RODGERS :: LYRICS : MUSIC
    (a) Lyricist Lorenz *Hart* and composer Richard *Rodgers* collaborated on such musicals
    as *On Your Toes* and *Pal Joey*. **Object/Action**

65. ST. PAUL'S : ST. PETER'S :: (*a.* New York, *b.* Florence, *c.* **London**, *d.* Paris) : ROME
    (c) *St. Paul's* Cathedral designed by architect Christopher Wren is in *London*; *St. Peter's*
    Cathedral designed by architect Giacomo Della Porta is the main church of the
    Vatican, in *Rome*. **Characteristic**

66. PORTENTOUS : PORTABLE :: MODEST : (*a.* **permanent**, *b.* unassuming,
    c. convenient, *d.* arrogant)

(**a**) A *portentous* (pompous) person is not *modest*. A *portable* (movable) object is not *permanent*. **Antonym**

67. DOCTOR : PROCTOR :: CLINIC : (*a*. church, ***b*. school**, *c*. hospital, *d*. alleyway)
    (**b**) A *doctor* may work at a *clinic*. A *proctor*, who may supervise exams, generally works at a *school*. **Characteristic**

68. NAST : STUART :: (*a*. landscape, *b*. sketch, *c*. watercolor, ***d*. cartoon**) : PORTRAIT
    (**d**) Thomas *Nast* (1737–1831) was an early American political *cartoonist*. Gilbert *Stuart* (1755–1828) was an American *portrait* painter. **Object/Action**

69. (*a*. Kilimanjaro, *b*. Mount Everest, ***c*. K2**, *d*. Makalu) : KORAKARAM :: MONT BLANC : ALPS
    (**c**) *K2* is the highest peak in the *Korakaram* range in Central Asia. *Mont Blanc* is the highest peak in the *Alps* in Europe. **Characteristic**

70. GREECE : EGYPT :: APOLLO : (*a*. Amun, ***b*. Ra**, *c*. Osiris, *d*. Pharaoh)
    (**b**) *Apollo* was a sun god in ancient *Greek* myth. *Ra* was a sun god in ancient *Egyptian* myth. **Characteristic**

71. (***a*. pituitary**, *b*. adrenal, *c*. oxytocin, *d*. endocrine) : ADH :: PANCREAS : INSULIN
    (**a**) The *pituitary* gland produces *ADH* (antidiuretic hormone). The *pancreas* produces *insulin*. **Object/Action**

72. FLAMENCO : SPAIN :: (*a*. troika, ***b*. mazurka**, *c*. polka, *d*. schottische) : POLAND
    (**b**) The *flamenco* is a *Spanish* dance; the *mazurka* is a *Polish* dance. (The other dances are Russian, Czech, and German.) **Characteristic**

73. WALKING STICK : CAMOUFLAGE :: HAWK MOTH : (***a*. mimicry**, *b*. prey, *c*. coloration, *d*. distraction)
    (**a**) The *walking stick* and the *hawk moth* are both insects. The first uses *camouflage* to avoid capture; the second uses *mimicry*, imitating the appearance of a raptor. Both camouflage and the hawk moth's mimicry may be considered forms of coloration. **Object/Action**

74. MILLARD FILLMORE : (*a*. Democrat, *b*. Tory, *c*. Federalist, ***d*. Whig**) :: ABRAHAM LINCOLN : REPUBLICAN
    (**d**) *Millard Fillmore* became president in 1850 after Zachary Taylor died. The pair had run on the *Whig* ticket. *Abraham Lincoln* won the presidency a decade later, running as a *Republican*. **Characteristic**

75. ID : SUPEREGO :: INSTINCT : (*a*. impulse, ***b*. morality**, *c*. personality, *d*. heroism)
    (**b**) In Freudian theory, the *id* is the part of the self that is responsible for *instinctual* behavior. The *superego* (essentially the conscience) is the part responsible for *morality*. **Object/Action**

76. PATENT : (*a*. contract, *b*. inventor, ***c*. device**, *d*. application) :: COPYRIGHT : DOCUMENT
    (**c**) You can *patent* a *device* in the same way that you would *copyright* a *document*. In both cases, the action is to protect the creator's ownership of the material. **Object/Action**

77. TANKARD : FLUTE :: PEWTER : (*a.* tin, *b.* ale, *c.* goblet, ***d.* crystal**)
    (**d**) A *tankard* is a drinking vessel often made of *pewter*. A *flute* is a wineglass often made of *crystal.* **Characteristic**

78. FISSION : (*a.* missile, ***b.* A-bomb**, *c.* automatic weapon, *d.* nuclear energy) :: FUSION : H-BOMB
    (**b**) Nuclear *fission*, or the splitting of atoms, is the process that controls the workings of the *A-bomb* (atomic bomb). Nuclear *fusion*, or the joining of nuclei, is the process that controls the workings of the *H-bomb* (hydrogen bomb). **Object/Action**

79. (***a.* quarter**, *b.* dime, *c.* nickel, *d.* penny) : HALF-DOLLAR :: WASHINGTON : KENNEDY
    (**a**) George *Washington* is on the face of a *quarter*, and John F. *Kennedy* is on the face of a *half-dollar.* **Characteristic**

80. NOVEMBER : OCTOBER :: WEDNESDAY : (*a.* Thursday, *b.* weekend, ***c.* Tuesday**, *d.* Sunday)
    (**c**) The month before *November* is *October*. The day before *Wednesday* is *Tuesday.* **Sequence**

81. (*a.* rings, *b.* moon, ***c.* Venus**, *d.* planet) : 2 :: SATURN : 6
    (**c**) *Venus* is the *second* planet from the sun, and *Saturn* is the *sixth* planet from the sun. **Sequence**

82. ATAXIA : (*a.* hearing, *b.* oration, ***c.* movement**, *d.* sight) :: APHASIA : SPEECH
    (**c**) If you suffer from *ataxia*, your *movement* is impaired. If you suffer from *aphasia*, your *speech* is impaired. **Object/Action**

83. ERIC THE RED : LEIF ERICSSON :: HENRY VIII : (*a.* Henry VII, ***b.* Elizabeth I**, *c.* Anne Boleyn, *d.* James I)
    (**b**) *Eric the Red* was the father of *Leif Ericsson*. *Henry VIII* was the father of *Elizabeth I.* **Sequence**

84. ANTONY AND CLEOPATRA : CAESAR AND CLEOPATRA :: SHAKESPEARE : (*a.* Wilde, *b.* Jonson, *c.* Marlowe, ***d.* Shaw**)
    (**d**) In 1606, William *Shakespeare* wrote a play now called *Antony and Cleopatra*. In 1899, George Bernard *Shaw* wrote a play called *Caesar and Cleopatra.* **Object/Action**

85. TOPSOIL : (*a.* agrarianism, ***b.* subsoil**, *c.* loess, *d.* clay) :: SUBSOIL : BEDROCK
    (**b**) *Topsoil* is the soil that you see when you look at the ground. It lies on top of *subsoil. Subsoil*, on the other hand, lies on top of *bedrock.* **Sequence**

86. ANTIQUARIAN : STATIONER :: (***a.* jeroboam**, *b.* merlot, *c.* grape, *d.* wine cellar) : VINTNER
    (**a**) An *antiquarian* is the name of very large-sized paper sold by a *stationer*, or seller of writing materials. A *jeroboam* is the name of a very large bottle sold by a *vintner*, or wine seller. **Object/Action**

87. FLUTE : FLUGELHORN :: (*a.* silver, **b. woodwind**, *c.* tuba, *d.* sharp) : BRASS
    (**b**) A *flute* is a member of the *woodwind* family of instruments, and a *flugelhorn* is a member of the *brass* family of instruments. **Classification**

88. CLARENCE BIRDSEYE : FROZEN FOOD :: LADISLO BIRO :
    (*a.* fast food, *b.* freezer, **c. ballpoint pen**, *d.* electric shaver)
    (**c**) *Birdseye* invented a process to *freeze food* around 1924, and *Biro* invented the *ballpoint pen* in 1938. **Object/Action**

89. JUG : (*a.* **flagon**, *b.* vat, *c.* container, *d.* beaker) :: MUG : TANKARD
    (**a**) *Flagon* is another word for a *jug*, and *tankard* is another word for a *mug*. **Synonym**

90. WANT : LIKE :: (*a.* need, *b.* venerate, **c. crave**, *d.* loathe) : WORSHIP
    (**c**) If you really *want* something, you *crave* it. If you really *like* someone, you *worship* him or her. **Degree**

91. KING JOHN : MAGNA CARTA :: KING HENRY VIII : (*a.* **Church of England**, *b.* Synod of Whitby, *c.* Petition of Right, *d.* Atlantic Charter)
    (**a**) *King John* was forced to sign the *Magna Carta* in 1215. *King Henry VIII* was forced to create the *Church of England* in 1534 in order to split with Rome and divorce his wife. **Object/Action**

92. AUGUST : MARCH :: (*a.* dance, *b.* vagabond, *c.* harvest, ***d.* impressive**) : TRAMP
    (**d**) Beware of these multiple-meaning words! Someone who is *august* is *impressive*. To *march* is to *tramp* along. **Synonym**

93. (*a.* exist, *b.* lift, **c. exorcise**, *d.* hail) : SPIRIT :: EXCISE : TUMOR
    (**c**) A priest can try to *exorcise*, or remove, an evil *spirit*. A surgeon can try to *excise*, or remove, a *tumor*. **Object/Action**

94. FDIC : (*a.* stockbrokers, *b.* consumers, **c. bank depositors**, *d.* petitioners) :: FEMA : DISASTER VICTIMS
    (**c**) The *FDIC* (Federal Deposit Insurance Corporation) was created to secure *bank deposits* up to $100,000. *FEMA* (Federal Emergency Management Agency) was created to provide assistance to *disaster victims*. **Object/Action**

95. PHOBOS : MARS :: IO : (*a.* satellite, *b.* Saturn, *c.* sun, **d. Jupiter**)
    (**d**) *Phobos* is one of the moons of *Mars*. *Io* is one of the moons of *Jupiter*. **Characteristic**

96. WAVE : FAREWELL :: HANDSHAKE : (*a.* exit, *b.* summons, **c. agreement**, *d.* businessperson)
    (**c**) You might *wave* to signify *farewell*. You might *shake hands* to signify *agreement*. **Object/Action**

97. (*a.* luscious, *b.* pungent, **c. diminutive**, *d.* corpulent) : MINUSCULE :: AROMATIC : FRAGRANT
    (**c**) *Diminutive* and *minuscule* both mean "very small." *Aromatic* and *fragrant* both mean "sweet-smelling." **Synonym**

98. INDELIBLE : ERASURE :: (*a.* inexorable, *b.* **indisputable**, *c.* inaccurate, *d.* indirect) : ARGUMENT

    (**b**) Something that is *indelible* resists *erasure*. Something that is *indisputable* resists *argument*. **Object/Action**

99. EINE KLEINE NACHTMUSIC : A LITTLE NIGHT MUSIC :: MOZART : (*a.* **Sondheim**, *b.* Hammerstein, *c.* Copland, *d.* Ives)

    (**a**) Both titles mean the same thing, but the first is a composition by Wolfgang Amadeus *Mozart*, and the second is a musical by Stephen *Sondheim*. **Object/Action**

100. ALGAE : (*a.* spruce, *b.* **lichen**, *c.* bean, *d.* petunia) :: CACTUS : PALM

    (**b**) *Algae* and *lichen* are both examples of nonflowering plants. *Cactus* and *palm* are both examples of flowering plants. **Part/Whole**

PRACTICE TEST 3
ANSWER SHEET

1. Ⓐ Ⓑ Ⓒ Ⓓ
2. Ⓐ Ⓑ Ⓒ Ⓓ
3. Ⓐ Ⓑ Ⓒ Ⓓ
4. Ⓐ Ⓑ Ⓒ Ⓓ
5. Ⓐ Ⓑ Ⓒ Ⓓ
6. Ⓐ Ⓑ Ⓒ Ⓓ
7. Ⓐ Ⓑ Ⓒ Ⓓ
8. Ⓐ Ⓑ Ⓒ Ⓓ
9. Ⓐ Ⓑ Ⓒ Ⓓ
10. Ⓐ Ⓑ Ⓒ Ⓓ
11. Ⓐ Ⓑ Ⓒ Ⓓ
12. Ⓐ Ⓑ Ⓒ Ⓓ
13. Ⓐ Ⓑ Ⓒ Ⓓ
14. Ⓐ Ⓑ Ⓒ Ⓓ
15. Ⓐ Ⓑ Ⓒ Ⓓ
16. Ⓐ Ⓑ Ⓒ Ⓓ
17. Ⓐ Ⓑ Ⓒ Ⓓ
18. Ⓐ Ⓑ Ⓒ Ⓓ
19. Ⓐ Ⓑ Ⓒ Ⓓ
20. Ⓐ Ⓑ Ⓒ Ⓓ
21. Ⓐ Ⓑ Ⓒ Ⓓ
22. Ⓐ Ⓑ Ⓒ Ⓓ
23. Ⓐ Ⓑ Ⓒ Ⓓ
24. Ⓐ Ⓑ Ⓒ Ⓓ
25. Ⓐ Ⓑ Ⓒ Ⓓ

26. Ⓐ Ⓑ Ⓒ Ⓓ
27. Ⓐ Ⓑ Ⓒ Ⓓ
28. Ⓐ Ⓑ Ⓒ Ⓓ
29. Ⓐ Ⓑ Ⓒ Ⓓ
30. Ⓐ Ⓑ Ⓒ Ⓓ
31. Ⓐ Ⓑ Ⓒ Ⓓ
32. Ⓐ Ⓑ Ⓒ Ⓓ
33. Ⓐ Ⓑ Ⓒ Ⓓ
34. Ⓐ Ⓑ Ⓒ Ⓓ
35. Ⓐ Ⓑ Ⓒ Ⓓ
36. Ⓐ Ⓑ Ⓒ Ⓓ
37. Ⓐ Ⓑ Ⓒ Ⓓ
38. Ⓐ Ⓑ Ⓒ Ⓓ
39. Ⓐ Ⓑ Ⓒ Ⓓ
40. Ⓐ Ⓑ Ⓒ Ⓓ
41. Ⓐ Ⓑ Ⓒ Ⓓ
42. Ⓐ Ⓑ Ⓒ Ⓓ
43. Ⓐ Ⓑ Ⓒ Ⓓ
44. Ⓐ Ⓑ Ⓒ Ⓓ
45. Ⓐ Ⓑ Ⓒ Ⓓ
46. Ⓐ Ⓑ Ⓒ Ⓓ
47. Ⓐ Ⓑ Ⓒ Ⓓ
48. Ⓐ Ⓑ Ⓒ Ⓓ
49. Ⓐ Ⓑ Ⓒ Ⓓ
50. Ⓐ Ⓑ Ⓒ Ⓓ

51. Ⓐ Ⓑ Ⓒ Ⓓ
52. Ⓐ Ⓑ Ⓒ Ⓓ
53. Ⓐ Ⓑ Ⓒ Ⓓ
54. Ⓐ Ⓑ Ⓒ Ⓓ
55. Ⓐ Ⓑ Ⓒ Ⓓ
56. Ⓐ Ⓑ Ⓒ Ⓓ
57. Ⓐ Ⓑ Ⓒ Ⓓ
58. Ⓐ Ⓑ Ⓒ Ⓓ
59. Ⓐ Ⓑ Ⓒ Ⓓ
60. Ⓐ Ⓑ Ⓒ Ⓓ
61. Ⓐ Ⓑ Ⓒ Ⓓ
62. Ⓐ Ⓑ Ⓒ Ⓓ
63. Ⓐ Ⓑ Ⓒ Ⓓ
64. Ⓐ Ⓑ Ⓒ Ⓓ
65. Ⓐ Ⓑ Ⓒ Ⓓ
66. Ⓐ Ⓑ Ⓒ Ⓓ
67. Ⓐ Ⓑ Ⓒ Ⓓ
68. Ⓐ Ⓑ Ⓒ Ⓓ
69. Ⓐ Ⓑ Ⓒ Ⓓ
70. Ⓐ Ⓑ Ⓒ Ⓓ
71. Ⓐ Ⓑ Ⓒ Ⓓ
72. Ⓐ Ⓑ Ⓒ Ⓓ
73. Ⓐ Ⓑ Ⓒ Ⓓ
74. Ⓐ Ⓑ Ⓒ Ⓓ
75. Ⓐ Ⓑ Ⓒ Ⓓ

76. Ⓐ Ⓑ Ⓒ Ⓓ
77. Ⓐ Ⓑ Ⓒ Ⓓ
78. Ⓐ Ⓑ Ⓒ Ⓓ
79. Ⓐ Ⓑ Ⓒ Ⓓ
80. Ⓐ Ⓑ Ⓒ Ⓓ
81. Ⓐ Ⓑ Ⓒ Ⓓ
82. Ⓐ Ⓑ Ⓒ Ⓓ
83. Ⓐ Ⓑ Ⓒ Ⓓ
84. Ⓐ Ⓑ Ⓒ Ⓓ
85. Ⓐ Ⓑ Ⓒ Ⓓ
86. Ⓐ Ⓑ Ⓒ Ⓓ
87. Ⓐ Ⓑ Ⓒ Ⓓ
88. Ⓐ Ⓑ Ⓒ Ⓓ
89. Ⓐ Ⓑ Ⓒ Ⓓ
90. Ⓐ Ⓑ Ⓒ Ⓓ
91. Ⓐ Ⓑ Ⓒ Ⓓ
92. Ⓐ Ⓑ Ⓒ Ⓓ
93. Ⓐ Ⓑ Ⓒ Ⓓ
94. Ⓐ Ⓑ Ⓒ Ⓓ
95. Ⓐ Ⓑ Ⓒ Ⓓ
96. Ⓐ Ⓑ Ⓒ Ⓓ
97. Ⓐ Ⓑ Ⓒ Ⓓ
98. Ⓐ Ⓑ Ⓒ Ⓓ
99. Ⓐ Ⓑ Ⓒ Ⓓ
100. Ⓐ Ⓑ Ⓒ Ⓓ

PRACTICE TEST 3

Directions: For each question, you will see three capitalized words and four answer choices labeled *a, b, c,* and *d* in parentheses. Choose the answer that best completes the analogy posed by the three capitalized words. Use the answer sheet on page 81 to record your answers.

Time: 50 Minutes

1. GLUCOSE : SUGAR :: ETHANOL : (*a.* oil, *b.* gas, *c.* salt, *d.* alcohol)

2. CONVICTION : BELIEF :: (*a.* disorientation, *b.* convention, *c.* enigma, *d.* assurance) : MYSTERY

3. (*a.* Descartes, *b.* Ptolemy, *c.* Zeno, *d.* Newton) : ANALYTIC GEOMETRY :: ARCHIMEDES : PI

4. NEWT : TOAD :: SNAKE : (*a.* boa, *b.* turtle, *c.* worm, *d.* frog)

5. DECLARATION OF INDEPENDENCE : 1776 :: (*a.* Emancipation Proclamation, *b.* Homestead Act, *c.* Seneca Falls Declaration, *d.* Declaration of the Rights of Man) : 1848

6. VIRUS : COLD :: (*a.* pain, *b.* stress, *c.* bacterium, *d.* heat) : HEADACHE

7. WAGNER : (*a.* opera, *b.* Lohengrin, *c.* Tristan, *d.* Tosca) :: VERDI : AÏDA

8. (*a.* arch-, *b.* epi-, *c.* uni-, *d.* iso-) : EQUAL :: ETHNO- : PEOPLE

9. PRIOR : (*a.* behindhand, *b.* subsequently, *c.* however, *d.* heretofore) :: NEVERTHELESS : YET

10. ORIOLE : BIRD :: ORIEL : (*a.* window, *b.* paint, *c.* weasel, *d.* instrument)

11. CLEVELAND : (*a.* Pennsylvania, *b.* Erie, *c.* Ohio, *d.* Indiana) :: CHICAGO : MICHIGAN

12. 13 : 18 :: SLAVERY : (*a.* enfranchisement, *b.* weaponry, *c.* alcohol, *d.* state's rights)

13. (*a.* Washington, *b.* Kennedy, *c.* Jefferson, *d.* Bush) : UNITED STATES :: RHEE : KOREA

14. COSMOPOLITAN : (*a.* urbane, *b.* urban, *c.* fluid, *d.* cosmetic) :: SOPHISTICATED : DECORATIVE

15. (*a.* rotten, *b.* adapted, *c.* red herring, *d.* fostered) : DECAY :: ADOPTED : DECOY

16. FARRAGUT : NAVY :: (*a.* Decatur, *b.* Sherman, *c.* Perry, *d.* Rickover) : ARMY

17. (*a.* Teddy, *b.* Old Hickory, *c.* Tippecanoe, *d.* Henry) : HARRISON :: IKE : EISENHOWER

18. PALEONTOLOGIST : FOSSIL :: (*a.* potter, *b.* archeologist, *c.* vestige, *d.* geologist) : SHARD

19. (*a.* Elysium, *b.* Asgard, *c.* Jotunheimen, *d.* Trolltind) : SCANDINAVIAN :: OLYMPUS : GREEK

20. COOL : FROSTY :: HEAVY : (*a.* nippy, *b.* insubstantial, *c.* big, *d.* torrential)

21. (*a.* photograph, *b.* charcoal, *c.* tempera, *d.* clay) : OPAQUE :: WATERCOLOR : TRANSPARENT

22. PHILIPPINE REVOLUTION : (*a.* Philippines, *b.* Spain, *c.* Manila, *d.* China) :: AMERICAN REVOLUTION : ENGLAND

23. CORDAY : MARAT :: (*a.* Buchanan, *b.* Johnson, *c.* Booth, *d.* Todd) : LINCOLN

24. GREAT LAKES : (*a.* small lakes, *b.* Finger Lakes, *c.* Salt Lakes, *d.* rivers) :: HURON : CAYUGA

25. MOLECULE : ATOMS :: ELEMENT : (*a.* molecules, *b.* protons, *c.* iron, *d.* electrons)

26. (*a.* cor anglais, *b.* French horn, *c.* sousaphone, *d.* spinet) : WOODWIND :: TIMPANI : PERCUSSION

27. BEETHOVEN : FÜR ELISE :: (*a.* Mozart, *b.* Schubert, *c.* Tchaikovsky, *d.* Wagner) : AVE MARIA

28. (*a.* penguin, *b.* salamander, *c.* scorpion, *d.* clam) : SEAHORSE :: WARM-BLOODED : COLD-BLOODED

29. GENEROUS : PARSIMONIOUS :: (*a.* munificent, *b.* cooperative, *c.* obstinate, *d.* restive) : ACCOMMODATING

30. (*a.* Pasteur, *b.* Gauss, *c.* joule, *d.* kinetic) : ENERGY :: CURIE : RADIOACTIVITY

31. ALTER : PRESERVE :: FALTER : (*a.* persist, *b.* abate, *c.* amend, *d.* protect)

32. EUTERPE : (*a.* tragedy, *b.* poetry, *c.* history, *d.* music) :: THALIA : COMEDY

33. 210 : 310 :: 40 : (*a.* 50, *b.* 140, *c.* 400, *d.* 410)

34. WALTZ : 3/4 :: (*a.* merengue, *b.* polka, *c.* tarantella, *d.* minuet) : 6/8

35. (*a.* Antonia Fraser, *b.* Lanford Wilson, *c.* Alan Ayckbourn, *d.* Margaret Drabble) : HAROLD PINTER :: BIOGRAPHIES : PLAYS

36. GREECE : (*a.* dinar, *b.* zloty, *c.* drachma, *d.* khoum) :: JAPAN : YEN

37. OTTO HAHN : NUCLEAR FISSION :: (*a.* Amadeo Avogadro, *b.* Joseph Priestly, *c.* Niels Bohr, *d.* Edwin Hubble) : QUANTUM MECHANICS

38. (*a.* fletching, *b.* scumbling, *c.* stippling, *d.* crosshatching) : HATCHING :: DOTS : LINES

39. RIM : CUP :: (*a.* ladder, *b.* gunwale, *c.* rudder, *d.* kayak) : BOAT

40. UFFIZI : (*a.* Rome, *b.* Venice, *c.* Florence, *d.* Barcelona) :: TATE : LONDON

41. THROW : THROWN :: (*a.* captured, *b.* caw, *c.* catch, *d.* cough) : CAUGHT

42. KEEN : FANATICAL :: INTERESTED : (*a.* engrossed, *b.* indifferent, *c.* sharp, *d.* surprised)

43. NATION : (*a.* terrain, *b.* Caesar, *c.* ballot, *d.* temperance) :: ANTHONY : SUFFRAGE

44. -IST : (*a.* -ism, *b.* -ing, *c.* -ish, *d.* -ite) :: NOUN : ADJECTIVE

45. HOUSE OF REPRESENTATIVES : SENATE :: (*a.* 2, *b.* 50, *c.* 100, *d.* 435) : 100

46. (*a.* Martin, *b.* Calvin, *c.* Dryden, *d.* Haydn) : RESTORATION :: LUTHER : REFORMATION

47. DIVISOR : DIVIDEND :: SUBTRAHEND : (*a.* minuend, *b.* remainder, *c.* quotient, *d.* subtractor)

48. (*a.* reptiles, *b.* arthropods, *c.* fish, *d.* Aves) : AMPHIBIANS :: INVERTEBRATES : VERTEBRATES

49. EMBEZZLEMENT : (*a.* misdemeanor, *b.* burglary, *c.* larceny, *d.* negligence) :: ASSAULT : TORT

50. (*a.* faun, *b.* nanny, *c.* sileni, *d.* donkey) : GOAT :: HARPY : BIRD

51. RAUCOUS : MELLIFLUOUS :: UNYIELDING : (*a.* fluid, *b.* resonant, *c.* rigid, *d.* melancholic)

52. (*a.* Wim Wenders, *b.* Leni Reifenstahl, *c.* Fritz Lang, *d.* Dr. Caligari) : GERMAN EXPRESSIONISM :: FRANÇOIS TRUFFAUT : FRENCH NEW WAVE

53. πr^2 : (*a.* r^2, *b.* 2π, *c.* $2\pi r$, *d.* $2r$) :: AREA : PERIMETER

54. CHRONICLES : OLD TESTAMENT :: (*a.* Corinthians, *b.* Psalms, *c.* Ecclesiastes, *d.* Amos) : NEW TESTAMENT

55. COULTER : PLOW :: (*a.* smokestack, *b.* cowcatcher, *c.* wheel, *d.* railroad) : LOCOMOTIVE

56. AIRMAN : (*a.* cavalry, *b.* foot soldier, *c.* private, *d.* lieutenant) :: AIR FORCE : ARMY

57. WILL : HEIR :: (*a.* contract, *b.* pay stub, *c.* employer, *d.* human resources) : EMPLOYEE

58. U-BOAT : SUBMARINE :: PT BOAT : (*a.* speedboat, *b.* torpedo boat, *c.* floating hospital, *d.* hovercraft)

59. ANTAGONIST : PROTAGONIST :: (*a.* Claudius, *b.* Ophelia, *c.* Macbeth, *d.* Yorick) : HAMLET

60. SULFATE : ZINC SULFATE :: SALT : (*a.* phenylalanine, *b.* histamine, *c.* ketone, *d.* ammonium chloride)

61. (*a.* green, *b.* blue, *c.* lavender, *d.* royal) : PURPLE :: YELLOW : ORANGE

62. ADZE : (*a.* woodworking, *b.* bricklaying, *c.* plumbing, *d.* stonework) :: CHISEL : MASONRY

63. (*a.* disinfect, *b.* dissemble, *c.* displease, *d.* dismantle) : RAZE :: DISSATISFY : ANGER

64. DR. FAUSTUS : DR. JEKYLL :: MARLOWE : (*a.* Shelley, *b.* Hyde, *c.* Stevenson, *d.* Rabelais)

65. 10 : 100 :: (*a.* 11, *b.* 12, *c.* 14, *d.* 44) : 144

66. SCRIMSHAW : (*a.* ivory, *b.* carving, *c.* flooring, *d.* metal) :: PARQUET : WOOD

67. GAUL : HISPANIA :: (*a.* Roman Empire, *b.* Latin, *c.* France, *d.* Germany) : SPAIN

68. GOODALL : FOSSEY :: CHIMPANZEES : (*a.* insects, *b.* dancers, *c.* wolves, *d.* gorillas)

69. (*a.* Bundestag, *b.* Whigs, *c.* Socialists, *d.* Labour) : TORIES :: JACOBINS : GIRONDISTS

70. OHIO : OH :: NEVADA : (*a.* NE, *b.* ND, *c.* NV, *d.* NA)

71. GAIN : LOSS :: (*a.* reduction, *b.* profit, *c.* metabolism, *d.* combustion) : OXIDATION

72. BOAR : (*a.* sow, *b.* swine, *c.* sable, *d.* artist) :: HAIRBRUSH : PAINTBRUSH

73. CALYPSO : TRINIDAD :: GAMELAN : (*a.* West Africa, *b.* Jamaica, *c.* India, *d.* Indonesia)

74. PRE- : POST- :: A.M. : (*a.* F.M., *b.* P.M., *c.* M.A., *d.* Ph.D.)

75. INNOCENT : (*a.* purity, *b.* virtue, *c.* debris, *d.* evil) :: CLEAN : GRIME

76. AHAB : BLIGH :: (*a. Monitor, b. Golden Hind, c. Pequod, d. Victory*) : *BOUNTY*

77. YANKEE : NEW ENGLAND :: TAR HEEL : (*a.* Indiana, *b.* North Carolina, *c.* Tennessee, *d.* West Virginia)

78. (*a.* Prokofiev, *b.* Diaghilev, *c.* Akhmatova, *d.* Nesterov) : BALLETS RUSSES :: BALANCHINE : NEW YORK CITY BALLET

79. OP ART : POP ART :: VASARELY : (*a.* Pollock, *b.* Lichtenstein, *c.* Kandinsky, *d.* Rothko)

80. PALEOZOIC : REPTILES :: MESOZOIC : (*a.* sponges, *b.* brachiopods, *c.* birds, *d.* plants)

81. STOMACH : DIGESTION :: (*a.* diaphragm, *b.* cell, *c.* intestine, *d.* kidney) : RESPIRATION

82. (*a.* G, *b.* scale, *c.* natural, *d.* transposition) : FLAT :: SHARP : NATURAL

83. SIGNET : (*a.* impression, *b.* ring, *c.* king, *d.* official) :: PORTENT : PROPHESY

84. EXONERATE : EXORCISE :: (*a.* execrate, *b.* absolve, *c.* excommunicate, *d.* impel) : EXPEL

85. (*a.* Stokowski, *b.* Casals, *c.* Heifetz, *d.* Paderewski) : GOULD :: VIOLIN : PIANO

86. INEXTRICABLE : ESCAPE :: INEXPRESSIBLE : (*a.* diversion, *b.* alteration, *c.* evasion, *d.* description)

87. TRANSMISSION : GEARS :: (*a.* vehicle, *b.* suspension, *c.* absorbers, *d.* armature) : STRUTS

88. EULOGY : PRAISE :: ELEGY : (*a.* commendation, *b.* gratification, *c.* censure, *d.* lamentation)

89. EGG : LARVA :: (*a.* pupa, *b.* embryo, *c.* caterpillar, *d.* blastocyst) : IMAGO

90. GIDE : (*a. The Bald Soprano, b. The Immoralist, c. The Plague, d. The Prisoner*) :: CAMUS : THE STRANGER

91. SEEK : FIND :: ASK : (*a.* collect, *b.* query, *c.* appear, *d.* receive)

92. (*a.* Ringgold, *b.* Basquiat, *c.* Wegman, *d.* Wyeth) : PHOTOGRAPH :: RIVERA : MURAL

93. MOAT : INVASION :: (*a.* bacillus, *b.* injury, *c.* bandage, *d.* seepage) : INFECTION

94. (*a.* debauchery, *b.* dedication, *c.* deposition, *d.* dereliction) : DEPRECATION :: NEGLECT : DISAPPROVAL

95. VIAL : VAT :: FILAMENT : (*a.* hair, *b.* tub, *c.* strand, *d.* rope)

96. DOG : PAVLOV :: RAT : (*a.* Rorschach, *b.* Piaget, *c.* Adler, *d.* Skinner)

97. SHOCK : SCANDALIZE :: DEMORALIZE : (*a.* depress, *b.* appall, *c.* confirm, *d.* hearten)

98. (*a.* extender, *b.* pipe cleaner, *c.* flexor, *d.* knee) : BEND :: EXTENSOR : STRAIGHTEN

99. DYNAMITE : REVOLVER :: NOBEL : (*a.* Gatling, *b.* Colt, *c.* Maxim, *d.* Prize)

100. ACID : BASE :: 0 : (*a.* 2, *b.* 14, *c.* 38, *d.* 100)

STOP

If there is any time remaining, go back and check your work.

PRACTICE TEST 3
ANSWER KEY

1. d	26. a	51. a	76. c
2. c	27. b	52. c	77. b
3. a	28. a	53. c	78. b
4. b	29. c	54. a	79. b
5. c	30. c	55. b	80. c
6. b	31. a	56. c	81. a
7. b	32. d	57. a	82. c
8. d	33. b	58. b	83. a
9. d	34. c	59. a	84. b
10. a	35. a	60. d	85. c
11. b	36. c	61. b	86. d
12. c	37. c	62. a	87. b
13. a	38. c	63. d	88. d
14. d	39. b	64. c	89. a
15. b	40. c	65. b	90. b
16. b	41. c	66. a	91. d
17. c	42. a	67. c	92. c
18. b	43. d	68. d	93. c
19. b	44. c	69. b	94. d
20. d	45. d	70. c	95. d
21. c	46. c	71. a	96. d
22. b	47. a	72. c	97. a
23. c	48. b	73. d	98. c
24. b	49. c	74. b	99. b
25. a	50. a	75. d	100. b

PRACTICE TEST 3
EXPLANATORY ANSWERS

1. GLUCOSE : SUGAR :: ETHANOL : (*a.* oil, *b.* gas, *c.* salt, **d. alcohol**)
   (**d**) *Glucose* is one form of *sugar*, and *ethanol,* sometimes used as fuel, is one form of *alcohol.* **Classification**

2. CONVICTION : BELIEF :: (*a.* disorientation, *b.* convention, **c. enigma,**
   d. assurance) : MYSTERY
   (**c**) A *conviction* is the same as a *belief,* and an *enigma* is the same as a *mystery.*
   Synonym

3. (**a. Descartes,** *b.* Ptolemy, *c.* Zeno, *d.* Newton) : ANALYTIC GEOMETRY ::
   ARCHIMEDES : PI
   (**a**) *Descartes* is considered the father of *analytic geometry,* and *Archimedes* is believed to be the inventor of *pi.* **Object/Action**

4. NEWT : TOAD :: SNAKE : (*a.* boa, **b. turtle,** *c.* worm, *d.* frog)
   (**b**) Both *newts* and *toads* are amphibians. Both *snakes* and *turtles* are reptiles.
   Part/Whole

5. DECLARATION OF INDEPENDENCE : 1776 :: (*a.* Emancipation Proclamation,
   b. Homestead Act, **c. Seneca Falls Declaration,** *d.* Declaration of the Rights of Man) :
   1848
   (**c**) Everyone is familiar with the date of the *Declaration of Independence. 1848* was the date of the signing of Elizabeth Cady Stanton's *Seneca Falls Declaration,* which declared women equal to men. **Characteristic**

6. VIRUS : COLD :: (*a.* pain, **b. stress,** *c.* bacterium, *d.* heat) : HEADACHE
   (**b**) A *virus* is the cause of a *cold. Stress* may be the cause of a *headache.* **Object/Action**

7. WAGNER : (*a.* opera, **b. Lohengrin,** *c.* Tristan, *d.* Tosca) :: VERDI: AÏDA
   (**b**) Although *Wagner* used the characters Lohengrin and Tristan in his operas, only *Lohengrin,* like *Aïda,* is a female character whose name is also the name of the opera in which she appears. **Object/Action**

8. (*a.* arch-, *b.* epi-, *c.* uni-, **d. iso-**) : EQUAL :: ETHNO- : PEOPLE
   (**d**) The prefix *iso-* means "*equal,*" as in *isotope.* The prefix *ethno-* means "*people,*" as in *ethnocentric.* **Affix**

9. PRIOR : (*a.* behindhand, *b.* subsequently, *c.* however, **d. heretofore**) ::
   NEVERTHELESS : YET
   (**d**) *Prior,* or beforehand, means about the same thing as *heretofore. Nevertheless,* or however, means about the same thing as *yet.* **Synonym**

10. ORIOLE : BIRD :: ORIEL : (**a. window,** *b.* paint, *c.* weasel, *d.* instrument)
    (**a**) An *oriole* is a black and orange *songbird.* An *oriel* is a projecting bay *window.*
    Classification

11. CLEVELAND : (*a.* Pennsylvania, ***b.* Erie**, *c.* Ohio, *d.* Indiana) :: CHICAGO : MICHIGAN
    (**b**) The city of *Cleveland*, Ohio, lies along Lake *Erie*. The city of *Chicago*, Illinois, lies along Lake *Michigan*. **Characteristic**

12. 13 : 18 :: SLAVERY : (*a.* enfranchisement, *b.* weaponry, ***c.* alcohol**, *d.* state's rights)
    (**c**) The *Thirteenth* Amendment to the Constitution outlawed *slavery*. The *Eighteenth* Amendment to the Constitution outlawed the sale and manufacture of *alcohol*, and the Twenty-first Amendment repealed that amendment. **Object/Action**

13. (***a.* Washington**, *b.* Kennedy, *c.* Jefferson, *d.* Bush) : UNITED STATES :: RHEE : KOREA
    (**a**) Just as George *Washington* was the first president of the *United States*, Syngman *Rhee* was the first president of South *Korea* (from 1948 to 1960). **Characteristic**

14. COSMOPOLITAN : (*a.* urbane, *b.* urban, *c.* fluid, ***d.* cosmetic**) :: SOPHISTICATED : DECORATIVE
    (**d**) To be *cosmopolitan* is to be *sophisticated*, and to be *cosmetic* is to be *decorative*. **Synonym**

15. (*a.* rotten, ***b.* adapted**, *c.* red herring, *d.* fostered) : DECAY :: ADOPTED : DECOY
    (**b**) Changing the letter *a* to *o* changes *adapted* to *adopted*. The same change makes *decay* into *decoy*. **Conversion**

16. FARRAGUT : NAVY :: (*a.* Decatur, ***b.* Sherman**, *c.* Perry, *d.* Rickover) : ARMY
    (**b**) David *Farragut* was an admiral in the U.S. *Navy* during the Civil War. William Tecumseh *Sherman* was a general in the U.S. *Army* during the Civil War. **Characteristic**

17. (*a.* Teddy, *b.* Old Hickory, ***c.* Tippecanoe**, *d.* Henry) : HARRISON :: IKE : EISENHOWER
    (**c**) President William Henry *Harrison* became known as *Tippecanoe* following his success in the Battle of Tippecanoe when he was military governor of the territory of Indiana. President Dwight David *Eisenhower* was known as *Ike* from boyhood. Both nicknames figured in their presidential campaigns: "Tippecanoe and Tyler Too" and "I Like Ike" are among the most famous of campaign slogans. **Conversion**

18. PALEONTOLOGIST : FOSSIL :: (*a.* potter, ***b.* archeologist**, *c.* vestige, *d.* geologist) : SHARD
    (**b**) A *paleontologist* studies *fossils* to learn about ancient life, and an *archeologist* studies pottery *shards* to learn about ancient cultures. **Object/Action**

19. (*a.* Elysium, ***b.* Asgard**, *c.* Jotunheimen, *d.* Trolltind) : SCANDINAVIAN :: OLYMPUS : GREEK
    (**b**) In *Scandinavian* mythology, *Asgard* was the home of the Norse gods; in *Greek* mythology, *Olympus* was the home of the Greek gods. **Characteristic**

20. COOL : FROSTY :: HEAVY : (*a.* nippy, *b.* insubstantial, *c.* big, ***d.* torrential**)
    (**d**) A very *cool* morning might be *frosty*. A very *heavy* rain might be *torrential*. **Degree**

21. (*a.* photograph, *b.* charcoal, ***c.* tempera**, *d.* clay) : OPAQUE :: WATERCOLOR : TRANSPARENT

    (**c**) *Tempera* paints are *opaque*; they allow little light to pass through. *Watercolor* paints, on the other hand, are *transparent*. Both are paints, making *c* a better choice than *b* or *d*. **Characteristic**

22. PHILIPPINE REVOLUTION : (*a.* Philippines, ***b.* Spain**, *c.* Manila, *d.* China) :: AMERICAN REVOLUTION : ENGLAND

    (**b**) The *Philippine Revolution* signaled the end of *Spanish* reign in the Philippines. The *American Revolution* signaled the end of *English* reign here. **Object/Action**

23. CORDAY : MARAT :: (*a.* Buchanan, *b.* Johnson, ***c.* Booth**, *d.* Todd) : LINCOLN

    (**c**) In 1793, Charlotte *Corday* assassinated the French revolutionary Jean Paul *Marat*. In 1865, John Wilkes *Booth* assassinated the U.S. President Abraham *Lincoln*. **Object/Action**

24. GREAT LAKES : (*a.* small lakes, ***b.* Finger Lakes**, *c.* Salt Lakes, *d.* rivers) :: HURON : CAYUGA

    (**b**) Lake *Huron* is one of five *Great Lakes*; the others are Michigan, Erie, Superior, and Ontario. *Cayuga* Lake is one of the *Finger Lakes* in upstate New York. **Classification**

25. MOLECULE : ATOMS :: ELEMENT : (***a.* molecules**, *b.* protons, *c.* iron, *d.* electrons)

    (**a**) Just as *atoms* make up a *molecule*, so *molecules* make up an *element* such as helium, potassium, or iron. **Part/Whole**

26. (***a.* cor anglais**, *b.* French horn, *c.* sousaphone, *d.* spinet) : WOODWIND :: TIMPANI : PERCUSSION

    (**a**) The *cor anglais*, or English horn, is essentially a large oboe, placing it squarely in the *woodwind* family of instruments. The *timpani* is a brass or copper instrument with a tunable drumhead, making it a *percussion* instrument. **Classification**

27. BEETHOVEN : FÜR ELISE :: (*a.* Mozart, ***b.* Schubert**, *c.* Tchaikovsky, *d.* Wagner) : AVE MARIA

    (**b**) *Für Elise* is a composition by Ludwig van *Beethoven*. There are several *Ave Marias*; the most famous is by Franz *Schubert*. **Object/Action**

28. (***a.* penguin**, *b.* salamander, *c.* scorpion, *d.* clam) : SEAHORSE :: WARM-BLOODED : COLD-BLOODED

    (**a**) Like all birds, the *penguin* is *warm-blooded*; its temperature is internally regulated. Like all fish, the *seahorse* is *cold-blooded*; its temperature changes with that of its environment. **Characteristic**

29. GENEROUS : PARSIMONIOUS :: (*a.* munificent, *b.* cooperative, ***c.* obstinate**, *d.* restive) : ACCOMMODATING

    (**c**) If you are *generous*, you are not *parsimonious* (stingy). If you are *obstinate* (stubborn), you are not *accommodating* (cooperative). **Antonym**

30. (*a.* Pasteur, *b.* Gauss, ***c.* joule**, *d.* kinetic) : ENERGY :: CURIE : RADIOACTIVITY

    (**c**) The *joule* is a unit used to measure *energy*. The *curie* is a unit used to measure *radioactivity*. **Object/Action**

31. ALTER : PRESERVE :: FALTER : (*a.* **persist**, *b.* abate, *c.* amend, *d.* protect)
    (**a**) If you *alter* something, you fail to *preserve* it. If you *falter* in a task, you fail to *persist* at it. **Antonym**

32. EUTERPE : (*a.* tragedy, *b.* poetry, *c.* history, *d.* **music**) :: THALIA : COMEDY
    (**d**) Both Euterpe and Thalia were Greek muses, with *Euterpe* in charge of *music* and *Thalia* in charge of *comedy*. **Characteristic**

33. 210 : 310 :: 40 : (*a.* 50, *b.* **140**, *c.* 400, *d.* 410)
    (**b**) 310 is 100 more than 210, and 140 is 100 more than 40. **Sequence**

34. WALTZ : 3/4 :: (*a.* merengue, *b.* polka, *c.* **tarantella**, *d.* minuet) : 6/8
    (**c**) Most dances are in double or triple time. *Waltz* music has three quarter notes to a measure, which is indicated as *3/4*. *Tarantella* music, on the other hand, has six eighth notes to a measure, which is indicated as *6/8*. **Characteristic**

35. (*a.* **Antonia Fraser**, *b.* Lanford Wilson, *c.* Alan Ayckbourn, *d.* Margaret Drabble) : HAROLD PINTER :: BIOGRAPHIES : PLAYS
    (**a**) In addition to being married to the *playwright Harold Pinter*, Lady *Antonia Fraser* is a *biographer* of some repute. **Object/Action**

36. GREECE : (*a.* dinar, *b.* zloty, *c.* **drachma**, *d.* khoum) :: JAPAN : YEN
    (**c**) In pre-euro *Greece*, the major currency was the *drachma*. In *Japan*, the major currency remains the *yen*. **Characteristic**

37. OTTO HAHN : NUCLEAR FISSION :: (*a.* Amadeo Avogadro, *b.* Joseph Priestly, *c.* **Niels Bohr**, *d.* Edwin Hubble) : QUANTUM MECHANICS
    (**c**) The Austrian *Otto Hahn* was one of the first to discover *nuclear fission*. The Danish physicist *Niels Bohr* won the Nobel Prize for his advances in *quantum mechanics*. **Object/Action**

38. (*a.* fletching, *b.* scumbling, *c.* **stippling**, *d.* crosshatching) : HATCHING :: DOTS : LINES
    (**c**) In drawing, to *stipple* is to shade using a series of tiny *dots*. To *hatch* is to shade using a series of parallel *lines*. **Characteristic**

39. RIM : CUP :: (*a.* ladder, *b.* **gunwale**, *c.* rudder, *d.* kayak) : BOAT
    (**b**) The *rim* forms the top edge of a *cup*. The *gunwale* (pronounced "gunnel") forms the top edge of a canoe or other *boat*. **Part/Whole**

40. UFFIZI : (*a.* Rome, *b.* Venice, *c.* **Florence**, *d.* Barcelona) :: TATE : LONDON
    (**c**) The *Uffizi* is an art museum in *Florence*, Italy. The *Tate* is an art museum in *London*, England. **Characteristic**

41. THROW : THROWN :: (*a.* captured, *b.* caw, *c.* **catch**, *d.* cough) : CAUGHT
    (**c**) The past participle of *to throw* is *thrown*. The past participle of *to catch* is *caught*. **Conversion**

42. KEEN : FANATICAL :: INTERESTED : (*a.* **engrossed**, *b.* indifferent, *c.* sharp, *d.* surprised)

(a) If you were more than a little *keen* on a topic, one might say you were *fanatical*. If you were more than a little *interested* in some reading material, one might say you were *engrossed* in it. **Degree**

43. NATION : (*a.* terrain, *b.* Caesar, *c.* ballot, *d.* **temperance**) :: ANTHONY : SUFFRAGE
    (d) Carry *Nation* was a *temperance* (antiliquor) reformer. Susan B. *Anthony* was a *suffragist*; she worked toward obtaining voting rights for women. **Object/Action**

44. -IST : (*a.* -ism, *b.* -ing, *c.* **-ish**, *d.* -ite) :: NOUN : ADJECTIVE
    (c) The suffix *-ist* changes a noun into another *noun*, as in *pianist* or *Marxist*. The suffix *-ish* changes a noun into an *adjective*, as in *foolish* or *fiendish*. **Affix**

45. HOUSE OF REPRESENTATIVES : SENATE :: (*a.* 2, *b.* 50, *c.* 100, *d.* **435**) : 100
    (d) There are *435* voting members of the *House of Representatives* and *100* members of the *Senate*. **Classification**

46. (*a.* Martin, *b.* Calvin, *c.* **Dryden**, *d.* Haydn) : RESTORATION :: LUTHER : REFORMATION
    (c) John *Dryden* wrote during the reign of Charles II in England, known as the *Restoration* because the monarchy had been re-established. Martin *Luther* was a key figure in the Protestant *Reformation*, which began as an attempt to reform the Catholic Church. **Characteristic**

47. DIVISOR : DIVIDEND :: SUBTRAHEND : (*a.* **minuend**, *b.* remainder, *c.* quotient, *d.* subtractor)
    (a) The *dividend* is the number into which the *divisor* is divided. The *minuend* is the number from which the *subtrahend* is subtracted. **Object/Action**

48. (*a.* reptiles, *b.* **arthropods**, *c.* fish, *d.* Aves) : AMPHIBIANS :: INVERTEBRATES : VERTEBRATES
    (b) Of the answer choices, only *arthropods* (arachnids, insects, and crustaceans) lack backbones (are *invertebrates*). All the other groups listed have backbones (are *vertebrates*). **Classification**

49. EMBEZZLEMENT : (*a.* misdemeanor, *b.* burglary, *c.* **larceny**, *d.* negligence) :: ASSAULT : TORT
    (c) In law, *embezzlement* may be considered a form of *larceny*, whereas *assault* may be considered one kind of *tort*. **Classification**

50. (*a.* **faun**, *b.* nanny, *c.* sileni, *d.* donkey) : GOAT :: HARPY : BIRD
    (a) A *faun* is a mythical creature that is part man and part *goat*. A *harpy* is a mythical creature that is part woman and part *bird*. **Part/Whole**

51. RAUCOUS : MELLIFLUOUS :: UNYIELDING : (*a.* **fluid**, *b.* resonant, *c.* rigid, *d.* melancholic)
    (a) A sound that is *raucous* is not *mellifluous* (sweet-sounding). An object that is *unyielding* (rigid) is not *fluid*. **Antonym**

52. (*a.* Wim Wenders, *b.* Leni Reifenstahl, **c. Fritz Lang**, *d.* Dr. Caligari) : GERMAN EXPRESSIONISM :: FRANÇOIS TRUFFAUT : FRENCH NEW WAVE
(**c**) Both Fritz Lang and François Truffaut were filmmakers, with *Lang* classified as a *German expressionist* and *Truffaut* part of the *French new wave*. **Classification**

53. πr^2 : (*a.* r^2, *b.* 2π, **c. $2\pi r$**, *d.* $2r$) :: AREA : PERIMETER
(**c**) The *area* of a circle is defined as πr^2, where *r* equals the radius of the circle. A circle's *perimeter*, or circumference, is $2\pi r$. **Classification**

54. CHRONICLES : OLD TESTAMENT :: (**a. Corinthians**, *b.* Psalms, *c.* Ecclesiastes, *d.* Amos) : NEW TESTAMENT
(**a**) *Corinthians* is a book of the *New Testament*. All the other books listed are in the *Old Testament*. **Classification**

55. COULTER : PLOW :: (*a.* smokestack, **b. cowcatcher**, *c.* wheel, *d.* railroad) : LOCOMOTIVE
(**b**) A *coulter* is the forepart of a *plow*. Although it does not serve the same function, a *cowcatcher* is the forepart of a *locomotive*. **Part/Whole**

56. AIRMAN : (*a.* cavalry, *b.* foot soldier, **c. private**, *d.* lieutenant) :: AIR FORCE : ARMY
(**c**) In the *Air Force*, an enlisted man or woman of lowest rank is an *airman*. In the *Army*, such a recruit is a *private*. **Classification**

57. WILL : HEIR :: (**a. contract**, *b.* pay stub, *c.* employer, *d.* human resources) : EMPLOYEE
(**a**) A *will* tells an *heir* what to expect in the way of compensation, just as a *contract* does for an *employee*. **Object/Action**

58. U-BOAT : SUBMARINE :: PT BOAT : (*a.* speedboat, **b. torpedo boat**, *c.* floating hospital, *d.* hovercraft)
(**b**) *U-boat* is another name for a certain type of *submarine*, and a *PT boat* is a surface boat that carries *torpedoes*. **Synonym**

59. ANTAGONIST : PROTAGONIST :: (**a. Claudius**, *b.* Ophelia, *c.* Macbeth, *d.* Yorick) : HAMLET
(**a**) In literature, the tension between an antagonist and a protagonist, or main character, often creates much of the conflict. In Shakespeare's *Hamlet*, *Hamlet* is the *protagonist*, and his uncle *Claudius* is the chief *antagonist*, at least in Hamlet's mind. **Classification**

60. SULFATE : ZINC SULFATE :: SALT : (*a.* phenylalanine, *b.* histamine, *c.* ketone, **d. ammonium chloride**)
(**d**) *Zinc sulfate* is one kind of *sulfate*, and *ammonium chloride* is one kind of *salt*. **Classification**

61. (*a.* green, **b. blue**, *c.* lavender, *d.* royal) : PURPLE :: YELLOW : ORANGE
(**b**) The color *blue* is one part of *purple* (the other is red). The color *yellow* is one part of *orange* (again, the other is red). **Part/Whole**

62. ADZE : (*a.* **woodworking,** *b.* bricklaying, *c.* plumbing, *d.* stonework) :: CHISEL : MASONRY

    (**a**) The *adze* is an axelike tool used in *woodworking.* The *chisel* is another edged tool used in *masonry.* **Object/Action**

63. (*a.* disinfect, *b.* dissemble, *c.* displease, *d.* **dismantle**) : RAZE :: DISSATISFY : ANGER

    (**d**) To *dismantle* something thoroughly is to *raze,* or flatten, it. To *dissatisfy* someone thoroughly is probably to *anger* him or her. **Degree**

64. DR. FAUSTUS : DR. JEKYLL :: MARLOWE : (*a.* Shelley, *b.* Hyde, *c.* **Stevenson,** *d.* Rabelais)

    (**c**) Christopher *Marlowe* created *Dr. Faustus* in his play, *Faust.* Robert Louis *Stevenson* created *Dr. Jekyll* in his novel, *Dr. Jekyll and Mr. Hyde.* **Object/Action**

65. 10 : 100 :: (*a.* 11, *b.* **12,** *c.* 14, *d.* 44) : 144

    (**b**) The square root of *100* is *10;* the square root of *144* is *12.* **Conversion**

66. SCRIMSHAW : (*a.* **ivory,** *b.* carving, *c.* flooring, *d.* metal) :: PARQUET : WOOD

    (**a**) *Scrimshaw* is engraved *ivory* or bone. *Parquet* is a design of inlaid *wood.* **Characteristic**

67. GAUL : HISPANIA :: (*a.* Roman Empire, *b.* Latin, *c.* **France,** *d.* Germany) : SPAIN

    (**c**) In ancient times, *Gaul* was the name for what we now know as *France. Hispania* was the name for what we now know as *Spain.* **Conversion**

68. GOODALL : FOSSEY :: CHIMPANZEES : (*a.* insects, *b.* dancers, *c.* wolves, *d.* **gorillas**)

    (**d**) Jane *Goodall* is known for her work in the wild with *chimpanzees.* Dian *Fossey* was known for her work in the wild with *gorillas.* **Object/Action**

69. (*a.* Bundestag, *b.* **Whigs,** *c.* Socialists, *d.* Labour) : TORIES :: JACOBINS : GIRONDISTS

    (**b**) Around the time that the *Jacobins* and *Girondists* were political factions in France, two major political parties in England were the *Whigs* and the *Tories.* **Part/Whole**

70. OHIO : OH :: NEVADA : (*a.* NE, *b.* ND, *c.* **NV,** *d.* NA)

    (**c**) The postal abbreviation for *Ohio* is *OH,* and the postal abbreviation for *Nevada* is *NV.* **Conversion**

71. GAIN : LOSS :: (*a.* **reduction,** *b.* profit, *c.* metabolism, *d.* combustion) : OXIDATION

    (**a**) Just as *gain* is the opposite of *loss,* in chemistry *reduction* is the opposite of *oxidation.* In reduction, atoms gain electrons, and in oxidation, they lose electrons. **Antonym**

72. BOAR : (*a.* sow, *b.* swine, *c.* **sable,** *d.* artist) :: HAIRBRUSH : PAINTBRUSH

    (**c**) Fancy *hairbrushes* are made from *boar* hair. Fancy *paintbrushes* are made from *sable* hair. A sable is a weasellike mammal. **Object/Action**

73. CALYPSO : TRINIDAD :: GAMELAN : (*a.* West Africa, *b.* Jamaica, *c.* India, *d.* **Indonesia**)

    (**d**) *Calypso* is a form of music that originated in *Trinidad. Gamelan* is a form of music that originated in *Indonesia.* **Characteristic**

74. PRE- : POST- :: A.M. : (*a.* F.M., *b.* **P.M.**, *c.* M.A., *d.* Ph.D.)

    (**b**) The abbreviation *A.M.* means "ante meridiem," or *pre*-midday. The abbreviation *P.M.* means "*post* meridiem," or after midday. **Antonym**

75. INNOCENT : (*a.* purity, *b.* virtue, *c.* debris, *d.* **evil**) :: CLEAN : GRIME

    (**d**) To be *innocent* is to be without *evil,* just as to be *clean* is to be without *grime.* **Characteristic**

76. AHAB : BLIGH :: (*a. Caine, b. Golden Hind, c.* **Pequod,** *d. Victory*) : BOUNTY

    (**c**) In *Moby Dick,* Captain *Ahab* was the captain of the *Pequod,* a whaling vessel. Captain *Bligh* was the captain of the *Bounty,* object of a famous mutiny. **Object/Action**

77. YANKEE : NEW ENGLAND :: TAR HEEL : (*a.* Indiana, *b.* **North Carolina**, *c.* Tennessee, *d.* West Virginia)

    (**b**) A native of *New England* is familiarly known as a *Yankee.* A native of North Carolina is familiarly known as a *Tar Heel.* **Characteristic**

78. (*a.* Prokofiev, *b.* **Diaghilev**, *c.* Akhmatova, *d.* Nesterov) : BALLETS RUSSES :: BALANCHINE : NEW YORK CITY BALLET)

    (**b**) Serge *Diaghilev* was a choreographer and director of the *Ballets Russes.* George *Balanchine* was a choreographer and director of the *New York City Ballet.* **Characteristic**

79. OP ART : POP ART :: VASARELY : (*a.* Pollock, *b.* **Lichtenstein**, *c.* Kandinsky, *d.* Rothko)

    (**b**) Victor *Vasarely* was a key player in the early world of *op art,* or optical art. Roy *Lichtenstein's* comic-book paintings were part of the world of *pop art.* **Object/Action**

80. PALEOZOIC : REPTILES :: MESOZOIC : (*a.* sponges, *b.* brachiopods, *c.* **birds**, *d.* plants)

    (**c**) The end of the *Paleozoic* era (453 to 248 million years ago) saw the rise of the first *reptiles.* The end of the *Mesozoic* era (248 to 65 million years ago) saw the rise of the first *birds.* **Characteristic**

81. STOMACH : DIGESTION :: (*a.* **diaphragm**, *b.* cell, *c.* intestine, *d.* kidney) : RESPIRATION

    (**a**) The *stomach* is a muscular organ used in *digestion.* The *diaphragm* is a muscle used in *respiration.* Cells take part in respiration, but they are not muscular body parts. **Object/Action**

82. (*a.* G, *b.* scale, *c.* **natural**, *d.* transposition) : FLAT :: SHARP : NATURAL

    (**c**) In musical notation, a *natural* comes just after a *flat,* and a *sharp* comes just after a *natural.* For example, B follows B flat, and C sharp follows C. **Sequence**

83. SIGNET : (*a.* **impression**, *b.* ring, *c.* king, *d.* official) :: PORTENT : PROPHESY
    (a) A *signet* is a seal that is used to make an *impression* in sealing wax. A *portent* is an omen that is used to make a *prophesy* about upcoming events. **Object/Action**

84. EXONERATE : EXORCISE :: (*a.* execrate, *b.* **absolve**, *c.* excommunicate, *d.* impel) : EXPEL
    (b) If you *exonerate* someone, you *absolve* him or her of responsibility for a crime. If you *exorcise* evil spirits, you *expel* them from someone's soul. **Synonym**

85. (*a.* Stokowski, *b.* Casals, *c.* **Heifetz**, *d.* Paderewski) : GOULD :: VIOLIN : PIANO
    (c) Jascha *Heifetz* was a brilliant *violinist* of the twentieth century, and Glenn *Gould* was a brilliant *pianist.* **Object/Action**

86. INEXTRICABLE : ESCAPE :: INEXPRESSIBLE : (*a.* diversion, *b.* alteration, *c.* evasion, *d.* **description**)
    (d) Something that is *inextricable* resists *escape,* and something that is *inexpressible* resists *description.* **Object/Action**

87. TRANSMISSION : GEARS :: (*a.* vehicle, *b.* **suspension**, *c.* absorbers, *d.* armature) : STRUTS
    (b) *Gears* are part of a vehicle's *transmission,* and *struts* are part of its *suspension* system. **Part/Whole**

88. EULOGY : PRAISE :: ELEGY : (*a.* commendation, *b.* gratification, *c.* censure, *d.* **lamentation**)
    (d) One delivers a *eulogy* to *praise* a subject. One writes an *elegy* to *lament* a subject's passing. **Object/Action**

89. EGG : LARVA :: (*a.* **pupa**, *b.* embryo, *c.* caterpillar, *d.* blastocyst) : IMAGO
    (a) The four steps in the growth pattern of certain insects are from *egg* to *larva* to *pupa* to *imago.* **Sequence**

90. GIDE : (*a. The Bald Soprano*, *b. **The Immoralist***, *c. The Plague*, *d. The Prisoner*) :: CAMUS : THE STRANGER
    (b) André *Gide* is the author of *The Immoralist.* Albert *Camus* is the author of *The Stranger.* **Object/Action**

91. SEEK : FIND :: ASK : (*a.* collect, *b.* query, *c.* appear, *d.* **receive**)
    (d) The Biblical quotations you should recall here are "*Seek* and ye shall *find*" and "*Ask* and ye shall *receive.*" **Sequence**

92. (*a.* Ringgold, *b.* Basquiat, *c.* **Wegman**, *d.* Wyeth) : PHOTOGRAPH :: RIVERA : MURAL
    (c) William *Wegman* is known for his *photographs,* particularly those starring Weimaraners (dogs) in human clothing, settings, and situations. Diego *Rivera* is known for his *murals.* **Object/Action**

93. MOAT : INVASION :: (*a.* bacillus, *b.* injury, *c.* **bandage**, *d.* seepage) : INFECTION
    (c) A *moat* protects a castle from *invasion.* A *bandage* protects a wound from *infection.* **Object/Action**

94. (*a.* debauchery, *b.* dedication, *c.* deposition, ***d.* dereliction**) : DEPRECATION ::
NEGLECT : DISAPPROVAL
(**d**) *Dereliction* is similar to *neglect. Deprecation* is similar to *disapproval.* **Synonym**

95. VIAL : VAT :: FILAMENT : (*a.* hair, *b.* tub, *c.* strand, ***d.* rope**)
(**d**) A *vial* is a small container; a *vat* is a large container. A *filament* is a small thread;
a *rope* is a large thread. **Degree**

96. DOG : PAVLOV :: RAT : (*a.* Rorschach, *b.* Piaget, *c.* Adler, ***d.* Skinner**)
(**d**) Ivan *Pavlov* studied behavior, using *dogs* as his subject. B. F. *Skinner* studied
behavior, using *rats* as his subject. **Object/Action**

97. SHOCK : SCANDALIZE :: DEMORALIZE : (***a.* depress**, *b.* appall, *c.* confirm,
d. hearten)
(**a**) To *shock* is to *scandalize.* To *demoralize* is to *depress.* **Synonym**

98. (*a.* extender, *b.* pipe cleaner, ***c.* flexor**, *d.* knee) : BEND :: EXTENSOR :
STRAIGHTEN
(**c**) A *flexor* is a muscle that *bends* a limb. An *extensor* is a muscle that *straightens* a limb.
Object/Action

99. DYNAMITE : REVOLVER :: NOBEL : (*a.* Gatling, ***b.* Colt**, *c.* Maxim, *d.* Prize)
(**b**) The inventor of *dynamite* was Alfred *Nobel.* The inventor of the *revolver* was
Samuel *Colt.* **Object/Action**

100. ACID : BASE :: 0 : (*a.* 2, ***b.* 14**, *c.* 38, *d.* 100)
(**b**) The pH ("potential of hydrogen") scale is a logarithmic scale used to describe the
alkalinity or acidity of a substance. On the scale, which ranges from *0* to *14*, a pH of
less than 7 describes an *acid*, and a pH greater than 7 describes a *base.* **Characteristic**

PRACTICE TEST 4
ANSWER SHEET

1. Ⓐ Ⓑ Ⓒ Ⓓ	26. Ⓐ Ⓑ Ⓒ Ⓓ	51. Ⓐ Ⓑ Ⓒ Ⓓ	76. Ⓐ Ⓑ Ⓒ Ⓓ
2. Ⓐ Ⓑ Ⓒ Ⓓ	27. Ⓐ Ⓑ Ⓒ Ⓓ	52. Ⓐ Ⓑ Ⓒ Ⓓ	77. Ⓐ Ⓑ Ⓒ Ⓓ
3. Ⓐ Ⓑ Ⓒ Ⓓ	28. Ⓐ Ⓑ Ⓒ Ⓓ	53. Ⓐ Ⓑ Ⓒ Ⓓ	78. Ⓐ Ⓑ Ⓒ Ⓓ
4. Ⓐ Ⓑ Ⓒ Ⓓ	29. Ⓐ Ⓑ Ⓒ Ⓓ	54. Ⓐ Ⓑ Ⓒ Ⓓ	79. Ⓐ Ⓑ Ⓒ Ⓓ
5. Ⓐ Ⓑ Ⓒ Ⓓ	30. Ⓐ Ⓑ Ⓒ Ⓓ	55. Ⓐ Ⓑ Ⓒ Ⓓ	80. Ⓐ Ⓑ Ⓒ Ⓓ
6. Ⓐ Ⓑ Ⓒ Ⓓ	31. Ⓐ Ⓑ Ⓒ Ⓓ	56. Ⓐ Ⓑ Ⓒ Ⓓ	81. Ⓐ Ⓑ Ⓒ Ⓓ
7. Ⓐ Ⓑ Ⓒ Ⓓ	32. Ⓐ Ⓑ Ⓒ Ⓓ	57. Ⓐ Ⓑ Ⓒ Ⓓ	82. Ⓐ Ⓑ Ⓒ Ⓓ
8. Ⓐ Ⓑ Ⓒ Ⓓ	33. Ⓐ Ⓑ Ⓒ Ⓓ	58. Ⓐ Ⓑ Ⓒ Ⓓ	83. Ⓐ Ⓑ Ⓒ Ⓓ
9. Ⓐ Ⓑ Ⓒ Ⓓ	34. Ⓐ Ⓑ Ⓒ Ⓓ	59. Ⓐ Ⓑ Ⓒ Ⓓ	84. Ⓐ Ⓑ Ⓒ Ⓓ
10. Ⓐ Ⓑ Ⓒ Ⓓ	35. Ⓐ Ⓑ Ⓒ Ⓓ	60. Ⓐ Ⓑ Ⓒ Ⓓ	85. Ⓐ Ⓑ Ⓒ Ⓓ
11. Ⓐ Ⓑ Ⓒ Ⓓ	36. Ⓐ Ⓑ Ⓒ Ⓓ	61. Ⓐ Ⓑ Ⓒ Ⓓ	86. Ⓐ Ⓑ Ⓒ Ⓓ
12. Ⓐ Ⓑ Ⓒ Ⓓ	37. Ⓐ Ⓑ Ⓒ Ⓓ	62. Ⓐ Ⓑ Ⓒ Ⓓ	87. Ⓐ Ⓑ Ⓒ Ⓓ
13. Ⓐ Ⓑ Ⓒ Ⓓ	38. Ⓐ Ⓑ Ⓒ Ⓓ	63. Ⓐ Ⓑ Ⓒ Ⓓ	88. Ⓐ Ⓑ Ⓒ Ⓓ
14. Ⓐ Ⓑ Ⓒ Ⓓ	39. Ⓐ Ⓑ Ⓒ Ⓓ	64. Ⓐ Ⓑ Ⓒ Ⓓ	89. Ⓐ Ⓑ Ⓒ Ⓓ
15. Ⓐ Ⓑ Ⓒ Ⓓ	40. Ⓐ Ⓑ Ⓒ Ⓓ	65. Ⓐ Ⓑ Ⓒ Ⓓ	90. Ⓐ Ⓑ Ⓒ Ⓓ
16. Ⓐ Ⓑ Ⓒ Ⓓ	41. Ⓐ Ⓑ Ⓒ Ⓓ	66. Ⓐ Ⓑ Ⓒ Ⓓ	91. Ⓐ Ⓑ Ⓒ Ⓓ
17. Ⓐ Ⓑ Ⓒ Ⓓ	42. Ⓐ Ⓑ Ⓒ Ⓓ	67. Ⓐ Ⓑ Ⓒ Ⓓ	92. Ⓐ Ⓑ Ⓒ Ⓓ
18. Ⓐ Ⓑ Ⓒ Ⓓ	43. Ⓐ Ⓑ Ⓒ Ⓓ	68. Ⓐ Ⓑ Ⓒ Ⓓ	93. Ⓐ Ⓑ Ⓒ Ⓓ
19. Ⓐ Ⓑ Ⓒ Ⓓ	44. Ⓐ Ⓑ Ⓒ Ⓓ	69. Ⓐ Ⓑ Ⓒ Ⓓ	94. Ⓐ Ⓑ Ⓒ Ⓓ
20. Ⓐ Ⓑ Ⓒ Ⓓ	45. Ⓐ Ⓑ Ⓒ Ⓓ	70. Ⓐ Ⓑ Ⓒ Ⓓ	95. Ⓐ Ⓑ Ⓒ Ⓓ
21. Ⓐ Ⓑ Ⓒ Ⓓ	46. Ⓐ Ⓑ Ⓒ Ⓓ	71. Ⓐ Ⓑ Ⓒ Ⓓ	96. Ⓐ Ⓑ Ⓒ Ⓓ
22. Ⓐ Ⓑ Ⓒ Ⓓ	47. Ⓐ Ⓑ Ⓒ Ⓓ	72. Ⓐ Ⓑ Ⓒ Ⓓ	97. Ⓐ Ⓑ Ⓒ Ⓓ
23. Ⓐ Ⓑ Ⓒ Ⓓ	48. Ⓐ Ⓑ Ⓒ Ⓓ	73. Ⓐ Ⓑ Ⓒ Ⓓ	98. Ⓐ Ⓑ Ⓒ Ⓓ
24. Ⓐ Ⓑ Ⓒ Ⓓ	49. Ⓐ Ⓑ Ⓒ Ⓓ	74. Ⓐ Ⓑ Ⓒ Ⓓ	99. Ⓐ Ⓑ Ⓒ Ⓓ
25. Ⓐ Ⓑ Ⓒ Ⓓ	50. Ⓐ Ⓑ Ⓒ Ⓓ	75. Ⓐ Ⓑ Ⓒ Ⓓ	100. Ⓐ Ⓑ Ⓒ Ⓓ

PRACTICE TEST 4

Directions: For each question, you will see three capitalized words and four answer choices labeled *a, b, c,* and *d* in parentheses. Choose the answer that best completes the analogy posed by the three capitalized words. Use the answer sheet on page 101 to record your answers.

Time: 50 Minutes

1. (*a.* Leonardo's Horse, *b.* Eros, *c.* Winged Victory, *d.* Pietà) : PARIS :: MICHELANGELO'S DAVID : FLORENCE

2. WHEEL : SHIP :: (*a.* reins, *b.* west, *c.* horse, *d.* wagon box) : STAGECOACH

3. FORMOSA : TAIWAN :: CEYLON : (*a.* Pakistan, *b.* Sri Lanka, *c.* Madagascar, *d.* Tamil)

4. HEAT : (*a.* lamp, *b.* intensity, *c.* desiccation, *d.* fungus) :: DAMP : MOLD

5. TELO- : (*a.* far, *b.* end, *c.* earth, *d.* prior) :: TELE- : DISTANT

6. PLACATE : MOLLIFY :: (*a.* irk, *b.* comfort, *c.* mollify, *d.* attend to) : VEX

7. UNITARIANISM : (*a.* peace, *b.* Trinity, *c.* deity, *d.* community) :: ANGLICANISM : PAPACY

8. ALLY : COLLABORATOR :: DEVOTEE : (*a.* colleague, *b.* adjunct, *c.* champion, *d.* buff)

9. MELODY : ARIA :: (*a.* tune, *b.* dance, *c.* feast, *d.* promenade) : PROM

10. (*a.* marigold, *b.* foxglove, *c.* goldenrod, *d.* iris) : ANNUAL :: DAISY : PERENNIAL

11. AVIATOR : (*a.* aviators, *b.* aviatress, *c.* aviatrix, *d.* aviation) :: ACTOR : ACTRESS

12. PHOTORECEPTOR : SIGHT :: CHEMORECEPTOR : (*a.* smell, *b.* hearing, *c.* chemical, *d.* amphibian)

13. GRAND COULEE DAM : (*a.* Mississippi, *b.* Yangtze, *c.* Columbia, *d.* Colorado) :: ASWAN DAM : NILE

14. FUNICULAR : (*a.* cathedral, *b.* edifice, *c.* road, *d.* mountain) :: ELEVATOR : SKYSCRAPER

15. WYETH : PHOTOGRAPHIC REALISM :: KLEE : (*a.* constructivism, *b.* surrealism, *c.* primitivism, *d.* pointillism)

16. CHRONOMETER : (*a.* wind speed, *b.* time, *c.* distance, *d.* color variation) :: BAROMETER : PRESSURE

17. ADVERB : NOUN :: KINDLY : (*a.* kinder, *b.* kindle, *c.* kindness, *d.* kindhearted)

18. ERA : (*a.* time, *b.* Mesozoic, *c.* phase, *d.* period) :: EPOCH : AGE

19. ACIDIC : HYDROGEN :: BASIC : (*a.* hydrochloride, *b.* sulfurate, *c.* hydroxide, *d.* proton)

20. ETHNOLOGIST : ETYMOLOGIST :: (*a.* culture, *b.* speech, *c.* structure, *d.* government) : LANGUAGE

21. SEVEN : (*a.* oaths, *b.* sins, *c.* directives, *d.* dominions) :: TEN : COMMANDMENTS

22. FRENZY : SERENITY :: RAPTURE : (*a.* bliss, *b.* fascination, *c.* repose, *d.* gloom)

23. JAUNDICE : (*a.* artifice, *b.* cirrhosis, *c.* roseola, *d.* yellow fever) :: YELLOW : RED

24. (*a.* timorous, *b.* gluttonous, *c.* sated, *d.* heroic) : CRAVEN :: BEWILDERED : ENLIGHTENED

25. POL POT : CAMBODIA :: IDI AMIN : (*a.* Zimbabwe, *b.* Uganda, *c.* Congo, *d.* Ethiopia)

26. 3 : 5 :: (*a.* 4, *b.* 7, *c.* 9, *d.* 10) : 11

27. THESEUS : (*a.* Sparta, *b.* Rome, *c.* Athens, *d.* Crete) :: PRIAM : TROY

28. (*a.* decomposition, *b.* respiration, *c.* energy, *d.* transpiration) : CO_2 :: PHOTOSYNTHESIS : O_2

29. CHLOROPHYLL : SPINACH :: CAROTENOID : (*a.* fruit flies, *b.* cabbage, *c.* carrots, *d.* soybeans)

30. *DRACULA* : *FRANKENSTEIN* :: (*a.* King, *b.* Price, *c.* Stevenson, *d.* Stoker) : SHELLEY

31. (*a.* phony, *b.* pugilist, *c.* pacifist, *d.* swine) : SWINDLER :: FIGHTER : WARRIOR

32. CLARINET : SINGLE REED :: (*a.* flute, *b.* saxophone, *c.* oboe, *d.* recorder) : DOUBLE REED

33. SATYR : MAENAD :: RAM : (*a.* billy goat, *b.* horn, *c.* sheep, *d.* ewe)

34. LEVANTER : EAST :: (*a.* mistral, *b.* chinook, *c.* vendeval, *d.* sirocco) : NORTH

35. 1 : 0001 :: 10 : (*a.* 1001, *b.* 1010, *c.* 1100, *d.* 1000)

36. (*a.* parsec, *b.* ampere, *c.* calorie, *d.* candela) : HEAT :: DECIBEL : SOUND

37. BORON : ELEMENT :: BORAX : (*a.* atom, *b.* solution, *c.* compound, *d.* ion)

38. PENNY : (*a.* nickel, *b.* dime, *c.* quarter, *d.* five-dollar bill) :: LINCOLN MEMORIAL : MONTICELLO

39. WHITE FLAG : BLACK FLAG :: (*a.* law, *b.* fear, *c.* truce, *d.* health) : PIRACY

40. (*a.* Orthodox, *b.* Gregorian, *c.* Christian, *d.* Judaic) : ISLAMIC :: SEPTEMBER : RAMADAN

41. UKRAINIAN : SLAVIC :: WELSH : (*a.* English, *b.* Nordic, *c.* Celtic, *d.* Germanic)

42. FRANCE : (*a.* prefectures, *b.* districts, *c.* states, *d.* departments) :: CANADA : PROVINCES

43. CACOPHONY : EUPHONY :: (*a.* dissonance, *b.* cachet, *c.* despair, *d.* amphora) : EUPHORIA

44. OPERETTA : (*a.* opera, *b.* oratorio, *c.* symphonic poem, *d.* elegy) :: *THE MIKADO* : *THE MESSIAH*

45. RATIONALIST : (*a.* empiricist, *b.* relativist, *c.* deconstructionist, *d.* fatalist) :: DESCARTES : HUME

46. (*a.* tinnitus, *b.* eustachian tube, *c.* otology, *d.* audition) : HEARING :: VISION : SIGHT

47. WILLIAM JAMES : PRAGMATISM :: (*a.* Baruch Spinoza, *b.* Karl Marx, *c.* Herbert Marcuse, *d.* Immanuel Kant) : LIBERTARIANISM

48. (*a.* Earth, *b.* apple, *c.* center, *d.* cherry) : CORE :: PEACH : PIT

49. (*a.* avant garde, *b.* crash, *c.* neutralize, *d.* smog) : PORTMANTEAU :: SPLASH : ONOMATOPOEIA

50. MOTET : (*a.* prose, *b.* verse, *c.* song, *d.* epic) :: ODE : POEM

51. 35° : 145° :: 60° : (*a.* 45°, *b.* 80°, *c.* 105°, *d.* 120°)

52. FULTON : STEAMBOAT :: (*a.* Otis, *b.* Faraday, *c.* Yale, *d.* Westinghouse) : ELEVATOR

53. (*a.* worship, *b.* heresy, *c.* penance, *d.* devotion) : SACRILEGE :: REVERENCE : VENERATION

54. CRUSTACEA : (*a.* crab, *b.* Animalia, *c.* Arthropoda, *d.* Insectae) :: CLASS : PHYLUM

55. (*a.* limb, *b.* foot, *c.* ankle, *d.* arch) : TOE :: PALM : THUMB

56. CARDINAL : ORDINAL :: 24 : (*a.* 1/24, *b.* 0.12, *c.* 17th, *d.* 4275)

57. BASALT : TITANIUM :: (*a.* iron, *b.* alloy, *c.* rock, *d.* salt) : METAL

58. BATON : CONDUCT :: POINTER : (*a.* convey, *b.* hunt, *c.* indicate, *d.* confront)

59. (*a.* adagio, *b.* allegro, *c.* ostinato, *d.* pizzicato) : PRESTO :: BRISK : SPEEDY

60. GRIMACE : GROAN :: (*a.* distrust, *b.* dismay, *c.* disbelief, *d.* distaste) : DISCOMFORT

61. BLEED : BLED :: FEAR : (*a.* fearful, *b.* far, *c.* fled, *d.* afraid)

62. MARSEILLAISE : FRANCE :: (*a.* Land of Hope and Glory, *b.* White Cliffs of Dover, *c.* Rule Britannia, *d.* God Save the Queen) : BRITAIN

63. (*a.* Wesley, *b.* Calvin, *c.* Young, *d.* Loyola) : METHODISTS :: SMITH : MORMONS

64. TESSERAE : (*a.* collage, *b.* tile, *c.* mosaic, *d.* transparency) :: PIXELS : DIGITAL PHOTO

65. HADES : ARTEMIS :: PLUTO : (*a.* Diana, *b.* Uranus, *c.* Venus, *d.* Aurora)

66. (*a.* herb, *b.* wisdom, *c.* fool, *d.* wizard) : SAGE :: FIEND : SERAPH

67. DANIEL WEBSTER : ORATORY :: NOAH WEBSTER :
    (*a.* anthropology, *b.* composition, *c.* erudition, *d.* lexicography)

68. AERIE : EAGLE :: (*a.* burrow, *b.* formicary, *c.* rookery, *d.* apiary) : ANT

69. ARABLE : POTABLE :: LIFELESS : (*a.* dead, *b.* liquid, *c.* toxic, *d.* vital)

70. DESERT : SAND :: (*a.* tundra, *b.* taiga, *c.* savanna, *d.* swamp) : GRASS

71. FORESTER : *THE AFRICAN QUEEN* :: FORSTER : (*a. A Passage to India, b. Out of Africa, c. The Virgin Queen, d. An American Tragedy*)

72. PARTHENON : (*a.* Colosseum, *b.* San Niccolo, *c.* Doge's Palace, *d.* St. Mark's) :: ATHENS : ROME

73. CUTANEOUS : SKIN :: PILEOUS : (*a.* blood, *b.* lymph, *c.* scale, *d.* hair)

74. GUNNAR MYRDAL : (*a.* physics, *b.* economics, *c.* medicine, *d.* history) :: LINUS PAULING : CHEMISTRY

75. KUWAIT : (*a.* shekel, *b.* rial, *c.* dinar, *d.* shilling) :: LUXEMBOURG : EURO

76. HOLLYWOOD : FILM :: (*a.* Tokyo, *b.* Paris, *c.* New York, *d.* Caracas) : ANIME

77. LEAR : CORDELIA :: PROSPERO : (*a.* Regan, *b.* Olivia, *c.* Miranda, *d.* Gertrude)

78. (*a.* Britten, *b.* Balanchine, *c.* Bernstein, *d.* Baryshnikov) : STRAVINSKY :: CHOREOGRAPHY : COMPOSITION

79. FAUX PAS : GAFFE :: IDÉE FIXE : (*a.* correction, *b.* delight, *c.* brainstorm, *d.* obsession)

80. SALVADOR DALI : SURREALISM :: (*a.* Amedeo Modigliani, *b.* Claude Monet, *c.* Dante Gabriel Rossetti, *d.* Gustav Klimt) : IMPRESSIONISM

81. OENOLOGIST : ONCOLOGIST :: (*a.* eyes, *b.* birth, *c.* wine, *d.* viruses) : CANCER

82. EXECUTIVE : (*a.* Library of Congress, *b.* Court of Appeals, *c.* Parliament, *d.* Cabinet) :: JUDICIAL : SUPREME COURT

83. PORTFOLIO : ARTIST :: (*a.* folder, *b.* briefcase, *c.* oeuvre, *d.* composition) : COMPOSER

84. PRETEST : (*a.* invention, *b.* completion, *c.* additions, *d.* instruction) :: PRETAX : DEDUCTIONS

85. *CATCHER IN THE RYE* : *CATCH-22* :: SALINGER : (*a.* Heller, *b.* Saroyan, *c.* Vonnegut, *d.* Bellow)

86. VIII : (*a.* VI, *b.* X, *c.* L, *d.* C) :: IV : V

87. (*a.* botany, *b.* genetics, *c.* recombination, *d.* grafting) : HYBRIDS :: CLONING : DUPLICATES

88. WRIGHT : FALLINGWATER :: SAARINEN : (*a.* Museum of Modern Art, *b.* Gateway Arch, *c.* Washington Monument, *d.* Golden Gate Bridge)

89. (*a.* gregarious, *b.* ascetic, *c.* abstemious, *d.* superficial) : EXTROVERTED :: RECLUSIVE : INTROVERTED

90. CAMERA : (*a.* tripod, *b.* lens, *c.* eye, *d.* student) :: APERTURE : PUPIL

91. KITTY HAWK : (*a.* biplane, *b.* airfoil, *c.* kite, *d.* aileron) :: CAPE CANAVERAL : ROCKET

92. LITTLE DORRITT : DICKENS :: LITTLE EVA : (*a.* Alcott, *b.* Stowe, *c.* Eliot, *d.* Gilman)

93. (*a.* gnome, *b.* pixie, *c.* Leviathan, *d.* Swift) : ENORMITY :: LILLIPUTIAN : TININESS

94. MISDEMEANOR : (*a.* theft, *b.* burglary, *c.* felony, *d.* crime) :: PETIT LARCENY : GRAND LARCENY

95. AMPLE : (*a.* substantial, *b.* petty, *c.* scarce, *d.* incorrigible) :: TRIFLING : NEGLIGIBLE

96. (*a.* Natty Bumppo, *b.* James Fenimore Cooper, *c.* Mohican, *d.* Leatherstocking) : THE DEERSLAYER :: CHRISTOPHER NEWMAN : THE AMERICAN

97. SATURN : RINGS :: MOON : (*a.* lines, *b.* mares, *c.* haze, *d.* arrows)

98. OCTA- : (*a.* deca-, *b.* ennea-, *c.* dodeca-, *d.* binal) :: EIGHT : TWELVE

99. TIN MAN : HEART :: JASON : (*a.* brain, *b.* grail, *c.* fleece, *d.* Argo)

100. QUIXOTE : IDEALISM :: (*a.* Javert, *b.* Panza, *c.* Bovary, *d.* Raskolnikov) : DETERMINATION

STOP

If there is any time remaining, go back and check your work.

PRACTICE TEST 4
ANSWER KEY

1. c	26. b	51. d	76. a
2. a	27. c	52. a	77. c
3. b	28. b	53. b	78. b
4. c	29. c	54. c	79. d
5. b	30. d	55. d	80. b
6. a	31. a	56. c	81. c
7. b	32. c	57. c	82. d
8. d	33. d	58. c	83. c
9. b	34. a	59. b	84. d
10. a	35. b	60. d	85. a
11. c	36. c	61. b	86. b
12. a	37. c	62. d	87. d
13. c	38. a	63. a	88. b
14. d	39. c	64. c	89. a
15. c	40. b	65. a	90. c
16. b	41. c	66. c	91. a
17. c	42. d	67. d	92. b
18. d	43. c	68. b	93. c
19. c	44. b	69. c	94. c
20. a	45. a	70. c	95. a
21. b	46. d	71. a	96. a
22. d	47. c	72. a	97. b
23. c	48. b	73. d	98. c
24. d	49. d	74. b	99. c
25. b	50. c	75. c	100. a

PRACTICE TEST 4
EXPLANATORY ANSWERS

1. (*a.* Leonardo's Horse, *b.* Eros, *c.* **Winged Victory**, *d.* Pietà) : PARIS ::
   MICHELANGELO'S DAVID : FLORENCE
   (**c**) The Greek marble statue known as *Winged Victory* is housed at the Louvre in *Paris*,
   France, just as the Renaissance statue of *David* is now located in the Accademia
   Gallery in *Florence*, Italy. **Characteristic**

2. WHEEL : SHIP :: (*a.* **reins**, *b.* west, *c.* horse, *d.* wagon box) : STAGECOACH
   (**a**) You would use a *wheel* to steer a *ship*; you would use *reins* to steer a *stagecoach*.
   Object/Action

3. FORMOSA : TAIWAN :: CEYLON : (*a.* Pakistan, *b.* **Sri Lanka**, *c.* Madagascar,
   d. Tamil)
   (**b**) The island in the South China Sea once known as *Formosa* is now called *Taiwan*.
   The island in the Indian Ocean once called *Ceylon* is now called *Sri Lanka*.
   Conversion

4. HEAT : (*a.* lamp, *b.* intensity, *c.* **desiccation**, *d.* fungus) :: DAMP : MOLD
   (**c**) Too much *heat* can lead to *desiccation*, or drying out. Too much *damp* can lead to
   mold. **Object/Action**

5. TELO- : (*a.* far, *b.* **end**, *c.* earth, *d.* prior) :: TELE- : DISTANT
   (**b**) The prefix *telo-*, as in *telophase*, means "*end.*" The prefix *tele-*, as in *telescope*, means
   "*distant.*" **Affix**

6. PLACATE : MOLLIFY :: (*a.* **irk**, *b.* comfort, *c.* mollify, *d.* attend to) : VEX
   (**a**) To *placate* people is to *mollify*, or soothe, them. To *irk* people is to *vex*, or annoy,
   them. **Synonym**

7. UNITARIANISM : (*a.* peace, *b.* **Trinity**, *c.* deity, *d.* community) :: ANGLICANISM :
   PAPACY
   (**b**) *Unitarianism* is a religion that rejects the notion of the *Trinity*—the oneness of the
   Father, the Son, and the Holy Ghost. *Anglicanism* is a religion that rejects the *papacy*—
   the notion that the pope is a conduit between God and humankind. **Object/Action**

8. ALLY : COLLABORATOR :: DEVOTEE : (*a.* colleague, *b.* adjunct, *c.* champion,
   d. **buff**)
   (**d**) An *ally*, or partner, may be considered a *collaborator*. A *devotee*, or fan, may be
   considered a *buff*. **Synonym**

9. MELODY : ARIA :: (*a.* tune, *b.* **dance**, *c.* feast, *d.* promenade) : PROM
   (**b**) An *aria* may be considered a very fancy *melody*, and a *prom* may be considered a
   very fancy *dance*. **Degree**

10. (*a.* **marigold**, *b.* foxglove, *c.* goldenrod, *d.* iris) : ANNUAL :: DAISY : PERENNIAL
    (**a**) *Marigolds* are *annuals*—they must be planted anew each spring. *Daisies* are
    perennials—they die and renew themselves year after year. **Classification**

11. AVIATOR : (*a.* aviators, *b.* aviatress, ***c.* aviatrix**, *d.* aviation) :: ACTOR : ACTRESS
(**c**) The female form of the word *aviator* is *aviatrix*. The female form of the word *actor* is *actress*. **Conversion**

12. PHOTORECEPTOR : SIGHT :: CHEMORECEPTOR : (***a.* smell**, *b.* hearing, *c.* chemical, *d.* amphibian)
(**a**) We have *sight* when our *photoreceptors* convert light into electrical signals. We can *smell* when our *chemoreceptors* convert chemicals into electrical signals. **Object/Action**

13. GRAND COULEE DAM : (*a.* Mississippi, *b.* Yangtze, ***c.* Columbia**, *d.* Colorado) :: ASWAN DAM : NILE
(**c**) The *Grand Coulee Dam* is built in the *Columbia* River in central Washington state. The *Aswan Dam* is built in the *Nile* River in southern Egypt. **Characteristic**

14. FUNICULAR : (*a.* cathedral, *b.* edifice, *c.* road, ***d.* mountain**) :: ELEVATOR : SKYSCRAPER
(**d**) You might ride a *funicular*, or cable car, up a *mountain*. You might ride an *elevator* up a *skyscraper*. **Characteristic**

15. WYETH : PHOTOGRAPHIC REALISM :: KLEE : (*a.* constructivism, *b.* surrealism, ***c.* primitivism**, *d.* pointillism)
(**c**) Andrew Wyeth painted pictures with a real-life look known as *photographic realism*. Paul Klee created childlike paintings in the style known as *primitivism*. **Object/Action**

16. CHRONOMETER : (*a.* wind speed, ***b.* time**, *c.* distance, *d.* color variation) :: BAROMETER : PRESSURE
(**b**) A *chronometer* (think "chronology") measures *time*, usually very precisely. A *barometer* measures atmospheric *pressure*. **Object/Action**

17. ADVERB : NOUN :: KINDLY : (*a.* kinder, *b.* kindle, ***c.* kindness**, *d.* kindhearted)
(**c**) The word *kindly* is an *adverb*, a word that modifies a verb, adjective, or another adverb. The word *kindness* is a *noun*, a word that names a person, place, thing, or idea. **Classification**

18. ERA : (*a.* time, *b.* Mesozoic, *c.* phase, ***d.* period**) :: EPOCH : AGE
(**d**) The four units—*era, period, epoch,* and *age*—are all terms used to measure geologic time and thus are all related. They are listed here from longest to shortest. **Part/Whole**

19. ACIDIC : HYDROGEN :: BASIC : (*a.* hydrochloride, *b.* sulfurate, ***c.* hydroxide**, *d.* proton)
(**c**) An *acid* is a substance that increases the concentration of *hydrogen* ions (H^+) when dissolved in water. A *base* is a substance that increases the concentration of *hydroxide* ions (OH^-) when dissolved in water. **Classification**

20. ETHNOLOGIST : ETYMOLOGIST :: (***a.* culture**, *b.* speech, *c.* structure, *d.* government) : LANGUAGE
(**a**) An *ethnologist* might study the *culture* of a region; an *etymologist* might study its *language*. **Object/Action**

21. SEVEN : (*a.* oaths, ***b.* sins**, *c.* directives, *d.* dominions) :: TEN : COMMANDMENTS
    (**b**) The *seven* deadly *sins*, as named and refined by clerics throughout the Middle Ages, are pride, envy, gluttony, lust, anger, greed, and sloth. The *Ten Commandments* are laws given to Moses by God. **Characteristic**

22. FRENZY : SERENITY :: RAPTURE : (*a.* bliss, *b.* fascination, *c.* repose, ***d.* gloom**)
    (**d**) Someone who is in a *frenzy* lacks *serenity*, or calm. Someone who is in *rapture* lacks *gloom*, or sadness. **Antonym**

23. JAUNDICE : (*a.* artifice, *b.* cirrhosis, ***c.* roseola**, *d.* yellow fever) :: YELLOW : RED
    (**c**) *Jaundice* is a condition that causes the skin to take on a *yellowish* tint. *Roseola* is a disease that causes a *red* rash. **Object/Action**

24. (*a.* timorous, *b.* gluttonous, *c.* sated, ***d.* heroic**) : CRAVEN :: BEWILDERED : ENLIGHTENED
    (**d**) To be *heroic* is the opposite of being *craven*, or cowardly. To be *bewildered* is the opposite of being *enlightened*, or informed. **Antonym**

25. POL POT : CAMBODIA :: IDI AMIN : (*a.* Zimbabwe, ***b.* Uganda**, *c.* Congo, *d.* Ethiopia)
    (**b**) *Pol Pot* was a murderous tyrant who ran the country of *Cambodia* from 1976 to 1979. *Idi Amin* was a murderous tyrant who ran the country of *Uganda* from 1971 to 1979. **Characteristic**

26. 3 : 5 :: (*a.* 4, ***b.* 7**, *c.* 9, *d.* 10) : 11
    (**b**) The numbers *3, 5, 7,* and *11* are prime numbers in sequence. **Sequence**

27. THESEUS : (*a.* Sparta, *b.* Rome, ***c.* Athens**, *d.* Crete) :: PRIAM : TROY
    (**c**) In Greek mythology, *Theseus* was a king of *Athens*, and *Priam* was the last king of *Troy*. **Characteristic**

28. (*a.* decomposition, ***b.* respiration**, *c.* energy, *d.* transpiration) : CO_2 :: PHOTOSYNTHESIS : O_2
    (**b**) The end product of *respiration* is carbon dioxide (CO_2). The end product of *photosynthesis* is oxygen (O_2). **Object/Action**

29. CHLOROPHYLL : SPINACH :: CAROTENOID : (*a.* fruit flies, *b.* cabbage, ***c.* carrots**, *d.* soybeans)
    (**c**) *Chlorophyll* gives *spinach* its green color. *Carotenoid* gives *carrots* their orange color. **Characteristic**

30. *DRACULA* : *FRANKENSTEIN* :: (*a.* King, *b.* Price, *c.* Stevenson, ***d.* Stoker**) : SHELLEY
    (**d**) Bram *Stoker* wrote *Dracula* in 1897. Mary *Shelley* wrote *Frankenstein* in 1818. **Object/Action**

31. (***a.* phony**, *b.* pugilist, *c.* pacifist, *d.* swine) : SWINDLER :: FIGHTER : WARRIOR
    (**a**) An extreme *phony* might be called a *swindler*. An extreme *fighter* might be called a *warrior*. **Degree**

32. CLARINET : SINGLE REED :: (*a.* flute, *b.* saxophone, *c.* **oboe**, *d.* recorder) :
DOUBLE REED
(**c**) A *reed* is a strip of material placed in the mouthpiece of certain woodwind
instruments. It vibrates when air passes over it. *Clarinets* and saxophones are *single-reed*
instruments. *Oboes* and bassoons are *double-reed* instruments. **Characteristic**

33. SATYR : MAENAD :: RAM : (*a.* billy goat, *b.* horn, *c.* sheep, *d.* **ewe**)
(**d**) Satyrs and maenads took part in the Dionysian rites (called *Bacchanalias* in Roman
mythology). The *satyrs* were male, and the *maenads* were female, just as *rams* are male
sheep, and *ewes* are female sheep. **Part/Whole**

34. LEVANTER : EAST :: (*a.* **mistral**, *b.* chinook, *c.* vendeval, *d.* sirocco) : NORTH
(**a**) The *levanter* and *mistral* are both Mediterranean winds, the former from the *east*,
and the latter from the *north*. **Characteristic**

35. 1 : 0001 :: 10 : (*a.* 1001, *b.* **1010**, *c.* 1100, *d.* 1000)
(**b**) In our decimal system, the number 10 means one 10 and zero 1s. In the binary
system, the number 1010 means one 8, zero 4s, one 2, and zero 1s—for a total of 10
in all. **Conversion**

36. (*a.* parsec, *b.* ampere, *c.* **calorie**, *d.* candela) : HEAT :: DECIBEL : SOUND
(**c**) A *calorie* is a unit used to measure *heat*. A *decibel* is a unit used to measure *sound*.
Object/Action

37. BORON : ELEMENT :: BORAX : (*a.* atom, *b.* solution, *c.* **compound**, *d.* ion)
(**c**) *Boron* is an *element*, atomic number 5 on the periodic table of elements. *Borax* is a
compound made up primarily of sodium and boron. **Classification**

38. PENNY : (*a.* **nickel**, *b.* dime, *c.* quarter, *d.* five-dollar bill) :: LINCOLN MEMORIAL :
MONTICELLO
(**a**) The tail side of a *penny* shows the *Lincoln Memorial*. The tail side of a *nickel* shows
Jefferson's home, *Monticello*. **Characteristic**

39. WHITE FLAG : BLACK FLAG :: (*a.* law, *b.* fear, *c.* **truce**, *d.* health) : PIRACY
(**c**) A *white flag* is a universal symbol calling for a *truce*. A *black flag* was once the
symbol of a *pirate* ship. **Object/Action**

40. (*a.* Orthodox, *b.* **Gregorian**, *c.* Christian, *d.* Judaic) : ISLAMIC :: SEPTEMBER :
RAMADAN
(**b**) *September* is a month on our *Gregorian* calendar. *Ramadan* is a month on the
Islamic calendar. **Classification**

41. UKRAINIAN : SLAVIC :: WELSH : (*a.* English, *b.* Nordic, *c.* **Celtic**, *d.* Germanic)
(**c**) *Ukrainian* is a language within the *Slavic* family of languages. *Welsh* is a language
within the *Celtic* family of languages. **Classification**

42. FRANCE : (*a.* prefectures, *b.* districts, *c.* states, *d.* **departments**) :: CANADA :
PROVINCES
(**d**) The country of *France* is divided into large regions called *departments*. *Canada* is
divided into large regions called *provinces*. **Part/Whole**

43. CACOPHONY : EUPHONY :: (*a.* dissonance, *b.* cachet, **c. despair**, *d.* amphora) :
EUPHORIA

(**c**) *Cacophony*, which means "terrible din," is the opposite of *euphony*, which means
"pleasant sound." Similarly, *despair* is the opposite of *euphoria*. **Antonym**

44. OPERETTA : (*a.* opera, **b. oratorio**, *c.* symphonic poem, *d.* elegy) :: *THE MIKADO* :
THE MESSIAH

(**b**) *The Mikado*, with music by Arthur Sullivan and words by W. S. Gilbert, is a kind
of light, short opera with occasional spoken speech known as an *operetta*. *The Messiah*,
by George Frideric Handel, is a kind of dramatic, religious work performed without
staging known as an *oratorio*. **Classification**

45. RATIONALIST : (**a. empiricist**, *b.* relativist, *c.* deconstructionist, *d.* fatalist) ::
DESCARTES : HUME

(**a**) René *Descartes* was a *rationalist*, one who believes that knowledge derives from
reason. David *Hume* was an *empiricist*, one who believes that knowledge derives from
sensory experience. **Classification**

46. (*a.* tinnitus, *b.* eustachian tube, *c.* otology, **d. audition**) : HEARING :: VISION :
SIGHT

(**d**) *Audition* is *hearing*, and *vision* is *sight*. **Synonym**

47. WILLIAM JAMES : PRAGMATISM :: (*a.* Baruch Spinoza, *b.* Karl Marx, **c. Herbert
Marcuse**, *d.* Immanuel Kant) : LIBERTARIANISM

(**c**) *William James* (1842–1910) was a philosopher and psychologist who identified
with the *pragmatists*, people who believe that the truth of ideas or values is dependent
on their usefulness. *Herbert Marcuse* (1898–1979) was a Marxist philosopher who
followed the principles of *libertarianism*—that freedom from restraint takes precedence
over other rights. **Object/Action**

48. (*a.* Earth, **b. apple**, *c.* center, *d.* cherry) : CORE :: PEACH : PIT

(**b**) The inside part of an *apple* that contains its seeds is the *core*. The inside part of a
peach that contains its seeds is the *pit*. **Part/Whole**

49. (*a.* avant garde, *b.* crash, *c.* neutralize, **d. smog**) : PORTMANTEAU :: SPLASH :
ONOMATOPOEIA

(**d**) *Smog* is a *portmanteau* word, a word that is created from the merger of two other
words. In this case, the words are *smoke* and *fog*. *Splash* is an example of
onomatopoeia—a word that sounds like its meaning. **Classification**

50. MOTET : (*a.* prose, *b.* verse, **c. song**, *d.* epic) :: ODE : POEM

(**c**) A *motet* is one kind of *song*, usually a sacred song. An *ode* is one kind of *poem*,
usually a long, solemn, lyric poem. **Classification**

51. 35° : 145° :: 60° : (*a.* 45°, *b.* 80°, *c.* 105°, **d. 120°**)

(**d**) A line measures 180°. Two angles measuring *35°* and *145°* add up to 180°, as do
two angles measuring *60°* and *120°*. **Part/Whole**

52. FULTON : STEAMBOAT :: (*a.* **Otis**, *b.* Faraday, *c.* Yale, *d.* Westinghouse) : ELEVATOR
(a) Robert *Fulton* made the first practical *steamboat*, and Elisha *Otis* made the first practical *elevator*. **Object/Action**

53. (*a.* worship, *b.* **heresy**, *c.* penance, *d.* devotion) : SACRILEGE :: REVERENCE : VENERATION
(b) *Heresy* is similar to *sacrilege*; both are acts that go against religious orthodoxy. If you show *reverence* toward someone or something, that is the same as showing *veneration*. **Synonym**

54. CRUSTACEA : (*a.* crab, *b.* Animalia, *c.* **Arthropoda**, *d.* Insectae) :: CLASS : PHYLUM
(c) In the world of classification, a kingdom contains many phyla, and a phylum contains many classes. *Arthropoda* is the *phylum* that contains the *class Crustacea* (and the class Insectae). **Classification**

55. (*a.* limb, *b.* foot, *c.* ankle, *d.* **arch**) : TOE :: PALM : THUMB
(d) Both the *arch* and the *toe* are part of a foot. Both the *palm* and the *thumb* are part of a hand. **Part/Whole**

56. CARDINAL : ORDINAL :: 24 : (*a.* 1/24, *b.* 0.12, *c.* **17th**, *d.* 4275)
(c) *Cardinal* numbers are what we think of as counting numbers: 1, 2, 3, and so on. *Ordinal* numbers are numbers that show the order in a sequence: 1st, 2nd, 3rd, and so on. **Classification**

57. BASALT : TITANIUM :: (*a.* iron, *b.* alloy, *c.* **rock**, *d.* salt) : METAL
(c) *Basalt* is one kind of *rock*. *Titanium* is one kind of *metal*. **Classification**

58. BATON : CONDUCT :: POINTER : (*a.* convey, *b.* hunt, *c.* **indicate**, *d.* confront)
(c) You might use a *baton* to *conduct* an orchestra. You might use a similarly shaped object, a *pointer*, to *indicate* something on a chart or chalkboard. **Object/Action**

59. (*a.* adagio, *b.* **allegro**, *c.* ostinato, *d.* pizzicato) : PRESTO :: BRISK : SPEEDY
(b) *Allegro* is a direction in music that means "fast and lively." *Presto* is a direction in music that means "very quick." *Brisk* and *speedy* have similar degrees of difference. **Degree**

60. GRIMACE : GROAN :: (*a.* distrust, *b.* dismay, *c.* disbelief, *d.* **distaste**) : DISCOMFORT
(d) You would be likely to *grimace* as a sign of *distaste*, just as you might *groan* as a sign of *discomfort*. **Object/Action**

61. BLEED : BLED :: FEAR : (*a.* fearful, *b.* **far**, *c.* fled, *d.* afraid)
(b) Removing one *e* from *bleed* gives you *bled*. Removing one *e* from *fear* gives you *far*. **Conversion**

62. MARSEILLAISE : FRANCE :: (*a.* Land of Hope and Glory, *b.* White Cliffs of Dover, *c.* Rule Britannia, *d.* **God Save the Queen**) : BRITAIN
(d) *La Marseillaise* is the official national anthem of *France*, just as *God Save the Queen* is the official national anthem of Great *Britain*. **Characteristic**

63. (*a.* **Wesley,** *b.* Calvin, *c.* Young, *d.* Loyola) : METHODISTS :: SMITH : MORMONS
    (**a**) John *Wesley* (1703–1791) founded the *Methodist* Church. Joseph *Smith* (1805–1844) founded the Church of Jesus Christ of Latter Day Saints, commonly known as the *Mormons.* **Object/Action**

64. TESSERAE : (*a.* collage, *b.* tile, *c.* **mosaic,** *d.* transparency) :: PIXELS : DIGITAL PHOTO
    (**c**) *Tesserae* are the little tiles used to make a *mosaic. Pixels* are the smallest "picture element" of a *digital photo.* **Part/Whole**

65. HADES : ARTEMIS :: PLUTO : (*a.* **Diana,** *b.* Uranus, *c.* Venus, *d.* Aurora)
    (**a**) The Greek god of the Underworld, *Hades,* was called *Pluto* in Roman mythology. The Greek goddess of the hunt, *Artemis,* was called *Diana* in Roman mythology. **Conversion**

66. (*a.* herb, *b.* wisdom, *c.* **fool,** *d.* wizard) : SAGE :: FIEND : SERAPH
    (**c**) A *fool* is the opposite of a *sage.* A *fiend* (demon) is the opposite of a *seraph* (angel). **Antonym**

67. DANIEL WEBSTER : ORATORY :: NOAH WEBSTER : (*a.* anthropology, *b.* composition, *c.* erudition, *d.* **lexicography**)
    (**d**) *Daniel Webster* (1782–1852) was a statesman and lawyer known for his great speechifying, or *oratory. Noah Webster* (1758–1843) is best known as the writer of the first dictionary (*lexicon*) of the American language. **Object/Action**

68. AERIE : EAGLE :: (*a.* burrow, *b.* **formicary,** *c.* rookery, *d.* apiary) : ANT
    (**b**) An *eagle's* nest is properly called an *aerie.* An *ant's* nest is properly called a *formicary.* **Characteristic**

69. ARABLE : POTABLE :: LIFELESS : (*a.* dead, *b.* liquid, *c.* **toxic,** *d.* vital)
    (**c**) Land that is *arable* (cultivatable) is not *lifeless.* Drink that is *potable* (drinkable) is not *toxic.* **Antonym**

70. DESERT : SAND :: (*a.* tundra, *b.* taiga, *c.* **savanna,** *d.* swamp) : GRASS
    (**c**) A *desert* biome, or habitat, is primarily *sand.* A *savanna* biome is primarily *grass.* **Characteristic**

71. FORESTER : *THE AFRICAN QUEEN* :: FORSTER : (*a.* ***A Passage to India,*** *b.* Out of Africa, *c.* The Virgin Queen, *d.* An American Tragedy)
    (**a**) Cecil Scott *Forester* wrote the book *The African Queen,* which is better known as a movie directed by John Huston. E. M. *Forster* wrote *A Passage to India.* **Object/Action**

72. PARTHENON : (*a.* **Colosseum,** *b.* San Niccolo, *c.* Doge's Palace, *d.* St. Mark's) :: ATHENS : ROME
    (**a**) The *Parthenon* is an ancient structure found in *Athens,* Greece. The *Colosseum* is an ancient structure found in *Rome,* Italy. **Characteristic**

73. CUTANEOUS : SKIN :: PILEOUS : (*a.* blood, *b.* lymph, *c.* scale, *d.* **hair**)
    (**d**) *Cutaneous* means "having to do with *skin.*" *Pileous* means "having to do with *hair.*" **Characteristic**

74. GUNNAR MYRDAL : (*a.* physics, ***b.* economics**, *c.* medicine, *d.* history) :: LINUS PAULING : CHEMISTRY
    (b) *Gunnar Myrdal*, a Swede, won the Nobel Prize in Economics in 1974 for work regarding the interdependence of *economic* and social events. *Linus Pauling*, an American, won the Nobel Prize in Chemistry in 1954 for his research into *chemical* bonds. **Object/Action**

75. KUWAIT : (*a.* shekel, *b.* rial, ***c.* dinar**, *d.* shilling) :: LUXEMBOURG : EURO
    (c) The currency of *Kuwait* is the *dinar*; the currency of modern *Luxembourg* is the *euro*. **Characteristic**

76. HOLLYWOOD : FILM :: (***a.* Tokyo**, *b.* Paris, *c.* New York, *d.* Caracas) : ANIME
    (a) *Hollywood* is known for housing the *film* industry. *Tokyo* is the home of the cartoon style known as *anime*. **Object/Action**

77. LEAR : CORDELIA :: PROSPERO : (*a.* Regan, *b.* Olivia, ***c.* Miranda**, *d.* Gertrude)
    (c) All the characters listed are from plays by Shakespeare. *Cordelia* is one of the daughters of King *Lear*. *Miranda* is the daughter of *Prospero* in *The Tempest*. **Sequence**

78. (*a.* Britten, ***b.* Balanchine**, *c.* Bernstein, *d.* Baryshnikov) : STRAVINSKY :: CHOREOGRAPHY : COMPOSITION
    (b) George *Balanchine* was a *choreographer* and director of the New York City Ballet. Igor *Stravinsky* was a *composer* who often collaborated with Balanchine. **Object/Action**

79. FAUX PAS : GAFFE :: IDÉE FIXE : (*a.* correction, *b.* delight, *c.* brainstorm, ***d.* obsession**)
    (d) Certain French phrases have made their way into English usage. Examples include *faux pas,* which refers to a social *gaffe* or error, and *idée fixe,* which is an *obsession.* **Synonym**

80. SALVADOR DALI : SURREALISM :: (*a.* Amedeo Modigliani, ***b.* Claude Monet**, *c.* Dante Gabriel Rossetti, *d.* Gustav Klimt) : IMPRESSIONISM
    (b) The Spanish artist *Salvador Dali* worked in a style called *surrealism.* The French artist *Claude Monet* was part of the school known as *impressionism.* **Object/Action**

81. OENOLOGIST : ONCOLOGIST :: (*a.* eyes, *b.* birth, ***c.* wine**, *d.* viruses) : CANCER
    (c) An *oenologist* specializes in *winemaking.* An *oncologist* is a doctor whose specialty is *cancer* treatment. **Object/Action**

82. EXECUTIVE : (*a.* Library of Congress, *b.* Court of Appeals, *c.* Parliament, ***d.* Cabinet**) :: JUDICIAL : SUPREME COURT
    (d) The president's *Cabinet* is part of the *executive* branch of government. The *Supreme Court* is part of the *judicial* branch of government. **Part/Whole**

83. PORTFOLIO : ARTIST :: (*a.* folder, *b.* briefcase, ***c.* oeuvre**, *d.* composition) : COMPOSER
    (c) An *artist's* major works are part of his or her *portfolio.* A *composer's* major works are part of his or her *oeuvre.* **Object/Action**

84. PRETEST : (*a.* invention, *b.* completion, *c.* additions, **d. instruction**) :: PRETAX : DEDUCTIONS

    (**d**) A *pretest* is given prior to *instruction* in a subject. A *pretax* is levied prior to *deductions* being taken. **Sequence**

85. *CATCHER IN THE RYE* : *CATCH-22* :: SALINGER : (**a. Heller**, *b.* Saroyan, *c.* Vonnegut, *d.* Bellow)

    (**a**) J. D. *Salinger* wrote *Catcher in the Rye*. Joseph *Heller* wrote *Catch-22*. **Object/Action**

86. VIII : (*a.* VI, **b. X**, *c.* L, *d.* C) :: IV : V

    (**b**) Think of this as a ratio. *VIII* = 8, and *X* = 10. *IV* = 4 and *V* = 5. 8/10 = 4/5. **Sequence**

87. (*a.* botany, *b.* genetics, *c.* recombination, **d. grafting**) : HYBRIDS :: CLONING : DUPLICATES

    (**d**) In botany *grafting* is a kind of plant propagation that results in a *hybrid*, or crossbreed. *Cloning* is a kind of genetic manipulation that results in a *duplicate* organism. **Object/Action**

88. WRIGHT : FALLINGWATER :: SAARINEN : (*a.* Museum of Modern Art, **b. Gateway Arch**, *c.* Washington Monument, *d.* Golden Gate Bridge)

    (**b**) Both Frank Lloyd Wright and Eero Saarinen were twentieth-century architects. One of *Wright's* best-known works is the Pennsylvania house called "*Fallingwater.*" One of *Saarinen's* best-known works is St. Louis's *Gateway Arch*. **Object/Action**

89. (**a. gregarious**, *b.* ascetic, *c.* abstemious, *d.* superficial) : EXTROVERTED :: RECLUSIVE : INTROVERTED

    (**a**) If you are *gregarious*, or friendly, you might be called *extroverted*. If you are *reclusive*, or withdrawn, you might be called *introverted*. **Synonym**

90. CAMERA : (*a.* tripod, *b.* lens, **c. eye**, *d.* student) :: APERTURE : PUPIL

    (**c**) The *aperture* in a *camera* performs the same function—letting light in or closing light out—that a *pupil* does in an *eye*. **Object/Action**

91. KITTY HAWK : (**a. biplane**, *b.* airfoil, *c.* kite, *d.* aileron) :: CAPE CANAVERAL : ROCKET

    (**a**) The flying machine the Wright Brothers flew at *Kitty Hawk* was a *biplane*. The flying machines most often flown at *Cape Canaveral* are *rockets*. **Characteristic**

92. LITTLE DORRITT : DICKENS :: LITTLE EVA : (*a.* Alcott, **b. Stowe**, *c.* Eliot, *d.* Gilman)

    (**b**) *Little Dorritt* is a character in a novel by that same name by Charles *Dickens*. *Little Eva* is a character in *Uncle Tom's Cabin* by Harriet Beecher *Stowe*. **Object/Action**

93. (*a.* gnome, *b.* pixie, **c. Leviathan**, *d.* Swift) : ENORMITY :: LILLIPUTIAN : TININESS

    (**c**) The biblical *Leviathan* was a *enormous* and evil serpent. The *Lilliputs* in *Gulliver's Travels* were *tiny* elfin creatures. Both gave their names to adjectives that refer to size. **Characteristic**

94. MISDEMEANOR : (*a.* theft, *b.* burglary, *c.* **felony**, *d.* crime) :: PETIT LARCENY : GRAND LARCENY

    (**c**) A *misdemeanor* is a lesser crime than a *felony*. *Petit larceny* is a lesser crime than *grand larceny*. **Degree**

95. AMPLE : (***a.* substantial**, *b.* petty, *c.* scarce, *d.* incorrigible) :: TRIFLING : NEGLIGIBLE

    (**a**) Something that is *ample* is more than enough, or *substantial*. Something that is *trifling* is insignificant, or *negligible*. **Synonym**

96. (***a.* Natty Bumppo**, *b.* James Fenimore Cooper, *c.* Mohican, *d.* Leatherstocking) : THE DEERSLAYER :: CHRISTOPHER NEWMAN : THE AMERICAN

    (**a**) *Natty Bumppo* was the unlikely name of the character known as *The Deerslayer* in James Fenimore Cooper's book by that name. *Christopher Newman* was the character known as *The American* in Henry James's book by that name. **Conversion**

97. SATURN : RINGS :: MOON : (*a.* lines, ***b.* mares**, *c.* haze, *d.* arrows)

    (**b**) A key feature of *Saturn* is its *rings*. A key feature of our *moon* is its *mares*, or dry seas, which appear as craters from our vantage point on Earth. **Characteristic**

98. OCTA- : (*a.* deca-, *b.* ennea-, *c.* **dodeca-**, *d.* binal) :: EIGHT : TWELVE

    (**c**) *Octa-* is a Greek prefix that means "*eight*," as in *octagon*. *Dodeca-* is a Greek prefix that means "*twelve*"; a *dodecagon* has twelve sides. **Affix**

99. TIN MAN : HEART :: JASON : (*a.* brain, *b.* grail, *c.* **fleece**, *d.* Argo)

    (**c**) In *The Wizard of Oz*, the *Tin Man* goes on a quest to find a *heart*. In Greek mythology, *Jason* goes on a quest to find the golden *fleece*. **Object/Action**

100. QUIXOTE : IDEALISM :: (***a.* Javert**, *b.* Panza, *c.* Bovary, *d.* Raskolnikov) : DETERMINATION

    (**a**) Don *Quixote* is a character that is often used as the archetype of romantic *idealism*. Inspector *Javert* in Victor Hugo's *Les Misérables* is a character that represents dogged *determination*. **Characteristic**

PRACTICE TEST 5
ANSWER SHEET

1. (A) (B) (C) (D)
2. (A) (B) (C) (D)
3. (A) (B) (C) (D)
4. (A) (B) (C) (D)
5. (A) (B) (C) (D)
6. (A) (B) (C) (D)
7. (A) (B) (C) (D)
8. (A) (B) (C) (D)
9. (A) (B) (C) (D)
10. (A) (B) (C) (D)
11. (A) (B) (C) (D)
12. (A) (B) (C) (D)
13. (A) (B) (C) (D)
14. (A) (B) (C) (D)
15. (A) (B) (C) (D)
16. (A) (B) (C) (D)
17. (A) (B) (C) (D)
18. (A) (B) (C) (D)
19. (A) (B) (C) (D)
20. (A) (B) (C) (D)
21. (A) (B) (C) (D)
22. (A) (B) (C) (D)
23. (A) (B) (C) (D)
24. (A) (B) (C) (D)
25. (A) (B) (C) (D)

26. (A) (B) (C) (D)
27. (A) (B) (C) (D)
28. (A) (B) (C) (D)
29. (A) (B) (C) (D)
30. (A) (B) (C) (D)
31. (A) (B) (C) (D)
32. (A) (B) (C) (D)
33. (A) (B) (C) (D)
34. (A) (B) (C) (D)
35. (A) (B) (C) (D)
36. (A) (B) (C) (D)
37. (A) (B) (C) (D)
38. (A) (B) (C) (D)
39. (A) (B) (C) (D)
40. (A) (B) (C) (D)
41. (A) (B) (C) (D)
42. (A) (B) (C) (D)
43. (A) (B) (C) (D)
44. (A) (B) (C) (D)
45. (A) (B) (C) (D)
46. (A) (B) (C) (D)
47. (A) (B) (C) (D)
48. (A) (B) (C) (D)
49. (A) (B) (C) (D)
50. (A) (B) (C) (D)

51. (A) (B) (C) (D)
52. (A) (B) (C) (D)
53. (A) (B) (C) (D)
54. (A) (B) (C) (D)
55. (A) (B) (C) (D)
56. (A) (B) (C) (D)
57. (A) (B) (C) (D)
58. (A) (B) (C) (D)
59. (A) (B) (C) (D)
60. (A) (B) (C) (D)
61. (A) (B) (C) (D)
62. (A) (B) (C) (D)
63. (A) (B) (C) (D)
64. (A) (B) (C) (D)
65. (A) (B) (C) (D)
66. (A) (B) (C) (D)
67. (A) (B) (C) (D)
68. (A) (B) (C) (D)
69. (A) (B) (C) (D)
70. (A) (B) (C) (D)
71. (A) (B) (C) (D)
72. (A) (B) (C) (D)
73. (A) (B) (C) (D)
74. (A) (B) (C) (D)
75. (A) (B) (C) (D)

76. (A) (B) (C) (D)
77. (A) (B) (C) (D)
78. (A) (B) (C) (D)
79. (A) (B) (C) (D)
80. (A) (B) (C) (D)
81. (A) (B) (C) (D)
82. (A) (B) (C) (D)
83. (A) (B) (C) (D)
84. (A) (B) (C) (D)
85. (A) (B) (C) (D)
86. (A) (B) (C) (D)
87. (A) (B) (C) (D)
88. (A) (B) (C) (D)
89. (A) (B) (C) (D)
90. (A) (B) (C) (D)
91. (A) (B) (C) (D)
92. (A) (B) (C) (D)
93. (A) (B) (C) (D)
94. (A) (B) (C) (D)
95. (A) (B) (C) (D)
96. (A) (B) (C) (D)
97. (A) (B) (C) (D)
98. (A) (B) (C) (D)
99. (A) (B) (C) (D)
100. (A) (B) (C) (D)

PRACTICE TEST 5

Directions: For each question, you will see three capitalized words and four answer choices labeled *a, b, c,* and *d* in parentheses. Choose the answer that best completes the analogy posed by the three capitalized words. Use the answer sheet on page 121 to record your answers.

Time: 50 Minutes

1. CUBE : (*a.* prism, *b.* square, *c.* cone, *d.* rectangle) :: PYRAMID : TRIANGLE

2. MEUSE : FRANCE :: (*a.* Oise, *b.* Stuttgart, *c.* Volga, *d.* Danube) : GERMANY

3. PROD : STAB :: DISOBEY : (*a.* wound, *b.* punish, *c.* flout, *d.* conform)

4. IV : 4 :: (*a.* VI, *b.* XIIII, *c.* XIV, *d.* XVI) : 14

5. (*a.* temper, *b.* tempo, *c.* tempest, *d.* temp) : TEMPI :: CHORUS : CHORUSES

6. (*a.* elephant, *b.* antler, *c.* mammal, *d.* ungulate) : HOOF :: MARSUPIAL : POUCH

7. DICT : DUCT :: TO SPEAK : (*a.* to lead, *b.* to fall, *c.* to listen, *d.* to show)

8. PTOLEMY : COPERNICUS :: (*a.* moon, *b.* numbers, *c.* Earth, *d.* Egypt) : SUN

9. GOITER : (*a.* vitamin D, *b.* beriberi, *c.* iodine, *d.* iron) :: SCURVY : VITAMIN C

10. (*a.* debonair, *b.* noble, *c.* clever, *d.* naive) : SUAVE :: VALIANT : BRAVE

11. FARRIER : FURRIER :: (*a.* shoe, *b.* iron, *c.* beat, *d.* horse) : HIDE

12. FOX : OWL :: SLYNESS : (*a.* night vision, *b.* wisdom, *c.* predation, *d.* craftiness)

13. (*a.* goldenhair, *b.* saguaro, *c.* succulent, *d.* pteridophyte) : MAIDENHAIR :: CACTUS : FERN

14. AVARICE : ENVY :: EUCHARIST : (*a.* penance, *b.* lust, *c.* mystery, *d.* celebration)

15. NATURAL RESOURCES : HUMAN RESOURCES :: MINERALS : (*a.* ore, *b.* oil, *c.* labor, *d.* management)

16. MEPHISTOPHELES : (*a.* soul, *b.* bile, *c.* scar, *d.* manna) :: DRACULA : BLOOD

17. INTERCELLULAR : CELLS :: INTERCOSTAL : (*a.* coast, *b.* nuclei, *c.* ribs, *d.* heart)

18. (*a.* excessive, *b.* restrained, *c.* heinous, *d.* renowned) : GOOD :: SCANDALOUS : ADMIRABLE

19. MUTAGEN : MUTATION :: PREDATOR : (*a.* tiger, *b.* depopulation, *c.* carnivore, *d.* prey)

20. *PLESSY V. FERGUSON* : (*a.* 1862, *b.* 1896, *c.* 1917, *d.* 1963) :: *BROWN V. BOARD OF EDUCATION* : 1954

21. (*a.* Alaska, *b.* Maine, *c.* Florida, *d.* Delaware) : HAWAII :: A : Z

22. HEPTAGON : SEVEN :: TRAPEZOID : (*a.* three, *b.* four, *c.* five, *d.* six)

23. ZENO : (*a.* Stoicism, *b.* rationalism, *c.* fauvism, *d.* eclecticism) :: ANISTHENES : CYNICISM

24. GARCÍA LORCA : GARCÍA MÁRQUEZ :: SPAIN : (*a.* Mexico, *b.* Colombia, *c.* Cuba, *d.* Argentina)

25. FEYDEAU : FARCE :: (*a.* Jarry, *b.* Molière, *c.* Corneille, *d.* Ionesco) : TRAGEDY

26. (*a.* tinge, *b.* dehydrate, *c.* amuse, *d.* eliminate) : SATURATE :: SENTIMENTAL : MAUDLIN

27. DO : ONE :: (*a.* go, *b.* fa, *c.* sew, *d.* unto) : FOUR

28. CENTAUR : HORSE :: (*a.* Hydra, *b.* ogre, *c.* sphinx, *d.* cenotaph) : LION

29. VODKA : (*a.* grape, *b.* honey, *c.* sugar beet, *d.* potato) :: RUM : MOLASSES

30. (*a.* recession, *b.* monopoly, *c.* inflation, *d.* deflation) : COMPETITION :: DEPRESSION : BUSINESS ACTIVITY

31. $1 : $100 :: GEORGE WASHINGTON : (*a.* Thomas Jefferson, *b.* Alexander Hamilton, *c.* Andrew Johnson, *d.* Benjamin Franklin)

32. (*a.* Kelvin, *b.* Mach, *c.* lumen, *d.* rad) : TEMPERATURE :: CANDELA : LUMINOUS INTENSITY

33. CARTOON : (*a.* caricature, *b.* likeness, *c.* watercolor, *d.* fresco) :: SKETCH : PORTRAIT

34. HEARING AID : AUDIBILITY :: CANE : (*a.* sight, *b.* mobility, *c.* levitation, *d.* age)

35. PLATITUDE : (*a.* banality, *b.* irreverence, *c.* imagination, *d.* composure) :: AFFRONT : INSULT

36. (*a.* record player, *b.* video camera, *c.* kinetoscope, *d.* film) : MOVIE PROJECTOR :: GRAMOPHONE : CD PLAYER

37. RADIO : RADIUM :: (*a.* Pasteur, *b.* Murrow, *c.* Hertz, *d.* Marconi) : CURIE

38. (*a.* ionization, *b.* electrolyte, *c.* sodium hydroxide, *d.* nitric acid) : ALKALI :: HYDROCHLORIC ACID : ACID

39. GOLGOTHA : GOMORRAH :: (*a.* terror, *b.* suffering, *c.* lechery, *d.* joy) : WICKEDNESS

40. (*a.* pace, *b.* foot, *c.* centimeter, *d.* parsec) : DISTANCE :: TERAGRAM : MASS

41. ELIZABETH I : ELIZABETH II :: TUDOR : (*a.* Stuart, *b.* Wessex, *c.* Lancaster, *d.* Windsor)

42. (*a.* mistletoe, *b.* skunk, *c.* lemming, *d.* fern) : WOLF :: PARASITE : PREDATOR

43. ALBERTA : MANITOBA :: DURANGO : (*a.* Colorado, *b.* Oaxaca, *c.* Mexico, *d.* Quebec)

44. (*a.* carping, *b.* belligerent, *c.* frenetic, *d.* stoic) : COMPLAINING :: CALM : FRANTIC

45. SEVEN : (*a.* eight, *b.* Potemkin, *c.* twelve, *d.* stages) :: SEAS : STEPS

46. (*a.* Jude, *b.* Hebrews, *c.* Acts, *d.* Malachi) : OLD TESTAMENT :: REVELATION : NEW TESTAMENT

47. URSULA : GUDRUN :: REGAN : (*a.* Aileen, *b.* Reagan, *c.* Goneril, *d.* Ireland)

48. NEMATODE : ROUNDWORM :: (*a.* annelid, *b.* tube, *c.* rotifer, *d.* ceolomate) : SEGMENTED WORM

49. (*a.* partition, *b.* elevator, *c.* roof, *d.* girder) : SKYSCRAPER :: SKELETON : HUMAN

50. FREUD : LAING :: VEBLEN : (*a.* Barthes, *b.* Keynes, *c.* Skinner, *d.* Lorenz)

51. MINOTAUR : CHIMERA :: (*a.* Atlas, *b.* bull, *c.* mythic, *d.* Fin) : GIANT

52. WARSAW PACT : NATO :: (*a.* Greece, *b.* Bulgaria, *c.* Albania, *d.* Turkey) : CANADA

53. MORGAN : (*a.* General Motors, *b.* New York Public Library, *c.* U.S. Steel, *d.* General Electric) :: ROCKEFELLER : STANDARD OIL

54. LIEN : ENCUMBRANCE :: INDICTMENT : (*a.* accusation, *b.* confirmation, *c.* guilt, *d.* jurisprudence)

55. DON JUAN : DON QUIXOTE :: (*a.* drama, *b.* ballet, *c.* epic, *d.* novella) : NOVEL

56. TROUBADOUR : (*a.* lute, *b.* traveler, *c.* Middle Ages, *d.* minstrel) :: BALLERINA : DANCER

57. (*a.* braise, *b.* soda, *c.* sienna, *d.* apple) : BROWN :: AVOCADO : GREEN

58. PITH HELMET : (*a.* archeologist, *b.* Arctic explorer, *c.* deep sea diver, *d.* gaucho) :: HARDHAT : CONSTRUCTION WORKER

59. JOSTLE : MANHANDLE :: EMBRACE : (*a.* kiss, *b.* touch, *c.* cuddle, *d.* smother)

60. (*a.* gape, *b.* amazement, *c.* cry, *d.* ache) : AWE :: WINCE : PAIN

61. TABLESPOON : TEASPOON :: (*a.* 8, *b.* 4, *c.* 3, *d.* 2) : 1

62. (*a.* actor, *b.* scene, *c.* drama, *d.* interlude) : ACT :: NOVEL : CHAPTER

63. CORNWALLIS : YORKTOWN :: LEE : (*a.* Gettysburg, *b.* Appomattox, *c.* Antietam, *d.* Manassas)

64. PISTIL : PETAL :: (*a.* repel, *b.* manufacture, *c.* consume, *d.* reproduce) : ATTRACT

65. EWE : (*a.* tribe, *b.* congregate, *c.* flock, *d.* gaggle) :: COW : HERD

66. 100 : 212 :: 0 : (*a.* 32, *b.* 100, *c.* 120, *d.* 200)

67. (*a.* purple, *b.* blue, *c.* yellow, *d.* pink) : VIOLET :: GREEN : RED

68. PEARY : NORTH POLE :: (*a.* Henson, *b.* Amundsen, *c.* Hudson, *d.* Byrd) : SOUTH POLE

69. GUITAR : (*a.* 3, *b.* 6, *c.* 9, *d.* 10) :: VIOLIN : 4

70. (*a.* subsidized, *b.* assembled, *c.* veiled, *d.* beloved) : REVILED :: BENEFIT : DETRIMENT

71. TEAPOT DOME : (*a.* Roosevelt, *b.* Johnson, *c.* Harding, *d.* Cleveland) :: WATERGATE : NIXON

72. *THE SCHOOL FOR SCANDAL* : *THE SCHOOL FOR WIVES* :: (*a.* Sheridan, *b.* Beaumont, *c.* Wilde, *d.* Behan) : MOLIÈRE

73. VOWEL : CONSONANT :: (*a.* rhyme, *b.* synecdoche, *c.* alliteration, *d.* assonance) : CONSONANCE

74. SYBARITE : SELF-INDULGENCE :: EPICUREAN : (*a.* pleasure, *b.* self-loathing, *c.* generosity, *d.* self-expression)

75. (*a.* icon, *b.* apparition, *c.* pietà, *d.* basilica) : MOURNING :: ASSUMPTION : RISING

76. CRANIOTOMY : SKULL :: PHLEBOTOMY : (*a.* brain, *b.* limb, *c.* vein, *d.* sensory organ)

77. (*a.* major, *b.* colonel, *c.* admiral, *d.* ensign) : NAVY :: SECOND LIEUTENANT : ARMY

78. IRREFUTABLE : (*a.* disprove, *b.* throw away, *c.* refuse, *d.* err) :: IRREMEDIABLE : CORRECT

79. NILE : (*a.* Mississippi, *b.* Amazon, *c.* Yangtze, *d.* Niger) :: EVEREST : K2

80. THELONIOUS MONK : PIANO :: (*a.* John Coltrane, *b.* Stan Getz, *c.* Miles Davis, *d.* Dave Brubeck) : TRUMPET

81. (*a.* defamation, *b.* libel, *c.* regulation, *d.* intent) : SLANDER :: TORT : NEGLIGENCE

82. GRATEFUL : INDEBTED :: EAGER : (*a.* beholden, *b.* willing, *c.* adaptable, *d.* fervent)

83. RATIONAL : IRRATIONAL :: 2 : (*a.* 1/2, *b.* 0.2, *c.* −2, *d.* √2)

84. PLUM : (*a.* peach, *b.* pit, *c.* prune, *d.* apricot) :: GRAPE : RAISIN

85. (*a.* plasma, *b.* bile, *c.* cell, *d.* lymph) : DEFENSE :: BLOOD : TRANSPORT

86. COSSACK : HUSSAR :: RUSSIA : (*a.* Germany, *b.* Hungary, *c.* Ukraine, *d.* Poland)

87. ROLLS : AUTOMOBILES :: (*a.* Hepplewhite, *b.* Lenox, *c.* Spode, *d.* Staffordshire) : FURNITURE

88. FLEUR-DE-LIS : (*a.* lilac, *b.* daffodil, *c.* lion, *d.* dragon) :: FRANCE : ENGLAND

89. PORTENT : OMEN :: CONJECTURE : (*a.* forecast, *b.* magician, *c.* parameter, *d.* guess)

90. PRO BONO : (*a.* goodness, *b.* compensation, *c.* incidence, *d.* free will) :: IN ABSENTIA : ATTENDANCE

91. NIRVANA : MOKSHA :: BUDDHISM : (*a.* liberation, *b.* Taoism, *c.* Hinduism, *d.* Iroquois)

92. APLASTIC : FORM :: ACEPHELOUS : (*a.* function, *b.* head, *c.* center, *d.* meaning)

93. EAST : (*a.* northwest, *b.* north, *c.* southeast, *d.* west) :: NORTHEAST : SOUTHWEST

94. (*a.* St. John's, *b.* Labrador, *c.* Gander, *d.* St. Lawrence) : NEWFOUNDLAND :: HALIFAX : NOVA SCOTIA

95. JONAS SALK : POLIO VACCINE :: (*a.* Edward Jenner, *b.* Louis Pasteur, *c.* Linus Pauling, *d.* Albert Sabin) : SMALLPOX VACCINE

96. GREAT COMMONER : GREAT COMMUNICATOR :: (*a.* Daniel Boone, *b.* William Jennings Bryan, *c.* Stephen A. Douglas, *d.* Theodore Roosevelt) : RONALD REAGAN

97. (*a.* liter, *b.* furlong, *c.* fathom, *d.* angstrom) : DEPTH :: HECTARE : AREA

98. MIS- : (*a.* hardly, *b.* at, *c.* nothing, *d.* wrong) :: IM- : NOT

99. COMFORT : SOOTHE :: DIVERT : (*a.* distract, *b.* sully, *c.* disagree, *d.* unite)

100. BIZET : CARMEN :: (*a.* Rossini, *b.* Verdi, *c.* Scarpia, *d.* Puccini) : TOSCA

STOP

If there is any time remaining, go back and check your work.

PRACTICE TEST 5
ANSWER KEY

1. b	26. a	51. a	76. c
2. d	27. b	52. b	77. d
3. c	28. c	53. c	78. a
4. c	29. d	54. a	79. b
5. b	30. b	55. c	80. c
6. d	31. d	56. d	81. a
7. a	32. a	57. c	82. d
8. c	33. d	58. a	83. d
9. c	34. b	59. d	84. c
10. a	35. a	60. a	85. d
11. b	36. c	61. c	86. b
12. b	37. d	62. c	87. a
13. b	38. c	63. b	88. c
14. a	39. b	64. d	89. d
15. c	40. d	65. c	90. b
16. a	41. d	66. a	91. c
17. c	42. a	67. c	92. b
18. c	43. b	68. b	93. d
19. b	44. d	69. b	94. a
20. b	45. c	70. d	95. a
21. d	46. d	71. c	96. b
22. b	47. c	72. a	97. c
23. a	48. a	73. d	98. d
24. b	49. d	74. a	99. a
25. c	50. b	75. c	100. d

PRACTICE TEST 5
EXPLANATORY ANSWERS

1. CUBE : (*a.* prism, *b.* **square**, *c.* cone, *d.* rectangle) :: PYRAMID : TRIANGLE
   (**b**) A *cube's* faces are *squares,* and most or all of a *pyramid's* faces are *triangles.*
   Part/Whole

2. MEUSE : FRANCE :: (*a.* Oise, *b.* Stuttgart, *c.* Volga, *d.* **Danube**) : GERMANY
   (**d**) The headwaters of the *Meuse* River are in *France.* The headwaters of the *Danube*
   River are in *Germany.* **Characteristic**

3. PROD : STAB :: DISOBEY : (*a.* wound, *b.* punish, *c.* **flout**, *d.* conform)
   (**c**) To *prod* with vigor is to *stab.* To *disobey* with vigor is to *flout.* **Degree**

4. IV : 4 :: (*a.* VI, *b.* XIIII, *c.* **XIV**, *d.* XVI) : 14
   (**c**) The Roman numeral for *4* is *IV.* The Roman numeral for *14* is *XIV.* **Synonym**

5. (*a.* temper, *b.* **tempo**, *c.* tempest, *d.* temp) : TEMPI :: CHORUS : CHORUSES
   (**b**) *Tempi* is the plural form of *tempo.* *Choruses* is the plural form of *chorus.* **Conversion**

6. (*a.* elephant, *b.* antler, *c.* mammal, *d.* **ungulate**) : HOOF :: MARSUPIAL : POUCH
   (**d**) An *ungulate* is a *hoofed* mammal such as a horse, antelope, or bison. A *marsupial* is
   a mammal that typically uses a *pouch* rather than a placenta in which to carry its
   young. **Characteristic**

7. DICT : DUCT :: TO SPEAK : (*a.* **to lead**, *b.* to fall, *c.* to listen, *d.* to show)
   (**a**) The root *dict*, as in *dictation*, means "*to speak.*" The root *duct*, as in *conductor*,
   means "*to lead.*" **Affix**

8. PTOLEMY : COPERNICUS :: (*a.* moon, *b.* numbers, *c.* **Earth**, *d.* Egypt) : SUN
   (**c**) *Ptolemy* was an Alexandrian astronomer who theorized a system in which the
   planets and sun circled the *Earth. Copernicus* was a Polish astronomer who opposed
   this theory and placed the *sun* at the center of the solar system. **Object/Action**

9. GOITER : (*a.* vitamin D, *b.* beriberi, *c.* **iodine**, *d.* iron) :: SCURVY : VITAMIN C
   (**c**) Lack of *iodine* can cause the swelling of the thyroid known as a *goiter.* Lack of
   vitamin C can lead to the deficiency disease called *scurvy.* **Characteristic**

10. (*a.* **debonair**, *b.* noble, *c.* clever, *d.* naive) : SUAVE :: VALIANT : BRAVE
    (**a**) If you are *debonair,* or refined, you might also be called *suave.* If you are *valiant,* or
    intrepid, you might also be called *brave.* **Synonym**

11. FARRIER : FURRIER :: (*a.* shoe, *b.* **iron**, *c.* beat, *d.* horse) : HIDE
    (**b**) A *farrier* is a blacksmith who works with *iron* and shoes horses. A *furrier* makes
    or repairs fur (or *hide*) garments. **Object/Action**

12. FOX : OWL :: SLYNESS : (*a.* night vision, *b.* **wisdom**, *c.* predation, *d.* craftiness)
    (**b**) In literature, a *fox* is used as a symbol of *slyness,* and an *owl* is used as a symbol of
    wisdom. **Object/Action**

13. (*a.* goldenhair, **b. saguaro**, *c.* succulent, *d.* pteridophyte) : MAIDENHAIR ::
CACTUS : FERN
(**b**) The *saguaro* is one kind of *cactus.* The *maidenhair* is one kind of *fern.*
Classification

14. AVARICE : ENVY :: EUCHARIST : (**a. penance**, *b.* lust, *c.* mystery, *d.* celebration)
(**a**) *Avarice* and *envy* are two of the seven deadly sins. *Eucharist* and *penance* are two of
the seven sacraments. **Part/Whole**

15. NATURAL RESOURCES : HUMAN RESOURCES :: MINERALS : (*a.* ore, *b.* oil,
c. labor, *d.* management)
(**c**) In economics, *minerals* may be classified as *natural resources,* along with timber, oil,
natural gas, and so on. *Labor* (workers) may be classified as *human resources.*
Classification

16. MEPHISTOPHELES : (**a. soul**, *b.* bile, *c.* scar, *d.* manna) :: DRACULA : BLOOD
(**a**) In the legend of Faust, *Mephistopheles,* or Satan, steals humans' *souls.* In Bram
Stoker's novel, *Dracula* steals their *blood.* **Object/Action**

17. INTERCELLULAR : CELLS :: INTERCOSTAL : (*a.* coast, *b.* nuclei, **c. ribs**,
d. heart)
(**c**) *Intercellular* means "between the *cells.*" *Intercostal* means "between the *ribs.*"
Characteristic

18. (*a.* excessive, *b.* restrained, **c. heinous**, *d.* renowned) : GOOD :: SCANDALOUS :
ADMIRABLE
(**c**) Something that is *heinous* is anything but *good.* Something that is *scandalous* is
anything but *admirable.* **Antonym**

19. MUTAGEN : MUTATION :: PREDATOR : (*a.* tiger, **b. depopulation**, *c.* carnivore,
d. prey)
(**b**) A *mutagen* is something that causes *mutation.* A *predator* is something that causes
depopulation. **Object/Action**

20. *PLESSY V. FERGUSON* : (*a.* 1862, **b. 1896**, *c.* 1917, *d.* 1963) :: *BROWN V.
BOARD OF EDUCATION* : 1954
(**b**) The Supreme Court case known as *Plessy v. Ferguson* established the doctrine of
"separate but equal" in the year *1896.* The case known as *Brown v. Board of Education
of Topeka* overturned that doctrine in *1954.* **Characteristic**

21. (*a.* Alaska, *b.* Maine, *c.* Florida, **d. Delaware**) : HAWAII :: A : Z
(**d**) *Delaware* was the first state admitted to the Union, and *Hawaii* was the last.
A is the first letter of the alphabet, and *Z* is the last. **Sequence**

22. HEPTAGON : SEVEN :: TRAPEZOID : (*a.* three, **b. four**, *c.* five, *d.* six)
(**b**) A *heptagon* is a polygon with *seven* sides. A *trapezoid* is a polygon with *four* sides,
one pair of which is parallel. **Characteristic**

23. ZENO : (**a. Stoicism**, *b.* rationalism, *c.* fauvism, *d.* eclecticism) :: ANISTHENES :
CYNICISM

(a) The Greek philosopher *Zeno* founded the *Stoic* school, which suggested that followers accept all events indifferently as a sign of divine will. The Greek philosopher *Anisthenes* founded the *Cynic* school, which rejected most of the comforts of society and preached a return to a "natural" life. **Object/Action**

24. GARCÍA LORCA : GARCÍA MÁRQUEZ :: SPAIN : (*a.* Mexico, ***b.* Colombia**, *c.* Cuba, *d.* Argentina)
    (b) Federico *García Lorca* was a *Spanish* playwright and poet who was a martyr of the Spanish Civil War. Gabriel *García Márquez* is a *Colombian* Nobel Laureate who is best known for novels in the magic realist tradition. **Characteristic**

25. FEYDEAU : FARCE :: (*a.* Jarry, *b.* Molière, ***c.* Corneille**, *d.* Ionesco) : TRAGEDY
    (c) Georges *Feydeau* was a comic playwright of *La Belle Epoque* (the turn of the nineteenth century), best known for *farces* such as *A Flea in Her Ear*. Pierre *Corneille* was a seventeenth-century dramatist known for *tragedies* such as *Le Cid*. **Object/Action**

26. (***a.* tinge**, *b.* dehydrate, *c.* amuse, *d.* eliminate) : SATURATE :: SENTIMENTAL : MAUDLIN
    (a) If you *tinge* something, you add a bit of color or liquid to it. If you *saturate* something, you drench it. Something that is *sentimental* is a bit emotional. Something that is *maudlin* is over the top. **Degree**

27. DO : ONE :: (*a.* go, ***b.* fa**, *c.* sew, *d.* unto) : FOUR
    (b) In a major scale, the first tonic note is called *do*, and the fourth is called *fa*. **Characteristic**

28. CENTAUR : HORSE :: (*a.* Hydra, *b.* ogre, ***c.* sphinx**, *d.* cenotaph) : LION
    (c) A *centaur* is part human and part *horse*. A *sphinx* is part human and part *lion*. **Part/Whole**

29. VODKA : (*a.* grape, *b.* honey, *c.* sugar beet, ***d.* potato**) :: RUM : MOLASSES
    (d) *Vodka* is liquor traditionally made from *potatoes*. *Rum* is liquor traditionally made from *molasses*. **Characteristic**

30. (*a.* recession, ***b.* monopoly**, *c.* inflation, *d.* deflation) : COMPETITION :: DEPRESSION : BUSINESS ACTIVITY
    (b) A *monopoly* occurs when there is little *competition*. A *depression* occurs when there is little *business activity*. **Object/Action**

31. $1 : $100 :: GEORGE WASHINGTON : (*a.* Thomas Jefferson, *b.* Alexander Hamilton, *c.* Andrew Johnson, ***d.* Benjamin Franklin**)
    (d) *George Washington's* face is on the *$1* bill. *Benjamin Franklin's* face is on the *$100* bill. **Characteristic**

32. (***a.* Kelvin**, *b.* Mach, *c.* lumen, *d.* rad) : TEMPERATURE :: CANDELA : LUMINOUS INTENSITY
    (a) A *degree Kelvin* is used to measure *temperature*. A *candela* is used to measure *luminous intensity*. **Object/Action**

33. CARTOON : (*a.* caricature, *b.* likeness, *c.* watercolor, ***d.* fresco**) :: SKETCH : PORTRAIT
    (**d**) Before creating a *fresco*, artists once made full-scale preliminary drawings called *cartoons*. Before painting a *portrait*, artists usually make *sketches*. **Sequence**

34. HEARING AID : AUDIBILITY :: CANE : (*a.* sight, ***b.* mobility**, *c.* levitation, *d.* age)
    (**b**) A *hearing aid* assists with *audibility*. A *cane* assists with *mobility* (not sight—it does not help you see in the way that a hearing aid helps you hear). **Object/Action**

35. PLATITUDE : (***a.* banality**, *b.* irreverence, *c.* imagination, *d.* composure) :: AFFRONT : INSULT
    (**a**) A *platitude*, or cliché, is the same as a *banality*. An *affront*, or slight, is the same as an *insult*. **Synonym**

36. (*a.* record player, *b.* video camera, ***c.* kinetoscope**, *d.* film) : MOVIE PROJECTOR :: GRAMOPHONE : CD PLAYER
    (**c**) The *kinetoscope* was an early version of machines that project moving pictures (*movie projector*). A *gramophone* was an early version of machines that play recorded music (*CD player*). **Conversion**

37. RADIO : RADIUM :: (*a.* Pasteur, *b.* Murrow, *c.* Hertz, ***d.* Marconi**) : CURIE
    (**d**) Guglielmo *Marconi* worked on transmitting wireless signals, which resulted in the first *radio*. Marie *Curie* discovered the element *radium*. **Object/Action**

38. (*a.* ionization, *b.* electrolyte, ***c.* sodium hydroxide**, *d.* nitric acid) : ALKALI :: HYDROCHLORIC ACID : ACID
    (**c**) *Sodium hydroxide* is one kind of *alkali* substance, or base; *hydrochloric acid* is one kind of *acidic* substance. **Classification**

39. GOLGOTHA : GOMORRAH :: (*a.* terror, ***b.* suffering**, *c.* lechery, *d.* joy) : WICKEDNESS
    (**b**) *Golgotha* names the hill near Jerusalem where Jesus died. The word has come to mean "*suffering*." *Gomorrah* was a town that God destroyed because its residents were sinful and depraved. It has come to mean "*wickedness*." **Characteristic**

40. (*a.* pace, *b.* foot, *c.* centimeter, ***d.* parsec**) : DISTANCE :: TERAGRAM : MASS
    (**d**) All four answer choices may measure distance, but only a *parsec* measures enormous *distances* as a *teragram* measures enormous *mass*. **Object/Action**

41. ELIZABETH I : ELIZABETH II :: TUDOR : (*a.* Stuart, *b.* Wessex, *c.* Lancaster, ***d.* Windsor**)
    (**d**) *Elizabeth I* (1533–1603) was a scion of the House of *Tudor*. *Elizabeth II* (b. 1926) is a scion of the House of *Windsor*. **Classification**

42. (***a.* mistletoe**, *b.* skunk, *c.* lemming, *d.* fern) : WOLF :: PARASITE : PREDATOR
    (**a**) *Mistletoe*, a shrub that lives off the trees it chokes, is an example of a *parasite*. A *wolf* is an example of a *predator*. **Classification**

43. ALBERTA : MANITOBA :: DURANGO : (*a.* Colorado, ***b.* Oaxaca**, *c.* Mexico, *d.* Quebec)

(b) Both *Alberta* and *Manitoba* are Canadian provinces. Both *Durango* and *Oaxaca* are Mexican states. **Part/Whole**

44. (*a.* carping, *b.* belligerent, *c.* frenetic, *d.* **stoic**) : COMPLAINING :: CALM : FRANTIC
    (d) If you are *stoic*, you are patient and un*complaining*. If you are *calm*, you are not *frantic*. **Antonym**

45. SEVEN : (*a.* eight, *b.* Potemkin, *c.* **twelve**, *d.* stages) :: SEAS : STEPS
    (c) Ancient mapmakers and storytellers spoke of the *seven seas* (the Red Sea, the Mediterranean, the Black Sea, the Caspian Sea, the Adriatic, the Persian Gulf, and the Indian Ocean). Addiction therapy features *twelve steps*, which include admission of powerlessness and making amends. **Characteristic**

46. (*a.* Jude, *b.* Hebrews, *c.* Acts, *d.* **Malachi**) : OLD TESTAMENT :: REVELATION : NEW TESTAMENT
    (d) Of the books listed, only *Malachi* is found in the *Old Testament*.
    The others, including the book of *Revelation*, appear in the *New Testament*. **Classification**

47. URSULA : GUDRUN :: REGAN : (*a.* Aileen, *b.* Reagan, *c.* **Goneril**, *d.* Ireland)
    (c) *Ursula* and *Gudrun* are sisters in D. H. Lawrence's *Women in Love*. *Regan* and *Goneril* are sisters in Shakespeare's *King Lear*. **Sequence**

48. NEMATODE : ROUNDWORM :: (*a.* **annelid**, *b.* tube, *c.* rotifer, *d.* ceolomate) : SEGMENTED WORM
    (a) *Nematode* is another word for *roundworm*. *Annelid* is another word for *segmented worm*. **Synonym**

49. (*a.* partition, *b.* elevator, *c.* roof, *d.* **girder**) : SKYSCRAPER :: SKELETON : HUMAN
    (d) A *girder* forms part of the substructure of a *skyscraper*, just as a *skeleton* forms part of the substructure of a *human* being. **Object/Action**

50. FREUD : LAING :: VEBLEN : (*a.* Barthes, *b.* **Keynes**, *c.* Skinner, *d.* Lorenz)
    (b) Sigmund *Freud* and R. D. *Laing* were both psychoanalysts. Thorstein *Veblen* and John Maynard *Keynes* were both economists. **Part/Whole**

51. MINOTAUR : CHIMERA :: (*a.* **Atlas**, *b.* bull, *c.* mythic, *d.* Fin) : GIANT
    (a) In Greek mythology, the *Minotaur* was a kind of *chimera*, or animal formed from a mixture of two animals. *Atlas* was a *giant* who held up the heavens. **Classification**

52. WARSAW PACT : NATO :: (*a.* Greece, *b.* **Bulgaria**, *c.* Albania, *d.* Turkey) : CANADA
    (b) During the Cold War, *Bulgaria* was one of the *Warsaw Pact* nations, and *Canada* remains affiliated with *NATO*, the North Atlantic Treaty Organization. **Classification**

53. MORGAN : (*a.* General Motors, *b.* New York Public Library, *c.* **U.S. Steel**, *d.* General Electric) :: ROCKEFELLER : STANDARD OIL
    (c) J. P. *Morgan* bought a steel company from Andrew Carnegie and built it into *U.S. Steel*. John D. *Rockefeller* dominated the oil industry for decades with his company, *Standard Oil*. **Object/Action**

54. LIEN : ENCUMBRANCE :: INDICTMENT : (*a.* **accusation**, *b.* confirmation, *c.* guilt, *d.* jurisprudence)
(**a**) A *lien* is an *encumbrance* upon your property. An *indictment* is an *accusation* charging you with an offense. **Synonym**

55. DON JUAN : DON QUIXOTE :: (*a.* drama, *b.* ballet, ***c.* epic**, *d.* novella) : NOVEL
(**c**) *Don Juan* is the title character in an *epic* poem by George Gordon, Lord Byron. *Don Quixote* is the title character in a *novel* by Miguel de Cervantes. **Classification**

56. TROUBADOUR : (*a.* lute, *b.* traveler, *c.* Middle Ages, ***d.* minstrel**) :: BALLERINA : DANCER
(**d**) A *troubadour,* or traveling poet and singer, was a kind of medieval *minstrel.* A *ballerina* is one kind of *dancer.* **Classification**

57. (*a.* braise, *b.* soda, ***c.* sienna**, *d.* apple) : BROWN :: AVOCADO : GREEN
(**c**) *Sienna* is a particular shade of *brown. Avocado* is a particular shade of *green.* **Classification**

58. PITH HELMET : (***a.* archeologist**, *b.* Arctic explorer, *c.* deep sea diver, *d.* gaucho) :: HARDHAT : CONSTRUCTION WORKER
(**a**) An *archaeologist* might wear a *pith helmet* for protection from the sun. A *construction worker* might wear a *hardhat* for protection from falling objects. **Object/Action**

59. JOSTLE : MANHANDLE :: EMBRACE : (*a.* kiss, *b.* touch, *c.* cuddle, ***d.* smother**)
(**d**) To be over-*jostled* is to be *manhandled*. To be over-*embraced* is to be *smothered*. **Degree**

60. (***a.* gape**, *b.* amazement, *c.* cry, *d.* ache) : AWE :: WINCE : PAIN
(**a**) You might *gape*—stare openmouthed—in *awe*. You might *wince*—flinch—in *pain*. **Object/Action**

61. TABLESPOON : TEASPOON :: (*a.* 8, *b.* 4, ***c.* 3**, *d.* 2) : 1
(**c**) Think of this as a ratio. A teaspoon is 1/3 of a tablespoon. The ratio of a *teaspoon* to a *tablespoon* is *1 : 3.* **Conversion**

62. (*a.* actor, *b.* scene, ***c.* drama**, *d.* interlude) : ACT :: NOVEL : CHAPTER
(**c**) A *drama* is divided into parts called *acts.* A *novel* is divided into parts called *chapters.* **Part/Whole**

63. CORNWALLIS : YORKTOWN :: LEE : (*a.* Gettysburg, ***b.* Appomattox**, *c.* Antietam, *d.* Manassas)
(**b**) The American Revolution essentially ended with General *Cornwallis's* surrender at *Yorktown.* The Civil War essentially ended with General *Lee's* surrender at *Appomattox.* **Characteristic**

64. PISTIL : PETAL :: (*a.* repel, *b.* manufacture, *c.* consume, ***d.* reproduce**) : ATTRACT
(**d**) The *pistil* is the part of a flower whose job is *reproduction.* The *petal* is the part of a flower whose job is *attraction* (of birds, butterflies, and so on). **Object/Action**

65. EWE : (*a.* tribe, *b.* congregate, *c.* **flock**, *d.* gaggle) :: COW : HERD
(**c**) A *ewe*, or female sheep, is part of a *flock* of sheep. A *cow*, or female bovine, is part of a *herd* of cattle. **Part/Whole**

66. 100 : 212 :: 0 : (*a.* **32**, *b.* 100, *c.* 120, *d.* 200)
(**a**) On the Celsius scale, *100* is the boiling point of water, and *0* is the freezing point of water. On the Fahrenheit scale, *212* is the boiling point of water, and *32* is the freezing point of water. **Conversion**

67. (*a.* purple, *b.* blue, *c.* **yellow**, *d.* pink) : VIOLET :: GREEN : RED
(**c**) On a color wheel, *yellow* and *violet* are opposites, and *green* and *red* are opposites. **Antonym**

68. PEARY : NORTH POLE :: (*a.* Henson, *b.* **Amundsen**, *c.* Hudson, *d.* Byrd) : SOUTH POLE
(**b**) In 1909, Robert *Peary* led the first team of explorers to reach the *North Pole*. In 1911, Roald *Amundsen* led the first team of explorers to reach the *South Pole*. **Object/Action**

69. GUITAR : (*a.* 3, *b.* **6**, *c.* 9, *d.* 10) :: VIOLIN : 4
(**b**) A standard *guitar* has *6* strings, and a *violin* has *4.* **Characteristic**

70. (*a.* subsidized, *b.* assembled, *c.* veiled, *d.* **beloved**) : REVILED :: BENEFIT : DETRIMENT
(**d**) To be *beloved* is the opposite of being *reviled*, or hated. Something that is a *benefit* is the opposite of something that is a *detriment*, or loss. **Antonym**

71. TEAPOT DOME : (*a.* Roosevelt, *b.* Johnson, *c.* **Harding**, *d.* Cleveland) :: WATERGATE : NIXON
(**c**) President Warren *Harding's* brief administration was plagued by the *Teapot Dome* scandal, just as Richard *Nixon's* second term was cut short by the *Watergate* scandal. **Characteristic**

72. *THE SCHOOL FOR SCANDAL* : *THE SCHOOL FOR WIVES* :: (*a.* **Sheridan**, *b.* Beaumont, *c.* Wilde, *d.* Behan) : MOLIÈRE
(**a**) Politician-playwright Richard *Sheridan* (1751–1816) wrote *The School for Scandal* in 1777. Jean-Baptiste Poquelin, pen name *Molière* (1622–1673), wrote *The School for Wives* in 1662. **Object/Action**

73. VOWEL : CONSONANT :: (*a.* rhyme, *b.* synecdoche, *c.* alliteration, *d.* **assonance**) : CONSONANCE
(**d**) *Assonance* is a literary term that means "repetition of *vowel* sounds," as in this line: "The breeze revealed the kneeling trees." *Consonance* is a literary term that means "repetition of *consonant* sounds," as in this line: "At night the boats sit taut and tense." **Characteristic**

74. SYBARITE : SELF-INDULGENCE :: EPICUREAN : (*a.* **pleasure**, *b.* self-loathing, *c.* generosity, *d.* self-expression)
(**a**) A *sybarite's* motivation is *self-indulgence* and luxury. An *epicurean's* motivation is pure *pleasure*, especially that found in food and drink. **Characteristic**

75. (*a.* icon, *b.* apparition, ***c.* pietà**, *d.* basilica) : MOURNING :: ASSUMPTION : RISING

    (c) The form of religious art known as a *pietà* shows Mary *mourning* over her dead son. The form of religious art called an *assumption* shows Mary *rising* up to heaven. **Object/Action**

76. CRANIOTOMY : SKULL :: PHLEBOTOMY : (*a.* brain, *b.* limb, ***c.* vein**, *d.* sensory organ)

    (c) *Craniotomy* requires opening of the *skull*. *Phlebotomy* requires opening of a *vein*. **Object/Action**

77. (*a.* major, *b.* colonel, *c.* admiral, ***d.* ensign**) : NAVY :: SECOND LIEUTENANT : ARMY

    (d) The rank of *ensign* in the *navy* corresponds to the rank of *second lieutenant* in the *army*. **Part/Whole**

78. IRREFUTABLE : (***a.* disprove**, *b.* throw away, *c.* refuse, *d.* err) :: IRREMEDIABLE : CORRECT

    (a) If your argument is *irrefutable*, it cannot be *disproved*. If your actions are *irremediable*, they cannot be *corrected*. **Object/Action**

79. NILE : (*a.* Mississippi, ***b.* Amazon**, *c.* Yangtze, *d.* Niger) :: EVEREST : K2

    (b) The *Nile* is the longest river in the world, and the *Amazon* is second-longest. *Mount Everest* is the tallest mountain in the world, and *K2* is the second-tallest. **Sequence**

80. THELONIOUS MONK : PIANO :: (*a.* John Coltrane, *b.* Stan Getz, ***c.* Miles Davis**, *d.* Dave Brubeck): TRUMPET

    (c) *Thelonious Monk* was a jazz *pianist*, and *Miles Davis* was a jazz *trumpet* player. **Object/Action**

81. (***a.* defamation**, *b.* libel, *c.* regulation, *d.* intent) : SLANDER :: TORT : NEGLIGENCE

    (a) *Slander* is a form of *defamation* (libel is another). *Negligence* is a form of *tort*, or civil wrong. **Classification**

82. GRATEFUL : INDEBTED :: EAGER : (*a.* beholden, *b.* willing, *c.* adaptable, ***d.* fervent**)

    (d) If you are very *grateful*, you might feel *indebted*. If you are very *eager*, you might seem *fervent*. **Degree**

83. RATIONAL : IRRATIONAL :: 2 : (*a.* 1/2, *b.* 0.2, *c.* −2, ***d.* √2**)

    (d) A *rational* number can be expressed as a/b, where a and b are integers and b is not zero. For example, 2 may be expressed as 2/1, as 4/2, as 200/100, and so on. An *irrational* number such as $\sqrt{2}$ cannot be expressed as a/b. **Classification**

84. PLUM : (*a.* peach, *b.* pit, ***c.* prune**, *d.* apricot) :: GRAPE : RAISIN

    (c) A dried *plum* is a *prune*. A dried *grape* is a *raisin*. **Conversion**

85. (*a.* plasma, *b.* bile, *c.* cell, ***d.* lymph**) : DEFENSE :: BLOOD : TRANSPORT
    (**d**) *Lymph* is a clear fluid that contains antibodies and white blood cells. It is part of
    the body's *defense* against disease. *Blood* is a fluid made of platelets, red and white
    blood cells, and plasma. Among its key jobs is the *transport* of nourishment and
    oxygen. **Object/Action**

86. COSSACK : HUSSAR :: RUSSIA : (*a.* Germany, ***b.* Hungary**, *c.* Ukraine, *d.* Poland)
    (**b**) The *Cossacks* were a cavalry corps in czarist *Russia.* The *Hussars* were
    a cavalry corps in *Hungary.* **Characteristic**

87. ROLLS : AUTOMOBILES :: (***a.* Hepplewhite**, *b.* Lenox, *c.* Spode, *d.* Staffordshire) :
    FURNITURE
    (**a**) Charles *Rolls*, with his partner F. H. Royce, was an English manufacturer of
    automobiles. George *Hepplewhite* was a cabinetmaker and manufacturer of fine
    furniture. **Object/Action**

88. FLEUR-DE-LIS : (*a.* lilac, *b.* daffodil, ***c.* lion**, *d.* dragon) :: FRANCE : ENGLAND
    (**c**) The *fleur-de-lis* (a kind of iris) is the symbol of *France.* The *lion* is the symbol of
    England. **Object/Action**

89. PORTENT : OMEN :: CONJECTURE : (*a.* forecast, *b.* magician, *c.* parameter,
    ***d.* guess**)
    (**d**) A *portent,* or sign, is the same as an *omen.* A *conjecture,* or speculation, is the same
    as a *guess.* **Synonym**

90. PRO BONO : (*a.* goodness, ***b.* compensation**, *c.* incidence, *d.* free will) :: IN
    ABSENTIA : ATTENDANCE
    (**b**) If you work *pro bono,* you do it without *compensation.* If you work
    in absentia, you do it without *attendance.* **Object/Action**

91. NIRVANA : MOKSHA :: BUDDHISM : (*a.* liberation, *b.* Taoism, ***c.* Hinduism**,
    d. Iroquois)
    (**c**) *Nirvana,* a state without suffering, is the goal of *Buddhism.* Achievement of nirvana
    means liberation from the wheel of life, and it is therefore equated with the Christian
    view of heaven. The same is true of *moksha* in *Hinduism.* **Characteristic**

92. APLASTIC : FORM :: ACEPHELOUS : (*a.* function, ***b.* head**, *c.* center, *d.* meaning)
    (**b**) Something that is *aplastic* lacks *form.* Something that is *acephelous* lacks a *head.*
    Object/Action

93. EAST : (*a.* northwest, *b.* north, *c.* southeast, ***d.* west**) :: NORTHEAST : SOUTHWEST
    (**d**) On a compass, *east* lies opposite *west,* and *northeast* lies opposite *southwest.*
    Antonym

94. (***a.* St. John's**, *b.* Labrador, *c.* Gander, *d.* St. Lawrence) : NEWFOUNDLAND ::
    HALIFAX : NOVA SCOTIA
    (**a**) *St. John's* is the capital of *Newfoundland,* and *Halifax* is the capital of *Nova Scotia.*
    Characteristic

95. JONAS SALK : POLIO VACCINE :: (*a.* **Edward Jenner**, *b.* Louis Pasteur, *c.* Linus Pauling, *d.* Albert Sabin) : SMALLPOX VACCINE
(**a**) *Jonas Salk* developed a *polio vaccine* in 1952 at the height of the polio epidemic. *Edward Jenner* developed a *smallpox vaccine* in 1796. **Object/Action**

96. GREAT COMMONER : GREAT COMMUNICATOR :: (*a.* Daniel Boone, *b.* **William Jennings Bryan**, *c.* Stephen A. Douglas, *d.* Theodore Roosevelt) : RONALD REAGAN
(**b**) William Pitt was the first *Great Commoner*, but orator *William Jennings Bryan* was given that nickname because of his conservative, "everyman" values. President *Ronald Reagan's* acting skills and upbeat message earned him the nickname the *Great Communicator.* **Conversion**

97. (*a.* liter, *b.* furlong, *c.* **fathom**, *d.* angstrom) : DEPTH :: HECTARE : AREA
(**c**) The *fathom* is a unit used to measure *depth* of water. One fathom equals six feet. The *hectare* is a unit used to measure *area* of land. One hectare equals 10,000 square meters. **Object/Action**

98. MIS- : (*a.* hardly, *b.* at, *c.* nothing, *d.* **wrong**) :: IM- : NOT
(**d**) The prefix *mis-* means "*wrong,*" as in *misspoke.* The prefix *im-* means "*not,*" as in *impossible.* **Affix**

99. COMFORT : SOOTHE :: DIVERT : (*a.* **distract**, *b.* sully, *c.* disagree, *d.* unite)
(**a**) To *comfort* someone is to *soothe* him or her. To *divert* someone is to *distract* him or her. **Synonym**

100. BIZET : CARMEN :: (*a.* Rossini, *b.* Verdi, *c.* Scarpia, *d.* **Puccini**) : TOSCA
(**d**) Georges *Bizet* (1838–1875) created the character of *Carmen* in the opera of the same name. Giacomo *Puccini* (1858–1924) created the character of *Tosca* in the opera of the same name. **Object/Action**

PRACTICE TEST 6
ANSWER SHEET

1. (A)(B)(C)(D)　　26. (A)(B)(C)(D)　　51. (A)(B)(C)(D)　　76. (A)(B)(C)(D)

2. (A)(B)(C)(D)　　27. (A)(B)(C)(D)　　52. (A)(B)(C)(D)　　77. (A)(B)(C)(D)

3. (A)(B)(C)(D)　　28. (A)(B)(C)(D)　　53. (A)(B)(C)(D)　　78. (A)(B)(C)(D)

4. (A)(B)(C)(D)　　29. (A)(B)(C)(D)　　54. (A)(B)(C)(D)　　79. (A)(B)(C)(D)

5. (A)(B)(C)(D)　　30. (A)(B)(C)(D)　　55. (A)(B)(C)(D)　　80. (A)(B)(C)(D)

6. (A)(B)(C)(D)　　31. (A)(B)(C)(D)　　56. (A)(B)(C)(D)　　81. (A)(B)(C)(D)

7. (A)(B)(C)(D)　　32. (A)(B)(C)(D)　　57. (A)(B)(C)(D)　　82. (A)(B)(C)(D)

8. (A)(B)(C)(D)　　33. (A)(B)(C)(D)　　58. (A)(B)(C)(D)　　83. (A)(B)(C)(D)

9. (A)(B)(C)(D)　　34. (A)(B)(C)(D)　　59. (A)(B)(C)(D)　　84. (A)(B)(C)(D)

10. (A)(B)(C)(D)　　35. (A)(B)(C)(D)　　60. (A)(B)(C)(D)　　85. (A)(B)(C)(D)

11. (A)(B)(C)(D)　　36. (A)(B)(C)(D)　　61. (A)(B)(C)(D)　　86. (A)(B)(C)(D)

12. (A)(B)(C)(D)　　37. (A)(B)(C)(D)　　62. (A)(B)(C)(D)　　87. (A)(B)(C)(D)

13. (A)(B)(C)(D)　　38. (A)(B)(C)(D)　　63. (A)(B)(C)(D)　　88. (A)(B)(C)(D)

14. (A)(B)(C)(D)　　39. (A)(B)(C)(D)　　64. (A)(B)(C)(D)　　89. (A)(B)(C)(D)

15. (A)(B)(C)(D)　　40. (A)(B)(C)(D)　　65. (A)(B)(C)(D)　　90. (A)(B)(C)(D)

16. (A)(B)(C)(D)　　41. (A)(B)(C)(D)　　66. (A)(B)(C)(D)　　91. (A)(B)(C)(D)

17. (A)(B)(C)(D)　　42. (A)(B)(C)(D)　　67. (A)(B)(C)(D)　　92. (A)(B)(C)(D)

18. (A)(B)(C)(D)　　43. (A)(B)(C)(D)　　68. (A)(B)(C)(D)　　93. (A)(B)(C)(D)

19. (A)(B)(C)(D)　　44. (A)(B)(C)(D)　　69. (A)(B)(C)(D)　　94. (A)(B)(C)(D)

20. (A)(B)(C)(D)　　45. (A)(B)(C)(D)　　70. (A)(B)(C)(D)　　95. (A)(B)(C)(D)

21. (A)(B)(C)(D)　　46. (A)(B)(C)(D)　　71. (A)(B)(C)(D)　　96. (A)(B)(C)(D)

22. (A)(B)(C)(D)　　47. (A)(B)(C)(D)　　72. (A)(B)(C)(D)　　97. (A)(B)(C)(D)

23. (A)(B)(C)(D)　　48. (A)(B)(C)(D)　　73. (A)(B)(C)(D)　　98. (A)(B)(C)(D)

24. (A)(B)(C)(D)　　49. (A)(B)(C)(D)　　74. (A)(B)(C)(D)　　99. (A)(B)(C)(D)

25. (A)(B)(C)(D)　　50. (A)(B)(C)(D)　　75. (A)(B)(C)(D)　　100. (A)(B)(C)(D)

PRACTICE TEST 6

Directions: For each question, you will see three capitalized words and four answer choices labeled *a, b, c,* and *d* in parentheses. Choose the answer that best completes the analogy posed by the three capitalized words. Use the answer sheet on page 141 to record your answers.

Time: 50 Minutes

1. WILSON : (*a.* Fair Deal, *b.* New Deal, *c.* New Frontier, *d.* New Freedom) :: JOHNSON : GREAT SOCIETY

2. SCOPES : TEACHING EVOLUTION :: DREYFUS : (*a.* insubordination, *b.* treason, *c.* desertion, *d.* felonious assault)

3. HARDWARE : SOFTWARE :: (*a.* spreadsheet, *b.* operations, *c.* keyboard, *d.* applications) : PROGRAM

4. (*a.* jaundice, *b.* tannin, *c.* carotenoid, *d.* hemoglobin) : RED :: CHLOROPHYLL : GREEN

5. MOSES : TORAH :: JOHN : (*a.* Revelation, *b.* Genesis, *c.* Hebrews, *d.* Psalms)

6. DEIMOS : (*a.* Titania, *b.* Ganymede, *c.* Phobos, *d.* Europa) :: CALLISTO : IO

7. MICAH : PROPHET :: MICHAEL : (*a.* disciple, *b.* archangel, *c.* pope, *d.* pharisee)

8. OERSTED : (*a.* electromagnetism, *b.* telepathy, *c.* cosmology, *d.* fluid mechanics) :: BECQUEREL : RADIOACTIVITY

9. (*a.* petal, *b.* stamen, *c.* sepal, *d.* style) : PISTIL :: MALE : FEMALE

10. WRONGHEADED : ASTUTE :: PHLEGMATIC : (*a.* parched, *b.* healthy, *c.* incisive, *d.* energetic)

11. *METAMORPHOSES* : *THE METAMORPHOSIS* :: (*a.* Ovid, *b.* Virgil, *c.* Aeschylus, *d.* Sophocles) : KAFKA

12. FORT MCHENRY : (*a.* French and Indian War, *b.* American Revolution, *c.* War of 1812, *d.* Spanish-American War) :: FORT SUMTER : CIVIL WAR

13. PRELUDE : FINALE :: ZENITH : (*a.* pinnacle, *b.* terminal, *c.* nadir, *d.* acme)

14. $5 : (*a.* $10, *b.* $20, *c.* $50, *d.* $100) :: ABRAHAM LINCOLN : ALEXANDER HAMILTON

15. (*a.* Nevelson, *b.* O'Keeffe, *c.* Lange, *d.* Bonheur) : PHOTOGRAPHY :: CASSATT : PAINTING

16. TRAFALGAR SQUARE : PICCADILLY CIRCUS :: (*a.* Nelson, *b.* Henry VIII, *c.* Peter Pan, *d.* Venus) : EROS

17. ANTIBIOTIC : INFECTION :: (*a.* fungicide, *b.* statin, *c.* antiviral, *d.* analgesic) : PAIN

18. (*a.* serene, *b.* disgruntled, *c.* restive, *d.* hysterical) : LIVID :: RESTLESS : FRANTIC

19. SYMMETRY : ASYMMETRY :: ISOSCELES : (*a.* scalene, *b.* equiangular, *c.* obtuse, *d.* acute)

20. SKUNK : (*a.* stripe, *b.* elimination, *c.* odor, *d.* ammunition) :: SKINK : AMPUTATION

21. FRANKLIN ROOSEVELT : FELIX FRANKFURTER :: RONALD REAGAN : (*a.* George H. W. Bush, *b.* Sandra Day O'Connor, *c.* Alexander Haig, *d.* Donald Regan)

22. TAJ MAHAL : AGRA :: GREAT PYRAMID : (*a.* Accra, *b.* Aswan, *c.* Suez, *d.* Giza)

23. (*a.* vacuum, *b.* pulley, *c.* valve, *d.* gauge) : CONTROL :: SIPHON : TRANSFER

24. (*a.* hostilities, *b.* damage, *c.* wound, *d.* ambush) : POSTWAR :: INJURY : POSTTRAUMATIC

25. HERTZ : (*a.* tempo, *b.* volume, *c.* frequency, *d.* force) :: OHM : RESISTANCE

26. BALLPARK : BALLPOINT :: (*a.* mound, *b.* approximate, *c.* fence, *d.* competition) : PEN

27. WHINE : (*a.* left, *b.* howl, *c.* correct, *d.* wine) :: WRITE : RIGHT

28. (*a.* Calloway, *b.* Miller, *c.* Ellington, *d.* Goodman) : PIANO :: ARMSTRONG : TRUMPET

29. LEARNED BEHAVIOR : IMPRINTING :: INHERITED BEHAVIOR : (*a.* habituation, *b.* reflex, *c.* conditioning, *d.* sensitization)

30. COLORATURA : ORNAMENTATION :: (*a.* pitch, *b.* accelerando, *c.* tenor, *d.* polyphony) : COUNTERPOINT

31. GULF : (*a.* sea, *b.* strait, *c.* bay, *d.* canal) :: AQABA : BENGAL

32. (*a.* trochee, *b.* foot, *c.* anapest, *d.* noun) : IAMB :: CON'·DUCT : CON·DUCT'

33. EARMARK : IDENTIFY :: EYELET : (*a.* bore, *b.* fasten, *c.* distinguish, *d.* finish)

34. 1.5 : 6/4 :: (*a.* 4/4, *b.* 1.0, *c.* 2.5, *d.* 3.5) : 10/4

35. (*a.* Jupiter, *b.* Hera, *c.* Kronos, *d.* Neptune) : TITANS :: ZEUS : OLYMPIANS

36. GLIDER : MOTOR :: INTEGRATED CIRCUIT : (*a.* transistor, *b.* wires, *c.* crystal, *d.* semiconductor)

37. EXHIBIT : (*a.* flaunt, *b.* impart, *c.* harass, *d.* express) :: ANNOY : TORMENT

38. MAGELLAN : PACIFIC OCEAN :: (*a.* Cabot, *b.* Drake, *c.* Pizarro, *d.* Vancouver) : PUGET SOUND

39. UNION : CONFEDERACY :: (*a.* Tennessee, *b.* Arkansas, *c.* Ohio, *d.* Texas) : ALABAMA

40. POLAND : (*a.* Bulgaria, *b.* Romania, *c.* Czech Republic, *d.* Albania) :: WARSAW : BUCHAREST

41. FAD : MANIA :: ENJOYMENT : (*a.* impulse, *b.* crush, *c.* encouragement, *d.* enthrallment)

42. ALLEVIATE : ASSUAGE :: HARBOR : (*a.* entertain, *b.* fjord, *c.* omen, *d.* collect)

43. (*a.* 1.4, *b.* 10, *c.* 12, *d.* 14) : 144 :: 20 : 400

44. PALM TREE : BRANCHES :: (*a.* book, *b.* volume, *c.* periodical, *d.* pamphlet) : BINDING

45. MICRO- : MILLIONTH :: NANO- : (*a.* thousandth, *b.* ten-thousandth, *c.* ten-millionth, *d.* billionth)

46. STEINBECK : (*a.* Gibbses, *b.* Babbitts, *c.* Joads, *d.* Sartorises) :: FAULKNER : SNOPESES

47. (*a.* Gagarin, *b.* Khrushchev, *c.* Chernenko, *d.* Severin) : RUSSIA :: SHEPARD : UNITED STATES

48. SCANDALOUS : (*a.* salacious, *b.* humorous, *c.* venerable, *d.* lackluster) :: DROLL : AMUSING

49. BUCKEYE : HAWKEYE :: OHIO : (*a.* Maine, *b.* Iowa, *c.* Kentucky, *d.* Colorado)

50. (*a.* iron, *b.* pumice, *c.* halite, *d.* argon) : BUTANE :: ALUMINUM : BARIUM

51. SHAKESPEARE : ELIZABETHAN :: (*a.* Donne, *b.* Brooke, *c.* Tennyson, *d.* Burns) : VICTORIAN

52. MIGRATE : HIBERNATE :: (*a.* rabbit, *b.* opossum, *c.* cougar, *d.* elk) : BEAR

53. GERMAN SHEPHERD : (*a.* Bavaria, *b.* collie, *c.* working dog, *d.* guardian) :: HOLSTEIN : JERSEY

54. ME : MINE :: THEM : (*a.* they, *b.* those, *c.* their, *d.* theirs)

55. (*a.* erratic, *b.* preponderant, *c.* exclusive, *d.* obvious) : UNCOMMON :: PREDICTABLE : UNEXPECTED

56. PENGUIN : FLY :: RAT : (*a.* mouse, *b.* vomit, *c.* skulk, *d.* swim)

57. (*a.* madras, *b.* chapati, *c.* sari, *d.* masala) : INDIA :: LEDERHOSEN : GERMANY

58. GIACOMETTI : (*a.* sculpture, *b.* landscapes, *c.* collage, *d.* photography) :: GAINSBOROUGH : PORTRAITS

59. COVALENT BOND : SHARING :: IONIC BOND : (*a.* holding, *b.* transferring, *c.* maintaining, *d.* isolating)

60. VICE PRESIDENT : (*a.* sinecure, *b.* succession, *c.* formal, *d.* executive) :: SENATOR : LEGISLATIVE

61. STRIKE-SLIP : FAULT :: (*a.* thrust, *b.* butte, *c.* tree line, *d.* valley) : HILL

62. TIBIA : (*a.* upper arm, *b.* thigh, *c.* calf, *d.* hip) :: RADIUS : FOREARM

63. (*a.* ballyhoo, *b.* hooligan, *c.* hootenanny, *d.* shoofly) : TRANQUILITY :: MOCKERY : RESPECT

64. FRET : GUITAR :: (*a.* ivory, *b.* tune, *c.* key, *d.* octave) : PIANO

65. NONVASCULAR : VASCULAR :: MOSS : (*a.* algae, *b.* liverwort, *c.* sponge, *d.* fern)

66. (*a.* adipose, *b.* adenine, *c.* thyroxine, *d.* edentate) : THYMINE :: GUANINE : CYTOSINE

67. GAMUT : RANGE :: GAMIN : (*a.* humbug, *b.* victory, *c.* neighborhood, *d.* urchin)

68. DIPHTHERIA : MUCOUS MEMBRANES :: (*a.* botulism, *b.* anemia, *c.* bruxism, *d.* dengue) : NERVE TISSUE

69. QUORUM : BOARD :: MINYAN : (*a.* plank, *b.* congregation, *c.* council, *d.* surface)

70. (*a.* hive, *b.* sugar, *c.* nectar, *d.* bee) : HONEY :: SAP : SYRUP

71. CHLOROPLAST : ENERGY PROCESSING :: VACUOLE : (*a.* digestion, *b.* membrane, *c.* transport, *d.* inoculation)

72. FORTUNATE : (*a.* providential, *b.* cataclysmic, *c.* notorious, *d.* surreptitious) :: REPUTABLE : INFAMOUS

73. TORTILLA : CORNMEAL :: (*a.* hotcake, *b.* crepe, *c.* latke, *d.* blini) : BUCKWHEAT FLOUR

74. PRODUCER : FINANCING :: GAFFER : (*a.* casting, *b.* lighting, *c.* directing, *d.* set design)

75. NEW HAMPSHIRE : (*a.* Granite State, *b.* Gem State, *c.* Pine Tree State, *d.* Constitution State) :: NEW JERSEY : GARDEN STATE

76. ELEPHANT : (*a.* "Star-Spangled Banner," *b.* donkey, *c.* Uncle Sam, *d.* Statue of Liberty) :: GOP : UNITED STATES

77. (*a.* dimwitted, *b.* commonplace, *c.* erudite, *d.* notable) :
    INTELLECTUAL :: MUNDANE : REMARKABLE

78. UBIQUITOUS : (*a.* universal, *b.* effective, *c.* almighty, *d.* servile) ::
    OMNIPRESENT : OMNIPOTENT

79. WASHINGTON : MOUNT VERNON :: JEFFERSON : (*a.* Sagamore,
    b. Beaufort, *c.* Montpelier, *d.* Monticello)

80. (*a.* meal, *b.* fast, *c.* overeating, *d.* expansion) : BINGE :: GROWTH :
    CUTBACK

81. CHILE : PESO :: SAUDI ARABIA : (*a.* pound, *b.* dinar, *c.* riyal,
    d. dollar)

82. *FATHERS AND SONS* : *SONS AND LOVERS* :: (*a.* Turgenev, *b.* Balzac,
    c. Zola, *d.* Tolstoy) : LAWRENCE

83. PRISONER : (*a.* crime, *b.* bars, *c.* liberty, *d.* warden) :: AMPUTEE :
    LIMB

84. (*a.* grief, *b.* tear, *c.* bereavement, *d.* bow) : SORROW :: CURTSY :
    RESPECT

85. ISLAND : MOUNTAIN :: ATOLL : (*a.* hill, *b.* Alp, *c.* vale, *d.* range)

86. PRIMATOLOGIST : (*a.* creation, *b.* apes, *c.* ancient cultures,
    d. composition) :: CETOLOGIST : WHALES

87. XX : L :: CC : (*a.* D, *b.* M, *c.* LL, *d.* CD)

88. (*a.* Vichy, *b.* collaborators, *c.* Axis, *d.* Nazis) : GERMANY :: ALLIES :
    GREAT BRITAIN

89. SCHIZOPHRENIA : PSYCHOSIS :: (*a.* bipolar disorder, *b.* paranoia,
    c. hallucinations, *d.* anxiety) : NEUROSIS

90. GREMLIN : MISCHIEF :: (*a.* genie, *b.* leprechaun, *c.* jinx, *d.* goblin) :
    BEHEST

91. TRIANGLE : ANGLES :: CIRCLE : (*a.* radii, *b.* arcs, *c.* circumference,
    d. pi)

92. (*a.* Kabuki, *b.* tercet, *c.* tanka, *d.* ghazal) : NOH :: POETRY : DRAMA

93. WAVE : TSUNAMI :: HOLLOW : (*a.* hole, *b.* ripple, *c.* gap, *d.* chasm)

94. (*a. Measure for Measure, b. Coriolanus, c. Cymbeline, d. King John*) : TRAGEDY :: *TWELFTH NIGHT* : COMEDY

95. © : ™ :: (*a.* circa, *b.* company, *c.* copyright, *d.* center) : TRADEMARK

96. TARIFF : IMPORTS :: VALUE-ADDED TAX : (*a.* profits, *b.* exports, *c.* luxuries, *d.* property)

97. (*a.* Hera, *b.* Helen, *c.* Leda, *d.* Arachne) : BEAUTY :: ATHENA : WISDOM

98. HEART : (*a.* kidney, *b.* bladder, *c.* lung, *d.* aorta) :: PUMP : FILTER

99. (*a.* ecstasy, *b.* anger, *c.* grief, *d.* wonder) : ULULATION :: JOY : EXULTATION

100. REPARATION : COMPENSATION :: SEPARATION : (*a.* remuneration, *b.* amalgamation, *c.* condensation, *d.* partition)

STOP

If there is any time remaining, go back and check your work.

PRACTICE TEST 6
ANSWER KEY

1. d	26. b	51. c	76. c
2. b	27. d	52. d	77. a
3. c	28. c	53. b	78. c
4. d	29. b	54. d	79. d
5. a	30. d	55. b	80. b
6. c	31. c	56. b	81. c
7. b	32. a	57. c	82. a
8. a	33. b	58. a	83. c
9. b	34. c	59. b	84. b
10. d	35. c	60. d	85. d
11. a	36. b	61. b	86. b
12. c	37. a	62. c	87. a
13. c	38. d	63. a	88. c
14. a	39. c	64. c	89. d
15. c	40. b	65. d	90. a
16. a	41. d	66. b	91. b
17. d	42. a	67. d	92. c
18. b	43. c	68. a	93. d
19. a	44. d	69. b	94. b
20. c	45. d	70. c	95. c
21. b	46. c	71. a	96. a
22. d	47. a	72. b	97. b
23. c	48. a	73. d	98. a
24. a	49. b	74. b	99. c
25. c	50. d	75. a	100. d

PRACTICE TEST 6
EXPLANATORY ANSWERS

1. WILSON : (*a.* Fair Deal, *b.* New Deal, *c.* New Frontier, ***d.* New Freedom**) :: JOHNSON : GREAT SOCIETY
   (**d**) Woodrow *Wilson's New Freedom* platform called for reforms to protect workers and limit the power of corporations. Lyndon *Johnson's Great Society* established social programs designed to alleviate racial and economic injustice. **Object/Action**

2. SCOPES : TEACHING EVOLUTION :: DREYFUS : (*a.* insubordination, ***b.* treason**, *c.* desertion, *d.* felonious assault)
   (**b**) In 1925, John *Scopes* was put on trial for *teaching evolution* in a Tennessee school. In 1884, Alfred *Dreyfus* of the French Army was put on trial for *treason*. **Object/Action**

3. HARDWARE : SOFTWARE :: (*a.* spreadsheet, *b.* operations, ***c.* keyboard**, *d.* applications) : PROGRAM
   (**c**) Computer *hardware* includes the mechanical devices that make up a computer system, such as the CPU, the monitor, and the *keyboard*. Computer *software* includes the *programs* and instructions that allow the computer to function. **Classification**

4. (*a.* jaundice, *b.* tannin, *c.* carotenoid, ***d.* hemoglobin**) : RED :: CHLOROPHYLL : GREEN
   (**d**) Iron-rich *hemoglobin* is what makes red blood cells *red*. *Chlorophyll* is what makes green plants *green*. **Characteristic**

5. MOSES : TORAH :: JOHN : (***a.* Revelation**, *b.* Genesis, *c.* Hebrews, *d.* Psalms)
   (**a**) Although not everyone agrees, some scholars believe that *Moses* wrote or communicated the first five books of the Bible, known as the *Torah*, and that the apostle *John* wrote the chapter of the New Testament known as the book of *Revelation*. **Object/Action**

6. DEIMOS : (*a.* Titania, *b.* Ganymede, ***c.* Phobos**, *d.* Europa) :: CALLISTO : IO
   (**c**) *Deimos* and *Phobos* are the two moons of Mars. *Callisto* and *Io* are two of the moons of Jupiter. **Part/Whole**

7. MICAH : PROPHET :: MICHAEL : (*a.* disciple, ***b.* archangel**, *c.* pope, *d.* pharisee)
   (**b**) *Micah* was a *prophet* who foretold the destruction of Jerusalem. *Michael* was an *archangel* who was the protector of Israel. **Classification**

8. OERSTED : (***a.* electromagnetism**, *b.* telepathy, *c.* cosmology, *d.* fluid mechanics) :: BECQUEREL : RADIOACTIVITY
   (**a**) Hans Christian *Oersted* (1777–1851) discovered the connection between electricity and magnetism, *electromagnetism*. Henri *Becquerel* (1852–1908) shared the Nobel Prize with Pierre and Marie Curie for discovering *radioactivity*. **Object/Action**

9. (*a.* petal, ***b.* stamen**, *c.* sepal, *d.* style) : PISTIL :: MALE : FEMALE
 (b) The *stamen* is the *male*, pollen-bearing structure of a flower. The *pistil* is the *female* organ, which contains the ovary, stigma, and style. **Characteristic**

10. WRONGHEADED : ASTUTE :: PHLEGMATIC : (*a.* parched, *b.* healthy, *c.* incisive, ***d.* energetic**)
 (d) If you are *wrongheaded,* you are not very *astute,* or incisive. If you are *phlegmatic,* you are not very *energetic.* **Antonym**

11. *METAMORPHOSES* : *THE METAMORPHOSIS* :: (***a.* Ovid**, *b.* Virgil, *c.* Aeschylus, *d.* Sophocles) : KAFKA
 (a) *Ovid* wrote the epic poem *Metamorphoses* around the time of the birth of Jesus. Franz *Kafka* published his novella *The Metamorphosis* in 1915. **Object/Action**

12. FORT McHENRY : (*a.* French and Indian War, *b.* American Revolution, ***c.* War of 1812**, *d.* Spanish-American War) :: FORT SUMTER : CIVIL WAR
 (c) The view of *Fort McHenry* during the Battle of Baltimore in the *War of 1812* inspired Francis Scott Key to write "The Star-Spangled Banner" in 1814. The battle at *Fort Sumter* in 1861 was the beginning of the *Civil War*. **Characteristic**

13. PRELUDE : FINALE :: ZENITH : (*a.* pinnacle, *b.* terminal, ***c.* nadir**, *d.* acme)
 (c) A *prelude* begins a musical work, and a *finale* ends it. The *zenith* is the very top of something, and the *nadir* is the very bottom. **Sequence**

14. $5 : (***a.* $10**, *b.* $20, *c.* $50, *d.* $100) :: ABRAHAM LINCOLN : ALEXANDER HAMILTON
 (a) *Abraham Lincoln* is pictured on the *$5* bill, and *Alexander Hamilton* is pictured on the *$10* bill. **Characteristic**

15. (*a.* Nevelson, *b.* O'Keeffe, ***c.* Lange**, *d.* Bonheur) : PHOTOGRAPHY :: CASSATT : PAINTING
 (c) Dorothea *Lange* is known for her *photographs* of workers and the poor during the Depression and World War II. Mary *Cassatt* was an American impressionist *painter.* **Object/Action**

16. TRAFALGAR SQUARE : PICCADILLY CIRCUS :: (***a.* Nelson**, *b.* Henry VIII, *c.* Peter Pan, *d.* Venus) : EROS
 (a) A statue of Admiral *Nelson* stands in London's *Trafalgar Square.* A statue of *Eros* stands in London's *Piccadilly Circus.* **Characteristic**

17. ANTIBIOTIC : INFECTION :: (*a.* fungicide, *b.* statin, *c.* antiviral, ***d.* analgesic**) : PAIN
 (d) An *antibiotic* such as penicillin fights *infection,* and an *analgesic* such as aspirin fights *pain.* **Object/Action**

18. (*a.* serene, ***b.* disgruntled**, *c.* restive, *d.* hysterical) : LIVID :: RESTLESS : FRANTIC
 (b) If you are very *disgruntled,* or displeased, you may be *livid.* If you are very *restless,* or on edge, you may be *frantic.* **Degree**

19. SYMMETRY : ASYMMETRY :: ISOSCELES : (*a.* **scalene**, *b.* equiangular, *c.* obtuse, *d.* acute)

    (**a**) An *isosceles* triangle has two *symmetrical* angles. A *scalene* triangle has no two sides the same length. **Characteristic**

20. SKUNK : (*a.* stripe, *b.* elimination, *c.* **odor**, *d.* ammunition) :: SKINK : AMPUTATION

    (**c**) A *skunk* emits an *odor* to fend off predators. A *skink* (a kind of lizard) uses self-*amputation* to avoid capture. **Characteristic**

21. FRANKLIN ROOSEVELT : FELIX FRANKFURTER :: RONALD REAGAN : (*a.* George H. W. Bush, *b.* **Sandra Day O'Connor**, *c.* Alexander Haig, *d.* Donald Regan)

    (**b**) President *Franklin Roosevelt* nominated *Felix Frankfurter* to serve on the Supreme Court, and President *Ronald Reagan* did the same for *Sandra Day O'Connor*. **Object/Action**

22. TAJ MAHAL : AGRA :: GREAT PYRAMID : (*a.* Accra, *b.* Aswan, *c.* Suez, *d.* **Giza**)

    (**d**) The *Taj Mahal* is a mausoleum in *Agra*, India. The *Great Pyramid* is a mausoleum in *Giza*, Egypt. **Characteristic**

23. (*a.* vacuum, *b.* pulley, *c.* **valve**, *d.* gauge) : CONTROL :: SIPHON : TRANSFER

    (**c**) The purpose of a *valve* is to *control* flow (of gas or fluid). The purpose of a *siphon* is to *transfer* fluid from one place to another. **Object/Action**

24. (*a.* **hostilities**, *b.* damage, *c.* wound, *d.* ambush) : POSTWAR :: INJURY : POSTTRAUMATIC

    (**a**) Something that is *postwar* takes place following *hostilities*. Something that is *posttraumatic* takes place following an *injury*. **Sequence**

25. HERTZ : (*a.* tempo, *b.* volume, *c.* **frequency**, *d.* force) :: OHM : RESISTANCE

    (**c**) A *hertz* is a unit used to measure *frequency*. An *ohm* is a unit used to measure *resistance*. **Object/Action**

26. BALLPARK : BALLPOINT :: (*a.* mound, *b.* **approximate**, *c.* fence, *d.* competition) : PEN

    (**b**) A *ballpark* figure is an *approximate* figure. A *ballpoint* is a *pen*. **Synonym**

27. WHINE : (*a.* left, *b.* howl, *c.* correct, *d.* **wine**) :: WRITE : RIGHT

    (**d**) The two pairs of words are homophones—words that sound alike but are spelled differently and have different meanings. **Conversion**

28. (*a.* Calloway, *b.* Miller, *c.* **Ellington**, *d.* Goodman) : PIANO :: ARMSTRONG : TRUMPET

    (**c**) Duke *Ellington* was a jazz bandleader who played the *piano*. Louis *Armstrong* was a jazz bandleader who played the *trumpet*. **Object/Action**

29. LEARNED BEHAVIOR : IMPRINTING :: INHERITED BEHAVIOR : (*a.* habituation, *b.* **reflex**, *c.* conditioning, *d.* sensitization)

    (**b**) *Imprinting* is an example of a *learning* process that takes place early in life. *Reflex* is an example of an innate, or *inherited*, reaction to a stimulus. **Classification**

30. COLORATURA : ORNAMENTATION :: (*a.* pitch, *b.* accelerando, *c.* tenor, *d.* **polyphony**) : COUNTERPOINT
    (**d**) *Coloratura* is a form of vocal *ornamentation* or embellishment of the melodic line. *Counterpoint,* a combination of simultaneous melodic lines, is an example of *polyphony,* or variety of tones. **Characteristic**

31. GULF : (*a.* sea, *b.* strait, *c.* **bay**, *d.* canal) :: AQABA : BENGAL
    (**c**) The *Gulf* of *Aqaba* lies along the eastern shore of the Sinai Peninsula. The *Bay* of *Bengal* lies along the eastern shore of India. **Classification**

32. (*a.* **trochee**, *b.* foot, *c.* anapest, *d.* noun) : IAMB :: CON'·DUCT : CON·DUCT'
    (**a**) A *trochee* is a two-syllable metrical foot in which the first syllable is stressed and the second is unstressed. An *iamb* is a two-syllable metrical foot in which the first syllable is unstressed and the second is stressed. **Classification**

33. EARMARK : IDENTIFY :: EYELET : (*a.* bore, *b.* **fasten**, *c.* distinguish, *d.* finish)
    (**b**) You would use an *earmark* to *identify* an object or animal. You would use an *eyelet* to *fasten* a garment. **Object/Action**

34. 1.5 : 6/4 :: (*a.* 4/4, *b.* 1.0, *c.* **2.5**, *d.* 3.5) : 10/4
    (**c**) *1.5* and *6/4* name the same number. *2.5* and *10/4* name the same number. **Synonym**

35. (*a.* Jupiter, *b.* Hera, *c.* **Kronos**, *d.* Neptune) : TITANS :: ZEUS : OLYMPIANS
    (**c**) *Kronos* was one of the *Titans,* the primordial giant gods in Greek mythology. *Zeus* was one of the *Olympians,* the gods who inhabited Mount Olympus. **Classification**

36. GLIDER : MOTOR :: INTEGRATED CIRCUIT : (*a.* transistor, *b.* **wires**, *c.* crystal, *d.* semiconductor)
    (**b**) A *glider* is marked by its lack of a *motor,* and an integrated *circuit* is marked by its lack of *wires.* **Characteristic**

37. EXHIBIT : (*a.* **flaunt**, *b.* impart, *c.* harass, *d.* express) :: ANNOY : TORMENT
    (**a**) To *exhibit* on a grand scale is to *flaunt.* To *annoy* on a grand scale is to *torment.* **Degree**

38. MAGELLAN : PACIFIC OCEAN :: (*a.* Cabot, *b.* Drake, *c.* Pizarro, *d.* **Vancouver**) : PUGET SOUND
    (**d**) The Portuguese explorer Ferdinand *Magellan* was the first European to sail the *Pacific Ocean* (while circumnavigating the Earth). The English navigator George *Vancouver* explored much of the Pacific coastline, including *Puget Sound* among his discoveries. **Object/Action**

39. UNION : CONFEDERACY :: (*a.* Tennessee, *b.* Arkansas, *c.* **Ohio**, *d.* Texas) : ALABAMA
    (**c**) During the Civil War, *Ohio* was a blue state, or part of the *Union,* and all the other states listed were gray states, or part of the *Confederacy.* **Part/Whole**

40. POLAND : (*a.* Bulgaria, *b.* **Romania**, *c.* Czech Republic, *d.* Albania) :: WARSAW : BUCHAREST

(**b**) *Warsaw* is the capital of *Poland*, and *Bucharest* is the capital of *Romania*.
Characteristic

41. FAD : MANIA :: ENJOYMENT : (*a.* impulse, *b.* crush, *c.* encouragement,
    d. **enthrallment**)
    (**d**) A *fad* taken too far might be a *mania*. *Enjoyment* taken too far might be
    enthrallment. **Degree**

42. ALLEVIATE : ASSUAGE :: HARBOR : (*a.* **entertain**, *b.* fjord, *c.* omen, *d.* collect)
    (**a**) If you *alleviate* someone's suffering, you *assuage*, or lessen, it. If you *harbor*
    suspicions, you *entertain* thoughts about them. **Synonym**

43. (*a.* 1.4, *b.* 10, *c.* **12**, *d.* 14) : 144 :: 20 : 400
    (**c**) *12* squared is *144*. *20* squared is *400*. **Conversion**

44. PALM TREE : BRANCHES :: (*a.* book, *b.* volume, *c.* periodical, *d.* **pamphlet**) :
    BINDING
    (**d**) A *palm tree* typically lacks *branches*. A *pamphlet* typically lacks a *binding*.
    Characteristic

45. MICRO- : MILLIONTH :: NANO- : (*a.* thousandth, *b.* ten-thousandth,
    c. ten-millionth, *d.* **billionth**)
    (**d**) The prefix *micro-* means "*millionth*," as in *microgram*. The prefix *nano-* means
    "*billionth*," as in *nanometer*. **Affix**

46. STEINBECK : (*a.* Gibbses, *b.* Babbitts, *c.* **Joads**, *d.* Sartorises) :: FAULKNER :
    SNOPESES
    (**c**) In *The Grapes of Wrath*, John *Steinbeck* introduced readers to the *Joad* family. In
    The Hamlet and various other tales, William *Faulkner* introduced readers to the *Snopes*
    family. **Object/Action**

47. (*a.* **Gagarin**, *b.* Khrushchev, *c.* Chernenko, *d.* Severin) : RUSSIA :: SHEPARD :
    UNITED STATES
    (**a**) In April of 1961, Yuri *Gagarin* was the first *Russian* cosmonaut in space. In May of
    that same year, Alan *Shepard* was the first astronaut in space from the *United States*.
    Characteristic

48. SCANDALOUS : (*a.* **salacious**, *b.* humorous, *c.* venerable, *d.* lackluster) :: DROLL :
    AMUSING
    (**a**) Something that is *scandalous* is also *salacious*. Something that is *droll* is also
    amusing. **Synonym**

49. BUCKEYE : HAWKEYE :: OHIO : (*a.* Maine, *b.* **Iowa**, *c.* Kentucky, *d.* Colorado)
    (**b**) A resident of *Ohio* may be referred to as a *Buckeye*. A resident of *Iowa* may be
    referred to as a *Hawkeye*. **Conversion**

50. (*a.* iron, *b.* pumice, *c.* halite, *d.* **argon**) : BUTANE :: ALUMINUM : BARIUM
    (**d**) *Argon* and *butane* are both gases. *Aluminum* and *barium* are both metals.
    Part/Whole

51. SHAKESPEARE : ELIZABETHAN :: (*a.* Donne, *b.* Brooke, *c.* **Tennyson**, *d.* Burns) :
VICTORIAN
(**c**) William *Shakespeare* was a writer of the *Elizabethan* Age (the reign of Elizabeth I).
Alfred, Lord *Tennyson* was a writer of the *Victorian* Age (the reign of Victoria).
Characteristic

52. MIGRATE : HIBERNATE :: (*a.* rabbit, *b.* opossum, *c.* cougar, *d.* **elk**) : BEAR
(**d**) *Elk* and some other large ungulates tend to *migrate*, or move from one location to
another. *Bears*, on the other hand, *hibernate*, slowing down their body processes and
sleeping through the winter. **Object/Action**

53. GERMAN SHEPHERD : (*a.* Bavaria, *b.* **collie**, *c.* working dog, *d.* guardian) ::
HOLSTEIN : JERSEY
(**b**) *German shepherds* and *collies* are both breeds of dogs. *Holsteins* and *Jerseys* are both
breeds of cattle. **Part/Whole**

54. ME : MINE :: THEM : (*a.* they, *b.* those, *c.* their, *d.* **theirs**)
(**d**) *Me* and *them* are both object pronouns. *Mine* and *theirs* are both possessive
pronouns that are not used to modify nouns but instead stand alone. **Conversion**

55. (*a.* erratic, *b.* **preponderant**, *c.* exclusive, *d.* obvious) : UNCOMMON ::
PREDICTABLE : UNEXPECTED
(**b**) If something is *preponderant*, it is very common. If something is *predictable*, it is to
be expected. **Antonym**

56. PENGUIN : FLY :: RAT : (*a.* mouse, *b.* **vomit**, *c.* skulk, *d.* swim)
(**b**) A *penguin* cannot *fly*. A *rat* cannot *vomit* (making it easily subject to poisoning).
Object/Action

57. (*a.* madras, *b.* chapati, *c.* **sari**, *d.* masala) : INDIA :: LEDERHOSEN : GERMANY
(**c**) A *sari* is native dress in *India*. *Lederhosen* are native dress in *Germany*.
Characteristic

58. GIACOMETTI : (*a.* **sculpture**, *b.* landscapes, *c.* collage, *d.* photography) ::
GAINSBOROUGH : PORTRAITS
(**a**) Alberto *Giacometti* was a Swiss artist famous for his *sculpture*, especially his
elongated human figures. Thomas *Gainsborough* was a painter known for his *portraits*;
for example, *The Blue Boy*. **Object/Action**

59. COVALENT BOND : SHARING :: IONIC BOND : (*a.* holding, *b.* **transferring**,
c. maintaining, *d.* isolating)
(**b**) In a *covalent bond* between two atoms, the atoms *share* electrons. In an *ionic bond*,
electrons are *transferred* from one atom to another. **Object/Action**

60. VICE PRESIDENT : (*a.* sinecure, *b.* succession, *c.* formal, *d.* **executive**) :: SENATOR :
LEGISLATIVE
(**d**) The *vice president* is a member of the *executive* branch of the government. A *senator*
is a member of the *legislative* branch of the government. **Classification**

61. STRIKE-SLIP : FAULT :: (*a.* thrust, *b.* **butte**, *c.* tree line, *d.* valley) : HILL
(**b**) *Strike-slip* names a vertical fracture in the earth, or *fault.* A *butte* is the name of one kind of *hill.* **Classification**

62. TIBIA : (*a.* upper arm, *b.* thigh, *c.* **calf**, *d.* hip) :: RADIUS : FOREARM
(**c**) The *tibia* is a bone in the *calf* of the leg. The *radius* is a bone in the *forearm.* **Part/Whole**

63. (*a.* **ballyhoo**, *b.* hooligan, *c.* hootenanny, *d.* shoofly) : TRANQUILITY :: MOCKERY : RESPECT
(**a**) *Ballyhoo*, or uproar, is the opposite of *tranquility.* *Mockery*, or ridicule, is the opposite of *respect.* **Antonym**

64. FRET : GUITAR :: (*a.* ivory, *b.* tune, *c.* **key**, *d.* octave) : PIANO
(**c**) A *fret* indicates pitch on a *guitar.* A *key* indicates pitch on a *piano.* **Characteristic**

65. NONVASCULAR : VASCULAR :: MOSS : (*a.* algae, *b.* liverwort, *c.* sponge, *d.* **fern**)
(**d**) *Moss* is one kind of *nonvascular* plant (liverwort is another). A *fern* is one kind of *vascular* plant—its tissues conduct fluids throughout the plant. **Classification**

66. (*a.* adipose, *b.* **adenine**, *c.* thyroxine, *d.* edentate) : THYMINE :: GUANINE : CYTOSINE
(**b**) In a DNA sequence, the purine base *adenine* pairs with the pyrimidine base *thymine,* and the purine base *guanine* pairs with the pyrimidine base *cytosine.* **Sequence**

67. GAMUT : RANGE :: GAMIN : (*a.* humbug, *b.* victory, *c.* neighborhood, *d.* **urchin**)
(**d**) A *gamut* is a *range*, as of colors or emotions. A *gamin* is a male *urchin*, or waif. **Synonym**

68. DIPHTHERIA : MUCOUS MEMBRANES :: (*a.* **botulism**, *b.* anemia, *c.* bruxism, *d.* dengue) : NERVE TISSUE
(**a**) The disease *diphtheria* attacks the *mucous membranes.* The toxin *botulism* attacks *nerve tissue.* **Object/Action**

69. QUORUM : BOARD :: MINYAN : (*a.* plank, *b.* **congregation**, *c.* council, *d.* surface)
(**b**) A *quorum* is the minimum number of members of a *board* or legislature that must be present to conduct business. A *minyan* is the minimum number of Jewish men (ten) who must be present to conduct a service. **Part/Whole**

70. (*a.* hive, *b.* sugar, *c.* **nectar**, *d.* bee) : HONEY :: SAP : SYRUP
(**c**) *Honey* is a sweetener that derives from flower *nectar.* *Syrup* is a sweetener that derives from tree *sap.* **Characteristic**

71. CHLOROPLAST : ENERGY PROCESSING :: VACUOLE : (*a.* **digestion**, *b.* membrane, *c.* transport, *d.* inoculation)
(**a**) In plant physiology, the *chloroplast* is that part of the plant in which *energy is processed.* The *vacuole* is that part of the plant in which food is stored and *digested.* **Object/Action**

72. FORTUNATE : (*a.* providential, ***b.* cataclysmic**, *c.* notorious, *d.* surreptitious) ::
REPUTABLE : INFAMOUS
(**b**) The opposite of *fortunate* is *cataclysmic*, or disastrous. The opposite
of *reputable* is *infamous*, or notorious. **Antonym**

73. TORTILLA : CORNMEAL :: (*a.* hotcake, *b.* crepe, *c.* latke, ***d.* blini**) :
BUCKWHEAT FLOUR
(**d**) A *tortilla* is a flat Mexican bread made from *cornmeal*. A *blini* is a flat Russian
pancake made from *buckwheat flour*. **Characteristic**

74. PRODUCER : FINANCING :: GAFFER : (*a.* casting, ***b.* lighting**, *c.* directing,
d. set design)
(**b**) In film production, the *producer* is generally responsible for the film's *financing*,
and the *gaffer* is in charge of *lighting* the set. **Object/Action**

75. NEW HAMPSHIRE : (***a.* Granite State**, *b.* Gem State, *c.* Pine Tree State,
d. Constitution State) :: NEW JERSEY : GARDEN STATE
(**a**) *New Hampshire's* nickname is "the *Granite State*." *New Jersey's* nickname is "the
Garden State." **Conversion**

76. ELEPHANT : (*a.* "Star-Spangled Banner," *b.* donkey, ***c.* Uncle Sam**, *d.* Statue of
Liberty) :: GOP : UNITED STATES
(**c**) The *elephant* symbolizes the *GOP*, or Republican Party. *Uncle Sam* is a character
that symbolizes the *United States*. **Object/Action**

77. (***a.* dimwitted**, *b.* commonplace, *c.* erudite, *d.* notable) : INTELLECTUAL ::
MUNDANE : REMARKABLE
(**a**) To be *dimwitted* is to be anything but *intellectual*. To be *mundane* is to be anything
but *remarkable*. **Antonym**

78. UBIQUITOUS : (*a.* universal, *b.* effective, ***c.* almighty**, *d.* servile) :: OMNIPRESENT :
OMNIPOTENT
(**c**) Something that is *ubiquitous* is *omnipresent*, or available everywhere. Someone who
is *almighty* is *omnipotent*, or all-powerful. **Synonym**

79. WASHINGTON : MOUNT VERNON :: JEFFERSON : (*a.* Sagamore, *b.* Beaufort,
c. Montpelier, ***d.* Monticello**)
(**d**) George *Washington's* home in Virginia was *Mount Vernon*. Thomas *Jefferson's* home
in Virginia was *Monticello*. **Object/Action**

80. (*a.* meal, ***b.* fast**, *c.* overeating, *d.* expansion) : BINGE :: GROWTH : CUTBACK
(**b**) The opposite of a *fast*, or refusal to eat, might be a *binge*. The opposite of *growth*
(in business, for example) might be a *cutback*. **Antonym**

81. CHILE : PESO :: SAUDI ARABIA : (*a.* pound, *b.* dinar, ***c.* riyal**, *d.* dollar)
(**c**) The *peso* is the currency of *Chile*. The *riyal* is the currency of *Saudi Arabia*.
Characteristic

82. *FATHERS AND SONS* : *SONS AND LOVERS* :: (***a.* Turgenev**, *b.* Balzac, *c.* Zola,
d. Tolstoy) : LAWRENCE

(a) Ivan *Turgenev* (1818–1883) wrote the novel *Fathers and Sons*. D. H. *Lawrence* (1885–1930) wrote the novel *Sons and Lovers*. **Object/Action**

83. PRISONER : (*a.* crime, *b.* bars, *c.* **liberty**, *d.* warden) :: AMPUTEE : LIMB
    (**c**) A *prisoner* lacks *liberty*. An *amputee* lacks a *limb*. **Characteristic**

84. (*a.* grief, *b.* **tear**, *c.* bereavement, *d.* bow) : SORROW :: CURTSY : RESPECT
    (**b**) A *tear* is a sign of *sorrow*. A *curtsy* is a sign of *respect*. **Object/Action**

85. ISLAND : MOUNTAIN :: ATOLL : (*a.* hill, *b.* Alp, *c.* vale, *d.* **range**)
    (**d**) A long string of *islands* is called an *atoll*. A long string of *mountains* is called a *range*. **Part/Whole**

86. PRIMATOLOGIST : (*a.* Creation, *b.* **apes**, *c.* ancient cultures, *d.* composition) :: CETOLOGIST : WHALES
    (**b**) A *primatologist* studies *apes*, and a *cetologist* studies *whales*. **Object/Action**

87. XX : L :: CC : (*a.* **D**, *b.* M, *c.* LL, *d.* CD)
    (**a**) *XX* = 20, and *L* = 50. This forms the same ratio as *CC* (200) to *D* (500). **Sequence**

88. (*a.* Vichy, *b.* collaborators, *c.* **Axis**, *d.* Nazis) : GERMANY :: ALLIES : GREAT BRITAIN
    (**c**) During World War II, *Germany* and its allies were called the *Axis*, and *Great Britain* and its allies were called the *Allies*. **Classification**

89. SCHIZOPHRENIA : PSYCHOSIS :: (*a.* bipolar disorder, *b.* paranoia, *c.* hallucinations, *d.* **anxiety**) : NEUROSIS
    (**d**) *Schizophrenia* is one form of *psychosis*, a severe mental illness. *Anxiety* is one form of *neurosis*, a milder disorder. **Classification**

90. GREMLIN : MISCHIEF :: (*a.* **genie**, *b.* leprechaun, *c.* jinx, *d.* goblin) : BEHEST
    (**a**) In the literature of fantasy, a *gremlin* is a creature that perpetrates *mischief*, whereas a *genie* is a creature that grants wishes, or *behests*. **Object/Action**

91. TRIANGLE : ANGLES :: CIRCLE : (*a.* radii, *b.* **arcs**, *c.* circumference, *d.* pi)
    (**b**) *Angles* make up the exterior of polygons such as the *triangle*. *Arcs* make up the exterior of a *circle*. **Part/Whole**

92. (*a.* Kabuki, *b.* tercet, *c.* **tanka**, *d.* ghazal) : NOH :: POETRY : DRAMA
    (**c**) A *tanka* is a form of Japanese *poem* having five lines with syllables as follows: five, seven, five, seven, seven. *Noh* is a form of stylized Japanese *drama*. **Classification**

93. WAVE : TSUNAMI :: HOLLOW : (*a.* hole, *b.* ripple, *c.* gap, *d.* **chasm**)
    (**d**) A huge *wave* is a *tsunami*. A huge *hollow* is a *chasm*. **Degree**

94. (*a. Measure for Measure*, *b.* **Coriolanus**, *c. Cymbeline*, *d. King John*) : TRAGEDY :: *TWELFTH NIGHT* : COMEDY
    (**b**) *Coriolanus* is a Shakespearean *tragedy*, and *Twelfth Night* is a Shakespearean *comedy*. **Classification**

95. © : ™ :: (*a.* circa, *b.* company, *c.* **copyright**, *d.* center) : TRADEMARK
   (**c**) The symbols shown stand for *copyright* and *trademark*. **Conversion**

96. TARIFF : IMPORTS :: VALUE-ADDED TAX : (*a.* **profits**, *b.* exports, *c.* luxuries, *d.* property)
   (**a**) A *tariff* is a tax on *imports*. A *value-added tax* is a tax on *profits*. **Object/Action**

97. (*a.* Hera, *b.* **Helen**, *c.* Leda, *d.* Arachne) : BEAUTY :: ATHENA : WISDOM
   (**b**) In Greek mythology, *Helen* of Troy was known for her *beauty*, and the goddess *Athena* was known for her *wisdom*. **Characteristic**

98. HEART : (*a.* **kidney**, *b.* bladder, *c.* lung, *d.* aorta) :: PUMP : FILTER
   (**a**) The *heart* performs actions much like those of any *pump*, and the *kidneys'* main function is to *filter* waste. **Object/Action**

99. (*a.* ecstasy, *b.* anger, *c.* **grief**, *d.* wonder) : ULULATION :: JOY : EXULTATION
   (**c**) *Ululation* is an expression of *grief*. *Exultation* is an expression of *joy*. **Object/Action**

100. REPARATION : COMPENSATION :: SEPARATION : (*a.* remuneration, *b.* amalgamation, *c.* condensation, *d.* **partition**)
   (**d**) *Reparation* is *compensation*, especially for an injury or wrong. A *separation* is a *partition*. **Synonym**

PRACTICE TEST 7
ANSWER SHEET

1. Ⓐ Ⓑ Ⓒ Ⓓ	26. Ⓐ Ⓑ Ⓒ Ⓓ	51. Ⓐ Ⓑ Ⓒ Ⓓ	76. Ⓐ Ⓑ Ⓒ Ⓓ
2. Ⓐ Ⓑ Ⓒ Ⓓ	27. Ⓐ Ⓑ Ⓒ Ⓓ	52. Ⓐ Ⓑ Ⓒ Ⓓ	77. Ⓐ Ⓑ Ⓒ Ⓓ
3. Ⓐ Ⓑ Ⓒ Ⓓ	28. Ⓐ Ⓑ Ⓒ Ⓓ	53. Ⓐ Ⓑ Ⓒ Ⓓ	78. Ⓐ Ⓑ Ⓒ Ⓓ
4. Ⓐ Ⓑ Ⓒ Ⓓ	29. Ⓐ Ⓑ Ⓒ Ⓓ	54. Ⓐ Ⓑ Ⓒ Ⓓ	79. Ⓐ Ⓑ Ⓒ Ⓓ
5. Ⓐ Ⓑ Ⓒ Ⓓ	30. Ⓐ Ⓑ Ⓒ Ⓓ	55. Ⓐ Ⓑ Ⓒ Ⓓ	80. Ⓐ Ⓑ Ⓒ Ⓓ
6. Ⓐ Ⓑ Ⓒ Ⓓ	31. Ⓐ Ⓑ Ⓒ Ⓓ	56. Ⓐ Ⓑ Ⓒ Ⓓ	81. Ⓐ Ⓑ Ⓒ Ⓓ
7. Ⓐ Ⓑ Ⓒ Ⓓ	32. Ⓐ Ⓑ Ⓒ Ⓓ	57. Ⓐ Ⓑ Ⓒ Ⓓ	82. Ⓐ Ⓑ Ⓒ Ⓓ
8. Ⓐ Ⓑ Ⓒ Ⓓ	33. Ⓐ Ⓑ Ⓒ Ⓓ	58. Ⓐ Ⓑ Ⓒ Ⓓ	83. Ⓐ Ⓑ Ⓒ Ⓓ
9. Ⓐ Ⓑ Ⓒ Ⓓ	34. Ⓐ Ⓑ Ⓒ Ⓓ	59. Ⓐ Ⓑ Ⓒ Ⓓ	84. Ⓐ Ⓑ Ⓒ Ⓓ
10. Ⓐ Ⓑ Ⓒ Ⓓ	35. Ⓐ Ⓑ Ⓒ Ⓓ	60. Ⓐ Ⓑ Ⓒ Ⓓ	85. Ⓐ Ⓑ Ⓒ Ⓓ
11. Ⓐ Ⓑ Ⓒ Ⓓ	36. Ⓐ Ⓑ Ⓒ Ⓓ	61. Ⓐ Ⓑ Ⓒ Ⓓ	86. Ⓐ Ⓑ Ⓒ Ⓓ
12. Ⓐ Ⓑ Ⓒ Ⓓ	37. Ⓐ Ⓑ Ⓒ Ⓓ	62. Ⓐ Ⓑ Ⓒ Ⓓ	87. Ⓐ Ⓑ Ⓒ Ⓓ
13. Ⓐ Ⓑ Ⓒ Ⓓ	38. Ⓐ Ⓑ Ⓒ Ⓓ	63. Ⓐ Ⓑ Ⓒ Ⓓ	88. Ⓐ Ⓑ Ⓒ Ⓓ
14. Ⓐ Ⓑ Ⓒ Ⓓ	39. Ⓐ Ⓑ Ⓒ Ⓓ	64. Ⓐ Ⓑ Ⓒ Ⓓ	89. Ⓐ Ⓑ Ⓒ Ⓓ
15. Ⓐ Ⓑ Ⓒ Ⓓ	40. Ⓐ Ⓑ Ⓒ Ⓓ	65. Ⓐ Ⓑ Ⓒ Ⓓ	90. Ⓐ Ⓑ Ⓒ Ⓓ
16. Ⓐ Ⓑ Ⓒ Ⓓ	41. Ⓐ Ⓑ Ⓒ Ⓓ	66. Ⓐ Ⓑ Ⓒ Ⓓ	91. Ⓐ Ⓑ Ⓒ Ⓓ
17. Ⓐ Ⓑ Ⓒ Ⓓ	42. Ⓐ Ⓑ Ⓒ Ⓓ	67. Ⓐ Ⓑ Ⓒ Ⓓ	92. Ⓐ Ⓑ Ⓒ Ⓓ
18. Ⓐ Ⓑ Ⓒ Ⓓ	43. Ⓐ Ⓑ Ⓒ Ⓓ	68. Ⓐ Ⓑ Ⓒ Ⓓ	93. Ⓐ Ⓑ Ⓒ Ⓓ
19. Ⓐ Ⓑ Ⓒ Ⓓ	44. Ⓐ Ⓑ Ⓒ Ⓓ	69. Ⓐ Ⓑ Ⓒ Ⓓ	94. Ⓐ Ⓑ Ⓒ Ⓓ
20. Ⓐ Ⓑ Ⓒ Ⓓ	45. Ⓐ Ⓑ Ⓒ Ⓓ	70. Ⓐ Ⓑ Ⓒ Ⓓ	95. Ⓐ Ⓑ Ⓒ Ⓓ
21. Ⓐ Ⓑ Ⓒ Ⓓ	46. Ⓐ Ⓑ Ⓒ Ⓓ	71. Ⓐ Ⓑ Ⓒ Ⓓ	96. Ⓐ Ⓑ Ⓒ Ⓓ
22. Ⓐ Ⓑ Ⓒ Ⓓ	47. Ⓐ Ⓑ Ⓒ Ⓓ	72. Ⓐ Ⓑ Ⓒ Ⓓ	97. Ⓐ Ⓑ Ⓒ Ⓓ
23. Ⓐ Ⓑ Ⓒ Ⓓ	48. Ⓐ Ⓑ Ⓒ Ⓓ	73. Ⓐ Ⓑ Ⓒ Ⓓ	98. Ⓐ Ⓑ Ⓒ Ⓓ
24. Ⓐ Ⓑ Ⓒ Ⓓ	49. Ⓐ Ⓑ Ⓒ Ⓓ	74. Ⓐ Ⓑ Ⓒ Ⓓ	99. Ⓐ Ⓑ Ⓒ Ⓓ
25. Ⓐ Ⓑ Ⓒ Ⓓ	50. Ⓐ Ⓑ Ⓒ Ⓓ	75. Ⓐ Ⓑ Ⓒ Ⓓ	100. Ⓐ Ⓑ Ⓒ Ⓓ

PRACTICE TEST 7

> **Directions**: For each question, you will see three capitalized words and four answer choices labeled *a, b, c,* and *d* in parentheses. Choose the answer that best completes the analogy posed by the three capitalized words. Use the answer sheet on page 161 to record your answers.

Time: 50 Minutes

1. (*a.* holiness, *b.* unity, *c.* ceremony, *d.* initiation) : RITUAL ::
   COMMUNION : SACRAMENT

2. QUACK : AUTHENTICITY :: IGNORAMUS : (*a.* obedience,
   b. scholarship, *c.* legitimacy, *d.* forensics)

3. RUBELLA : RASH :: (*a.* mumps, *b.* tetanus, *c.* German measles,
   d. influenza) : LOCKJAW

4. MAGGOT : FLY :: NYMPH : (*a.* bird, *b.* imago, *c.* dragonfly, *d.* satyr)

5. GOTHS : GERMANIC :: (*a.* Berbers, *b.* Visigoths, *c.* Huns, *d.* Alans) :
   NORTH AFRICAN

6. PLATO : ARISTOTLE :: ARISTOTLE : (*a.* Socrates, *b.* Pythagoras,
   c. Euripedes, *d.* Alexander)

7. (*a.* Aga Khan, *b.* Shi Huangdi, *c.* Genghis Khan, *d.* Rasputin) :
   MONGOL :: HANNIBAL : CARTHAGINIAN

8. AUGUSTE COMTE : (*a.* positivism, *b.* realism, *c.* pragmatism,
   d. sciencism) :: RENÉ DESCARTES : RATIONALISM

9. AUDUBON : BIRDS :: LINNAEUS : (*a.* apes, *b.* insects, *c.* plants,
   d. fish)

10. HILARITY : MELANCHOLY :: (*a.* fecundity, *b.* mirth, *c.* spite,
    d. benevolence) : MALICE

11. JOHN BOYD DUNLOP : (*a.* mountain bike, *b.* pneumatic tire,
    c. catalytic converter, *d.* motorcycle) :: LINUS YALE : CYLINDER
    LOCK

12. (*a*. Quebec City, *b*. Calgary, *c*. Toronto, *d*. Saskatoon) : ONTARIO :: WINNIPEG : MANITOBA

13. GREEN : (*a*. defiance, *b*. despair, *c*. joy, *d*. envy) :: BLUE : SORROW

14. TORQUEMADA : MENGELE :: INQUISITION : (*a*. Holocaust, *b*. sedition, *c*. surgery, *d*. Reichstag)

15. FOG : (*a*. translucency, *b*. droplets, *c*. visibility, *d*. pollutant) :: DIET : WEIGHT

16. (*a*. delicate, *b*. incapacitated, *c*. adequate, *d*. stalwart) : FEEBLE :: FIT : BRAWNY

17. KARATE : TAI CHI :: JAPAN : (*a*. China, *b*. Korea, *c*. Malaysia, *d*. Nepal)

18. REFEREE : (*a*. game, *b*. ruling, *c*. competition, *d*. amendment) :: NAVIGATOR : COURSE

19. (*a*. Abram, *b*. Joshua, *c*. David, *d*. Ishmael) : HAGAR :: HAMLET : GERTRUDE

20. TROLL : TEUTONIC :: (*a*. ogre, *b*. brownie, *c*. dryad, *d*. imp) : SCOTTISH

21. VACCINATION : INFECTION :: INSULATION : (*a*. building, *b*. infestation, *c*. heating, *d*. conduction)

22. GROUNDHOG : WOODCHUCK :: (*a*. bobcat, *b*. raccoon, *c*. skunk, *d*. cougar) : POLECAT

23. (*a*. Zeus, *b*. Atlas, *c*. Minerva, *d*. Prometheus) : JUPITER :: CRONUS : SATURN

24. ICHTHYOLOGIST : (*a*. Atlantic, *b*. cod, *c*. cobra, *d*. macaw) :: HERPETOLOGIST : PYTHON

25. JEROME : JEREMIAH :: SAINT : (*a*. sinner, *b*. angel, *c*. prophet, *d*. apostle)

26. (*a*. Momotaro, *b*. Canute, *c*. Achilles, *d*. Gilgamesh) : BABYLON :: BEOWULF : SCANDINAVIA

27. STRATUS : CINDER CONE :: CLOUD : (*a*. tornado, *b*. cyclone, *c*. volcano, *d*. fire)

28. (*a.* cow, *b.* ram, *c.* billy, *d.* bull) : OVINE :: TOM : FELINE

29. HERCULES : HYDRA :: (*a.* Perseus, *b.* Athena, *c.* Medusa, *d.* Heracles) : GORGON

30. REFUSE : (*a.* monarch, *b.* dross, *c.* defiance, *d.* correlation) :: RULER : SOVEREIGN

31. GYMNOSPERM : ANGIOSPERM :: (*a.* pine, *b.* algae, *c.* maple, *d.* corn) : OAK

32. (*a.* airstream, *b.* gale, *c.* doldrums, *d.* current) : WIND :: STALEMATE : MOVEMENT

33. ENCOURAGE : INCITE :: DISAGREE : (*a.* rebel, *b.* disapprove, *c.* concur, *d.* insist)

34. KENNEDY : JOHNSON :: (*a.* Carter, *b.* Nixon, *c.* Reagan, *d.* Dole) : FORD

35. PABLO PICASSO : (*a.* Gala, *b.* Malaga, *c.* Gertrude Stein, *d.* Guernica) :: ANDREW WYETH : HELGA

36. PLANET : SOLAR SYSTEM :: STAR : (*a.* planet, *b.* supernova, *c.* gas, *d.* galaxy)

37. DIENBIENPHU : (*a.* Chinese, *b.* Vietnamese, *c.* French, *d.* Americans) :: YORKTOWN : BRITISH

38. (*a.* damaging, *b.* elderly, *c.* fond, *d.* uncaring) : DOTING :: HARMFUL : DESTRUCTIVE

39. GRANDILOQUENT : (*a.* straightforward, *b.* clumsy, *c.* pompous, *d.* lissome) :: GRACEFUL : UNGAINLY

40. HELIX : HELICES :: AX : (*a.* axe, *b.* axis, *c.* axes, *d.* aces)

41. KRONE : (*a.* Berlin, *b.* Bonn, *c.* bund, *d.* mark) :: NORWAY : GERMANY

42. OMNI- : PERI- :: ALL : (*a.* around, *b.* approximately, *c.* outside, *d.* made of)

43. RIIS : NEW YORK TENEMENTS :: (*a.* Tarbell, *b.* Lewis, *c.* Sinclair, *d.* Agee) : CHICAGO STOCKYARDS

44. (*a.* Esperanza, *b.* Good Will, *c.* Santiago, *d.* Horn) : GOOD HOPE :: CHILE : SOUTH AFRICA

45. BLACK GOLD : FOOL'S GOLD :: OIL : (*a.* mineral, *b.* pyrite, *c.* water, *d.* mica)

46. DAPHNE : (*a.* fawn, *b.* reflection, *c.* laurel tree, *d.* amaryllis) :: CALLISTO : BEAR

47. NOSE : FACE :: DIAL : (*a.* knob, *b.* visage, *c.* touchtone, *d.* watch)

48. (*a.* Balmoral Castle, *b.* Buckingham Palace, *c.* Royal Mews, *d.* Winchester Cathedral) : QUEEN ELIZABETH II :: VATICAN : POPE BENEDICT XVI

49. PICA : (*a.* agate, *b.* stone, *c.* type, *d.* leather) :: BOLT : CLOTH

50. BRASS : COPPER :: (*a.* aluminum, *b.* steel, *c.* nickel, *d.* tungsten) : IRON

51. CHARLES LAMB : ELIA :: CHARLES DICKENS : (*a.* Boz, *b.* Pickwick, *c.* Pip, *d.* Dora)

52. (*a.* climax, *b.* denouement, *c.* structure, *d.* overture) : BEGINNING :: FINALE : PRELUDE

53. SOLZHENITSYN : CANCER WARD :: (*a.* Kesey, *b.* Grass, *c.* Bellow, *d.* Mann) : SANATORIUM

54. (*a.* Orinoco, *b.* Guyana, *c.* Amazon, *d.* Tierra del Fuego) : SOUTH AMERICA :: YANGTZE : ASIA

55. SHRUG : NONCHALANCE :: NOD : (*a.* insouciance, *b.* acquiescence, *c.* alliance, *d.* ascendancy)

56. SURREALISM : REALISM :: DALÍ : (*a.* Ernst, *b.* Gorky, *c.* Chagall, *d.* Daumier)

57. SQUARE : CUBE :: (*a.* rectangle, *b.* triangle, *c.* rhombus, *d.* pentagon) : TETRAHEDRON

58. (*a.* philatelist, *b.* numismatist, *c.* audiophile, *d.* phillumenist) : STAMPS :: BIBLIOPHILE : BOOKS

59. RETICENT : RETICULE :: RESERVED : (*a.* shyness, *b.* superstition, *c.* purse, *d.* compost)

60. 1948 : (*a.* scooter and deodorant, *b.* skateboard and polystyrene, *c.* Frisbee and Velcro, *d.* Slinky and hairspray) :: 1958 : HULA HOOP AND LASER

61. (*a.* moon, *b.* planet, *c.* rocket, *d.* aircraft) : SATELLITE :: EUROPA : SPUTNIK

62. CIVIL WAR : (*a.* Confederacy, *b.* Reconstruction, *c.* War Between the States, *d.* uprising) :: WORLD WAR I : WEIMAR REPUBLIC

63. (*a.* industrious, *b.* aloof, *c.* collegial, *d.* unflappable) : SOCIABLE :: UNPRODUCTIVE : BARREN

64. EDEN : JUDAS :: (*a.* innocence, *b.* fidelity, *c.* garden, *d.* forgetfulness) : BETRAYAL

65. (*a.* shire, *b.* canton, *c.* province, *d.* stadt) : SWITZERLAND :: DEPARTMENT : FRANCE

66. COMMUNARD : DECEMBRIST :: PARIS : (*a.* London, *b.* Berlin, *c.* St. Petersburg, *d.* Tehran)

67. GALEN : (*a.* philosophy, *b.* politics, *c.* poetry, *d.* medicine) :: HERODOTUS : HISTORY

68. COLLECTED : DISPERSED :: CLEANSED : (*a.* polluted, *b.* dissolved, *c.* purified, *d.* baptized)

69. THREE : TWO :: (*a.* semicircle, *b.* sphere, *c.* radius, *d.* orbit) : CIRCLE

70. DOSTOEVSKY : *THE IDIOT* :: GIDE : (*a. The Innocents Abroad*, *b. The Independent*, *c. The Inheritors*, *d. The Immoralist*)

71. (*a.* ukulele, *b.* flute, *c.* fruit, *d.* superior) : LUTE :: FLOWER : LOWER

72. PREVALENT : ATYPICAL :: (*a.* hygienic, *b.* contiguous, *c.* common, *d.* decadent) : UNSULLIED

73. SMARMY : (*a.* unctuous, *b.* trite, *c.* audacious, *d.* misshapen) :: BLAND : INSIPID

74. REINS : HORSE :: (*a.* hatch, *b.* motor, *c.* rudder, *d.* mainsail) : VESSEL

75. SHORTCOMING : VIRTUE :: ENTROPY : (*a.* time, *b.* order, *c.* exit, *d.* vice)

76. THUMB : GRASPING :: (*a.* fibula, *b.* wrist, *c.* arch, *d.* ligament) : SHOCK ABSORPTION

77. ANIMAL CELL : (*a.* cell wall, *b.* nucleus, *c.* mitochondrion, *d.* vacuole) :: PLANT CELL : CENTRIOLE

78. ROSSINI : PUCCINI :: *THE BARBER OF SEVILLE* : (*a. The Magic Flute, b. La Traviata, c. Parsifal, d. Madame Butterfly*)

79. MY LAI : (*a.* Ruby Ridge, *b.* Bitterroot Valley, *c.* Wounded Knee, *d.* Battle of Fallen Timbers) :: VIETNAM WAR : INDIAN WARS

80. (*a.* hammer, *b.* pulley, *c.* vice, *d.* handshake) : GRIP :: CORKSCREW : PULL

81. BOBCAT : OCELOT :: WOLF : (*a.* puma, *b.* coyote, *c.* elk, *d.* panther)

82. MARIA TALLCHIEF : (*a.* watercolor, *b.* folkdance, *c.* photography, *d.* ballet) :: ELEANOR POWELL : TAP

83. 2% : 5% :: 40% : (*a.* 1%, *b.* 50%, *c.* 60%, *d.* 100%)

84. QUILTING : FOLK ART :: (*a.* retablo, *b.* basketry, *c.* portraiture, *d.* embroidery) : FINE ART

85. COUSTEAU : UNDERSEA :: SHEPARD : (*a.* mountains, *b.* space, *c.* underground, *d.* overland)

86. BECKETT : GODOT :: ODETS : (*a.* Moe, *b.* Golden Boy, *c.* Lefty, *d.* McCarthy)

87. (*a.* enzyme, *b.* steroid, *c.* lipid, *d.* catalyst) : PROGESTERONE :: VITAMIN : FOLIC ACID

88. (*a.* Balboa, *b.* Velasquez, *c.* Chevrolet, *d.* Cabrillo) : CALIFORNIA :: CADILLAC : MICHIGAN

89. FENCING : PENTATHLON :: (*a.* pole vaulting, *b.* swimming, *c.* archery, *d.* equestrian show jumping) : DECATHLON

90. BEHAVIORISM : (*a.* sociology, *b.* psychology, *c.* zoology, *d.* archeology) :: AESTHETICS : PHILOSOPHY

91. SHOWY : GARISH :: (*a.* sturdy, *b.* blowsy, *c.* gaudy, *d.* wordy) : PROLIX

92. *LA BOHÈME* : (*a. Les Sylphides, b. Les Troyens, c. Les Huguenots, d. La Belle Hélène*) :: OPERA : BALLET

93. ACOUSTICS : (*a.* visions, *b.* lumière, *c.* optics, *d.* prism) :: SOUND : LIGHT

94. (*a.* etymology, *b.* verbosity, *c.* otiology, *d.* entomology) : WORDS :: GERONTOLOGY : AGING

95. MERRILY : (*a.* merriment, *b.* merrymaking, *c.* merry, *d.* merry-go-round) :: ADVERB : ADJECTIVE

96. (*a.* Honduras, *b.* Belize, *c.* Brunei, *d.* Botswana) : BRITISH HONDURAS :: GUYANA : BRITISH GUIANA

97. SMUG : SMUT :: HUMBLE : (*a.* subservience, *b.* superciliousness, *c.* plenitude, *d.* wholesomeness)

98. (*a.* hatchery, *b.* fisher, *c.* tarn, *d.* egg) : FISH :: NURSERY : TREE

99. SOCCER : SHIN GUARDS :: (*a.* polo, *b.* softball, *c.* hockey, *d.* lacrosse) : ARM PADS

100. AESOP : FABLES :: (*a.* Perrault, *b.* Singer, *c.* Lindgren, *d.* Alcott) : FAIRY TALES

STOP

If there is any time remaining, go back and check your work.

PRACTICE TEST 7
ANSWER KEY

1. d	26. d	51. a	76. c
2. b	27. c	52. b	77. a
3. b	28. b	53. d	78. d
4. c	29. a	54. c	79. c
5. a	30. b	55. b	80. c
6. d	31. a	56. d	81. b
7. c	32. c	57. b	82. d
8. a	33. a	58. a	83. d
9. c	34. b	59. c	84. c
10. d	35. c	60. c	85. b
11. b	36. d	61. a	86. c
12. c	37. c	62. b	87. b
13. d	38. c	63. c	88. d
14. a	39. a	64. a	89. a
15. c	40. c	65. b	90. b
16. a	41. d	66. c	91. d
17. a	42. a	67. d	92. a
18. b	43. c	68. a	93. c
19. d	44. d	69. b	94. a
20. b	45. b	70. d	95. c
21. d	46. c	71. b	96. b
22. c	47. d	72. d	97. d
23. a	48. b	73. a	98. a
24. b	49. c	74. c	99. d
25. c	50. b	75. b	100. a

PRACTICE TEST 7 EXPLANATORY ANSWERS

1. (*a.* holiness, *b.* unity, *c.* ceremony, ***d.* initiation**) : RITUAL :: COMMUNION : SACRAMENT
   (**d**) An *initiation* is one kind of *ritual. Communion* is one of the seven *sacraments.*
   Classification

2. QUACK : AUTHENTICITY :: IGNORAMUS : (*a.* obedience, ***b.* scholarship,** *c.* legitimacy, *d.* forensics)
   (**b**) A *quack,* or fake doctor, lacks *authenticity,* just as an *ignoramus,* or know-nothing, lacks *scholarship.* **Characteristic**

3. RUBELLA : RASH :: (*a.* mumps, ***b.* tetanus,** *c.* German measles, *d.* influenza) : LOCKJAW
   (**b**) A *rash* may be a sign of *rubella* (German measles). *Lockjaw* may be a sign of *tetanus.* **Object/Action**

4. MAGGOT : FLY :: NYMPH : (*a.* bird, *b.* imago, ***c.* dragonfly,** *d.* satyr)
   (**c**) The larva of a *fly* is called a *maggot.* The larva of a *dragonfly* is called a *nymph.*
   Part/Whole

5. GOTHS : GERMANIC :: (***a.* Berbers,** *b.* Visigoths, *c.* Huns, *d.* Alans) : NORTH AFRICAN
   (**a**) The *Goths* were a *Germanic* people known for invading the Roman Empire.
   The *Berbers* are a people of *Northern Africa* who have lived there since before the Arab conquest of the region. **Classification**

6. PLATO : ARISTOTLE :: ARISTOTLE : (*a.* Socrates, *b.* Pythagoras, *c.* Euripedes, ***d.* Alexander**)
   (**d**) *Plato* was *Aristotle's* teacher, and *Aristotle* tutored *Alexander* the Great. (Long before that, Socrates taught Plato.) **Object/Action**

7. (*a.* Aga Khan, *b.* Shi Huangdi, ***c.* Genghis Khan,** *d.* Rasputin) : MONGOL :: HANNIBAL : CARTHAGINIAN
   (**c**) *Genghis Khan* was a *Mongolian* emperor, and *Hannibal* was a *Carthaginian* general.
   Characteristic

8. AUGUSTE COMTE : (***a.* positivism,** *b.* realism, *c.* pragmatism, *d.* sciencism) :: RENÉ DESCARTES : RATIONALISM
   (**a**) *Auguste Comte* was the founder of the *positivist* movement, which declared that human knowledge is limited to what can be observed. *René Descartes* was his polar opposite, a *rationalist* who felt that knowledge is derived through reason and logic.
   Object/Action

9. AUDUBON : BIRDS :: LINNAEUS : (*a.* apes, *b.* insects, ***c.* plants,** *d.* fish)
   (**c**) John James *Audubon* (1785–1851) was an artist and ornithologist known for his paintings of *birds.* Carl *Linnaeus* (1707–1778) was a botanist who was one of the first to classify the kingdom of *plants.* **Object/Action**

10. HILARITY : MELANCHOLY :: (*a.* fecundity, *b.* mirth, *c.* spite, *d.* **benevolence**) :
    MALICE
    (**d**) *Hilarity* is the opposite of *melancholy*, and *benevolence* (kindness) is the opposite of
    malice (meanness). **Antonym**

11. JOHN BOYD DUNLOP : (*a.* mountain bike, *b.* **pneumatic tire**, *c.* catalytic converter,
    d. motorcycle) :: LINUS YALE : CYLINDER LOCK
    (**b**) *John Boyd Dunlop* invented a *tire* in 1888, and Dunlop tires still come from the
    corporation he founded. *Linus Yale* invented a *cylinder lock* in the 1860s, and Yale
    locks still come from the corporation he founded. **Object/Action**

12. (*a.* Quebec City, *b.* Calgary, *c.* **Toronto**, *d.* Saskatoon) : ONTARIO :: WINNIPEG :
    MANITOBA
    (**c**) *Toronto* is the largest city in *Ontario*, Canada. *Winnipeg* is the largest city in
    Manitoba, Canada. **Characteristic**

13. GREEN : (*a.* defiance, *b.* despair, *c.* joy, *d.* **envy**) :: BLUE : SORROW
    (**d**) The color *green* represents *envy*. The color *blue* represents *sorrow*, or sadness.
    Object/Action

14. TORQUEMADA : MENGELE :: INQUISITION : (*a.* **Holocaust**, *b.* sedition,
    c. surgery, *d.* Reichstag)
    (**a**) Tomás de *Torquemada* was a key figure in the Spanish *Inquisition*, and Dr. Josef
    Mengele was a key figure in the *Holocaust*. Both names are now bywords for sadism.
    Characteristic

15. FOG : (*a.* translucency, *b.* droplets, *c.* **visibility**, *d.* pollutant) :: DIET : WEIGHT
    (**c**) *Fog* reduces *visibility*, and a *diet* reduces *weight*. **Object/Action**

16. (*a.* **delicate**, *b.* incapacitated, *c.* adequate, *d.* stalwart) : FEEBLE :: FIT : BRAWNY
    (**a**) If you are very *delicate*, you might be termed *feeble*. If you are very *fit*, you might
    be termed *brawny*. **Degree**

17. KARATE : TAI CHI :: JAPAN : (*a.* **China**, *b.* Korea, *c.* Malaysia, *d.* Nepal)
    (**a**) *Karate* is a *Japanese* martial art that emphasizes striking movements. *Tai chi* is a
    Chinese martial art that emphasizes balance and slow, repetitive movements.
    Characteristic

18. REFEREE : (*a.* game, *b.* **ruling**, *c.* competition, *d.* amendment) :: NAVIGATOR :
    COURSE
    (**b**) A *referee* generates a *ruling*, and a *navigator* generates a *course*. **Object/Action**

19. (*a.* Abram, *b.* Joshua, *c.* David, *d.* **Ishmael**) : HAGAR :: HAMLET : GERTRUDE
    (**d**) In the book of Genesis, *Ishmael* was the son of *Hagar*. In the Shakespearean
    tragedy that bears his name, *Hamlet* was the son of *Gertrude*. **Sequence**

20. TROLL : TEUTONIC :: (*a.* ogre, *b.* **brownie**, *c.* dryad, *d.* imp) : SCOTTISH
    (**b**) A *troll* is a creature from *Teutonic* folklore. A *brownie* is a creature from *Scottish*
    folklore. **Characteristic**

21. VACCINATION : INFECTION :: INSULATION : (*a.* building, *b.* infestation, *c.* heating, *d.* **conduction**)
    (**d**) A *vaccination* can prevent *infection*. *Insulation* can prevent *conduction* (transfer of heat). **Object/Action**

22. GROUNDHOG : WOODCHUCK :: (*a.* bobcat, *b.* raccoon, *c.* **skunk**, *d.* cougar) : POLECAT
    (**c**) *Groundhog* and *woodchuck* are regional names for the same rodent. *Skunk* and *polecat* are regional names for the same mustelid. **Synonym**

23. (*a.* **Zeus**, *b.* Atlas, *c.* Minerva, *d.* Prometheus) : JUPITER :: CRONUS : SATURN
    (**a**) *Zeus* is the Greek name for the god known as *Jupiter* by the Romans. *Cronus* (or Kronos) is the Greek name for the Titan known as *Saturn* by the Romans. **Conversion**

24. ICHTHYOLOGIST : (*a.* Atlantic, *b.* **cod**, *c.* cobra, *d.* macaw) :: HERPETOLOGIST : PYTHON
    (**b**) An *ichthyologist* might study *cod* or other species of fish. A *herpetologist* might study *pythons* or other species of snake. **Object/Action**

25. JEROME : JEREMIAH :: SAINT : (*a.* sinner, *b.* angel, *c.* **prophet**, *d.* apostle)
    (**c**) *Jerome* was an early translator of the Scriptures who was later *sainted*. *Jeremiah* was an Old Testament *prophet* known for his "jeremiads," or lamentations, on the fate of Jerusalem. **Classification**

26. (*a.* Momotaro, *b.* Canute, *c.* Achilles, *d.* **Gilgamesh**) : BABYLON :: BEOWULF : SCANDINAVIA
    (**d**) *Gilgamesh* was a hero of *Babylonian* and Sumerian legend. *Beowulf* was a hero of *Scandinavian* legend. **Characteristic**

27. STRATUS : CINDER CONE :: CLOUD : (*a.* tornado, *b.* cyclone, *c.* **volcano**, *d.* fire)
    (**c**) *Stratus* is one kind of *cloud*—a low, flat cloud. *Cinder cone* is one kind of *volcano*—a simple volcano with a single vent in a crater at the summit. **Classification**

28. (*a.* cow, *b.* **ram**, *c.* billy, *d.* bull) : OVINE :: TOM : FELINE
    (**b**) A *ram* is a male *ovine*, or sheep. A *tom* is a male *feline*, or cat. **Classification**

29. HERCULES : HYDRA :: (*a.* **Perseus**, *b.* Athena, *c.* Medusa, *d.* Heracles) : GORGON
    (**a**) According to legend, *Hercules* killed the *Hydra,* a monster with multiple heads, and *Perseus* killed the *Gorgon* Medusa, a monster with snakes for hair. **Object/Action**

30. REFUSE : (*a.* monarch, *b.* **dross**, *c.* defiance, *d.* correlation) :: RULER : SOVEREIGN
    (**b**) In its meaning of "garbage," *refuse* means the same as *dross*. In its meaning of "leader," *ruler* means the same as *sovereign*. **Synonym**

31. GYMNOSPERM : ANGIOSPERM :: (*a.* **pine**, *b.* algae, *c.* maple, *d.* corn) : OAK
    (**a**) *Gymnosperms* such as *pine* trees have no flowers to protect their seeds. *Angiosperms* such as *oak* trees have seed-bearing flowers. **Classification**

32. (*a.* airstream, *b.* gale, *c.* **doldrums**, *d.* current) : WIND :: STALEMATE : MOVEMENT
(**c**) *Doldrums* are characterized by a lack of *wind*. A *stalemate*, as in a battle or game of chess, is characterized by a lack of *movement*. **Characteristic**

33. ENCOURAGE : INCITE :: DISAGREE : (*a.* **rebel**, *b.* disapprove, *c.* concur, *d.* insist)
(**a**) To *encourage* strongly is to *incite*. To *disagree* strongly is to *rebel*. **Degree**

34. KENNEDY : JOHNSON :: (*a.* Carter, *b.* **Nixon**, *c.* Reagan, *d.* Dole) : FORD
(**b**) Lyndon *Johnson* was John F. *Kennedy's* vice president and completed his unfinished term of office. Gerald *Ford* was one of Richard *Nixon's* vice presidents and completed his unfinished term of office. **Sequence**

35. PABLO PICASSO : (*a.* Gala, *b.* Malaga, *c.* **Gertrude Stein**, *d.* Guernica) :: ANDREW WYETH : HELGA
(**c**) One of *Picasso's* most famous human subjects was the poet *Gertrude Stein*. One of *Andrew Wyeth's* most famous human subjects was his neighbor *Helga*. **Object/Action**

36. PLANET : SOLAR SYSTEM :: STAR : (*a.* planet, *b.* supernova, *c.* gas, *d.* **galaxy**)
(**d**) A *planet* is part of the *solar system*. A *star* is part of a *galaxy*. **Part/Whole**

37. DIENBIENPHU : (*a.* Chinese, *b.* Vietnamese, *c.* **French**, *d.* Americans) :: YORKTOWN : BRITISH
(**c**) A battle at *Dienbienphu* marked the *French* defeat in Indochina. A battle at *Yorktown* marked the *British* defeat in America. **Characteristic**

38. (*a.* damaging, *b.* elderly, *c.* **fond**, *d.* uncaring) : DOTING :: HARMFUL : DESTRUCTIVE
(**c**) To be overly *fond* is to be *doting*. To be overly *harmful* is to be *destructive*. **Degree**

39. GRANDILOQUENT : (*a.* **straightforward**, *b.* clumsy, *c.* pompous, *d.* lissome) :: GRACEFUL : UNGAINLY
(**a**) *Grandiloquent*, or long-winded, is the opposite of *straightforward*. *Graceful* is the opposite of *ungainly*. **Antonym**

40. HELIX : HELICES :: AX : (*a.* axe, *b.* axis, *c.* **axes**, *d.* aces)
(**c**) The plural of *helix* is *helices*. The plural of *ax* is *axes*. **Conversion**

41. KRONE : (*a.* Berlin, *b.* Bonn, *c.* bund, *d.* **mark**) :: NORWAY : GERMANY
(**d**) The *krone* is the traditional currency of *Norway*. The *mark* is the traditional currency of *Germany*. **Characteristic**

42. OMNI- : PERI- :: ALL : (*a.* **around**, *b.* approximately, *c.* outside, *d.* made of)
(**a**) The prefix *omni-*, as in *omnipresent*, means "*all*." The prefix *peri-*, as in *pericardium*, means "*around*." **Affix**

43. RIIS : NEW YORK TENEMENTS :: (*a.* Tarbell, *b.* Lewis, *c.* **Sinclair**, *d.* Agee) : CHICAGO STOCKYARDS
(**c**) Muckraker Jacob *Riis* was one of the first photojournalists. His photographs of life in the slums, published in a book called *How the Other Half Lives,* led to reforms. Muckraker Upton *Sinclair's* exposé of the *Chicago stockyards*, *The Jungle*, had a similar effect. **Object/Action**

44. (*a.* Esperanza, *b.* Good Will, *c.* Santiago, *d.* **Horn**) : GOOD HOPE :: CHILE : SOUTH AFRICA
    (**d**) Cape *Horn*, the southernmost tip of South America, is part of *Chile*. Cape of *Good Hope*, the southernmost tip of Africa, is in *South Africa*. **Characteristic**

45. BLACK GOLD : FOOL'S GOLD :: OIL : (*a.* mineral, *b.* **pyrite**, *c.* water, *d.* mica)
    (**b**) *Black gold* is a nickname for *oil*. *Fool's gold* is a nickname for the brass-colored mineral called *pyrite*. **Synonym**

46. DAPHNE : (*a.* fawn, *b.* reflection, *c.* **laurel tree**, *d.* amaryllis) :: CALLISTO : BEAR
    (**c**) According to myth, the nymph *Daphne* was transformed into a *laurel tree* to escape Apollo's clutches. The nymph *Callisto* was changed into a *bear* as punishment for having an affair with Zeus. **Conversion**

47. NOSE : FACE :: DIAL : (*a.* knob, *b.* visage, *c.* touchtone, *d.* **watch**)
    (**d**) A *nose* is part of a *face*, and a *dial* is part of a *watch*. **Part/Whole**

48. (*a.* Balmoral Castle, *b.* **Buckingham Palace**, *c.* Royal Mews, *d.* Winchester Cathedral) : QUEEN ELIZABETH II :: VATICAN : POPE BENEDICT XVI
    (**b**) *Buckingham Palace* is a primary residence of *Queen Elizabeth*, and the *Vatican* is the primary residence of the *pope*. **Characteristic**

49. PICA : (*a.* agate, *b.* stone, *c.* **type**, *d.* leather) :: BOLT : CLOTH
    (**c**) The *pica* is a unit (equal to 1/6 inch) used to measure *type* size. The *bolt* is a unit used to measure *cloth*. **Object/Action**

50. BRASS : COPPER :: (*a.* aluminum, *b.* **steel**, *c.* nickel, *d.* tungsten) : IRON
    (**b**) One ingredient of *brass* is *copper*. One ingredient of *steel* is *iron*. **Part/Whole**

51. CHARLES LAMB : ELIA :: CHARLES DICKENS : (*a.* **Boz**, *b.* Pickwick, *c.* Pip, *d.* Dora)
    (**a**) *Charles Lamb* wrote essays under the pen name *Elia*. *Charles Dickens* wrote essays under the pen name *Boz*. **Conversion**

52. (*a.* climax, *b.* **denouement**, *c.* structure, *d.* overture) : BEGINNING :: FINALE : PRELUDE
    (**b**) The *denouement* of a story is the ending, or the opposite of the *beginning*. The *finale* of a composition is the ending, or the opposite of the *prelude*. **Antonym**

53. SOLZHENITSYN : CANCER WARD :: (*a.* Kesey, *b.* Grass, *c.* Bellow, *d.* **Mann**) : SANATORIUM
    (**d**) The setting of Alexander *Solzhenitsyn's* novel *The Cancer Ward* is a *cancer ward*. The setting of Thomas Mann's novel *The Magic Mountain* is a tuberculosis *sanatorium*. **Object/Action**

54. (*a.* Orinoco, *b.* Guyana, *c.* **Amazon**, *d.* Tierra del Fuego) : SOUTH AMERICA :: YANGTZE : ASIA
    (**c**) The *Amazon* is the longest river in *South America*. The *Yangtze* is the longest river in *Asia*. (The Orinoco is in South America, but it is not the longest river there.) **Characteristic**

55. SHRUG : NONCHALANCE :: NOD : (*a.* insouciance, *b.* **acquiescence**, *c.* alliance, *d.* ascendancy)
(**b**) You might *shrug* to show *nonchalance*, or indifference. You might *nod* to show *acquiescence*, or agreement. **Object/Action**

56. SURREALISM : REALISM :: DALÍ : (*a.* Ernst, *b.* Gorky, *c.* Chagall, *d.* **Daumier**)
(**d**) Salvador *Dalí* was a painter of *surrealist* paintings. Honoré *Daumier* is known for his *realistic* lithographs of the lower classes. **Classification**

57. SQUARE : CUBE :: (*a.* rectangle, *b.* **triangle**, *c.* rhombus, *d.* pentagon) : TETRAHEDRON
(**b**) A *cube* has six *square* faces. A *tetrahedron* has four *triangular* faces. **Part/Whole**

58. (*a.* **philatelist**, *b.* numismatist, *c.* audiophile, *d.* phillumenist) : STAMPS :: BIBLIOPHILE : BOOKS
(**a**) A *philatelist* is a *stamp* collector, and a *bibliophile* is a lover of *books*. **Object/Action**

59. RETICENT : RETICULE :: RESERVED : (*a.* shyness, *b.* superstition, *c.* **purse**, *d.* compost)
(**c**) If you are *reticent*, you are *reserved*, or shy. A *reticule* is a small drawstring *purse*. **Synonym**

60. 1948 : (*a.* scooter and deodorant, *b.* skateboard and polystyrene, *c.* **Frisbee and Velcro**, *d.* Slinky and hairspray) :: 1958 : HULA HOOP AND LASER
(**c**) The year *1948* saw the invention of the *Frisbee and Velcro*. The year *1958* saw the invention of the *hula hoop and laser*. **Characteristic**

61. (*a.* **moon**, *b.* planet, *c.* rocket, *d.* aircraft) : SATELLITE :: EUROPA : SPUTNIK
(**a**) *Europa* is one of the *moons* of Jupiter. *Sputnik* was an early mechanical *satellite*. **Classification**

62. CIVIL WAR : (*a.* Confederacy, *b.* **Reconstruction**, *c.* War Between the States, *d.* uprising) :: WORLD WAR I : WEIMAR REPUBLIC
(**b**) *Reconstruction* named the post-*Civil War* period in the South. The *Weimar Republic* named the post-*World War I* period in Germany. **Sequence**

63. (*a.* industrious, *b.* aloof, *c.* **collegial**, *d.* unflappable) : SOCIABLE :: UNPRODUCTIVE : BARREN
(**c**) To be *collegial* is to be *sociable*, or friendly. To be *unproductive* is to be *barren*, or infertile. **Synonym**

64. EDEN : JUDAS :: (*a.* **innocence**, *b.* fidelity, *c.* garden, *d.* forgetfulness) : BETRAYAL
(**a**) Based on their images in the Bible, *Eden*, the home of Adam and Eve, often represents *innocence*, whereas *Judas*, who pointed out Jesus to the Romans, represents *betrayal*. **Object/Action**

65. (*a.* shire, *b.* **canton**, *c.* province, *d.* stadt) : SWITZERLAND :: DEPARTMENT : FRANCE
(**b**) The country of *Switzerland* is divided into administrative units called *cantons*. Similar units in *France* are called *departments*. **Part/Whole**

66. COMMUNARD : DECEMBRIST :: PARIS : (*a.* London, *b.* Berlin, *c.* **St. Petersburg**, *d.* Tehran)
   (**c**) The original *Communards* were members of the socialist *Paris* Commune of 1871. The *Decembrists* were participants in an 1825 rebellion against Czar Nicholas I in *St. Petersburg*, Russia. **Characteristic**

67. GALEN : (*a.* philosophy, *b.* politics, *c.* poetry, *d.* **medicine**) :: HERODOTUS : HISTORY
   (**d**) *Galen* was a physician of ancient Greece whose views dominated *medicine* well into the middle ages. *Herodotus* was a historian whose writings on the Persian Wars altered the way humans recorded *history*—from the narrative poem to the well-researched, philosophical treatise. **Object/Action**

68. COLLECTED : DISPERSED :: CLEANSED : (*a.* **polluted**, *b.* dissolved, *c.* purified, *d.* baptized)
   (**a**) *Collected* is the opposite of *dispersed*, or scattered. *Cleansed* is the opposite of *polluted*, or contaminated. **Antonym**

69. THREE : TWO :: (*a.* semicircle, *b.* **sphere**, *c.* radius, *d.* orbit) : CIRCLE
   (**b**) A *sphere* has three *dimensions*, and a *circle* has *two*. **Characteristic**

70. DOSTOEVSKY : *THE IDIOT* :: GIDE : (*a. The Innocents Abroad*, *b. The Independent*, *c. The Inheritors*, *d. **The Immoralist***)
   (**d**) Fyodor *Dostoevsky's The Idiot* tells the story of a saintly fool. André *Gide's The Immoralist* is the tale of a man whose brush with death leads him to indulge his passions at the expense of those around him. **Object/Action**

71. (*a.* ukulele, *b.* **flute**, *c.* fruit, *d.* superior) : LUTE :: FLOWER : LOWER
   (**b**) Removing the *f* from *flute* leaves *lute*. Removing the *f* from *flower* leaves *lower*. **Conversion**

72. PREVALENT : ATYPICAL :: (*a.* hygienic, *b.* contiguous, *c.* common, *d.* **decadent**) : UNSULLIED
   (**d**) If something is *prevalent*, or common, it is not *atypical*. If something is *decadent*, or corrupt, it is not *unsullied*. **Antonym**

73. SMARMY : (*a.* **unctuous**, *b.* trite, *c.* audacious, *d.* misshapen) :: BLAND : INSIPID
   (**a**) *Smarmy* means "oily," or *unctuous*. *Bland* means "dull," or *insipid*. **Synonym**

74. REINS : HORSE :: (*a.* hatch, *b.* motor, *c.* **rudder**, *d.* mainsail) : VESSEL
   (**c**) You would use *reins* to steer a *horse*, and you would use a *rudder* to steer a *vessel*. **Object/Action**

75. SHORTCOMING : VIRTUE :: ENTROPY : (*a.* time, *b.* **order**, *c.* exit, *d.* vice)
   (**b**) A *shortcoming* is the antithesis of a *virtue*. In physics, *entropy* is a measure of disorder and is thus the antithesis of *order*. **Antonym**

76. THUMB : GRASPING :: (*a.* fibula, *b.* wrist, *c.* **arch**, *d.* ligament) : SHOCK ABSORPTION
   (**c**) Your *thumb* aids in *grasping* objects. The *arch* of your foot aids in *shock absorption* from the weight of your body against the floor or ground. **Object/Action**

77. ANIMAL CELL : (*a.* **cell wall**, *b.* nucleus, *c.* mitochondrion, *d.* vacuole) :: PLANT CELL : CENTRIOLE
(**a**) Unlike a plant cell, an *animal cell* lacks a *cell wall.* Unlike an animal cell, a *plant cell* lacks a *centriole.* **Characteristic**

78. ROSSINI : PUCCINI :: *THE BARBER OF SEVILLE* : (*a. The Magic Flute,* *b. La Traviata, c. Parsifal,* ***d. Madame Butterfly***)
(**d**) *The Barber of Seville* is an 1816 opera by Gioacchino *Rossini. Madame Butterfly* is a 1904 opera by Giacomo *Puccini.* **Object/Action**

79. MY LAI : (*a.* Ruby Ridge, *b.* Bitterroot Valley, *c.* **Wounded Knee**, *d.* Battle of Fallen Timbers) :: VIETNAM WAR : INDIAN WARS
(**c**) *My Lai* was the site of a massacre during the *Vietnam War. Wounded Knee* was the site of a massacre during the *Indian Wars.* **Characteristic**

80. (*a.* hammer, *b.* pulley, *c.* **vice**, *d.* handshake) : GRIP :: CORKSCREW : PULL
(**c**) A *vice* is a tool whose purpose is to *grip.* A *corkscrew* is a tool whose purpose is to *pull.* **Object/Action**

81. BOBCAT : OCELOT :: WOLF : (*a.* puma, *b.* **coyote**, *c.* elk, *d.* panther)
(**b**) *Bobcats* and *ocelots* are felines. *Wolves* and *coyotes* are canines. **Part/Whole**

82. MARIA TALLCHIEF : (*a.* watercolor, *b.* folkdance, *c.* photography, *d.* **ballet**) :: ELEANOR POWELL : TAP
(**d**) *Maria Tallchief* was a prima *ballerina* with the Ballet Russe de Monte Carlo and the New York City Ballet. *Eleanor Powell* was a movie actress and *tap* dancer of the 1930s. **Object/Action**

83. 2% : 5% :: 40% : (*a.* 1%, *b.* 50%, *c.* 60%, *d.* **100%**)
(**d**) If this were set up as a ratio, the relationship between *2%* and *5%* would be equivalent to that between *40%* and *100%*—2 to 5. **Sequence**

84. QUILTING : FOLK ART :: (*a.* retablo, *b.* basketry, *c.* **portraiture**, *d.* embroidery) : FINE ART
(**c**) All the art forms listed are *folk art* with the exception of *portraiture*, which is *fine art*—art produced for beauty rather than usefulness. **Classification**

85. COUSTEAU : UNDERSEA :: SHEPARD : (*a.* mountains, *b.* **space**, *c.* underground, *d.* overland)
(**b**) Jacques *Cousteau* was an explorer of the *undersea* world, and Alan *Shepard* was an explorer of outer *space.* **Characteristic**

86. BECKETT : GODOT :: ODETS : (*a.* Moe, *b.* Golden Boy, *c.* **Lefty**, *d.* McCarthy)
(**c**) Samuel *Beckett* wrote a play entitled *Waiting for Godot.* Clifford *Odets* wrote a play entitled *Waiting for Lefty.* **Object/Action**

87. (*a.* enzyme, *b.* **steroid**, *c.* lipid, *d.* catalyst) : PROGESTERONE :: VITAMIN : FOLIC ACID
(**b**) *Progesterone* is one kind of *steroid. Folic acid* is one kind of *vitamin.* **Classification**

88. (*a.* Balboa, *b.* Velasquez, *c.* Chevrolet, ***d.* Cabrillo**) : CALIFORNIA :: CADILLAC : MICHIGAN

    (d) Portuguese explorer Juan Rodriguez *Cabrillo* sailed up the *California* coast, discovering and naming San Diego Bay and Santa Barbara as he went. French explorer Antonie de *Cadillac* explored the Great Lakes region and founded the city of Detroit, *Michigan*. **Object/Action**

89. FENCING : PENTATHLON :: (***a.* pole vaulting**, *b.* swimming, *c.* archery, *d.* equestrian show jumping) : DECATHLON

    (a) The modern *pentathlon* is an athletic contest that features five events—running, swimming, horseback riding, *fencing*, and pistol shooting. A *decathlon* is an athletic contest that features ten track-and-field events, including *pole vaulting*. **Part/Whole**

90. BEHAVIORISM : (*a.* sociology, ***b.* psychology**, *c.* zoology, *d.* archeology) :: AESTHETICS : PHILOSOPHY

    (b) *Behaviorism*—the study of stimulus and response—is one branch of *psychology*. *Aesthetics*—the study of art and beauty—is one branch of *philosophy*. **Classification**

91. SHOWY : GARISH :: (*a.* sturdy, *b.* blowsy, *c.* gaudy, ***d.* wordy**) : PROLIX

    (d) Something that is terribly *showy* is *garish*. Something that is terribly *wordy* is *prolix*. **Degree**

92. *LA BOHÈME* : (***a. Les Sylphides***, *b. Les Troyens*, *c. Les Huguenots*, *d. La Belle Hélène*) :: OPERA : BALLET

    (a) *La Bohème* is an *opera* by Puccini. *Les Sylphides* is a *ballet* set to music by Chopin. **Classification**

93. ACOUSTICS : (*a.* visions, *b.* lumière, ***c.* optics**, *d.* prism) :: SOUND : LIGHT

    (c) *Acoustics* is the science of *sound*. *Optics* is the science of *light*. **Characteristic**

94. (***a.* etymology**, *b.* verbosity, *c.* otiology, *d.* entomology) : WORDS :: GERONTOLOGY : AGING

    (a) An *etymologist* studies language and *words*. A *gerontologist* specializes in *aging*. **Object/Action**

95. MERRILY : (*a.* merriment, *b.* merrymaking, ***c.* merry**, *d.* merry-go-round) :: ADVERB : ADJECTIVE

    (c) The word *merrily* is an *adverb*. It modifies the verb *roll* in "Merrily we roll along." The word *merry* is an *adjective*. It modifies the noun *Christmas* in "We wish you a merry Christmas." **Classification**

96. (*a.* Honduras, ***b.* Belize**, *c.* Brunei, *d.* Botswana) : BRITISH HONDURAS :: GUYANA : BRITISH GUIANA

    (b) The Central American country of *Belize* was formerly known as *British Honduras*. The South American country of *Guyana* was formerly known as *British Guiana*. **Conversion**

97. SMUG : SMUT :: HUMBLE : (*a.* subservience, *b.* superciliousness, *c.* plenitude, *d.* **wholesomeness**)

(**d**) The opposite of *smug*, or self-satisfied, is *humble*. The opposite of *smut*, or obscenity, is *wholesomeness*. **Antonym**

98. (*a.* **hatchery**, *b.* fisher, *c.* tarn, *d.* egg) : FISH :: NURSERY : TREE

(**a**) You can raise *fish* in a *hatchery*, and you can raise *trees* in a *nursery*. **Object/Action**

99. SOCCER : SHIN GUARDS :: (*a.* polo, *b.* softball, *c.* hockey, *d.* **lacrosse**) : ARM PADS

(**d**) *Soccer* players wear protective *shin guards*. *Lacrosse* players wear protective *arm pads*. **Characteristic**

100. AESOP : FABLES :: (*a.* **Perrault**, *b.* Singer, *c.* Lindgren, *d.* Alcott) : FAIRY TALES

(**a**) *Aesop* was a Greek *fabulist* who lived around 600 B.C. Charles *Perrault* (1628–1703) was a French writer known for collecting and publishing *fairy tales*. **Object/Action**

PRACTICE TEST 8
ANSWER SHEET

1. Ⓐ Ⓑ Ⓒ Ⓓ
2. Ⓐ Ⓑ Ⓒ Ⓓ
3. Ⓐ Ⓑ Ⓒ Ⓓ
4. Ⓐ Ⓑ Ⓒ Ⓓ
5. Ⓐ Ⓑ Ⓒ Ⓓ
6. Ⓐ Ⓑ Ⓒ Ⓓ
7. Ⓐ Ⓑ Ⓒ Ⓓ
8. Ⓐ Ⓑ Ⓒ Ⓓ
9. Ⓐ Ⓑ Ⓒ Ⓓ
10. Ⓐ Ⓑ Ⓒ Ⓓ
11. Ⓐ Ⓑ Ⓒ Ⓓ
12. Ⓐ Ⓑ Ⓒ Ⓓ
13. Ⓐ Ⓑ Ⓒ Ⓓ
14. Ⓐ Ⓑ Ⓒ Ⓓ
15. Ⓐ Ⓑ Ⓒ Ⓓ
16. Ⓐ Ⓑ Ⓒ Ⓓ
17. Ⓐ Ⓑ Ⓒ Ⓓ
18. Ⓐ Ⓑ Ⓒ Ⓓ
19. Ⓐ Ⓑ Ⓒ Ⓓ
20. Ⓐ Ⓑ Ⓒ Ⓓ
21. Ⓐ Ⓑ Ⓒ Ⓓ
22. Ⓐ Ⓑ Ⓒ Ⓓ
23. Ⓐ Ⓑ Ⓒ Ⓓ
24. Ⓐ Ⓑ Ⓒ Ⓓ
25. Ⓐ Ⓑ Ⓒ Ⓓ

26. Ⓐ Ⓑ Ⓒ Ⓓ
27. Ⓐ Ⓑ Ⓒ Ⓓ
28. Ⓐ Ⓑ Ⓒ Ⓓ
29. Ⓐ Ⓑ Ⓒ Ⓓ
30. Ⓐ Ⓑ Ⓒ Ⓓ
31. Ⓐ Ⓑ Ⓒ Ⓓ
32. Ⓐ Ⓑ Ⓒ Ⓓ
33. Ⓐ Ⓑ Ⓒ Ⓓ
34. Ⓐ Ⓑ Ⓒ Ⓓ
35. Ⓐ Ⓑ Ⓒ Ⓓ
36. Ⓐ Ⓑ Ⓒ Ⓓ
37. Ⓐ Ⓑ Ⓒ Ⓓ
38. Ⓐ Ⓑ Ⓒ Ⓓ
39. Ⓐ Ⓑ Ⓒ Ⓓ
40. Ⓐ Ⓑ Ⓒ Ⓓ
41. Ⓐ Ⓑ Ⓒ Ⓓ
42. Ⓐ Ⓑ Ⓒ Ⓓ
43. Ⓐ Ⓑ Ⓒ Ⓓ
44. Ⓐ Ⓑ Ⓒ Ⓓ
45. Ⓐ Ⓑ Ⓒ Ⓓ
46. Ⓐ Ⓑ Ⓒ Ⓓ
47. Ⓐ Ⓑ Ⓒ Ⓓ
48. Ⓐ Ⓑ Ⓒ Ⓓ
49. Ⓐ Ⓑ Ⓒ Ⓓ
50. Ⓐ Ⓑ Ⓒ Ⓓ

51. Ⓐ Ⓑ Ⓒ Ⓓ
52. Ⓐ Ⓑ Ⓒ Ⓓ
53. Ⓐ Ⓑ Ⓒ Ⓓ
54. Ⓐ Ⓑ Ⓒ Ⓓ
55. Ⓐ Ⓑ Ⓒ Ⓓ
56. Ⓐ Ⓑ Ⓒ Ⓓ
57. Ⓐ Ⓑ Ⓒ Ⓓ
58. Ⓐ Ⓑ Ⓒ Ⓓ
59. Ⓐ Ⓑ Ⓒ Ⓓ
60. Ⓐ Ⓑ Ⓒ Ⓓ
61. Ⓐ Ⓑ Ⓒ Ⓓ
62. Ⓐ Ⓑ Ⓒ Ⓓ
63. Ⓐ Ⓑ Ⓒ Ⓓ
64. Ⓐ Ⓑ Ⓒ Ⓓ
65. Ⓐ Ⓑ Ⓒ Ⓓ
66. Ⓐ Ⓑ Ⓒ Ⓓ
67. Ⓐ Ⓑ Ⓒ Ⓓ
68. Ⓐ Ⓑ Ⓒ Ⓓ
69. Ⓐ Ⓑ Ⓒ Ⓓ
70. Ⓐ Ⓑ Ⓒ Ⓓ
71. Ⓐ Ⓑ Ⓒ Ⓓ
72. Ⓐ Ⓑ Ⓒ Ⓓ
73. Ⓐ Ⓑ Ⓒ Ⓓ
74. Ⓐ Ⓑ Ⓒ Ⓓ
75. Ⓐ Ⓑ Ⓒ Ⓓ

76. Ⓐ Ⓑ Ⓒ Ⓓ
77. Ⓐ Ⓑ Ⓒ Ⓓ
78. Ⓐ Ⓑ Ⓒ Ⓓ
79. Ⓐ Ⓑ Ⓒ Ⓓ
80. Ⓐ Ⓑ Ⓒ Ⓓ
81. Ⓐ Ⓑ Ⓒ Ⓓ
82. Ⓐ Ⓑ Ⓒ Ⓓ
83. Ⓐ Ⓑ Ⓒ Ⓓ
84. Ⓐ Ⓑ Ⓒ Ⓓ
85. Ⓐ Ⓑ Ⓒ Ⓓ
86. Ⓐ Ⓑ Ⓒ Ⓓ
87. Ⓐ Ⓑ Ⓒ Ⓓ
88. Ⓐ Ⓑ Ⓒ Ⓓ
89. Ⓐ Ⓑ Ⓒ Ⓓ
90. Ⓐ Ⓑ Ⓒ Ⓓ
91. Ⓐ Ⓑ Ⓒ Ⓓ
92. Ⓐ Ⓑ Ⓒ Ⓓ
93. Ⓐ Ⓑ Ⓒ Ⓓ
94. Ⓐ Ⓑ Ⓒ Ⓓ
95. Ⓐ Ⓑ Ⓒ Ⓓ
96. Ⓐ Ⓑ Ⓒ Ⓓ
97. Ⓐ Ⓑ Ⓒ Ⓓ
98. Ⓐ Ⓑ Ⓒ Ⓓ
99. Ⓐ Ⓑ Ⓒ Ⓓ
100. Ⓐ Ⓑ Ⓒ Ⓓ

PRACTICE TEST 8

Directions: For each question, you will see three capitalized words and four answer choices labeled *a, b, c,* and *d* in parentheses. Choose the answer that best completes the analogy posed by the three capitalized words. Use the answer sheet on page 181 to record your answers.

Time: 50 Minutes

1. BOTICELLI : FLORENTINE :: BRUEGEL : (*a.* French, *b.* Teutonic, *c.* Flemish, *d.* Venetian)

2. MUTTON : SHEEP :: (*a.* veal, *b.* venison, *c.* tenderloin, *d.* prime rib) : CALF

3. JOCASTA : (*a.* Oedipus, *b.* Eurydice, *c.* Laius, *d.* Antigone) :: CASSIOPEIA : ANDROMEDA

4. (*a.* intelligentsia, *b.* absolute ruler, *c.* Satan, *d.* wealthy) : PLUTOCRACY :: GOD : THEOCRACY

5. CRINGE : FEAR :: SNEER : (*a.* courage, *b.* indifference, *c.* contempt, *d.* indignation)

6. CONNECTION : CORRELATION :: (*a.* granite, *b.* division, *c.* bond, *d.* vacuum) : SCHISM

7. (*a.* Frederick II, *b.* Henry II, *c.* Philip II, *d.* George II) : THE GREAT :: IVAN IV : THE TERRIBLE

8. SHAW : (*a.* radical individualism, *b.* satirical utopianism, *c.* Fabian socialism, *d.* millennialism) :: SARTRE : EXISTENTIALISM

9. SHOAT : PIG :: CYGNET : (*a.* swan, *b.* stork, *c.* swallow, *d.* sandpiper)

10. STOMATA : (*a.* differentiation, *b.* respiration, *c.* growth, *d.* circulation) :: STOMACH : DIGESTION

11. FOURTH ESTATE : PRESS :: FIFTH COLUMN : (*a.* poor, *b.* upper classes, *c.* subversives, *d.* plebes)

12. UNTOUCHABLE : CASTE :: (*a.* Muslim, *b.* Athenian, *c.* Hutterite, *d.* Pict) : SECT

13. (*a.* moonstone, *b.* beryl, *c.* spinel, *d.* sapphire) : AMETHYST :: YELLOW : PURPLE

14. OPTIMISTIC : TRIUMPHANT :: LUKEWARM : (*a.* celebratory, *b.* keen, *c.* fluid, *d.* apathetic)

15. (*a.* New Year, *b.* Boxing Day, *c.* Advent, *d.* gifted) : LENT :: CHRISTMAS : EASTER

16. *WAR AND PEACE* : *CRIME AND PUNISHMENT* :: (*a.* Chekhov, *b.* Tolstoy, *c.* Pasternak, *d.* Gogol) : DOSTOEVSKY

17. (*a.* Proverbs, *b.* Judges, *c.* Numbers, *d.* Matthew) : PENTATEUCH :: MARK : GOSPEL

18. ELLESMERE : ARCTIC OCEAN :: (*a.* Ibiza, *b.* Malta, *c.* Vanuatu, *d.* Sumatra) : INDIAN OCEAN

19. JAR : (*a.* container, *b.* confound, *c.* scrape, *d.* jolt) :: STARTLE : STUN

20. (*a.* hue, *b.* color, *c.* tint, *d.* pale) : WHITE :: SHADE : BLACK

21. BURR : (*a.* sticking, *b.* sprinkling, *c.* digging, *d.* filing) :: SHEARS : PRUNING

22. VITREOUS HUMOR : EYE :: (*a.* gray matter, *b.* lens, *c.* vertebra, *d.* column) : SPINAL CORD

23. ABLE : (*a.* dossier, *b.* life, *c.* escape, *d.* flee) :: BALE : FILE

24. GARRULOUS : TACITURN :: ARTICULATE : (*a.* expressive, *b.* reticulate, *c.* pacific, *d.* incoherent)

25. CALVIN CYCLE : GLUCOSE :: CELLULAR RESPIRATION : (*a.* sucrose, *b.* H_2O, *c.* carbon, *d.* ATP)

26. (*a.* Ulysses, *b.* Vulcan, *c.* Mercury, *d.* Apollo) : SPEED :: VENUS : BEAUTY

27. (*a.* phrenologist, *b.* pharmacist, *c.* pathologist, *d.* psychometrist) : DISEASE :: SEISMOLOGIST : EARTHQUAKE

28. EPISTOLARY : PICARESQUE :: (*a. Emma*, *b. Jane Eyre*, *c. Daisy Miller*, *d. Pamela*) : *CANDIDE*

29. SCALE : FISH :: (*a.* chimney, *b.* shingle, *c.* insulation, *d.* ceiling) : ROOF

30. WILLIAM THE CONQUEROR : (*a.* Versailles, *b.* Hampton Court, *c.* Windsor Castle, *d.* Kensington Palace) :: KING LUDWIG : LINDERHOF CASTLE

31. (*a.* noxious, *b.* righteous, *c.* fractious, *d.* imperturbable) : EVEN-TEMPERED :: UNFAIR : EVEN-HANDED

32. HEDONISM : PLEASURE :: UTILITARIANISM : (*a.* work, *b.* prosperity, *c.* harmony, *d.* happiness)

33. SILICON : (*a.* conductivity, *b.* rarity, *c.* magnetism, *d.* irregularity) :: X-RAY : PENETRATION

34. FURY : HOLY :: (*a.* ire, *b.* Noël, *c.* hallowed, *d.* furry) : HOLLY

35. (*a.* intrepid, *b.* pusillanimous, *c.* complex, *d.* unsophisticated) : INTRICATE :: COWARDLY : SIMPLE

36. KINDLE : IGNITE :: DWINDLE : (*a.* detonate, *b.* reduce, *c.* spin, *d.* embed)

37. PACKHORSE : (*a.* tote, *b.* bundle, *c.* hoof, *d.* saddle) :: WATCHDOG : GUARD

38. (*a.* nervous, *b.* eventful, *c.* energetic, *d.* congested) : ENERVATED :: POPULOUS : DESOLATE

39. CHRISTIAN : SALVATION :: (*a.* Pilgrim, *b.* Perceval, *c.* Buddhist, *d.* Avalon) : GRAIL

40. WOODWORKER : (*a.* nail, *b.* lathe, *c.* carpenter, *d.* frame) :: SCULPTOR : CHISEL

41. (*a.* composer, *b.* perishable, *c.* producer, *d.* collector) : SEAWEED :: DECOMPOSER : FUNGUS

42. (*a.* remote control, *b.* digital camera, *c.* robot, *d.* photocopier) : STATIC ELECTRICITY :: DISK DRIVE : ELECTROMAGNETISM

43. SPIRACLE : (*a.* grasshopper, *b.* palmetto, *c.* oyster, *d.* moss) :: GILL : FISH

44. BASIL : GINGER :: (*a.* fruit, *b.* pod, *c.* leaf, *d.* stem) : ROOT

45. ABRUPT : RUDE :: LONG : (*a.* coarse, *b.* brief, *c.* thin, *d.* protracted)

46. HENRY IV : (*a.* House of York, *b.* House of Windsor, *c.* House of Lancaster, *d.* House of Stuart) :: HENRY VIII : HOUSE OF TUDOR

47. SALTPETER : EXPLOSIVES :: METHANE : (*a.* cattle, *b.* natural gas, *c.* ethanol, *d.* petroleum)

48. (*a.* Isaac Stern, *b.* Yehudi Menuhin, *c.* Yo Yo Ma, *d.* Pinchas Zukerman) : CELLO :: ITZHAK PERLMAN : VIOLIN

49. ECRU : BEIGE :: CHARTREUSE : (*a.* red, *b.* yellow, *c.* orange, *d.* green)

50. AMOEBA : (*a.* protozoan, *b.* hydra, *c.* cytoplasm, *d.* pseudopod) :: PARAMECIUM : CILIA

51. (*a.* vascular, *b.* digitalis, *c.* inhibitor, *d.* platelet) : BLOOD FLOW :: COAGULANT : BLOOD CLOT

52. PRADO : (*a.* Madrid, *b.* Lisbon, *c.* Venice, *d.* Rome) :: LOUVRE : PARIS

53. *ILIAD : AENEID* :: HOMER : (*a.* Ovid, *b.* Dryden, *c.* Aeschylus, *d.* Virgil)

54. (*a.* egret, *b.* sandpiper, *c.* osprey, *d.* loon) : BITTERN :: GULL : TERN

55. LINES : (*a.* polygon, *b.* arc, *c.* end point, *d.* perpendicular) :: PARALLEL LINES : INTERSECTION

56. (*a.* C, *b.* E, *c.* F, *d.* B) : D :: G : A

57. HEBREW : SEMITIC :: TAHITIAN : (*a.* Chinese, *b.* Polynesian, *c.* Samoan, *d.* Christian)

58. (*a.* Copley Square, *b.* London, *c.* Prague, *d.* Berlin) : 1968 :: TIANANMEN SQUARE : 1989

59. 1/2 : (*a.* 2/3, *b.* 1/4, *c.* 1/10, *d.* 2/5) :: 1/3 : 1/9

60. HUDSON : NORTHEAST :: (*a.* Aviles, *b.* De Soto, *c.* Coronado, *d.* Vespucci) : SOUTHWEST

61. (*a.* predictive, *b.* close-minded, *c.* far-fetched, *d.* doomed) : PROPHETIC :: TACTLESS : INSENSITIVE

62. WALT WHITMAN : RUPERT BROOKE :: CIVIL WAR : (*a.* Spanish-American War, *b.* Boer War, *c.* World War I, *d.* World War II)

63. BACTERIOPHAGE : VIRUS :: (*a.* inoculation, *b.* amoeba, *c.* yeast, *d.* potato) : FUNGUS

64. 1 : HYDROGEN :: 2 : (*a.* water, *b.* helium, *c.* oxygen, *d.* nitrogen)

65. FRAUGHT : (*a.* appalled, *b.* afraid, *c.* educated, *d.* laden) :: TAUGHT : TRAINED

66. (*a.* Ibsen, *b.* Dickens, *c.* Stendhal, *d.* Strindberg) : NORA :: FLAUBERT : EMMA

67. PINT : HALF-GALLON :: (*a.* half-pint, *b.* cup, *c.* quart, *d.* half-gallon) : GALLON

68. NICAEA EMPIRE : BYZANTINES :: (*a.* Roman Empire, *b.* Mali Empire, *c.* Aztec Empire, *d.* Ottoman Empire) : MANDINKA

69. MARS : TERRESTRIAL :: SATURN : (*a.* aquatic, *b.* interplanetary, *c.* Jovian, *d.* ringed)

70. MAMBO : (*a.* Cuba, *b.* Brazil, *c.* Haiti, *d.* Jamaica) :: TANGO : ARGENTINA

71. APENNINE : SARDINIA :: (*a.* bay, *b.* peninsula, *c.* mountain, *d.* archipelago) : ISLAND

72. IMPETUS : (*a.* torpor, *b.* rashness, *c.* value, *d.* momentum) :: INERTIA : INACTION

73. SHAWM : OBOE :: REBEC : (*a.* trumpet, *b.* clarinet, *c.* piano, *d.* violin)

74. (*a.* ophthalmalgia, *b.* otalgia, *c.* mastalgia, *d.* cephalgia) : EAR :: NEURALGIA : NERVE

75. INFRA : INTRA :: (*a.* beneath, *b.* instead, *c.* without, *d.* over) : WITHIN

76. (*a.* thyroid, *b.* testes, *c.* kidneys, *d.* pancreas) : INSULIN :: OVARIES : ESTROGEN

77. VITAMIN D : RICKETS :: VITAMIN A : (*a.* scurvy, *b.* night blindness, *c.* beriberi, *d.* pellagra)

78. TIBIA : SHINBONE :: (*a.* femur, *b.* fibula, *c.* patella, *d.* scapula) : KNEECAP

79. BEETHOVEN'S THIRD : BEETHOVEN'S SIXTH :: EROICA : (*a.* Pastoral, *b.* Choral, *c.* Pathétique, *d.* Moonlight)

80. (*a.* Catholics, *b.* Presbyterians, *c.* Anabaptists, *d.* Lutherans) : MENNONITES :: MUSLIMS : SUNNI

81. TENACIOUS : TENABLE :: IRRESOLUTE : (*a.* firm, *b.* dogged, *c.* unsound, *d.* unfastened)

82. DAIMLER : (*a.* Benz, *b.* Fokker, *c.* Diesel, *d.* Horch) :: AUTOMOBILE : AIRCRAFT

83. CAVALRY : HORSEBACK :: (*a.* armored, *b.* infantry, *c.* lancers, *d.* dragoons) : FOOT

84. ELIZABETH BLACKWELL : (*a.* medicine, *b.* chemistry, *c.* geology, *d.* politics) :: MARIA MITCHELL : ASTRONOMY

85. (*a.* indebted, *b.* feral, *c.* derisive, *d.* intense) : APPRECIATIVE :: FEROCIOUS : PLACID

86. GRIMM BROTHERS : VAN EYCK BROTHERS :: FOLKLORE : (*a.* poetry, *b.* painting, *c.* fairy tales, *d.* fashion)

87. JULY 4 : UNITED STATES :: SEPTEMBER 16 : (*a.* Canada, *b.* Russia, *c.* Venezuela, *d.* Mexico)

88. (*a.* conduction, *b.* convection, *c.* condensation, *d.* conflation) : EVAPORATION :: LIQUID : GAS

89. CARSON CITY : SALT LAKE CITY :: (*a.* Wyoming, *b.* Nevada, *c.* Montana, *d.* Oregon) : UTAH

90. ABSALOM AND ACHITOPHEL : ABSALOM, ABSALOM! :: (*a.* John Donne, *b.* John Milton, *c.* John Bunyan, *d.* John Dryden) : WILLIAM FAULKNER

91. APPROVE : BLESS :: DISAPPROVE : (*a.* repel, *b.* desecrate, *c.* disagree, *d.* censure)

92. (*a.* Charles Ives, *b.* Aaron Copland, *c.* Richard Rodgers, *d.* Martha Graham) : RODEO :: MAURICE RAVEL : BOLÉRO

93. SIMPLE : AGGREGATE :: PEACH : (*a.* pear, *b.* raspberry, *c.* grape, *d.* apple)

94. COMMEDIA DELL'ARTE : (*a.* haiku, *b.* Nihonga, *c.* Kabuki, *d.* shamisen) :: ITALY : JAPAN

95. (*a.* sword, *b.* scepter, *c.* distance, *d.* inch) : RULER :: GAVEL : JUDGE

96. CENTAVOS : (*a.* centime, *b.* dollar, *c.* córdoba, *d.* piastre) ::
    CENTIMES : FRANC

97. PRE-RAPHAELITES : ROSSETTI :: POSTIMPRESSIONISTS :
    (*a.* Watteau, *b.* Dufy, *c.* Renoir, *d.* Gauguin)

98. *U.S.S. CAINE* : HERMAN WOUK :: (*a. Andrea Doria, b. Nautilus,
    c. Endeavor, d. H.M.S. Bounty*) : JULES VERNE

99. (*a.* Colossus, *b.* Sphinx, *c.* library, *d.* gold mine) : RHODES ::
    HANGING GARDENS : BABYLON

100. WATT : POWER :: (*a.* mole, *b.* faraday, *c.* dram, *d.* tesla) : MAGNETIC
     FLUX

STOP

If there is any time remaining, go back and check your work.

PRACTICE TEST 8
ANSWER KEY

1. c	26. c	51. b	76. d
2. a	27. c	52. a	77. b
3. d	28. d	53. d	78. c
4. d	29. b	54. a	79. a
5. c	30. c	55. c	80. c
6. b	31. c	56. a	81. c
7. a	32. d	57. b	82. b
8. c	33. a	58. c	83. b
9. a	34. d	59. b	84. a
10. b	35. a	60. c	85. c
11. c	36. b	61. a	86. b
12. c	37. a	62. c	87. d
13. b	38. c	63. c	88. c
14. d	39. b	64. b	89. b
15. c	40. b	65. d	90. d
16. b	41. c	66. a	91. d
17. c	42. d	67. c	92. b
18. d	43. a	68. b	93. b
19. d	44. c	69. c	94. c
20. c	45. d	70. a	95. b
21. d	46. c	71. c	96. c
22. a	47. b	72. d	97. d
23. b	48. c	73. d	98. b
24. d	49. d	74. b	99. a
25. d	50. d	75. a	100. d

PRACTICE TEST 8
EXPLANATORY ANSWERS

1. BOTICELLI : FLORENTINE :: BRUEGEL : (*a.* French, *b.* Teutonic, **c. Flemish**, *d.* Venetian)
   (c) Allesandro *Boticelli* was a Renaissance painter from *Florence*. Pieter *Breugel* was a Renaissance painter from *Flanders* (now Belgium). **Characteristic**

2. MUTTON : SHEEP :: (**a. veal**, *b.* venison, *c.* tenderloin, *d.* prime rib) : CALF
   (a) The meat called *mutton* comes from a *sheep*. The meat called *veal* comes from a *calf*. **Object/Action**

3. JOCASTA : (*a.* Oedipus, *b.* Eurydice, *c.* Laius, *d.* **Antigone**) :: CASSIOPEIA : ANDROMEDA
   (d) *Jocasta* (Oedipus's wife and mother) was the mother of *Antigone*. *Cassiopeia* was the mother of *Andromeda*. **Sequence**

4. (*a.* intelligentsia, *b.* absolute ruler, *c.* Satan, *d.* **wealthy**) : PLUTOCRACY :: GOD : THEOCRACY
   (d) A *plutocracy* is ruled by the *wealthy*. A *theocracy* is ruled by *God* via the controlling religions in the region. **Characteristic**

5. CRINGE : FEAR :: SNEER : (*a.* courage, *b.* indifference, **c. contempt**, *d.* indignation)
   (c) *Fear* might cause you to *cringe*, or shrink back. *Contempt* might cause you to *sneer*, or turn your nose up. **Object/Action**

6. CONNECTION : CORRELATION :: (*a.* granite, **b. division**, *c.* bond, *d.* vacuum) : SCHISM
   (b) *Connection* and *correlation* are synonyms, as are *division* and *schism*. **Synonym**

7. (**a. Frederick II**, *b.* Henry II, *c.* Philip II, *d.* George II) : THE GREAT :: IVAN IV : THE TERRIBLE
   (a) For modernizing Prussia, *Frederick II* was known as "*the Great*." The Russian czar *Ivan IV* was known as "*the Terrible*." **Conversion**

8. SHAW : (*a.* radical individualism, *b.* satirical utopianism, **c. Fabian socialism**, *d.* millennialism) :: SARTRE : EXISTENTIALISM
   (c) Along with other intellectuals such as Havelock Ellis and Emmeline Pankhurst, British playwright George Bernard *Shaw* was drawn to a kind of socialism known as *Fabian*. The French author Jean-Paul *Sartre* was an *existentialist*, someone who believes that the act of being alive leads to the creation of meaning. **Object/Action**

9. SHOAT : PIG :: CYGNET : (**a. swan**, *b.* stork, *c.* swallow, *d.* sandpiper)
   (a) A *shoat* is a baby *pig*. A *cygnet* is a baby *swan*. **Classification**

10. STOMATA : (*a.* differentiation, **b. respiration**, *c.* growth, *d.* circulation) :: STOMACH : DIGESTION
    (b) *Stomata* are pores on the underside of leaves used by a plant in *respiration*, or gas exchange. The *stomach* is an organ in larger animals used in *digestion*. **Object/Action**

11. FOURTH ESTATE : PRESS :: FIFTH COLUMN : (*a.* poor, *b.* upper classes, *c.* **subversives**, *d.* plebes)

(c) The *fourth estate* refers to the *press*. In the time of the French Revolution, the first estate was the clergy; the second estate, the nobility; and the third estate, the commoners. *Fifth column* was a term coined by a Nationalist general during the Spanish Civil War to refer to his clandestine supporters (*subversives*) during an assault on Madrid by four of his army columns. **Synonym**

12. UNTOUCHABLE : CASTE :: (*a.* Muslim, *b.* Athenian, *c.* **Hutterite**, *d.* Pict) : SECT

(c) In Hindu social stratification, or caste system, the *untouchables* are below the four traditional *castes*. The *Hutterites* are a Protestant *sect*. **Classification**

13. (*a.* moonstone, *b.* **beryl**, *c.* spinel, *d.* sapphire) : AMETHYST :: YELLOW : PURPLE

(b) A *beryl* is a *yellow* gem. An *amethyst* is a *purple* gem. **Characteristic**

14. OPTIMISTIC : TRIUMPHANT :: LUKEWARM : (*a.* celebratory, *b.* keen, *c.* fluid, *d.* **apathetic**)

(d) If you are very *optimistic* about an occurrence, you might be *triumphant*. If you are very *lukewarm* on a subject, you might be *apathetic*. **Degree**

15. (*a.* New Year, *b.* Boxing Day, *c.* **Advent**, *d.* gifted) : LENT :: CHRISTMAS : EASTER

(c) *Advent* is the name for the period of time that leads up to *Christmas*. *Lent* is the name for the period of time that leads up to *Easter*. **Sequence**

16. *WAR AND PEACE : CRIME AND PUNISHMENT* :: (*a.* Chekhov, *b.* **Tolstoy**, *c.* Pasternak, *d.* Gogol) : DOSTOEVSKY

(b) Leo *Tolstoy* completed the novel *War and Peace* in 1869. Fyodor *Dostoevsky* completed the novel *Crime and Punishment* in 1866. **Object/Action**

17. (*a.* Proverbs, *b.* Judges, *c.* **Numbers**, *d.* Matthew) : PENTATEUCH :: MARK : GOSPEL

(c) The book of *Numbers* is one of the first five books (*Pentateuch*) of the Bible. The Gospel of *Mark* is part of the *Gospel*. **Part/Whole**

18. ELLESMERE : ARCTIC OCEAN :: (*a.* Ibiza, *b.* Malta, *c.* Vanuatu, *d.* **Sumatra**) : INDIAN OCEAN

(d) *Ellesmere* is a large island in the *Arctic Ocean*, and *Sumatra* is a large island in the *Indian Ocean*. **Characteristic**

19. JAR : (*a.* container, *b.* confound, *c.* scrape, *d.* **jolt**) :: STARTLE : STUN

(d) If you *jar* something hard, you *jolt* it. If you *startle* someone greatly, you *stun* him or her. **Degree**

20. (*a.* hue, *b.* color, *c.* **tint**, *d.* pale) : WHITE :: SHADE : BLACK

(c) To *tint* a color, you add *white*. To *shade* a color, you add *black*. **Characteristic**

21. BURR : (*a.* sticking, *b.* sprinkling, *c.* digging, *d.* **filing**) :: SHEARS : PRUNING

(d) A *burr* is a tool used for *filing* metal. *Shears* are a tool used for *pruning* shrubbery. **Object/Action**

22. VITREOUS HUMOR : EYE :: (**a. gray matter**, *b.* lens, *c.* vertebra, *d.* column) : SPINAL CORD

    (**a**) The gelatinous material that fills the *eyeball* is called the *vitreous humor*. The gelatinous material that lines the *spinal cord* is called *gray matter*. **Part/Whole**

23. ABLE : (*a.* dossier, ***b.* life**, *c.* escape, *d.* flee) :: BALE : FILE

    (**b**) *Able* and *bale* contain the same letters in a different order. *Life* and *file* contain the same letters in a different order. **Conversion**

24. GARRULOUS : TACITURN :: ARTICULATE : (*a.* expressive, *b.* reticulate, *c.* pacific, ***d.* incoherent**)

    (**d**) To be *garrulous* is to talk a lot; to be *taciturn* is to talk very little. To be *articulate* is to express yourself clearly; to be *incoherent* is to be unable to express yourself. **Antonym**

25. CALVIN CYCLE : GLUCOSE :: CELLULAR RESPIRATION : (*a.* sucrose, *b.* H_2O, *c.* carbon, ***d.* ATP**)

    (**d**) The end product of the *Calvin cycle* (the second step in photosynthesis) is *glucose*. The end product of *cellular respiration* is *ATP*, or adenosine triphosphate. **Object/Action**

26. (*a.* Ulysses, *b.* Vulcan, ***c.* Mercury**, *d.* Apollo) : SPEED :: VENUS : BEAUTY

    (**c**) The god *Mercury*, messenger to the gods, was known for his *speed*. The goddess *Venus* was known for her *beauty*. **Characteristic**

27. (*a.* phrenologist, *b.* pharmacist, ***c.* pathologist**, *d.* psychometrist) : DISEASE :: SEISMOLOGIST : EARTHQUAKE

    (**c**) A *pathologist* is a physician who specializes in diagnosis of *disease*. A *seismologist* is a geologist who specializes in causes and effects of *earthquakes*. **Object/Action**

28. EPISTOLARY : PICARESQUE :: (*a.* Emma, *b.* Jane Eyre, *c.* Daisy Miller, ***d.* Pamela**) : *CANDIDE*

    (**d**) *Pamela*, a 1742 novel by Samuel Richardson, is *epistolary*; it is written in the form of letters. *Candide*, a 1759 novel by Voltaire, is *picaresque*; it relates the adventures of a clever rogue. **Classification**

29. SCALE : FISH :: (*a.* chimney, ***b.* shingle**, *c.* insulation, *d.* ceiling) : ROOF

    (**b**) A *scale* is part of the skin of a *fish*; a *shingle* is part of the "skin" of a *roof*. **Part/Whole**

30. WILLIAM THE CONQUEROR : (*a.* Versailles, *b.* Hampton Court, ***c.* Windsor Castle**, *d.* Kensington Palace) :: KING LUDWIG : LINDERHOF CASTLE

    (**c**) Construction of *Windsor Castle* was begun under *William the Conqueror* in 1075. *King Ludwig* of Bavaria built *Linderhof Castle* in the 1870s. **Object/Action**

31. (*a.* noxious, *b.* righteous, ***c.* fractious**, *d.* imperturbable) : EVEN-TEMPERED :: UNFAIR : EVEN-HANDED

    (**c**) To be *fractious* is the opposite of being *even-tempered*. To be *unfair* is the opposite of being *even-handed*. **Antonym**

32. HEDONISM : PLEASURE :: UTILITARIANISM : (*a.* work, *b.* prosperity, *c.* harmony, ***d.* happiness**)

(**d**) The goal of *hedonism* is *pleasure*, primarily self-indulgence. The goal of *utilitarianism* is *happiness*, particularly happiness of the community. **Characteristic**

33. SILICON : (***a.* conductivity**, *b.* rarity, *c.* magnetism, *d.* irregularity) :: X-RAY : PENETRATION

(**a**) The element *silicon* is useful for its *conductivity*, which makes it a key element in integrated circuits. *X-rays* are a form of radiation useful for their ability to *penetrate* skin tissue. **Object/Action**

34. FURY : HOLY :: (*a.* ire, *b.* Noël, *c.* hallowed, ***d.* furry**) : HOLLY

(**d**) Doubling the *r* in *fury* produces *furry*. Doubling the *l* in *holy* produces *holly*. **Conversion**

35. (***a.* intrepid**, *b.* pusillanimous, *c.* complex, *d.* unsophisticated) : INTRICATE :: COWARDLY : SIMPLE

(**a**) If you are *intrepid*, you are brave, not *cowardly*. If something is *intricate*, it is complex, not *simple*. **Antonym**

36. KINDLE : IGNITE :: DWINDLE : (*a.* detonate, ***b.* reduce**, *c.* spin, *d.* embed)

(**b**) To *kindle* something is to *ignite* it, or set it afire. To *dwindle* is to *reduce*, or shrink. **Synonym**

37. PACKHORSE : (***a.* tote**, *b.* bundle, *c.* hoof, *d.* saddle) :: WATCHDOG : GUARD

(**a**) You would use a *packhorse* to *tote* a load. You would use a *watchdog* to *guard* your property. **Object/Action**

38. (*a.* nervous, *b.* eventful, ***c.* energetic**, *d.* congested) : ENERVATED :: POPULOUS : DESOLATE

(**c**) To be *energetic* is the opposite of being *enervated*. To be *populous* is the opposite of being *desolate*. **Antonym**

39. CHRISTIAN : SALVATION :: (*a.* Pilgrim, ***b.* Perceval**, *c.* Buddhist, *d.* Avalon) : GRAIL

(**b**) In *A Pilgrim's Progress* (1678–1684) by John Bunyan, *Christian* overcomes many obstacles in search of *salvation*. In the legend of the Holy *Grail*, *Perceval* overcomes many obstacles in search of that sacred object. **Object/Action**

40. WOODWORKER : (*a.* nail, ***b.* lathe**, *c.* carpenter, *d.* frame) :: SCULPTOR : CHISEL

(**b**) A *woodworker* uses a *lathe* to shape wood. A *sculptor* uses a *chisel* to shape stone. **Object/Action**

41. (*a.* composer, *b.* perishable, ***c.* producer**, *d.* collector) : SEAWEED :: DECOMPOSER : FUNGUS

(**c**) In the food chain, *seaweed* and other green plants are classified as *producers*. *Fungus* is classified as a *decomposer*. **Classification**

42. (*a.* remote control, *b.* digital camera, *c.* robot, ***d.* photocopier**) : STATIC ELECTRICITY :: DISK DRIVE : ELECTROMAGNETISM

(**d**) A *photocopier* relies on *static electricity* to run, and a *disk drive* relies on *electromagnetism.* **Object/Action**

43. SPIRACLE : (*a.* **grasshopper**, *b.* palmetto, *c.* oyster, *d.* moss) :: GILL : FISH
(**a**) *Grasshoppers* and other insects breathe through slits called *spiracles.* *Fish* breathe through slits called *gills.* **Part/Whole**

44. BASIL : GINGER :: (*a.* fruit, *b.* pod, *c.* **leaf**, *d.* stem) : ROOT
(**c**) The edible part of *basil* is the *leaf.* The edible part of *ginger* is the *root.* **Classification**

45. ABRUPT : RUDE :: LONG : (*a.* coarse, *b.* brief, *c.* thin, *d.* **protracted**)
(**d**) An action that is very *abrupt* might be considered *rude.* A discussion that is very *long* might be considered *protracted.* **Degree**

46. HENRY IV : (*a.* House of York, *b.* House of Windsor, *c.* **House of Lancaster**, *d.* House of Stuart) :: HENRY VIII : HOUSE OF TUDOR
(**c**) King *Henry IV* of England was a member of the *House of Lancaster.* King *Henry VIII* of England was a member of the *House of Tudor.* **Classification**

47. SALTPETER : EXPLOSIVES :: METHANE : (*a.* cattle, *b.* **natural gas**, *c.* ethanol, *d.* petroleum)
(**b**) *Saltpeter* (potassium nitrate) can be used to make *explosives.* *Methane* is the primary ingredient in *natural gas.* **Part/Whole**

48. (*a.* Isaac Stern, *b.* Yehudi Menuhin, *c.* **Yo Yo Ma**, *d.* Pinchas Zukerman) : CELLO :: ITZHAK PERLMAN : VIOLIN
(**c**) All the men listed are virtuoso violinists with the exception of *Yo Yo Ma*, who plays the *cello.* **Object/Action**

49. ECRU : BEIGE :: CHARTREUSE : (*a.* red, *b.* yellow, *c.* orange, *d.* **green**)
(**d**) *Ecru* is a particular shade of *beige.* *Chartreuse* is a particular shade of *green.* **Classification**

50. AMOEBA : (*a.* protozoan, *b.* hydra, *c.* cytoplasm, *d.* **pseudopod**) :: PARAMECIUM : CILIA
(**d**) An *amoeba* may move by means of a *pseudopod.* A *paramecium* may move by means of *cilia.* **Characteristic**

51. (*a.* vascular, *b.* **digitalis**, *c.* inhibitor, *d.* platelet) : BLOOD FLOW :: COAGULANT : BLOOD CLOT
(**b**) *Digitalis* is a drug derived from the foxglove plant. It can increase *blood flow.* A *coagulant* is any agent that causes blood to *clot.* **Object/Action**

52. PRADO : (*a.* **Madrid**, *b.* Lisbon, *c.* Venice, *d.* Rome) :: LOUVRE : PARIS
(**a**) The *Prado* is an art museum in *Madrid*, Spain. The *Louvre* is an art museum in *Paris*, France. **Characteristic**

53. *ILIAD : AENEID* :: HOMER : (*a.* Ovid, *b.* Dryden, *c.* Aeschylus, *d.* **Virgil**)
(**d**) *Homer* wrote the *Iliad*, and *Virgil* wrote the *Aeneid.* **Object/Action**

54. (*a.* **egret**, *b.* sandpiper, *c.* osprey, *d.* loon) : BITTERN :: GULL : TERN
    (**a**) *Egrets* and *bitterns* are long-legged wading birds in the same family. *Gulls* and *terns* are fish-eating aquatic birds in the same family. **Part/Whole**

55. LINES : (*a.* polygon, *b.* arc, *c.* **end point**, *d.* perpendicular) :: PARALLEL LINES : INTERSECTION
    (**c**) *Lines* have no *end point*; *parallel lines* have no *intersection*. **Characteristic**

56. (*a.* **C**, *b.* E, *c.* F, *d.* B) : D :: G : A
    (**a**) In the tonic scale, *C* comes just before *D*, and *G* comes just before *A*. **Sequence**

57. HEBREW : SEMITIC :: TAHITIAN : (*a.* Chinese, *b.* **Polynesian**, *c.* Samoan, *d.* Christian)
    (**b**) *Hebrew* is one of several *Semitic* languages. *Tahitian* is one of several *Polynesian* languages. **Classification**

58. (*a.* Copley Square, *b.* London, *c.* **Prague**, *d.* Berlin) : 1968 :: TIANANMEN SQUARE : 1989
    (**c**) In *1968*, *Prague* was the scene of an uprising that was quickly quashed by the ruling Soviets. In *1989*, *Tiananmen Square* was the scene of an uprising that was quickly quashed by the Chinese government. **Characteristic**

59. 1/2 : (*a.* 2/3, *b.* **1/4**, *c.* 1/10, *d.* 2/5) :: 1/3 : 1/9
    (**b**) *1/2* squared is *1/4*. *1/3* squared is *1/9*. **Conversion**

60. HUDSON : NORTHEAST :: (*a.* Aviles, *b.* De Soto, *c.* **Coronado**, *d.* Vespucci) : SOUTHWEST
    (**c**) Henry *Hudson* (1565–1611) explored the North American *Northeast*. Francisco Vásquez de *Coronado* (1510–1554) explored the American *Southwest*. **Object/Action**

61. (*a.* **predictive**, *b.* close-minded, *c.* far-fetched, *d.* doomed) : PROPHETIC :: TACTLESS : INSENSITIVE
    (**a**) Something that is *predictive* might be called *prophetic*. Someone who is *tactless* might be called *insensitive*. **Synonym**

62. WALT WHITMAN : RUPERT BROOKE :: CIVIL WAR : (*a.* Spanish-American War, *b.* Boer War, *c.* **World War I**, *d.* World War II)
    (**c**) American poet and essayist *Walt Whitman* served (as a nurse) in the *Civil War* and wrote extensively about his experiences. English poet *Rupert Brooke* wrote about *World War I* and died on his way to serve in Gallipoli. **Characteristic**

63. BACTERIOPHAGE : VIRUS :: (*a.* inoculation, *b.* amoeba, *c.* **yeast**, *d.* potato) : FUNGUS
    (**c**) A *bacteriophage* is a kind of *virus*. *Yeast* is a kind of *fungus*. **Classification**

64. 1 : HYDROGEN :: 2 : (*a.* water, *b.* **helium**, *c.* oxygen, *d.* nitrogen)
    (**b**) The element *hydrogen* has the atomic number *1*. *Helium* has the atomic number *2*. **Sequence**

65. FRAUGHT : (*a.* appalled, *b.* afraid, *c.* educated, *d.* **laden**) :: TAUGHT : TRAINED
(**d**) To be *fraught* with something is to be *laden*, or weighed down. To be *taught* is to be *trained.* **Synonym**

66. (*a.* **Ibsen**, *b.* Dickens, *c.* Stendhal, *d.* Strindberg) : NORA :: FLAUBERT : EMMA
(**a**) Henrik *Ibsen* created the character *Nora* Helmer in his 1879 play *A Doll's House.* Gustave *Flaubert* created the character *Emma* Bovary in his 1856 novel *Madame Bovary.* **Object/Action**

67. PINT : HALF-GALLON :: (*a.* half-pint, *b.* cup, *c.* **quart**, *d.* half-gallon) : GALLON
(**c**) There are four *pints* in a *half-gallon* and four *quarts* in a *gallon.* **Part/Whole**

68. NICAEA EMPIRE : BYZANTINES :: (*a.* Roman Empire, *b.* **Mali Empire**, *c.* Aztec Empire, *d.* Ottoman Empire) : MANDINKA
(**b**) The *Nicaea Empire* was founded at Nicaea when the *Byzantine* emperors fled Constantinople to escape the Crusaders. The *Mali Empire* was an Islamic empire of the *Mandinka* people in western Africa. **Characteristic**

69. MARS : TERRESTRIAL :: SATURN : (*a.* aquatic, *b.* interplanetary, *c.* **Jovian**, *d.* ringed)
(**c**) There are two main classifications of the planets in our solar system. The *terrestrial,* rocky planets include Mercury, Venus, Earth, and *Mars.* The *Jovian* planets are the outlying, huge, gaseous planets—Jupiter, *Saturn,* Uranus, and Neptune. Pluto does not fit into either category—it is rocky and small but far colder than the terrestrial planets. **Classification**

70. MAMBO : (*a.* **Cuba**, *b.* Brazil, *c.* Haiti, *d.* Jamaica) :: TANGO : ARGENTINA
(**a**) The *mambo* is an Afro-*Cuban* dance in 4/4 time. The *tango* is an *Argentinian* dance, usually in 2/4 time. **Characteristic**

71. APENNINE : SARDINIA :: (*a.* bay, *b.* peninsula, *c.* **mountain**, *d.* archipelago) : ISLAND
(**c**) The *Apennines* are a *mountain* range in Italy. *Sardinia* is an Italian-owned *island* in the Mediterranean. **Classification**

72. IMPETUS : (*a.* torpor, *b.* rashness, *c.* value, *d.* **momentum**) :: INERTIA : INACTION
(**d**) *Impetus* and *momentum* both refer to the force that moves an object. *Inertia* and *inaction* both refer to the tendency of an object to remain at rest. **Synonym**

73. SHAWM : OBOE :: REBEC : (*a.* trumpet, *b.* clarinet, *c.* piano, *d.* **violin**)
(**d**) The *shawm* was a medieval *oboe.* The *rebec* was a medieval *violin.* **Conversion**

74. (*a.* ophthalmalgia, *b.* **otalgia**, *c.* mastalgia, *d.* cephalgia) : EAR :: NEURALGIA : NERVE
(**b**) *Otalgia* is pain in the *ear. Neuralgia* is pain along a *nerve.* **Characteristic**

75. INFRA : INTRA :: (*a.* **beneath**, *b.* instead, *c.* without, *d.* over) : WITHIN
(**a**) The root *infra-*, as in *infrastructure*, means "*beneath*." The root *intra-*, as in *intramural*, means "*within*." **Affix**

76. (*a*. thyroid, *b*. testes, *c*. kidneys, **d. pancreas**) : INSULIN :: OVARIES : ESTROGEN
(**d**) The *pancreas* is the organ that produces *insulin*. The *ovaries* are the organs that produce *estrogen*. **Object/Action**

77. VITAMIN D : RICKETS :: VITAMIN A : (*a*. scurvy, **b. night blindness**, *c*. beriberi, *d*. pellagra)
(**b**) Deficiency of *vitamin D* can lead to a disease called *rickets*. Deficiency of *vitamin A* can lead to *night blindness*. **Characteristic**

78. TIBIA : SHINBONE :: (*a*. femur, *b*. fibula, *c*. patella, *d*. scapula) : KNEECAP
(**c**) *Tibia* is the medical name for the *shinbone*, and *patella* is the medical name for the *kneecap*. **Synonym**

79. BEETHOVEN'S THIRD : BEETHOVEN'S SIXTH :: EROICA :
(**a. Pastoral**, *b*. Choral, *c*. Pathétique, *d*. Moonlight)
(**a**) Many of Beethoven's works have nicknames, among them his *third* symphony, called *Eroica*, and his *sixth* symphony, called *Pastoral*. **Conversion**

80. (*a*. Catholics, *b*. Presbyterians, **c. Anabaptists**, *d*. Lutherans) : MENNONITES ::
MUSLIMS : SUNNI
(**c**) The *Mennonites* are a sect of the *Anabaptists,* a group of Protestants who believe in rebaptizing new members (and not baptizing infants). The *Sunni* are a sect of *Muslims* who hold that the true succession of Muslim leadership comes not from Muhammad's son-in-law Ali, but rather from the original four Caliphs. **Part/Whole**

81. TENACIOUS : TENABLE :: IRRESOLUTE : (*a*. firm, *b*. dogged, **c. unsound**, *d*. unfastened)
(**c**) If you are *tenacious*, or stubborn, you are not *irresolute* (indecisive). If a theory is *tenable*, or plausible, it is not *unsound* (illogical). **Antonym**

82. DAIMLER : (*a*. Benz, **b. Fokker**, *c*. Diesel, *d*. Horch) :: AUTOMOBILE :
AIRCRAFT
(**b**) Gottlieb *Daimler* was a German engineer and manufacturer who designed the first high-speed internal combustion engine. Anthony *Fokker* was a Dutch engineer and manufacturer who designed Germany's World War I combat planes. **Object/Action**

83. CAVALRY : HORSEBACK :: (*a*. armored, **b. infantry**, *c*. lancers, *d*. dragoons) :
FOOT
(**b**) Traditionally, the *cavalry* is a mounted (on *horseback*) army component, and the *infantry* consists of soldiers who fight on *foot*. **Characteristic**

84. ELIZABETH BLACKWELL : (**a. medicine**, *b*. chemistry, *c*. geology, *d*. politics) ::
MARIA MITCHELL : ASTRONOMY
(**a**) *Elizabeth Blackwell* was the first American woman to receive a doctor of *medicine* degree (in 1849). *Maria Mitchell* was a professor of *astronomy* at Vassar College and the first woman elected to the American Academy of Arts and Sciences. She discovered a comet in 1847. **Object/Action**

85. (*a.* indebted, *b.* feral, *c.* **derisive**, *d.* intense) : APPRECIATIVE :: FEROCIOUS :
PLACID
(c) To be *derisive,* or scornful, is to be *unappreciative.* To be *ferocious* is to be wild,
or the opposite of *placid.* **Antonym**

86. GRIMM BROTHERS : VAN EYCK BROTHERS :: FOLKLORE :
(*a.* poetry, *b.* **painting**, *c.* fairy tales, *d.* fashion)
(b) Jacob and Wilhelm *Grimm* collected *folktales* and published their first collection in
1812. Hubert and Jan *van Eyck* were fifteenth-century Dutch *painters.* **Object/Action**

87. JULY 4 : UNITED STATES :: SEPTEMBER 16 : (*a.* Canada, *b.* Russia, *c.* Venezuela,
d. **Mexico**)
(d) Independence Day in the *United States* is celebrated on *July 4.* Independence Day
in *Mexico* is celebrated on *September 16.* **Characteristic**

88. (*a.* conduction, *b.* convection, *c.* **condensation**, *d.* conflation) : EVAPORATION ::
LIQUID : GAS
(c) *Condensation* produces *liquid,* and *evaporation* produces *gas.* **Object/Action**

89. CARSON CITY : SALT LAKE CITY :: (*a.* Wyoming, *b.* **Nevada**, *c.* Montana,
d. Oregon) : UTAH
(b) *Carson City* is the capital of *Nevada. Salt Lake City* is the capital of *Utah.*
Characteristic

90. ABSALOM AND ACHITOPHEL : *ABSALOM, ABSALOM!* :: (*a.* John Donne,
b. John Milton, *c.* John Bunyan, *d.* **John Dryden**) : WILLIAM FAULKNER
(d) In 1681, *John Dryden* published the political satire called *Absalom and Achitophel.*
In 1936, *William Faulkner* published the novel *Absalom, Absalom!* Absalom is a Biblical
character who plotted unsuccessfully against his father, King David. **Object/Action**

91. APPROVE : BLESS :: DISAPPROVE : (*a.* repel, *b.* desecrate, *c.* disagree, *d.* **censure**)
(d) If you *approved* enormously of a plan, you might *bless* it. If you *disapproved*
enormously, you might *censure,* or condemn it. **Degree**

92. (*a.* Charles Ives, *b.* **Aaron Copland**, *c.* Richard Rodgers, *d.* Martha Graham) :
RODEO :: MAURICE RAVEL : BOLÉRO
(b) *Aaron Copland* was the composer of the one-act ballet *Rodeo. Maurice Ravel* was
the composer of the one-act ballet *Boléro.* **Object/Action**

93. SIMPLE : AGGREGATE :: PEACH : (*a.* pear, *b.* **raspberry**, *c.* grape, *d.* apple)
(b) A *peach* is an example of a *simple* fruit—fruit derived from a single ovary. A
raspberry is an example of an *aggregate* fruit—fruit consisting of many small fruits.
Classification

94. COMMEDIA DELL'ARTE : (*a.* haiku, *b.* Nihonga, *c.* **Kabuki**, *d.* shamisen) :: ITALY :
JAPAN
(c) *Commedia dell'Arte* is a form of theater from *Italy. Kabuki* is a form of theater from
Japan. **Characteristic**

95. (*a.* sword, ***b.* scepter**, *c.* distance, *d.* inch) : RULER :: GAVEL : JUDGE
    (**b**) A *scepter* is a symbol of a *ruler's* power. A *gavel* is a symbol of a *judge's* power. **Object/Action**

96. CENTAVOS : (*a.* centime, *b.* dollar, ***c.* córdoba**, *d.* piastre) :: CENTIMES : FRANC
    (**c**) In Nicaragua, 100 *centavos* equal 1 *córdoba*. In many French-speaking nations, 100 *centimes* equal 1 *franc*. **Part/Whole**

97. PRE-RAPHAELITES : ROSSETTI :: POSTIMPRESSIONISTS : (*a.* Watteau, *b.* Dufy, *c.* Renoir, ***d.* Gauguin**)
    (**d**) Dante Gabriel *Rossetti* (1828–1882) led the *pre-Raphaelite* movement, artists interested in restoring early Renaissance qualities and ideals. Paul *Gauguin* (1848–1903) was one of the *postimpressionists*, late-nineteenth-century artists who reacted against impressionism. **Classification**

98. *U.S.S. CAINE* : HERMAN WOUK :: (*a. Andrea Doria*, ***b. Nautilus***, *c. Endeavor*, *d. H.M.S. Bounty*) :: JULES VERNE
    (**b**) *Herman Wouk* wrote of the craft the *U.S.S. Caine* in his 1951 novel *The Caine Mutiny*. *Jules Verne* wrote of the craft *Nautilus* in his 1870 novel, *Twenty Thousand Leagues Under the Sea*. **Object/Action**

99. (***a.* Colossus**, *b.* Sphinx, *c.* library, *d.* gold mine) : RHODES :: HANGING GARDENS : BABYLON
    (**a**) Two of the seven wonders of the world were the *Colossus* (giant statue) of *Rhodes* and the *Hanging Gardens* of *Babylon*. **Characteristic**

100. WATT : POWER :: (*a.* mole, *b.* faraday, *c.* dram, ***d.* tesla**) : MAGNETIC FLUX
    (**d**) A *watt* is a unit that is used to measure *power*. A *tesla* is a unit that is used to measure *magnetic flux*. **Object/Action**

PRACTICE TEST 9
ANSWER SHEET

1. Ⓐ Ⓑ Ⓒ Ⓓ	26. Ⓐ Ⓑ Ⓒ Ⓓ	51. Ⓐ Ⓑ Ⓒ Ⓓ	76. Ⓐ Ⓑ Ⓒ Ⓓ
2. Ⓐ Ⓑ Ⓒ Ⓓ	27. Ⓐ Ⓑ Ⓒ Ⓓ	52. Ⓐ Ⓑ Ⓒ Ⓓ	77. Ⓐ Ⓑ Ⓒ Ⓓ
3. Ⓐ Ⓑ Ⓒ Ⓓ	28. Ⓐ Ⓑ Ⓒ Ⓓ	53. Ⓐ Ⓑ Ⓒ Ⓓ	78. Ⓐ Ⓑ Ⓒ Ⓓ
4. Ⓐ Ⓑ Ⓒ Ⓓ	29. Ⓐ Ⓑ Ⓒ Ⓓ	54. Ⓐ Ⓑ Ⓒ Ⓓ	79. Ⓐ Ⓑ Ⓒ Ⓓ
5. Ⓐ Ⓑ Ⓒ Ⓓ	30. Ⓐ Ⓑ Ⓒ Ⓓ	55. Ⓐ Ⓑ Ⓒ Ⓓ	80. Ⓐ Ⓑ Ⓒ Ⓓ
6. Ⓐ Ⓑ Ⓒ Ⓓ	31. Ⓐ Ⓑ Ⓒ Ⓓ	56. Ⓐ Ⓑ Ⓒ Ⓓ	81. Ⓐ Ⓑ Ⓒ Ⓓ
7. Ⓐ Ⓑ Ⓒ Ⓓ	32. Ⓐ Ⓑ Ⓒ Ⓓ	57. Ⓐ Ⓑ Ⓒ Ⓓ	82. Ⓐ Ⓑ Ⓒ Ⓓ
8. Ⓐ Ⓑ Ⓒ Ⓓ	33. Ⓐ Ⓑ Ⓒ Ⓓ	58. Ⓐ Ⓑ Ⓒ Ⓓ	83. Ⓐ Ⓑ Ⓒ Ⓓ
9. Ⓐ Ⓑ Ⓒ Ⓓ	34. Ⓐ Ⓑ Ⓒ Ⓓ	59. Ⓐ Ⓑ Ⓒ Ⓓ	84. Ⓐ Ⓑ Ⓒ Ⓓ
10. Ⓐ Ⓑ Ⓒ Ⓓ	35. Ⓐ Ⓑ Ⓒ Ⓓ	60. Ⓐ Ⓑ Ⓒ Ⓓ	85. Ⓐ Ⓑ Ⓒ Ⓓ
11. Ⓐ Ⓑ Ⓒ Ⓓ	36. Ⓐ Ⓑ Ⓒ Ⓓ	61. Ⓐ Ⓑ Ⓒ Ⓓ	86. Ⓐ Ⓑ Ⓒ Ⓓ
12. Ⓐ Ⓑ Ⓒ Ⓓ	37. Ⓐ Ⓑ Ⓒ Ⓓ	62. Ⓐ Ⓑ Ⓒ Ⓓ	87. Ⓐ Ⓑ Ⓒ Ⓓ
13. Ⓐ Ⓑ Ⓒ Ⓓ	38. Ⓐ Ⓑ Ⓒ Ⓓ	63. Ⓐ Ⓑ Ⓒ Ⓓ	88. Ⓐ Ⓑ Ⓒ Ⓓ
14. Ⓐ Ⓑ Ⓒ Ⓓ	39. Ⓐ Ⓑ Ⓒ Ⓓ	64. Ⓐ Ⓑ Ⓒ Ⓓ	89. Ⓐ Ⓑ Ⓒ Ⓓ
15. Ⓐ Ⓑ Ⓒ Ⓓ	40. Ⓐ Ⓑ Ⓒ Ⓓ	65. Ⓐ Ⓑ Ⓒ Ⓓ	90. Ⓐ Ⓑ Ⓒ Ⓓ
16. Ⓐ Ⓑ Ⓒ Ⓓ	41. Ⓐ Ⓑ Ⓒ Ⓓ	66. Ⓐ Ⓑ Ⓒ Ⓓ	91. Ⓐ Ⓑ Ⓒ Ⓓ
17. Ⓐ Ⓑ Ⓒ Ⓓ	42. Ⓐ Ⓑ Ⓒ Ⓓ	67. Ⓐ Ⓑ Ⓒ Ⓓ	92. Ⓐ Ⓑ Ⓒ Ⓓ
18. Ⓐ Ⓑ Ⓒ Ⓓ	43. Ⓐ Ⓑ Ⓒ Ⓓ	68. Ⓐ Ⓑ Ⓒ Ⓓ	93. Ⓐ Ⓑ Ⓒ Ⓓ
19. Ⓐ Ⓑ Ⓒ Ⓓ	44. Ⓐ Ⓑ Ⓒ Ⓓ	69. Ⓐ Ⓑ Ⓒ Ⓓ	94. Ⓐ Ⓑ Ⓒ Ⓓ
20. Ⓐ Ⓑ Ⓒ Ⓓ	45. Ⓐ Ⓑ Ⓒ Ⓓ	70. Ⓐ Ⓑ Ⓒ Ⓓ	95. Ⓐ Ⓑ Ⓒ Ⓓ
21. Ⓐ Ⓑ Ⓒ Ⓓ	46. Ⓐ Ⓑ Ⓒ Ⓓ	71. Ⓐ Ⓑ Ⓒ Ⓓ	96. Ⓐ Ⓑ Ⓒ Ⓓ
22. Ⓐ Ⓑ Ⓒ Ⓓ	47. Ⓐ Ⓑ Ⓒ Ⓓ	72. Ⓐ Ⓑ Ⓒ Ⓓ	97. Ⓐ Ⓑ Ⓒ Ⓓ
23. Ⓐ Ⓑ Ⓒ Ⓓ	48. Ⓐ Ⓑ Ⓒ Ⓓ	73. Ⓐ Ⓑ Ⓒ Ⓓ	98. Ⓐ Ⓑ Ⓒ Ⓓ
24. Ⓐ Ⓑ Ⓒ Ⓓ	49. Ⓐ Ⓑ Ⓒ Ⓓ	74. Ⓐ Ⓑ Ⓒ Ⓓ	99. Ⓐ Ⓑ Ⓒ Ⓓ
25. Ⓐ Ⓑ Ⓒ Ⓓ	50. Ⓐ Ⓑ Ⓒ Ⓓ	75. Ⓐ Ⓑ Ⓒ Ⓓ	100. Ⓐ Ⓑ Ⓒ Ⓓ

PRACTICE TEST 9

Directions: For each question, you will see three capitalized words and four answer choices labeled *a, b, c,* and *d* in parentheses. Choose the answer that best completes the analogy posed by the three capitalized words. Use the answer sheet on page 201 to record your answers.

Time: 50 Minutes

1. (*a.* Bre'r, *b.* Reynard, *c.* Remus, *d.* Mole) : FOX :: CHANTICLEER : ROOSTER

2. POLLUTION : (*a.* effluence, *b.* rain, *c.* sanitation, *d.* saturation) :: SMOG : FOG

3. (*a.* turtle, *b.* newt, *c.* spring peeper, *d.* eft) : FROG :: REPTILE : AMPHIBIAN

4. LADY CHATTERLEY : LADY WINDERMERE :: LAWRENCE : (*a.* Sheridan, *b.* Wilde, *c.* Thackery, *d.* Trollope)

5. WORRISOME : (*a.* disquieting, *b.* ambiguous, *c.* enlightening, *d.* noteworthy) :: SUSPICIOUS : DUBIOUS

6. DEIFIED : HISS :: (*a.* allegory, *b.* litotes, *c.* palindrome, *d.* tautology) : ONOMATOPOEIA

7. (*a.* Castile, *b.* Bourbon, *c.* Aragon, *d.* Jacques) : FRANCE :: STUART : ENGLAND

8. DANIEL : LION :: JONAH : (*a.* tiger, *b.* bear, *c.* lamb, *d.* whale)

9. BEAUMONT : (*a.* Mulligan, *b.* Beauchamp, *c.* Fletcher, *d.* Hart) :: GILBERT : SULLIVAN

10. POLYNESIAN : SAMOAN :: CHINESE : (*a.* Thai, *b.* Tahitian, *c.* Cantonese, *d.* Confucianism)

11. EDGAR LEE MASTERS : SPOON RIVER :: (*a.* Thornton Wilder, *b.* Sinclair Lewis, *c.* Washington Irving, *d.* Flannery O'Connor) : GROVER'S CORNERS

12. ANNAPURNA : NEPAL :: ARARAT : (*a.* Iraq, *b.* Israel, *c.* Lebanon, *d.* Turkey)

13. JOHN McADAM : (*a.* air travel, *b.* space travel, *c.* road travel, *d.* train travel) :: ROBERT FULTON : RIVER TRAVEL

14. ISHTAR : ISIS :: BABYLON : (*a.* Greece, *b.* Egypt, *c.* Rome, *d.* Persia)

15. ACHIEVE : THRIVE :: (*a.* profit, *b.* scuffle, *c.* realize, *d.* worry) : AGONIZE

16. ALPHA : OMEGA :: GENESIS : (*a.* Exodus, *b.* Psalms, *c.* Revelation, *d.* Romans)

17. WHITNEY MUSEUM : (*a.* Metropolitan Museum, *b.* Guggenheim Museum, *c.* Museum of Modern Art, *d.* Frick Museum) :: BREUER : WRIGHT

18. JAPAN : HONSHU :: INDONESIA : (*a.* Java, *b.* Malaysia, *c.* Luzon, *d.* Tasmania)

19. ELEVATE : (*a.* revoke, *b.* denigrate, *c.* glorify, *d.* assuage) :: MOCK : RIDICULE

20. PAKISTAN : (*a.* Philippines, *b.* Mongolia, *c.* Laos, *d.* Thailand) :: RUPEE : BAHT

21. (*a.* moue, *b.* pout, *c.* smirk, *d.* snivel) : DISPLEASURE :: LEER : LECHERY

22. SENTENCE : PARAGRAPH :: (*a.* poem, *b.* paragraph, *c.* verse, *d.* line) : STANZA

23. GROUT : FILL :: SPOUT : (*a.* remark, *b.* plug, *c.* discharge, *d.* sink)

24. (*a.* inoffensive, *b.* affable, *c.* poisonous, *d.* unreceptive) : INNOCUOUS :: HOSTILE : CONGENIAL

25. TISSUE : (*a.* wood, *b.* glass, *c.* gauze, *d.* net) :: TRANSLUCENT : OPAQUE

26. JACQUES COUSTEAU : ROBERT JARVIK :: AQUALUNG : (*a.* wheelchair, *b.* iron lung, *c.* bifocals, *d.* artificial heart)

27. DERMA : SKIN :: (*a.* armed, *b.* pen, *c.* colors, *d.* drawing) : INKS

28. CREATIVE : RESTIVE :: DERIVATIVE : (*a.* imitative, *b.* serene, *c.* inventive, *d.* festive)

29. (*a.* litigious, *b.* functional, *c.* credible, *d.* limited) : BELIEVABLE :: CONTENTIOUS : DEBATABLE

30. MURDER : CROW :: SETT : (*a.* trap, *b.* badger, *c.* fox, *d.* otter)

31. *KING LEAR* : TRAGEDY :: (*a. Pericles, Prince of Tyre, b. Timon of Athens, c. King John, d. Julius Caesar*) : HISTORY

32. (*a.* direct, *b.* unerring, *c.* offhand, *d.* sloppy) : UNDEVIATING :: BRIEF : BRUSQUE

33. (*a.* gorilla, *b.* stork, *c.* bumblebee, *d.* marmoset) : APIAN :: CHIMPANZEE : SIMIAN

34. MENINGES : BRAIN :: MYELIN : (*a.* sheath, *b.* muscle, *c.* heart, *d.* axon)

35. OLIVE BRANCH : PEACE :: (*a.* white, *b.* lily, *c.* halo, *d.* star) : SAINTHOOD

36. CAYUGA : (*a.* Five Federations, *b.* Tribal Alliance, *c.* Seven Eastern Tribes, *d.* Five Nations) :: CHEROKEE : FIVE CIVILIZED TRIBES

37. (*a.* reptile, *b.* mollusk, *c.* nematode, *d.* shark) : MANTLE :: AMPHIBIAN : SKIN

38. EPISTEMOLOGY : (*a.* knowledge, *b.* letters, *c.* plants, *d.* science) :: AESTHETICS : ART

39. (*a.* twenties, *b.* forties, *c.* sixties, *d.* eighties) : NINETIES :: ROARING : GAY

40. RECREANT : (*a.* recreation, *b.* dominance, *c.* food, *d.* courage) :: PAUPER : MONEY

41. 1/64 : 1/8 :: 0.016 : (*a.* 0.25, *b.* 0.025, *c.* 0.125, *d.* 0.32)

42. BALI : EAST INDIES :: (*a.* Bonaire, *b.* Bermuda, *c.* Mooréa, *d.* Ibiza) : WEST INDIES

43. (*a.* weave, *b.* worsted, *c.* viscose, *d.* sheep) : WOOL :: SHANTUNG : SILK

44. IMPETIGO : SKIN :: PHLEBITIS : (*a.* limb, *b.* skull, *c.* vein, *d.* sinus)

45. KINGDOM : (*a.* class, *b.* order, *c.* phylum, *d.* family) :: GENUS : SPECIES

46. (*a.* ad hominem, *b.* ad libitum, *c.* ad interim, *d.* ad valorem) : AT PLEASURE :: AD INFINITUM : TO INFINITY

47. HAYSTACKS : (*a.* Monet, *b.* Renoir, *c.* Cezanne, *d.* Toulouse-Lautrec) :: DANCERS : DEGAS

48. IMPROVE : DETERIORATE :: IMPRESS : (*a.* electrify, *b.* disappoint, *c.* decline, *d.* bolster)

49. (*a.* Stephens, *b.* Rockefeller, *c.* Roosevelt, *d.* Tarbell) : OIL INDUSTRY :: NADER : AUTOMOBILE INDUSTRY

50. ENGELS : DIALECTIC MATERIALISM :: (*a.* James, *b.* Bentham, *c.* Kant, *d.* Marx) : UTILITARIANISM

51. BASALT : (*a.* pumice, *b.* limestone, *c.* granite, *d.* slate) :: IGNEOUS : METAMORPHIC

52. PHONOLOGY : PHRENOLOGY :: SPEECH : (*a.* skull, *b.* skin, *c.* motion, *d.* language)

53. FAHRENHEIT : THERMOMETER :: (*a.* Ohm, *b.* Hertz, *c.* Tesla, *d.* Volta) : OSCILLATOR

54. (*a.* tibia, *b.* ilium, *c.* femur, *d.* radius) : THIGH :: ULNA : FOREARM

55. HUSSEIN : IRAQ :: (*a.* Ceausescu, *b.* Tito, *c.* Hoxha, *d.* Pompey) : YUGOSLAVIA

56. OXYGEN : ELEMENT :: WATER : (*a.* property, *b.* atom, *c.* ion, *d.* molecule)

57. NICKEL : (*a.* penny, *b.* dime, *c.* quarter, *d.* silver dollar) :: JEFFERSON : ROOSEVELT

58. (*a.* genuine, *b.* genius, *c.* genuflect, *d.* genetics) : VERB :: GENUINE : ADJECTIVE

59. DIATRIBE : (*a.* chronicle, *b.* clan, *c.* accolade, *d.* rant) :: ACCLAIM : TRIBUTE

60. VIBRAPHONE : MARIMBA :: ELECTRIC GUITAR : (*a.* bongo, *b.* electric violin, *c.* acoustic guitar, *d.* guitar pick)

61. SORORAL : (*a.* aunt, *b.* sister, *c.* grandmother, *d.* girl) :: AVUNCULAR : UNCLE

62. GASTRO- : HEPATO- :: STOMACH : (*a.* blood, *b.* lung, *c.* cell, *d.* liver)

63. PERISTALSIS : (*a.* propulsion, *b.* stasis, *c.* growth, *d.* digestion) :: GRIDLOCK : STANDSTILL

64. (*a.* area, *b.* square, *c.* perimeter, *d.* side) : POLYGON :: CIRCUMFERENCE : CIRCLE

65. FRAUDULENT : FLAVORFUL :: COUNTERFEIT : (*a.* faux, *b.* currency, *c.* savory, *d.* featureless)

66. ACT : (*a.* action, *b.* scene, *c.* actively, *d.* drama) :: VIEW : PREVIEWING

67. COAL : OIL :: WIND : (*a.* gas, *b.* weather, *c.* typhoon, *d.* sun)

68. (*a.* agoraphobia, *b.* acrophobia, *c.* ailurophobia, *d.* androphobia) : HYDROPHOBIA :: OPEN SPACES : WATER

69. XANTHIPPE : SOCRATES :: (*a.* Elba, *b.* Corsica, *c.* Josephine, *d.* Wellington) : NAPOLEON

70. ELIZABETHAN : ELIZABETH I :: JACOBEAN : (*a.* Jacob II, *b.* James I, *c.* John, *d.* Jane Grey)

71. MAINE : ALAMO :: (*a.* War of 1812, *b.* Civil War, *c.* Spanish-American War, *d.* Indian Wars) : MEXICAN-AMERICAN WAR

72. (*a.* Siam, *b.* Kampuchea, *c.* Côte d'Ivoire, *d.* East Pakistan) : BANGLADESH :: BURMA : MYANMAR

73. CONSTABLE : (*a.* sculpture, *b.* still life, *c.* landscapes, *d.* seascapes) :: REYNOLDS : PORTRAITS

74. WARP : (*a.* woven, *b.* cloth, *c.* twist, *d.* weft) :: LONGITUDE : LATITUDE

75. PERPETUAL : PROVISIONAL :: (*a.* charitable, *b.* compulsory, *c.* optional, *d.* regular) : VOLUNTARY

76. *CAKES AND ALE* : *TEA AND SYMPATHY* :: (*a.* Maugham, *b.* Greene, *c.* Waugh, *d.* Albee) : ANDERSON

77. ZIP CODE : AREA CODE :: FIVE : (*a.* two, *b.* three, *c.* seven, *d.* nine)

78. SCRUPLES : (*a.* apothecary, *b.* attorney, *c.* cleric, *d.* rancher) :: FATHOMS : SAILOR

79. (*a.* truculent, *b.* puerile, *c.* veteran, *d.* adamant) : PUGNACIOUS :: MATURE : PEACEABLE

80. *EREWHON* : SAMUEL BUTLER :: *UTOPIA* : (*a.* Plato, *b.* Aldous Huxley, *c.* Thomas More, *d.* James Hilton)

81. ANION : (*a.* ion, *b.* cation, *c.* union, *d.* inion) :: NEGATIVE : POSITIVE

82. DAVID LIVINGSTONE : NILE RIVER :: MUNGO PARK : (*a.* Amazon River, *b.* Mississippi River, *c.* Niger River, *d.* Ganges River)

83. (*a.* adagio, *b.* piano, *c.* animato, *d.* allegro) : ANDANTE :: SLOW : MODERATE

84. RIYADH : SAUDI ARABIA :: (*a.* Abu Dhabi, *b.* Aden, *c.* Qatar, *d.* Muscat) : UNITED ARAB EMIRATES

85. CALORIE : HEAT :: JOULE : (*a.* quality, *b.* luminosity, *c.* work, *d.* radioactivity)

86. REPTILIA : REPTILES :: (*a.* passerine, *b.* vertebrate, *c.* archaeopteryx, *d.* Aves) : BIRDS

87. (*a.* Captain Cook, *b.* Father Serra, *c.* Father Hennepin, *d.* Father Damien) : HAWAII :: MOTHER TERESA : INDIA

88. ISRAEL : STAR OF DAVID :: TURKEY : (*a.* sickle, *b.* crescent, *c.* cross, *d.* sun)

89. LETTERPRESS : RAISED LETTERS :: (*a.* gravure, *b.* offset, *c.* roller, *d.* silkscreen) : RECESSED LETTERS

90. (*a.* complementary, *b.* acute, *c.* obtuse, *d.* vertical) : SUPPLEMENTARY :: 90 : 180

91. TAME : SUBJUGATE :: USE : (*a.* treat, *b.* squander, *c.* vanquish, *d.* tarnish)

92. (*a.* Marx, *b.* Friedman, *c.* Malthus, *d.* Keynes) : NEW ECONOMICS :: MAILER : NEW JOURNALISM

93. DUCHY : (*a.* Estonia, *b.* Belgium, *c.* Luxembourg, *d.* Monaco) :: MONARCHY : SPAIN

94. α : ϕ :: ALPHA : (*a.* phi, *b.* theta, *c.* psi, *d.* omega)

95. DREAD : (*a.* anticipate, *b.* fear, *c.* defend, *d.* unnerve) :: DISAPPROVE : SUPPORT

96. *SISTER CARRIE : MOTHER COURAGE* :: (*a.* James, *b.* Dreiser, *c.* Wharton, *d.* Howells) : BRECHT

97. BACH : (*a.* Chopin, *b.* Schubert, *c.* Beethoven, *d.* Purcell) :: BAROQUE : CLASSICAL

98. JUDGE : LAW :: ACTUARY : (*a.* probability, *b.* premium, *c.* accident, *d.* mathematics)

99. (*a.* enzyme, *b.* tissue, *c.* lutein, *d.* xylem) : PROTEIN :: BACILLUS : BACTERIUM

100. PANEL : TRIPTYCH :: (*a.* pane, *b.* note, *c.* page, *d.* form) : TRIPLET

STOP

If there is any time remaining, go back and check your work.

PRACTICE TEST 9
ANSWER KEY

1. b	26. d	51. d	76. a
2. d	27. a	52. a	77. b
3. a	28. b	53. b	78. a
4. b	29. c	54. c	79. b
5. a	30. b	55. b	80. c
6. c	31. c	56. d	81. b
7. b	32. a	57. b	82. c
8. d	33. c	58. c	83. a
9. c	34. d	59. d	84. a
10. c	35. c	60. c	85. c
11. a	36. d	61. b	86. d
12. d	37. b	62. d	87. d
13. c	38. a	63. a	88. b
14. b	39. a	64. c	89. a
15. d	40. d	65. c	90. a
16. c	41. c	66. c	91. b
17. b	42. a	67. d	92. d
18. a	43. b	68. a	93. c
19. c	44. c	69. c	94. b
20. d	45. c	70. b	95. a
21. b	46. b	71. c	96. b
22. d	47. a	72. d	97. c
23. c	48. b	73. c	98. a
24. c	49. d	74. d	99. a
25. a	50. b	75. b	100. b

PRACTICE TEST 9
EXPLANATORY ANSWERS

1. (*a.* Bre'r, **b. Reynard**, *c.* Remus, *d.* Mole) : FOX :: CHANTICLEER : ROOSTER
   (**b**) In medieval fables, *Reynard* is a cunning *fox*, and *Chanticleer* is a *rooster*.
   Conversion

2. POLLUTION : (*a.* effluence, *b.* rain, *c.* sanitation, ***d.* saturation**) :: SMOG : FOG
   (**d**) *Smog* is the result of *pollution*, and *fog* is the result of *saturation*. **Object/Action**

3. (*a.* **turtle**, *b.* newt, *c.* spring peeper, *d.* eft) : FROG :: REPTILE : AMPHIBIAN
   (**a**) All the animals listed are *amphibians* except for the *turtle*, which is a *reptile*.
   Classification

4. LADY CHATTERLEY : LADY WINDERMERE :: LAWRENCE :
   (*a.* Sheridan, ***b.* Wilde**, *c.* Thackery, *d.* Trollope)
   (**b**) Lady Chatterley is a character created by D. H. *Lawrence* in the 1928 novel *Lady Chatterley's Lover*. Lady Windermere is a character created by Oscar *Wilde* in the 1892 play *Lady Windermere's Fan*. **Object/Action**

5. WORRISOME : (*a.* **disquieting**, *b.* ambiguous, *c.* enlightening, *d.* noteworthy) ::
   SUSPICIOUS : DUBIOUS
   (**a**) *Worrisome* and *disquieting* both mean "troubling." *Suspicious* and *dubious* both mean "mistrustful." **Synonym**

6. DEIFIED : HISS :: (*a.* allegory, *b.* litotes, ***c.* palindrome**, *d.* tautology) :
   ONOMATOPOEIA
   (**c**) The word *deified* is spelled the same backward and forward, making it a *palindrome*. The word *hiss* sounds like what it means, making it an example of *onomatopoeia*. **Classification**

7. (*a.* Castile, ***b.* Bourbon**, *c.* Aragon, *d.* Jacques) : FRANCE :: STUART : ENGLAND
   (**b**) The *Bourbons* were a *French* royal family. The *Stuarts* were a *British* royal family.
   Characteristic

8. DANIEL : LION :: JONAH : (*a.* tiger, *b.* bear, *c.* lamb, ***d.* whale**)
   (**d**) According to the Old Testament, *Daniel* received divine protection when he was thrown into a *lion's* den. *Jonah* was equally protected when he rode to safety in the belly of a *whale*. **Object/Action**

9. BEAUMONT : (*a.* Mulligan, *b.* Beauchamp, ***c.* Fletcher**, *d.* Hart) :: GILBERT :
   SULLIVAN
   (**c**) Francis *Beaumont* and John *Fletcher* were Elizabethan dramatists and collaborators.
   W. S. *Gilbert* and Arthur *Sullivan* collaborated on a number of light operas in the late nineteenth century. **Part/Whole**

10. POLYNESIAN : SAMOAN :: CHINESE : (*a.* Thai, *b.* Tahitian, *c.* **Cantonese**, *d.* Confucianism)
    (c) *Samoan* is classified as one of the *Polynesian* languages. *Cantonese* is one of the *Chinese* languages. **Classification**

11. EDGAR LEE MASTERS : SPOON RIVER :: (*a.* **Thornton Wilder**, *b.* Sinclair Lewis, *c.* Washington Irving, *d.* Flannery O'Connor) : GROVER'S CORNERS
    (a) *Edgar Lee Masters* introduced readers to the fictional community of *Spoon River* in his 1915 *Spoon River Anthology*. *Thornton Wilder* created the fictional community of *Grover's Corners* in his 1938 play, *Our Town*. **Object/Action**

12. ANNAPURNA : NEPAL :: ARARAT : (*a.* Iraq, *b.* Israel, *c.* Lebanon, *d.* **Turkey**)
    (d) *Annapurna* is a mountain in *Nepal*. Mount *Ararat*, where Noah's Ark is supposed to have landed, is a mountain in *Turkey*. **Characteristic**

13. JOHN McADAM : (*a.* air travel, *b.* space travel, *c.* **road travel**, *d.* train travel) :: ROBERT FULTON : RIVER TRAVEL
    (c) In the early 1800s Scottish engineer *John McAdam* developed the method of road making called *macadamization*—raising the road bed and constructing the road of layered rocks and gravel. At around the same time, *Robert Fulton* began experimenting with versions of the steamboat. **Object/Action**

14. ISHTAR : ISIS :: BABYLON : (*a.* Greece, *b.* **Egypt**, *c.* Rome, *d.* Persia)
    (b) *Ishtar* was the *Babylonian* goddess of fertility. *Isis* was the *Egyptian* goddess of fertility. **Characteristic**

15. ACHIEVE : THRIVE :: (*a.* profit, *b.* scuffle, *c.* realize, *d.* **worry**) : AGONIZE
    (d) To *thrive* is to *achieve* greatly. To *agonize* is to *worry* greatly. **Degree**

16. ALPHA : OMEGA :: GENESIS : (*a.* Exodus, *b.* Psalms, *c.* **Revelation**, *d.* Romans)
    (c) Just as *alpha* and *omega* are the first and last letters of the Greek alphabet, so Genesis and Revelation are the first and last books of the Bible. **Sequence**

17. WHITNEY MUSEUM : (*a.* Metropolitan Museum, *b.* **Guggenheim Museum**, *c.* Museum of Modern Art, *d.* Frick Museum) :: BREUER : WRIGHT
    (b) Marcel *Breuer* did the original design for New York's *Whitney Museum*. Frank Lloyd *Wright* did the original design for New York's *Guggenheim Museum*. **Object/Action**

18. JAPAN : HONSHU :: INDONESIA : (*a.* **Java**, *b.* Malaysia, *c.* Luzon, *d.* Tasmania)
    (a) *Honshu* is the island that is the center of population for *Japan*. *Java* is the island that is the center of population for *Indonesia*. **Part/Whole**

19. ELEVATE : (*a.* revoke, *b.* denigrate, *c.* **glorify**, *d.* assuage) :: MOCK : RIDICULE
    (c) To *elevate* significantly is to *glorify*. To *mock* significantly is to *ridicule*. **Degree**

20. PAKISTAN : (*a.* Philippines, *b.* Mongolia, *c.* Laos, *d.* **Thailand**) :: RUPEE : BAHT
    (d) The *rupee* is the monetary unit used in *Pakistan*. The *baht* is the monetary unit used in *Thailand*. **Characteristic**

21. (*a.* moue, *b.* **pout**, *c.* smirk, *d.* snivel) : DISPLEASURE :: LEER : LECHERY
    (b) A *pout* signifies *displeasure*. A *leer* signifies *lechery*. **Object/Action**

22. SENTENCE : PARAGRAPH :: (*a.* poem, *b.* paragraph, *c.* verse, *d.* **line**) : STANZA
    (**d**) Just as a *sentence* may be part of a *paragraph,* so a *line* may be part of a *stanza* (in poetry). **Part/Whole**

23. GROUT : FILL :: SPOUT : (*a.* remark, *b.* plug, *c.* **discharge**, *d.* sink)
    (**c**) The purpose of *grout* is to *fill* (for example, the spaces between tiles). The purpose of a *spout* is to *discharge* (for example, water). **Object/Action**

24. (*a.* inoffensive, *b.* affable, *c.* **poisonous**, *d.* unreceptive) : INNOCUOUS :: HOSTILE : CONGENIAL
    (**c**) If something is *poisonous,* it is anything but *innocuous,* or harmless.
    If someone is *hostile,* he or she is anything but *congenial,* or friendly. **Antonym**

25. TISSUE : (*a.* **wood**, *b.* glass, *c.* gauze, *d.* net) :: TRANSLUCENT : OPAQUE
    (**a**) *Tissue* is *translucent;* it allows some light to penetrate. *Wood* is *opaque;* it prevents light from penetrating. **Characteristic**

26. JACQUES COUSTEAU : ROBERT JARVIK :: AQUALUNG : (*a.* wheelchair, *b.* iron lung, *c.* bifocals, *d.* **artificial heart**)
    (**d**) In 1943, *Jacques Cousteau* was one of the inventors of the *aqualung,* which allowed divers to stay underwater for hours at a time. In the 1980s, *Robert Jarvik* designed an *artificial heart,* which allowed some patients to survive long enough to obtain a human transplant. **Object/Action**

27. DERMA : SKIN :: (*a.* **armed**, *b.* pen, *c.* colors, *d.* drawing) : INKS
    (**a**) The letters in *derma* may be mixed to form the word *armed.* The letters in *skin* may be mixed to form the word *inks.* **Conversion**

28. CREATIVE : RESTIVE :: DERIVATIVE : (*a.* imitative, *b.* **serene**, *c.* inventive, *d.* festive)
    (**b**) Something that is *creative* is not *derivative,* or imitative. Someone who is *restive,* or restless, is not *serene.* **Antonym**

29. (*a.* litigious, *b.* functional, *c.* **credible**, *d.* limited) : BELIEVABLE :: CONTENTIOUS : DEBATABLE
    (**c**) A *credible* story is *believable.* A *contentious* story is *debatable.* **Synonym**

30. MURDER : CROW :: SETT : (*a.* trap, *b.* **badger**, *c.* fox, *d.* otter)
    (**b**) A group of *crows* is called a *murder.* A group of *badgers* is called a *sett.* **Part/Whole**

31. *KING LEAR* : TRAGEDY :: (*a. Pericles, Prince of Tyre, b. Timon of Athens, c. King John, d. Julius Caesar*) : HISTORY
    (**c**) Shakespearean drama is classified as comedy, tragedy, or history. *King Lear* is a *tragedy. King John* is a *history.* **Classification**

32. (*a.* **direct**, *b.* unerring, *c.* offhand, *d.* sloppy) : UNDEVIATING :: BRIEF : BRUSQUE
    (**a**) To be extremely *direct* is to be *undeviating.* To be extremely *brief* is to be *brusque.* **Degree**

33. (*a.* gorilla, *b.* stork, *c.* **bumblebee**, *d.* marmoset) : APIAN :: CHIMPANZEE : SIMIAN

    (**c**) The Latin word *apis* means "*bee.*" The Latin word *sīmia* means "*ape.*" **Classification**

34. MENINGES : BRAIN :: MYELIN : (*a.* sheath, *b.* muscle, *c.* heart, *d.* **axon**)

    (**d**) *Meninges* are membranes that surround and protect the *brain. Myelin* is a layer of fatty substances that surrounds and protects nerve cells *(axons).* **Part/Whole**

35. OLIVE BRANCH : PEACE :: (*a.* white, *b.* lily, *c.* **halo**, *d.* star) : SAINTHOOD

    (**c**) Especially in art, the *olive branch* is a symbol of *peace,* and the *halo* is a symbol of *sainthood.* **Object/Action**

36. CAYUGA : (*a.* Five Federations, *b.* Tribal Alliance, *c.* Seven Eastern Tribes, *d.* **Five Nations**) :: CHEROKEE : FIVE CIVILIZED TRIBES

    (**d**) The *Five Nations* include the *Cayuga,* Seneca, Oneida, Mohawk, and Onondaga tribes. The *Five Civilized Tribes* include the *Cherokee,* Seminole, Choctaw, Creek, and Chickasaw tribes. **Classification**

37. (*a.* reptile, *b.* **mollusk**, *c.* nematode, *d.* shark) : MANTLE :: AMPHIBIAN : SKIN

    (**b**) The *mantle* of a *mollusk* such as the squid functions in much the same way as the *skin* of an *amphibian* does. **Characteristic**

38. EPISTEMOLOGY : (*a.* **knowledge**, *b.* letters, *c.* plants, *d.* science) :: AESTHETICS : ART

    (**a**) *Epistemology* is the philosophical study of *knowledge.* A*esthetics* (or "*esthetics*") is the philosophical study of *art.* **Object/Action**

39. (*a.* **twenties**, *b.* forties, *c.* sixties, *d.* eighties) : NINETIES :: ROARING : GAY

    (**a**) The 1920s were known as the *Roaring Twenties.* The 1890s were known as the *Gay Nineties.* **Characteristic**

40. RECREANT : (*a.* recreation, *b.* dominance, *c.* food, *d.* **courage**) :: PAUPER : MONEY

    (**d**) A *recreant,* or coward, lacks *courage.* A *pauper,* or poor person, lacks *money.* **Object/Action**

41. 1/64 : 1/8 :: 0.016 : (*a.* 0.25, *b.* 0.025, *c.* **0.125**, *d.* 0.32)

    (**c**) *0.016* is the decimal equivalent of *1/64. 0.125* is the decimal equivalent of *1/8.* **Conversion**

42. BALI : EAST INDIES :: (*a.* **Bonaire**, *b.* Bermuda, *c.* Mooréa, *d.* Ibiza) : WEST INDIES

    (**a**) *Bali* is an island in the *East Indies* (the Malay archipelago). *Bonaire* is an island in the *West Indies* (a string of Caribbean islands). **Characteristic**

43. (*a.* weave, *b.* **worsted**, *c.* viscose, *d.* sheep) : WOOL :: SHANTUNG : SILK

    (**b**) *Worsted* is one kind of *wool* cloth. *Shantung* is one kind of *silk* cloth. **Classification**

44. IMPETIGO : SKIN :: PHLEBITIS : (*a.* limb, *b.* skull, ***c.* vein**, *d.* sinus)
   (**c**) *Impetigo* is an infection of the *skin*. *Phlebitis* is the inflammation of a *vein*. **Characteristic**

45. KINGDOM : (*a.* class, *b.* order, ***c.* phylum**, *d.* family) :: GENUS : SPECIES
   (**c**) In taxonomy, a *phylum* is a subclass of a *kingdom*, and a *species* is a subclass of a *genus*. **Sequence**

46. (*a.* ad hominem, ***b.* ad libitum**, *c.* ad interim, *d.* ad valorem) : AT PLEASURE :: AD INFINITUM : TO INFINITY
   (**b**) The Latin phrase *ad libitum*, more commonly known as "ad lib," translates to "*at pleasure.*" *Ad infinitum* translates to "*to infinity.*" **Synonym**

47. HAYSTACKS : (***a.* Monet**, *b.* Renoir, *c.* Cezanne, *d.* Toulouse-Lautrec) :: DANCERS : DEGAS
   (**a**) Impressionist artist Claude *Monet* is known for his studies of *haystacks*. Impressionist artist Edgar *Degas* is known for his studies of ballerinas. **Object/Action**

48. IMPROVE : DETERIORATE :: IMPRESS : (*a.* electrify, ***b.* disappoint**, *c.* decline, *d.* bolster)
   (**b**) To *improve* is the opposite of to *deteriorate*. To *impress* is the opposite of to *disappoint*. **Antonym**

49. (*a.* Stephens, *b.* Rockefeller, *c.* Roosevelt, ***d.* Tarbell**) : OIL INDUSTRY :: NADER : AUTOMOBILE INDUSTRY
   (**d**) Muckraker Ida *Tarbell* took on the *oil industry* in her 1904 book *The History of the Standard Oil Company*. Modern muckraker Ralph *Nader* took on the *automobile industry* in his 1965 book *Unsafe at Any Speed*. **Object/Action**

50. ENGELS : DIALECTIC MATERIALISM :: (*a.* James, ***b.* Bentham**, *c.* Kant, *d.* Marx) : UTILITARIANISM
   (**b**) German socialist Friedrich *Engels* was a proponent of what was later termed *dialectic materialism*, which uses the concepts of thesis, antithesis, and synthesis to explain the course of human history. English philosopher Jeremy *Bentham* was an early proponent of *utilitarianism*, which urges society to strive for the greatest good for the greatest number of people. **Object/Action**

51. BASALT : (*a.* pumice, *b.* limestone, *c.* granite, ***d.* slate**) :: IGNEOUS : METAMORPHIC
   (**d**) Rock comes in three main classifications: igneous, metamorphic, and sedimentary. *Basalt* is one type of *igneous* rock. *Slate* is one type of *metamorphic* rock. **Classification**

52. PHONOLOGY : PHRENOLOGY :: SPEECH : (***a.* skull**, *b.* skin, *c.* motion, *d.* language)
   (**a**) *Phonology* is the study of *speech* sounds. *Phrenology* is the study of the structure of the *skull*. At one time it was believed that such structure could affect personality or ability. **Object/Action**

53. FAHRENHEIT : THERMOMETER :: (*a.* Ohm, ***b.*** **Hertz**, *c.* Tesla, *d.* Volta) : OSCILLATOR

(**b**) German physicist Gabriel *Fahrenheit* (1686–1736) invented the mercury *thermometer.* German physicist Heinrich Rudolf *Hertz* (1857–1894) used a simple *oscillator* to prove that electricity could be transmitted in the form of electromagnetic waves. Both scientists gave their names to units of measure. **Object/Action**

54. (*a.* tibia, *b.* ilium, ***c.*** **femur**, *d.* radius) : THIGH :: ULNA : FOREARM

(**c**) The *femur* is the *thighbone.* The *ulna* is one bone found in the *forearm.* **Part/Whole**

55. HUSSEIN : IRAQ :: (*a.* Ceausescu, ***b.*** **Tito**, *c.* Hoxha, *d.* Pompey) : YUGOSLAVIA

(**b**) Saddam *Hussein* was a longtime dictator of *Iraq.* Joseph Broz (*Tito*) was a longtime dictator of *Yugoslavia.* **Characteristic**

56. OXYGEN : ELEMENT :: WATER : (*a.* property, *b.* atom, *c.* ion, ***d.*** **molecule**)

(**d**) *Oxygen* is an *element,* which may be defined as a substance that cannot be broken down into simpler substances. *Water* is a *molecule,* a group of two or more atoms held together by chemical bonds, that is also the smallest part of a compound that retains the properties of that compound. A water molecule contains two elements—two atoms of hydrogen and one of oxygen. **Classification**

57. NICKEL : (*a.* penny, ***b.*** **dime**, *c.* quarter, *d.* silver dollar) :: JEFFERSON : ROOSEVELT

(**b**) Thomas *Jefferson* appears on the heads side of a *nickel.* Franklin *Roosevelt* appears on the heads side of a *dime.* **Characteristic**

58. (*a.* genuine, *b.* genius, ***c.*** **genuflect**, *d.* genetics) : VERB :: GENUINE : ADJECTIVE

(**c**) To *genuflect,* or bend the knee, is an action, and therefore *genuflect* is a *verb.* The word *genuine* may describe a person or thing, making it an *adjective.* **Classification**

59. DIATRIBE : (*a.* chronicle, *b.* clan, *c.* accolade, ***d.*** **rant**) :: ACCLAIM : TRIBUTE

(**d**) A *diatribe,* or tirade, is a *rant. Acclaim,* or praise, is *tribute.* **Synonym**

60. VIBRAPHONE : MARIMBA :: ELECTRIC GUITAR : (*a.* bongo, *b.* electric violin, ***c.*** **acoustic guitar**, *d.* guitar pick)

(**c**) A *vibraphone* is like an electronic version of the pitched percussion instrument called the *marimba.* An *electric guitar* is an electronic version of an *acoustic guitar.* **Conversion**

61. SORORAL : (*a.* aunt, ***b.*** **sister**, *c.* grandmother, *d.* girl) :: AVUNCULAR : UNCLE

(**b**) The word *sororal* has to do with *sisterhood.* The word *avuncular* refers to actions befitting an *uncle.* **Characteristic**

62. GASTRO- : HEPATO- :: STOMACH : (*a.* blood, *b.* lung, *c.* cell, ***d.*** **liver**)

(**d**) The prefix *gastro-,* as in *gastric ulcer,* refers to the *stomach.* The prefix *hepato-,* as in *hepatic artery,* refers to the *liver.* **Affix**

63. PERISTALSIS : (***a.*** **propulsion**, *b.* stasis, *c.* growth, *d.* digestion) :: GRIDLOCK : STANDSTILL

(a) *Peristalsis* is the natural process that leads to *propulsion* of food through the esophagus and digestive tract. *Gridlock* is the human-made process that causes traffic to come to a *standstill*. **Object/Action**

64. (*a.* area, *b.* square, *c.* **perimeter**, *d.* side) : POLYGON :: CIRCUMFERENCE : CIRCLE
    (**c**) The distance around a *polygon* is its *perimeter*. The distance around a *circle* is its *circumference*. **Characteristic**

65. FRAUDULENT : FLAVORFUL :: COUNTERFEIT : (*a.* faux, *b.* currency, *c.* **savory**, *d.* featureless)
    (**c**) Something that is *fraudulent*, or fake, may be *counterfeit*. Something that is *flavorful*, or tasty, may be *savory*. **Synonym**

66. ACT : (*a.* action, *b.* scene, *c.* **actively**, *d.* drama) :: VIEW : PREVIEWING
    (**c**) The word *actively* contains the word *act* plus two affixes. The word *previewing* contains the word *view* plus two affixes. **Conversion**

67. COAL : OIL :: WIND : (*a.* gas, *b.* weather, *c.* typhoon, *d.* **sun**)
    (**d**) *Coal* and *oil* are nonrenewable resources, whereas *wind* and *sun* are renewable resources. **Part/Whole**

68. (*a.* **agoraphobia**, *b.* acrophobia, *c.* ailurophobia, *d.* androphobia) : HYDROPHOBIA :: OPEN SPACES : WATER
    (**a**) *Agoraphobia* is fear of the agora, or marketplace. It therefore refers to fear of *open spaces*. *Hydrophobia* is fear of *water*. **Characteristic**

69. XANTHIPPE : SOCRATES :: (*a.* Elba, *b.* Corsica, *c.* **Josephine**, *d.* Wellington) : NAPOLEON
    (**c**) *Xanthippe* was the wife of *Socrates*. *Josephine* was the wife of *Napoleon*. **Sequence**

70. ELIZABETHAN : ELIZABETH I :: JACOBEAN : (*a.* Jacob II, *b.* **James I**, *c.* John, *d.* Jane Grey)
    (**b**) The era during which *Elizabeth I* reigned is the *Elizabethan* era. The era during which *James I* reigned is the *Jacobean* era. **Classification**

71. MAINE : ALAMO :: (*a.* War of 1812, *b.* Civil War, *c.* **Spanish-American War**, *d.* Indian Wars) : MEXICAN-AMERICAN WAR
    (**c**) "Remember the [battleship] *Maine*" was a rallying cry of the *Spanish-American War*. "Remember the [fort] *Alamo*" was a rallying cry of the *Mexican-American War*. **Characteristic**

72. (*a.* Siam, *b.* Kampuchea, *c.* Côte d'Ivoire, *d.* **East Pakistan**) : BANGLADESH :: BURMA : MYANMAR
    (**d**) Prior to partition, the nation of *Bangladesh* was *East Pakistan*. *Myanmar* is the local name for the nation we still call *Burma*. **Conversion**

73. CONSTABLE : (*a.* sculpture, *b.* still life, *c.* **landscapes**, *d.* seascapes) :: REYNOLDS : PORTRAITS
    (**c**) John *Constable* (1776–1837) was an English *landscape* painter. Joshua *Reynolds* (1723–1792) was an English *portrait* painter. **Object/Action**

74. WARP : (*a.* woven, *b.* cloth, *c.* twist, ***d.* weft**) :: LONGITUDE : LATITUDE
    (**d**) In weaving, the *warp* is yarn arranged lengthwise on the loom, and the *weft* (or woof) is yarn running perpendicular to the warp. In geography, *longitude* is reference lines running north to south on the globe, and *latitude* is reference lines running perpendicular to those lines. **Part/Whole**

75. PERPETUAL : PROVISIONAL :: (*a.* charitable, ***b.* compulsory**, *c.* optional, *d.* regular) : VOLUNTARY
    (**b**) Something that is *perpetual*, or ongoing, is not *provisional*, or short term. Something that is *compulsory*, or required, is not *voluntary*. **Antonym**

76. *CAKES AND ALE* : *TEA AND SYMPATHY* :: (***a.* Maugham**, *b.* Greene, *c.* Waugh, *d.* Albee) : ANDERSON
    (**a**) *Cakes and Ale* (1930) is a satirical novel by W. Somerset *Maugham*. *Tea and Sympathy* (1953) is a play and screenplay by Robert W. *Anderson*. **Object/Action**

77. ZIP CODE : AREA CODE :: FIVE : (*a.* two, ***b.* three**, *c.* seven, *d.* nine)
    (**b**) The traditional *ZIP* code has *five* digits, and an *area code* has *three*. **Characteristic**

78. SCRUPLES : (***a.* apothecary**, *b.* attorney, *c.* cleric, *d.* rancher) :: FATHOMS : SAILOR
    (**a**) *Scruples* are a unit of measure used by *apothecaries* (pharmacists). *Fathom*s are a unit of measure used by *sailors*. **Object/Action**

79. (*a.* truculent, ***b.* puerile**, *c.* veteran, *d.* adamant) : PUGNACIOUS :: MATURE : PEACEABLE
    (**b**) If you are *puerile*, or juvenile, you are not *mature*. If you are *pugnacious*, or antagonistic, you are not *peaceable*. **Antonym**

80. *EREWHON* : SAMUEL BUTLER :: *UTOPIA* : (*a.* Plato, *b.* Aldous Huxley, ***c.* Thomas More**, *d.* James Hilton)
    (**c**) *Samuel Butler* wrote the Utopian satire *Erewhon* (*nowhere* backwards) in 1872. *Thomas More* wrote *Utopia* (*nowhere* in Greek) in 1516. **Object/Action**

81. ANION : (*a.* ion, ***b.* cation**, *c.* union, *d.* inion) :: NEGATIVE : POSITIVE
    (**b**) An *anion* is a *negatively* charged ion. A *cation* is a *positively* charged ion. **Characteristic**

82. DAVID LIVINGSTONE : NILE RIVER :: MUNGO PARK : (*a.* Amazon River, *b.* Mississippi River, ***c.* Niger River**, *d.* Ganges River)
    (**c**) Scottish explorer/missionary *David Livingstone* led several expeditions to search for the source of the *Nile*. Scottish explorer *Mungo Park* led an expedition to search for the source of the *Niger*. **Object/Action**

83. (***a.* adagio**, *b.* piano, *c.* animato, *d.* allegro) : ANDANTE :: SLOW : MODERATE
    (**a**) In musical notation, *adagio* means "*slow*," and *andante* means "*moderate*." **Sequence**

84. RIYADH : SAUDI ARABIA :: (***a.* Abu Dhabi**, *b.* Aden, *c.* Qatar, *d.* Muscat) : UNITED ARAB EMIRATES
    (**a**) *Riyadh* is the capital of *Saudi Arabia*. *Abu Dhabi* is the capital of the *United Arab Emirates*. **Characteristic**

85. CALORIE : HEAT :: JOULE : (*a.* quality, *b.* luminosity, *c.* **work**, *d.* radioactivity)
(**c**) The *calorie* is a unit used to measure *heat*. The *joule* is a unit used to measure *work* (energy). **Object/Action**

86. REPTILIA : REPTILES :: (*a.* passerine, *b.* vertebrate, *c.* archaeopteryx, ***d.* Aves**) : BIRDS
(**d**) *Reptilia* is the class of animals known as *reptiles*. *Aves* is the class of animals known as *birds*. **Synonym**

87. (*a.* Captain Cook, *b.* Father Serra, *c.* Father Hennepin, ***d.* Father Damien**) : HAWAII :: MOTHER TERESA : INDIA
(**d**) *Father Damien* (1840–1889) was a missionary in *Hawaii* known for his work with lepers. *Mother Teresa* (1910–1997) was a missionary in *India* known for her work with the poor. **Characteristic**

88. ISRAEL : STAR OF DAVID :: TURKEY : (*a.* sickle, ***b.* crescent**, *c.* cross, *d.* sun)
(**b**) The *Star of David*, a six-pointed star, is a symbol of *Israel*. The *crescent* moon is a symbol of *Turkey*. **Object/Action**

89. LETTERPRESS : RAISED LETTERS :: (***a.* gravure**, *b.* offset, *c.* roller, *d.* silkscreen) : RECESSED LETTERS
(**a**) Letterpress, gravure, and offset are three forms of printing. *Letterpress* is done with *raised letters* on a plate or drum, and *gravure* is done with *recessed letters* on a plate or drum. **Characteristic**

90. (***a.* complementary**, *b.* acute, *c.* obtuse, *d.* vertical) : SUPPLEMENTARY :: 90 : 180
(**a**) Two *complementary* angles have measures that add up to *90* degrees. Two *supplementary* angles have measures that add up to *180* degrees. **Object/Action**

91. TAME : SUBJUGATE :: USE : (*a.* treat, ***b.* squander**, *c.* vanquish, *d.* tarnish)
(**b**) A negative connotation of *tame* is *subjugate*. A negative connotation of *use* is *squander*. **Degree**

92. (*a.* Marx, *b.* Friedman, *c.* Malthus, ***d.* Keynes**) : NEW ECONOMICS :: MAILER : NEW JOURNALISM
(**d**) John Maynard *Keynes* is associated with the *New Economics*. Norman *Mailer* is associated with the *New Journalism*. Neither has been truly "new" for half a century or more. **Object/Action**

93. DUCHY : (*a.* Estonia, *b.* Belgium, ***c.* Luxembourg**, *d.* Monaco) :: MONARCHY : SPAIN
(**c**) Although it is really a constitutional monarchy, *Luxembourg* still refers to itself as a *duchy*. Its grand duke (Henri) has mostly symbolic power. *Spain* is a constitutional *monarchy* whose king (Juan Carlos I) has mostly symbolic power. **Classification**

94. α : ϕ :: ALPHA : (*a.* phi, ***b.* theta**, *c.* psi, *d.* omega)
(**b**) The first symbol is the Greek letter *alpha* (α). The second is the Greek letter *theta* (ϕ). **Conversion**

95. DREAD : (*a.* **anticipate**, *b.* fear, *c.* defend, *d.* unnerve) :: DISAPPROVE : SUPPORT
    (**a**) *Dread* is the opposite of the more positive *anticipate*. *Disapprove* is the opposite of the more positive *support*. **Antonym**

96. *SISTER CARRIE* : *MOTHER COURAGE* :: (*a.* James, *b.* **Dreiser**, *c.* Wharton, *d.* Howells) : BRECHT
    (**b**) American novelist Theodore *Dreiser* published *Sister Carrie* in 1900. German playwright Bertolt *Brecht* published *Mother Courage* (more properly known as *Mother Courage and Her Children*) in 1939. **Object/Action**

97. BACH : (*a.* Chopin, *b.* Schubert, *c.* **Beethoven**, *d.* Purcell) :: BAROQUE : CLASSICAL
    (**c**) Johann Sebastian *Bach* was a composer of the *baroque* period (around 1600–1750). Ludwig van *Beethoven* was a composer of the *classical* period (around 1750–1830). **Characteristic**

98. JUDGE : LAW :: ACTUARY : (*a.* **probability**, *b.* premium, *c.* accident, *d.* mathematics)
    (**a**) A *judge* interprets and applies the *law*. An *actuary* (a risk-management professional) interprets and applies *probability*. **Object/Action**

99. (*a.* **enzyme**, *b.* tissue, *c.* lutein, *d.* xylem) : PROTEIN :: BACILLUS : BACTERIUM
    (**a**) An *enzyme* is one kind of *protein*. A *bacillus* is one kind of *bacterium*. **Classification**

100. PANEL : TRIPTYCH :: (*a.* pane, *b.* **note**, *c.* page, *d.* form) : TRIPLET
    (**b**) A *triptych* is a work of art painted on three *panels*. A *triplet* is a group of three *notes* played in the time allotted for two. **Part/Whole**

PRACTICE TEST 10
ANSWER SHEET

1. Ⓐ Ⓑ Ⓒ Ⓓ	26. Ⓐ Ⓑ Ⓒ Ⓓ	51. Ⓐ Ⓑ Ⓒ Ⓓ	76. Ⓐ Ⓑ Ⓒ Ⓓ
2. Ⓐ Ⓑ Ⓒ Ⓓ	27. Ⓐ Ⓑ Ⓒ Ⓓ	52. Ⓐ Ⓑ Ⓒ Ⓓ	77. Ⓐ Ⓑ Ⓒ Ⓓ
3. Ⓐ Ⓑ Ⓒ Ⓓ	28. Ⓐ Ⓑ Ⓒ Ⓓ	53. Ⓐ Ⓑ Ⓒ Ⓓ	78. Ⓐ Ⓑ Ⓒ Ⓓ
4. Ⓐ Ⓑ Ⓒ Ⓓ	29. Ⓐ Ⓑ Ⓒ Ⓓ	54. Ⓐ Ⓑ Ⓒ Ⓓ	79. Ⓐ Ⓑ Ⓒ Ⓓ
5. Ⓐ Ⓑ Ⓒ Ⓓ	30. Ⓐ Ⓑ Ⓒ Ⓓ	55. Ⓐ Ⓑ Ⓒ Ⓓ	80. Ⓐ Ⓑ Ⓒ Ⓓ
6. Ⓐ Ⓑ Ⓒ Ⓓ	31. Ⓐ Ⓑ Ⓒ Ⓓ	56. Ⓐ Ⓑ Ⓒ Ⓓ	81. Ⓐ Ⓑ Ⓒ Ⓓ
7. Ⓐ Ⓑ Ⓒ Ⓓ	32. Ⓐ Ⓑ Ⓒ Ⓓ	57. Ⓐ Ⓑ Ⓒ Ⓓ	82. Ⓐ Ⓑ Ⓒ Ⓓ
8. Ⓐ Ⓑ Ⓒ Ⓓ	33. Ⓐ Ⓑ Ⓒ Ⓓ	58. Ⓐ Ⓑ Ⓒ Ⓓ	83. Ⓐ Ⓑ Ⓒ Ⓓ
9. Ⓐ Ⓑ Ⓒ Ⓓ	34. Ⓐ Ⓑ Ⓒ Ⓓ	59. Ⓐ Ⓑ Ⓒ Ⓓ	84. Ⓐ Ⓑ Ⓒ Ⓓ
10. Ⓐ Ⓑ Ⓒ Ⓓ	35. Ⓐ Ⓑ Ⓒ Ⓓ	60. Ⓐ Ⓑ Ⓒ Ⓓ	85. Ⓐ Ⓑ Ⓒ Ⓓ
11. Ⓐ Ⓑ Ⓒ Ⓓ	36. Ⓐ Ⓑ Ⓒ Ⓓ	61. Ⓐ Ⓑ Ⓒ Ⓓ	86. Ⓐ Ⓑ Ⓒ Ⓓ
12. Ⓐ Ⓑ Ⓒ Ⓓ	37. Ⓐ Ⓑ Ⓒ Ⓓ	62. Ⓐ Ⓑ Ⓒ Ⓓ	87. Ⓐ Ⓑ Ⓒ Ⓓ
13. Ⓐ Ⓑ Ⓒ Ⓓ	38. Ⓐ Ⓑ Ⓒ Ⓓ	63. Ⓐ Ⓑ Ⓒ Ⓓ	88. Ⓐ Ⓑ Ⓒ Ⓓ
14. Ⓐ Ⓑ Ⓒ Ⓓ	39. Ⓐ Ⓑ Ⓒ Ⓓ	64. Ⓐ Ⓑ Ⓒ Ⓓ	89. Ⓐ Ⓑ Ⓒ Ⓓ
15. Ⓐ Ⓑ Ⓒ Ⓓ	40. Ⓐ Ⓑ Ⓒ Ⓓ	65. Ⓐ Ⓑ Ⓒ Ⓓ	90. Ⓐ Ⓑ Ⓒ Ⓓ
16. Ⓐ Ⓑ Ⓒ Ⓓ	41. Ⓐ Ⓑ Ⓒ Ⓓ	66. Ⓐ Ⓑ Ⓒ Ⓓ	91. Ⓐ Ⓑ Ⓒ Ⓓ
17. Ⓐ Ⓑ Ⓒ Ⓓ	42. Ⓐ Ⓑ Ⓒ Ⓓ	67. Ⓐ Ⓑ Ⓒ Ⓓ	92. Ⓐ Ⓑ Ⓒ Ⓓ
18. Ⓐ Ⓑ Ⓒ Ⓓ	43. Ⓐ Ⓑ Ⓒ Ⓓ	68. Ⓐ Ⓑ Ⓒ Ⓓ	93. Ⓐ Ⓑ Ⓒ Ⓓ
19. Ⓐ Ⓑ Ⓒ Ⓓ	44. Ⓐ Ⓑ Ⓒ Ⓓ	69. Ⓐ Ⓑ Ⓒ Ⓓ	94. Ⓐ Ⓑ Ⓒ Ⓓ
20. Ⓐ Ⓑ Ⓒ Ⓓ	45. Ⓐ Ⓑ Ⓒ Ⓓ	70. Ⓐ Ⓑ Ⓒ Ⓓ	95. Ⓐ Ⓑ Ⓒ Ⓓ
21. Ⓐ Ⓑ Ⓒ Ⓓ	46. Ⓐ Ⓑ Ⓒ Ⓓ	71. Ⓐ Ⓑ Ⓒ Ⓓ	96. Ⓐ Ⓑ Ⓒ Ⓓ
22. Ⓐ Ⓑ Ⓒ Ⓓ	47. Ⓐ Ⓑ Ⓒ Ⓓ	72. Ⓐ Ⓑ Ⓒ Ⓓ	97. Ⓐ Ⓑ Ⓒ Ⓓ
23. Ⓐ Ⓑ Ⓒ Ⓓ	48. Ⓐ Ⓑ Ⓒ Ⓓ	73. Ⓐ Ⓑ Ⓒ Ⓓ	98. Ⓐ Ⓑ Ⓒ Ⓓ
24. Ⓐ Ⓑ Ⓒ Ⓓ	49. Ⓐ Ⓑ Ⓒ Ⓓ	74. Ⓐ Ⓑ Ⓒ Ⓓ	99. Ⓐ Ⓑ Ⓒ Ⓓ
25. Ⓐ Ⓑ Ⓒ Ⓓ	50. Ⓐ Ⓑ Ⓒ Ⓓ	75. Ⓐ Ⓑ Ⓒ Ⓓ	100. Ⓐ Ⓑ Ⓒ Ⓓ

PRACTICE TEST 10

Directions: For each question, you will see three capitalized words and four answer choices labeled *a, b, c,* and *d* in parentheses. Choose the answer that best completes the analogy posed by the three capitalized words. Use the answer sheet on page 221 to record your answers.

Time: 50 Minutes

1. T SQUARE : (*a.* architect, *b.* physicist, *c.* photographer, *d.* compass) :: MITER BOX : FRAMER

2. PLEAT : SKIRT :: CRENELLATION : (*a.* trousers, *b.* wharf, *c.* battlement, *d.* bookcase)

3. (*a.* rearm, *b.* finalize, *c.* generate, *d.* safeguard) : INSTIGATE :: ANNIHILATE : CREATE

4. BAUM : OZ :: LEWIS : (*a.* Aslan, *b.* Wonderland, *c.* Merlin, *d.* Narnia)

5. MECCA : MUHAMMAD :: (*a.* Jerusalem, *b.* Bethlehem, *c.* Nazareth, *d.* Calvary) : JESUS

6. RUBICON : (*a.* war, *b.* health, *c.* fortune, *d.* peace) :: STYX : DEATH

7. COMPLIMENT : CRITICISM :: COMPLEMENT : (*a.* conflict, *b.* critique, *c.* concealment, *d.* contempt)

8. (*a.* bowsprit, *b.* crossbow, *c.* cudgel, *d.* barb) : STRIKE :: SLINGSHOT : PROJECT

9. ANODE : (*a.* electrode, *b.* ion, *c.* electrolyte, *d.* cathode) :: POSITIVE : NEGATIVE

10. TERMINATE : FOUND :: EXTERMINATE : (*a.* hearten, *b.* revive, *c.* expire, *d.* dictate)

11. SALIVARY GLANDS : GASTRIC GLANDS :: MOUTH : (*a.* esophagus, *b.* stomach, *c.* small intestine, *d.* liver)

12. NOVA SCOTIA : PROVINCE :: NEW SOUTH WALES : (*a.* country, *b.* territory, *c.* republic, *d.* state)

13. THERMODYNAMICS : (*a.* electrodynamics, *b.* solid state physics, *c.* nuclear physics, *d.* quantum mechanics) :: HEAT : ATOMIC NUCLEI

14. ALHAMBRA : TAJ MAHAL :: (*a.* Spain, *b.* Morocco, *c.* Algeria, *d.* Portugal) : INDIA

15. *SWAN LAKE* : BALLET COMPANY :: (*a. Water Music, b. An American in Paris, c. The Stars and Stripes Forever, d. Hansel and Gretel*) : MARCHING BAND

16. VIRGINIA CREEPER : VINE :: SEQUOIA : (*a.* shrub, *b.* invasive, *c.* variegated, *d.* conifer)

17. NORTHERN HEMISPHERE : SOUTHERN HEMISPHERE :: (*a.* Peru, *b.* India, *c.* Tanzania, *d.* Fiji) : AUSTRALIA

18. (*a.* Jocasta, *b.* Hamlet, *c.* Polonius, *d.* Electra) : OPHELIA :: ORESTES : LAERTES

19. FORESTED : TIMBERED :: GRASSY : (*a.* barren, *b.* wooded, *c.* verdant, *d.* taiga)

20. MORSE : (*a.* communication, *b.* education, *c.* oratory, *d.* oceanography) :: LAND : PHOTOGRAPHY

21. (*a.* revered, *b.* vanquished, *c.* veritable, *d.* inventive) : VENERABLE :: FALSE : DISREPUTABLE

22. PICK : (*a.* plant, *b.* trowel, *c.* shard, *d.* foliage) :: ARCHAEOLOGIST : BOTANIST

23. WASHINGTON IRVING : RIP VAN WINKLE :: (*a.* Samuel Clemens, *b.* Booth Tarkington, *c.* Bret Harte, *d.* F. Scott Fitzgerald) : PUDD'NHEAD WILSON

24. SODIUM : ALKALI METAL :: URANIUM : (*a.* alloy, *b.* rare earth metal, *c.* transition metal, *d.* inert gas)

25. SQUARE UNIT : CUBIC UNIT :: (*a.* perimeter, *b.* distance, *c.* ratio, *d.* area) : VOLUME

26. UNITED NATIONS : NATO :: NEW YORK CITY : (*a.* Washington, *b.* London, *c.* Brussels, *d.* Geneva)

27. (*a.* benign, *b.* tasty, *c.* parched, *d.* cactus) : SUCCULENT :: ATTRACTIVE : GORGEOUS

28. PARR : (*a.* newt, *b.* rabbit, *c.* salmon, *d.* spider) :: TADPOLE : FROG

29. MILL : GRIND :: (*a.* iron, *b.* press, *c.* burden, *d.* motor) : SQUEEZE

30. (*a.* pack, *b.* mob, *c.* troop, *d.* herd) : BABOON :: ARMY : ANT

31. NEGLECT : (*a.* stalk, *b.* nurture, *c.* clamber, *d.* abandon) :: PESTER : HARASS

32. BLUEPRINT : HOUSE :: ORRERY : (*a.* solar system, *b.* skyscraper, *c.* factory, *d.* ocean)

33. CALDECOTT : (*a.* journalism, *b.* advertising, *c.* picture books, *d.* poetry) :: NEWBERY : CHILDREN'S LITERATURE

34. (*a.* bird, *b.* sibling, *c.* order, *d.* flight) : PARENT :: WING : BEAK

35. GEORGE PULLMAN : TRAIN TRAVEL :: RICHARD GATLING : (*a.* space travel, *b.* marine science, *c.* legislation, *d.* warfare)

36. POSSESSIVE : (*a.* pronoun, *b.* singular, *c.* objective, *d.* myself) :: MINE : ME

37. NILE : MEDITERRANEAN :: MEKONG : (*a.* South China Sea, *b.* Indian Ocean, *c.* Coral Sea, *d.* Arabian Sea)

38. STAMP : SQUASH :: SMACK : (*a.* hug, *b.* wedge, *c.* scale, *d.* clout)

39. UNICELLULAR : MULTICELLULAR :: YEAST : (*a.* amoeba, *b.* mouse, *c.* prokaryote, *d.* blue-green alga)

40. SAHARA : AFRICA :: (*a.* Mato Grosso, *b.* Kalahari, *c.* Yucatan, *d.* Patagonian) : SOUTH AMERICA

41. * : . . . . :: ASTERISK : (*a.* em space, *b.* ellipses, *c.* dash, *d.* omission)

42. DOGGED : RAGGED :: (*a.* steadfast, *b.* frayed, *c.* modish, *d.* irresolute) : ELEGANT

43. ETHICS : METAPHYSICS :: MORALITY : (*a.* reality, *b.* principles, *c.* pleasure, *d.* change)

44. PIRANDELLO : (*a.* Onegin, *b.* Ionesco, *c.* Albee, *d.* Machado) :: ITALIAN : FRENCH

45. ETIOLOGY : ETHOLOGY :: (*a.* language, *b.* disease, *c.* good and evil, *d.* sensation) : BEHAVIOR

46. (*a.* cranberry, *b.* Jerusalem artichoke, *c.* hop, *d.* crabapple) : FLOWER :: TOMATO : FRUIT

47. STAMP : (*a.* stick, *b.* mail, *c.* seal, *d.* pane) :: PAINT : CAN

48. KEYPAD : KEYBOARD :: (*a.* alarm system, *b.* electric piano, *c.* alphanumeric, *d.* typewriter) : COMPUTER

49. (*a.* Dinesen, *b.* Lindstrom, *c.* Strindberg, *d.* Forster) : DRAMA :: ANDERSEN : FAIRY TALES

50. DETERMINISM : CAUSALITY :: RATIONALISM : (*a.* epistemology, *b.* relativism, *c.* cosmology, *d.* semantics)

51. DIURNAL : (*a.* nocturnal, *b.* crepuscular, *c.* refractive, *d.* monocarpic) :: DAYTIME : DUSK

52. SEPTUM : DIVISION :: LATERAL LINE : (*a.* amalgamation, *b.* reproduction, *c.* classification, *d.* perception)

53. PERU : INCA :: (*a.* Colombia, *b.* Brazil, *c.* Mexico, *d.* Argentina) : AZTEC

54. PRESSURE : (*a.* force, *b.* voltage, *c.* reduction, *d.* saturation) :: PUMP : BATTERY

55. (*a.* 44, *b.* 24, *c.* 16, *d.* 8) : 4 :: 66 : 11

56. DRAWING : (*a.* sculpture, *b.* painting, *c.* watercolor, *d.* auction) :: TWO : THREE

57. (*a.* shell, *b.* cannon, *c.* caliber, *d.* agate) : AMMUNITION :: PICA : TYPE

58. PHALANX : (*a.* esophagus, *b.* sternum, *c.* shoulder, *d.* finger) :: MANDIBLE : JAW

59. (*a.* Hong Kong, *b.* Switzerland, *c.* Slovakia, *d.* South Korea) : DOLLAR :: SOUTH AFRICA : RAND

60. HORSE : DONKEY :: MARE : (*a.* molly, *b.* jenny, *c.* burro, *d.* hinny)

61. TRINIDAD : CARIBBEAN :: (*a.* Azores, *b.* Montserrat, *c.* Crete, *d.* Mauritius) : MEDITERRANEAN

62. (*a.* William I, *b.* Charles II, *c.* George I, *d.* Henry II) : PLANTAGENET :: ELIZABETH I : TUDOR

63. BAIL : HAIL :: (*a.* vessel, *b.* taxicab, *c.* amount, *d.* security) : SLEET

64. (*a.* wholly, *b.* blessed, *c.* pie, *d.* fragment) : PIECE :: HOLY : PEACE

65. SUPERIOR : NORTH AMERICA :: (*a.* anterior, *b.* Guinea, *c.* Victoria, *d.* Nyasa) : AFRICA

66. HEMO- : HEMI- :: (*a.* deficient, *b.* sleep, *c.* twice, *d.* blood) : HALF

67. (*a.* Rabelais, *b.* Poe, *c.* Defoe, *d.* Diderot) : GARGANTUA :: SHELLEY : FRANKENSTEIN'S MONSTER

68. WINTHROP : (*a.* Massachusetts, *b.* Rhode Island, *c.* New York, *d.* Virginia) :: PENN : PENNSYLVANIA

69. BLAMEWORTHY : REPREHENSIBLE :: PLAUSIBLE : (*a.* culpable, *b.* logical, *c.* oracular, *d.* influential)

70. VENUS : MARS :: (*a.* Artemis, *b.* Athena, *c.* Aphrodite, *d.* Minerva) : ARES

71. BIT : BYTE :: (*a.* cup, *b.* pint, *c.* quart, *d.* liter) : GALLON

72. LION : MANE :: TURKEY : (*a.* caruncle, *b.* spur, *c.* feather, *d.* beard)

73. (*a.* gavotte, *b.* minuet, *c.* polka, *d.* two-step) : FOXTROT :: NINETEENTH : TWENTIETH

74. HALLOWEEN : PAGAN :: (*a.* Sukkoth, *b.* Hanukkah, *c.* Passover, *d.* All Hallow's Eve) : JUDAISM

75. NIKE : (*a.* moon, *b.* sport, *c.* justice, *d.* victory) :: DEMETER : EARTH

76. (*a.* abacus, *b.* arithmetic, *c.* numerals, *d.* computer) : CALCULATOR :: TYPEWRITER : WORD PROCESSOR

77. GREGARIOUS : INTROVERTED :: CONFIDENT : (*a.* taciturn, *b.* vacillating, *c.* retrofitted, *d.* poised)

78. QUISLING : (*a.* Burr, *b.* Washington, *c.* Delaware, *d.* Hamilton) :: NORWAY : AMERICA

79. (*a.* HVAC, *b.* convection, *c.* refrigeration, *d.* cooling coils) : GAS :: CONDENSING COILS : LIQUID

80. GEORGIA : (*a.* fescue, *b.* peach, *c.* bulldog, *d.* rye) :: KENTUCKY : BLUEGRASS

81. REMARKABLE : MUNDANE :: FERAL : (*a.* humdrum, *b.* notable, *c.* domesticated, *d.* undaunted)

82. (*a.* pike, *b.* chickadee, *c.* stream, *d.* dolphin) : PICKEREL :: SPARROW : ROBIN

83. ROMULUS : REMUS :: (*a.* Achilles, *b.* Seine, *c.* Rome, *d.* Hector) : PARIS

84. ADDITION : DIVISION :: SUM : (*a.* divisor, *b.* quotient, *c.* dividend, *d.* remainder)

85. SCALES : JUDGMENT :: (*a.* kabballah, *b.* pentacle, *c.* seven seals, *d.* Lion of Judah) : LAST JUDGMENT

86. EARSPLITTING : BACKBREAKING :: (*a.* arduous, *b.* thunderous, *c.* heartbreaking, *d.* rail splitting) : LABORIOUS

87. 2 BILLION : (*a.* 1776, *b.* 1804, *c.* 1927, *d.* 1965) :: 4 BILLION : 1974

88. (*a.* illimitable, *b.* illicit, *c.* ill-equipped, *d.* illiberal) : CIRCUMSCRIBE :: ILLEGIBLE : DECIPHER

89. VIOLENT : AGGRESSIVE :: (*a.* brutal, *b.* passive, *c.* packaged, *d.* inferential) : SUBMISSIVE

90. VOSTOK : RUSSIA :: (*a.* Fundy, *b.* Carpenter, *c.* Mercury, *d.* Florida) : UNITED STATES

91. COOK : FROBISHER :: EASTER ISLAND : (*a.* Baffin Island, *b.* Isle of Man, *c.* Balearic Islands, *d.* Solomon Islands)

92. ARTERY : ARTERIOLE :: VEIN : (*a.* varicose, *b.* heart valve, *c.* venule, *d.* vena cava)

93. *YOU CAN'T GO HOME AGAIN* : *YOU CAN'T TAKE IT WITH YOU* :: (*a.* Fitzgerald, *b.* Hemingway, *c.* Welty, *d.* Wolfe) : HART/KAUFMAN

94. VERTEBRATE : INVERTEBRATE :: SNAKE : (*a.* bat, *b.* shrew, *c.* scorpion, *d.* eft)

95. LORD JIM : LUCKY JIM :: CONRAD : (*a.* Lardner, *b.* Perelman, *c.* Jerome, *d.* Amis)

96. THALIA : GRACES :: CLOTHO : (*a.* Fates, *b.* Muses, *c.* Horae, *d.* Danaids)

97. COIN : (*a.* mint, *b.* currency, *c.* financier, *d.* numismatist) :: STAMP : PHILATELIST

98. (*a.* clamorous, *b.* resonant, *c.* agreeable, *d.* reedy) : SONOROUS :: STRIDENT : SHRILL

99. RICHARD I : THE LIONHEARTED :: ETHELRED II : (*a.* the Peaceable, *b.* the Martyr, *c.* the Unready, *d.* the Confessor)

100. (*a.* spinach, *b.* beet, *c.* corn, *d.* potato) : BEAN :: MONOCOT : DICOT

STOP

If there is any time remaining, go back and check your work.

PRACTICE TEST 10
ANSWER KEY

1. a	26. c	51. b	76. a
2. c	27. b	52. d	77. b
3. b	28. c	53. c	78. a
4. d	29. b	54. b	79. d
5. b	30. c	55. b	80. b
6. a	31. d	56. a	81. c
7. a	32. a	57. c	82. a
8. c	33. c	58. d	83. d
9. d	34. b	59. a	84. b
10. b	35. d	60. b	85. c
11. b	36. c	61. c	86. b
12. d	37. a	62. d	87. c
13. c	38. d	63. d	88. a
14. a	39. b	64. a	89. b
15. c	40. d	65. c	90. c
16. d	41. b	66. d	91. a
17. b	42. d	67. a	92. c
18. d	43. a	68. a	93. d
19. c	44. b	69. b	94. c
20. a	45. b	70. c	95. d
21. c	46. c	71. b	96. a
22. b	47. d	72. d	97. d
23. a	48. a	73. c	98. b
24. b	49. c	74. a	99. c
25. d	50. a	75. d	100. c

PRACTICE TEST 10
EXPLANATORY ANSWERS

1. T SQUARE : (*a.* **architect**, *b.* physicist, *c.* photographer, *d.* compass) :: MITER BOX :
   FRAMER
   (a) A drafter or *architect* uses a *T square* as a guide in drawing parallel lines. A *framer*
   or carpenter uses a *miter box* as a guide in making crosscuts or beveled corners.
   Object/Action

2. PLEAT : SKIRT :: CRENELLATION : (*a.* trousers, *b.* wharf, *c.* **battlement**,
   d. bookcase)
   (c) A *pleat* is a fold in a garment such as a *skirt*. A *crenellation* is a notch in the wall of
   a *battlement*. **Part/Whole**

3. (*a.* rearm, *b.* **finalize**, *c.* generate, *d.* safeguard) : INSTIGATE :: ANNIHILATE :
   CREATE
   (b) To *finalize* is the opposite of to *instigate*, or bring about. To *annihilate* is the
   opposite of to *create*. **Antonym**

4. BAUM : OZ :: LEWIS : (*a.* Aslan, *b.* Wonderland, *c.* Merlin, *d.* **Narnia**)
   (d) L. Frank *Baum* created the land of *Oz* in a series of children's books. C. S. *Lewis*
   created the land of *Narnia* (ruled by Aslan) in a series of children's books.
   Object/Action

5. MECCA : MUHAMMAD :: (*a.* Jerusalem, *b.* **Bethlehem**, *c.* Nazareth, *d.* Calvary) :
   JESUS
   (b) *Mecca*, in Saudi Arabia, is the birthplace of *Muhammad*. *Bethlehem*, on the West
   Bank in Israel, is the birthplace of Jesus. **Characteristic**

6. RUBICON : (*a.* **war**, *b.* health, *c.* fortune, *d.* peace) :: STYX : DEATH
   (a) Crossing the river *Rubicon* was an act of *war* for Julius Caesar. In Greek mythology,
   crossing the river *Styx* meant traveling to the underworld. **Object/Action**

7. COMPLIMENT : CRITICISM :: COMPLEMENT : (*a.* **conflict**, *b.* critique,
   c. concealment, *d.* contempt)
   (a) To give *criticism*, or negative assessment, is the opposite of giving a *compliment*.
   A *conflict*, or divergence, is the opposite of a *complement*, or counterpart. **Antonym**

8. (*a.* bowsprit, *b.* crossbow, *c.* **cudgel**, *d.* barb) : STRIKE :: SLINGSHOT : PROJECT
   (c) A *cudgel*, or club, is used to *strike*. A *slingshot* is used to shoot, or *project*, a
   projectile. **Object/Action**

9. ANODE : (*a.* electrode, *b.* ion, *c.* electrolyte, *d.* **cathode**) :: POSITIVE : NEGATIVE
   (d) In a battery or other electric field, the *anode* is the *positive* end, and the *cathode* is
   the *negative* end. **Characteristic**

10. TERMINATE : FOUND :: EXTERMINATE : (*a.* hearten, ***b.* revive**, *c.* expire, *d.* dictate)
    (**b**) To *terminate* is to end, whereas to *found* is to start up. To *exterminate* is to kill, whereas to *revive* is to bring back to life. **Antonym**

11. SALIVARY GLANDS : GASTRIC GLANDS :: MOUTH : (*a.* esophagus, ***b.* stomach**, *c.* small intestine, *d.* liver)
    (**b**) The *salivary glands* are found in the *mouth*. The *gastric glands* are found in the *stomach*. **Part/Whole**

12. NOVA SCOTIA : PROVINCE :: NEW SOUTH WALES : (*a.* country, *b.* territory, *c.* republic, ***d.* state**)
    (**d**) *Nova Scotia* is a *province* in eastern Canada. *New South Wales* is a *state* in southeastern Australia. **Classification**

13. THERMODYNAMICS : (*a.* electrodynamics, *b.* solid state physics, ***c.* nuclear physics**, *d.* quantum mechanics) :: HEAT : ATOMIC NUCLEI
    (**c**) *Thermodynamics* is the branch of physics that studies *heat* and its properties. *Nuclear physics* is the branch of physics that studies *atomic nuclei* and their properties. **Object/Action**

14. ALHAMBRA : TAJ MAHAL :: (***a.* Spain**, *b.* Morocco, *c.* Algeria, *d.* Portugal) : INDIA
    (**a**) The *Alhambra* is a Moorish fortress in Granada, *Spain*. The *Taj Mahal* is a mausoleum in Agra, *India*. **Characteristic**

15. *SWAN LAKE* : BALLET COMPANY :: (*a. Water Music*, *b. An American in Paris*, ***c. The Stars and Stripes Forever***, *d. Hansel and Gretel*) : MARCHING BAND
    (**c**) *Swan Lake* (music by Tchaikovsky) is likely to be part of the repertoire of a *ballet company*, and *The Stars and Stripes Forever* (by John Philip Sousa) is likely to be part of the repertoire of a *marching band*. **Object/Action**

16. VIRGINIA CREEPER : VINE :: SEQUOIA : (*a.* shrub, *b.* invasive, *c.* variegated, ***d.* conifer**)
    (**d**) A *Virginia creeper* is one kind of *vine*. A *sequoia* is one kind of *conifer* (cone-bearing tree). **Classification**

17. NORTHERN HEMISPHERE : SOUTHERN HEMISPHERE :: (*a.* Peru, ***b.* India**, *c.* Tanzania, *d.* Fiji) : AUSTRALIA
    (**b**) All of *India* is north of the equator, placing it in the *northern hemisphere*. The other countries named are south of the equator. **Characteristic**

18. (*a.* Jocasta, *b.* Hamlet, *c.* Polonius, ***d.* Electra**) : OPHELIA :: ORESTES : LAERTES
    (**d**) In Greek mythology and drama, *Electra* and *Orestes* were sister and brother, as were *Ophelia* and *Laertes* in Shakespeare's *Hamlet*. **Sequence**

19. FORESTED : TIMBERED :: GRASSY : (*a.* barren, *b.* wooded, ***c.* verdant**, *d.* taiga)
    (**c**) A *forested* area may also be called *timbered*. A *grassy* area may be called *verdant* (green). **Synonym**

20. MORSE : (***a*. communication**, *b.* education, *c.* oratory, *d.* oceanography) :: LAND : PHOTOGRAPHY
    (**a**) Samuel *Morse's* key invention, the telegraph, led to progress in the area of *communication*. Edwin *Land's* key invention, instant photography, led to progress in the area of *photography*. **Object/Action**

21. (*a.* revered, *b.* vanquished, ***c*. veritable**, *d.* inventive) : VENERABLE :: FALSE : DISREPUTABLE
    (**c**) The opposite of *veritable* (true) is *false*. The opposite of *venerable* (respected) is *disreputable*. **Antonym**

22. PICK : (*a.* plant, ***b*. trowel**, *c.* shard, *d.* foliage) :: ARCHAEOLOGIST : BOTANIST
    (**b**) In the field, an *archaeologist* may use a *pick,* and a *botanist* may use a *trowel.* **Object/Action**

23. WASHINGTON IRVING : RIP VAN WINKLE :: (***a*. Samuel Clemens**, *b.* Booth Tarkington, *c.* Bret Harte, *d.* F. Scott Fitzgerald) : PUDD'NHEAD WILSON
    (**a**) In his *Sketch Book, Washington Irving* invented the character *Rip Van Winkle.* In *The Tragedy of Pudd'nhead Wilson, Samuel Clemens,* better known as Mark Twain, invented the character *Pudd'nhead Wilson.* **Object/Action**

24. SODIUM : ALKALI METAL :: URANIUM : (*a.* alloy, ***b*. rare earth metal**, *c.* transition metal, *d.* inert gas)
    (**b**) In the periodic table of elements, *sodium* is classified as an *alkali metal,* and *uranium* is classified as a *rare earth metal.* **Classification**

25. SQUARE UNIT : CUBIC UNIT :: (*a.* perimeter, *b.* distance, *c.* ratio, ***d*. area**) : VOLUME
    (**d**) You use *square units* to measure the *area* of an object. You use *cubic units* to measure the *volume* of an object. **Object/Action**

26. UNITED NATIONS : NATO :: NEW YORK CITY : (*a.* Washington, *b.* London, ***c*. Brussels**, *d.* Geneva)
    (**c**) The headquarters of the *United Nations* is in *New York City.* The headquarters of *NATO* is in *Brussels,* Belgium. **Characteristic**

27. (*a.* benign, ***b*. tasty**, *c.* parched, *d.* cactus) : SUCCULENT :: ATTRACTIVE : GORGEOUS
    (**b**) Something that is very *tasty* may be described as *succulent.* Someone who is very *attractive* may be described as *gorgeous.* **Degree**

28. PARR : (*a.* newt, *b.* rabbit, ***c*. salmon**, *d.* spider) :: TADPOLE : FROG
    (**c**) A *parr* is a young *salmon.* A *tadpole* is a young *frog.* **Sequence**

29. MILL : GRIND :: (*a.* iron, ***b*. press**, *c.* burden, *d.* motor) : SQUEEZE
    (**b**) The purpose of a *mill* (as a pepper mill) is to *grind.* The purpose of a *press* (as a cider press) is to *squeeze.* **Object/Action**

30. (*a.* pack, *b.* mob, ***c*. troop**, *d.* herd) : BABOON :: ARMY : ANT
    (**c**) A group of *baboons* is a *troop.* A group of *ants* is an *army.* **Part/Whole**

31. NEGLECT : (*a.* stalk, *b.* nurture, *c.* clamber, ***d.* abandon**) :: PESTER : HARASS
    (**d**) If you *neglect* someone entirely, you *abandon* him or her. If you *pester* someone unmercifully, you *harass* him or her. **Degree**

32. BLUEPRINT : HOUSE :: ORRERY : (***a.* solar system**, *b.* skyscraper, *c.* factory, *d.* ocean)
    (**a**) A *blueprint* is a schematic of a *house*. An *orrery* is a schematic of the *solar system*. **Characteristic**

33. CALDECOTT : (*a.* journalism, *b.* advertising, ***c.* picture books**, *d.* poetry) :: NEWBERY : CHILDREN'S LITERATURE
    (**c**) The *Caldecott* Award is given for the best *picture book* of the year. The *Newbery* Award is given for the best *children's literature* of the year. **Object/Action**

34. (*a.* bird, ***b.* sibling**, *c.* order, *d.* flight) : PARENT :: WING : BEAK
    (**b**) A *sibling* and a *parent* are both parts of a family. A *wing* and a *beak* are both parts of a bird. **Part/Whole**

35. GEORGE PULLMAN : TRAIN TRAVEL :: RICHARD GATLING : (*a.* space travel, *b.* marine science, *c.* legislation, ***d.* warfare**)
    (**d**) By inventing the sleeping car that bears his name, *George Pullman* updated *train travel*. By inventing the machine gun that bears his name, *Richard Gatling* updated *warfare*. **Object/Action**

36. POSSESSIVE : (*a.* pronoun, *b.* singular, ***c.* objective**, *d.* myself) :: MINE : ME
    (**c**) The pronoun *mine* is a *possessive* form. The pronoun *me* is in the *objective* case. **Classification**

37. NILE : MEDITERRANEAN :: MEKONG : (***a.* South China Sea**, *b.* Indian Ocean, *c.* Coral Sea, *d.* Arabian Sea)
    (**a**) The *Nile* River empties into the *Mediterranean*. The *Mekong* River empties into the *South China Sea*. **Object/Action**

38. STAMP : SQUASH :: SMACK : (*a.* hug, *b.* wedge, *c.* scale, ***d.* clout**)
    (**d**) To *stamp* thoroughly is to *squash*. To *smack* thoroughly is to *clout*. **Degree**

39. UNICELLULAR : MULTICELLULAR :: YEAST : (*a.* amoeba, ***b.* mouse**, *c.* prokaryote, *d.* blue-green alga)
    (**b**) *Yeast* is a one-celled, or *unicellular* organism. A *mouse* is a *multicellular* organism. **Classification**

40. SAHARA : AFRICA :: (*a.* Mato Grosso, *b.* Kalahari, *c.* Yucatan, ***d.* Patagonian**) : SOUTH AMERICA
    (**d**) The *Sahara* Desert is in *Africa*. The *Patagonian* Desert is in *South America*. **Characteristic**

41. * : . . . :: ASTERISK : (*a.* em space, ***b.* ellipses**, *c.* dash, *d.* omission)
    (**b**) The first symbol (*) is called an *asterisk*. The three dots (. . .) are known as *ellipses*. **Conversion**

42. DOGGED : RAGGED :: (*a.* steadfast, *b.* frayed, *c.* modish, ***d.* irresolute**) : ELEGANT
(**d**) If you are *dogged*, you are resolute, not *irresolute*. If you are *ragged*, you are inelegant, not *elegant*. **Antonym**

43. ETHICS : METAPHYSICS :: MORALITY : (***a.* reality**, *b.* principles, *c.* pleasure, *d.* change)
(**a**) In philosophy, *ethics* is the study of *morality*, and *metaphysics* is the study of *reality*. **Object/Action**

44. PIRANDELLO : (*a.* Onegin, ***b.* Ionesco**, *c.* Albee, *d.* Machado) :: ITALIAN : FRENCH
(**b**) The playwright Luigi *Pirandello* wrote in *Italian*. The playwright Eugene *Ionesco* wrote in *French*. **Characteristic**

45. ETIOLOGY : ETHOLOGY :: (*a.* language, ***b.* disease**, *c.* good and evil, *d.* sensation) : BEHAVIOR
(**b**) *Etiology* is the study of *disease* and its causes. *Ethology* is the study of *behavior* as it applies to animals in their natural habitats. **Object/Action**

46. (*a.* cranberry, *b.* Jerusalem artichoke, ***c.* hop**, *d.* crabapple) : FLOWER :: TOMATO : FRUIT
(**c**) The *flower* of the *hop* plant is used to make beer. The *fruit* of the *tomato* plant is used to make tomato sauce. **Classification**

47. STAMP : (*a.* stick, *b.* mail, *c.* seal, ***d.* pane**) :: PAINT : CAN
(**d**) Postage *stamps* are sold in flats called *panes*. *Paint* is sold in *cans*. **Part/Whole**

48. KEYPAD : KEYBOARD :: (***a.* alarm system**, *b.* electric piano, *c.* alphanumeric, *d.* typewriter) : COMPUTER
(**a**) A *keypad* with numbered push buttons may be part of an *alarm system*. A *keyboard* is part of the hardware of a *computer*. **Part/Whole**

49. (*a.* Dinesen, *b.* Lindstrom, ***c.* Strindberg**, *d.* Forster) : DRAMA :: ANDERSEN : FAIRY TALES
(**c**) August *Strindberg* (1849–1912) was a Swedish playwright. Hans Christian *Andersen* (1805–1875) was a Danish author of *fairy tales*. **Object/Action**

50. DETERMINISM : CAUSALITY :: RATIONALISM : (***a.* epistemology**, *b.* relativism, *c.* cosmology, *d.* semantics)
(**a**) *Determinism* is one branch of *causality*, the area of philosophy that looks at causes and their effects. *Rationalism* is one branch of *epistemology*, the area of philosophy that looks at knowledge and its achievement. **Classification**

51. DIURNAL : (*a.* nocturnal, ***b.* crepuscular**, *c.* refractive, *d.* monocarpic) :: DAYTIME : DUSK
(**b**) An animal that is *diurnal* is active during the *day*. An animal that is *crepuscular* is active at twilight (dawn or *dusk* or both). **Characteristic**

52. SEPTUM : DIVISION :: LATERAL LINE : (*a.* amalgamation, *b.* reproduction, *c.* classification, ***d.* perception**)
    (d) The purpose of a *septum* (as in the nose or the heart) is to *divide* one part from another. The purpose of a *lateral line* (as in a fish or amphibian) is to *perceive* changes in currents or water pressure. **Object/Action**

53. PERU : INCA :: (*a.* Colombia, *b.* Brazil, ***c.* Mexico**, *d.* Argentina) : AZTEC
    (c) The *Inca* ruled *Peru* from around 1100 until the early 1500s. The *Aztec* ruled *Mexico* during the same period of time. **Characteristic**

54. PRESSURE : (*a.* force, ***b.* voltage**, *c.* reduction, *d.* saturation) :: PUMP : BATTERY
    (b) A *pump* uses *pressure* to move gas or fluid. The *voltage* in a *battery* may be thought of as electrical pressure. **Object/Action**

55. (*a.* 44, ***b.* 24**, *c.* 16, *d.* 8) : 4 :: 66 : 11
    (b) *24* divided by *4* equals 6. *66* divided by *11* equals 6. **Conversion**

56. DRAWING : (***a.* sculpture**, *b.* painting, *c.* watercolor, *d.* auction) :: TWO : THREE
    (a) *Drawing* is a *two*-dimensional art form. *Sculpture* is a *three*-dimensional art form. **Characteristic**

57. (*a.* shell, *b.* cannon, ***c.* caliber**, *d.* agate) : AMMUNITION :: PICA : TYPE
    (c) The *caliber* is a unit used to measure *ammunition* size. The *pica* is a unit used to measure *type* size. **Object/Action**

58. PHALANX : (*a.* esophagus, *b.* sternum, *c.* shoulder, ***d.* finger**) :: MANDIBLE : JAW
    (d) A *phalanx* is any of the bones in the *fingers* or toes. The *mandible* is the lower bone of the *jaw*. **Part/Whole**

59. (***a.* Hong Kong**, *b.* Switzerland, *c.* Slovakia, *d.* South Korea) : DOLLAR :: SOUTH AFRICA : RAND
    (a) *Hong Kong's* unit of currency is the Hong Kong *dollar*. *South Africa's* unit of currency is the *rand*. **Characteristic**

60. HORSE : DONKEY :: MARE : (*a.* molly, ***b.* jenny**, *c.* burro, *d.* hinny)
    (b) A *mare* is a female *horse*. A *jenny* is a female *donkey*. **Classification**

61. TRINIDAD : CARIBBEAN :: (*a.* Azores, *b.* Montserrat, ***c.* Crete**, *d.* Mauritius) : MEDITERRANEAN
    (c) *Trinidad* is an island in the *Caribbean*. *Crete* is an island in the *Mediterranean*. **Characteristic**

62. (*a.* William I, *b.* Charles II, *c.* George I, ***d.* Henry II**) : PLANTAGENET :: ELIZABETH I : TUDOR
    (d) English king *Henry II* was a member of the *Plantagenet* line. English queen *Elizabeth I* was a member of the *Tudor* line. **Classification**

63. BAIL : HAIL :: (*a.* vessel, *b.* taxicab, *c.* amount, ***d.* security**) : SLEET
    (d) *Bail* is a *security* paid to allow an accused person to await trial outside of prison. *Hail* is a form of precipitation much like *sleet*. **Synonym**

64. (*a.* **wholly**, *b.* blessed, *c.* pie, *d.* fragment) : PIECE :: HOLY : PEACE
(**a**) *Wholly* and *holy* are homophones (words that sound the same but are spelled differently); so are *piece* and *peace*. **Conversion**

65. SUPERIOR : NORTH AMERICA :: (*a.* anterior, *b.* Guinea, *c.* **Victoria**, *d.* Nyasa) : AFRICA
(**c**) *Superior* is the largest lake in *North America*. *Victoria* is the largest lake in *Africa*. (Nyasa is a lake in Africa, but it is not the largest lake there.) **Characteristic**

66. HEMO- : HEMI- :: (*a.* deficient, *b.* sleep, *c.* twice, *d.* **blood**) : HALF
(**d**) The prefix *hemo-*, as in *hemoglobin*, means *blood*. The prefix *hemi-*, as in *hemisphere*, means *half*. **Affix**

67. (*a.* **Rabelais**, *b.* Poe, *c.* Defoe, *d.* Diderot) : GARGANTUA :: SHELLEY : FRANKENSTEIN'S MONSTER
(**a**) François *Rabelais* wrote the first book of *Gargantua et Pantagruel* in 1534. Mary *Shelley* wrote *Frankenstein, or the Modern Prometheus* in 1818. **Object/Action**

68. WINTHROP : (*a.* **Massachusetts**, *b.* Rhode Island, *c.* New York, *d.* Virginia) :: PENN : PENNSYLVANIA
(**a**) John *Winthrop* (1588–1649) was a Puritan leader and founder and longtime governor of the *Massachusetts* Bay Colony. William *Penn* (1644–1718) was a Quaker leader and founder and short-term governor of *Pennsylvania*. **Characteristic**

69. BLAMEWORTHY : REPREHENSIBLE :: PLAUSIBLE : (*a.* culpable, *b.* **logical**, *c.* oracular, *d.* influential)
(**b**) To be *blameworthy* (guilty) is to be *reprehensible*. To be *plausible* is to be *logical*. **Synonym**

70. VENUS : MARS :: (*a.* Artemis, *b.* Athena, *c.* **Aphrodite**, *d.* Minerva) : ARES
(**c**) *Venus* is the Roman name for the Greek goddess *Aphrodite*. *Mars* is the Roman name for the Greek god *Ares*. **Conversion**

71. BIT : BYTE :: (*a.* cup, *b.* **pint**, *c.* quart, *d.* liter) : GALLON
(**b**) There are eight *bits* in a *byte* (a unit of measure of computer memory). There are eight *pints* in a *gallon*. **Part/Whole**

72. LION : MANE :: TURKEY : (*a.* caruncle, *b.* spur, *c.* feather, *d.* **beard**)
(**d**) A *mane* of fur around the neck is typical of a male *lion*. A bristly *beard* extending from the neck is typical of a male *turkey*. **Characteristic**

73. (*a.* gavotte, *b.* minuet, *c.* **polka**, *d.* two-step) : FOXTROT :: NINETEENTH : TWENTIETH
(**c**) The *polka* is a Bohemian dance introduced in the *nineteenth* century. The *foxtrot* is an American ballroom dance introduced in the early *twentieth* century. **Sequence**

74. HALLOWEEN : PAGAN :: (*a.* **Sukkoth**, *b.* Hanukkah, *c.* Passover, *d.* All Hallow's Eve) : JUDAISM
(**a**) *Halloween* began as a *pagan* harvest festival. *Sukkoth* is a *Judaic* harvest festival. **Classification**

75. NIKE : (*a.* moon, *b.* sport, *c.* justice, ***d.* victory**) :: DEMETER : EARTH
    (**d**) In Greek mythology, *Nike* is the winged goddess of *victory*. *Demeter* is the goddess of the *Earth* and agriculture. **Characteristic**

76. (***a.* abacus**, *b.* arithmetic, *c.* numerals, *d.* computer) : CALCULATOR :: TYPEWRITER : WORD PROCESSOR
    (**a**) A *calculator* may be considered a modern version of the *abacus*. A *word processor* may be considered a modern version of the *typewriter*. **Conversion**

77. GREGARIOUS : INTROVERTED :: CONFIDENT : (*a.* taciturn, ***b.* vacillating**, *c.* retrofitted, *d.* poised)
    (**b**) If you are *gregarious*, or outgoing, you are not *introverted*. If you are *confident*, you are not *vacillating*, or indecisive. **Antonym**

78. QUISLING : (***a.* Burr**, *b.* Washington, *c.* Delaware, *d.* Hamilton) :: NORWAY : AMERICA
    (**a**) Vidkun *Quisling* was the Norwegian fascist leader who helped Germany plan its takeover of *Norway*. His last name has come to mean "traitor." Aaron *Burr*, formerly vice president of the United States, was convicted of treason for his part in a plot to separate the Western states from the Union. Because his actions did not meet the Constitutional definition of treason, he was finally acquitted. **Characteristic**

79. (*a.* HVAC, *b.* convection, *c.* refrigeration, ***d.* cooling coils**) : GAS :: CONDENSING COILS : LIQUID
    (**d**) In a refrigerator, for example, *cooling coils* turn liquid into *gas*. *Condensing coils* turn gas back into *liquid*. **Object/Action**

80. GEORGIA : (*a.* fescue, ***b.* peach**, *c.* bulldog, *d.* rye) :: KENTUCKY : BLUEGRASS
    (**b**) The symbol of *Georgia* is the *peach*; it is known as the Peach State. The symbol of *Kentucky* is *bluegrass*; it is known as the Bluegrass State. **Conversion**

81. REMARKABLE : MUNDANE :: FERAL : (*a.* humdrum, *b.* notable, ***c.* domesticated**, *d.* undaunted)
    (**c**) If an event is *remarkable*, it is not *mundane*, or everyday. If an animal is *feral*, or wild, it is not *domesticated*. **Antonym**

82. (***a.* pike**, *b.* chickadee, *c.* stream, *d.* dolphin) : PICKEREL :: SPARROW : ROBIN
    (**a**) Both *pike* and *pickerel* are fish. Both *sparrow* and *robin* are birds. **Part/Whole**

83. ROMULUS : REMUS :: (*a.* Achilles, *b.* Seine, *c.* Rome, ***d.* Hector**) : PARIS
    (**d**) In Roman mythology, *Romulus* and *Remus* were brothers. In Greek mythology, *Hector* and *Paris* were brothers. **Sequence**

84. ADDITION : DIVISION : SUM : (*a.* divisor, ***b.* quotient**, *c.* dividend, *d.* remainder)
    (**b**) The *sum* is the answer in an *addition* problem. The *quotient* is the answer in a *division* problem. **Characteristic**

85. SCALES : JUDGMENT :: (*a.* kabballah, *b.* pentacle, ***c.* seven seals**, *d.* Lion of Judah) : LAST JUDGMENT

(c) A balance *scale* is the symbol of *judgment*. *Seven seals* are a Biblical symbol of the *Last Judgment*. **Object/Action**

86. EARSPLITTING : BACKBREAKING :: (*a.* arduous, *b.* **thunderous**, *c.* heartbreaking, *d.* rail splitting) : LABORIOUS
(**b**) An *earsplitting* noise may be called *thunderous*. A *backbreaking* chore may be called *laborious*. **Synonym**

87. 2 BILLION : (*a.* 1776, *b.* 1804, *c.* **1927**, *d.* 1965) :: 4 BILLION : 1974
(**c**) In *1927*, the world's population was around *2 billion*. Less than 50 years later *(1974)*, it had doubled to around *4 billion*. **Characteristic**

88. (*a.* **illimitable**, *b.* illicit, *c.* ill-equipped, *d.* illiberal) : CIRCUMSCRIBE :: ILLEGIBLE : DECIPHER
(**a**) Something that is *illimitable*, or without limits, cannot be *circumscribed* (limited). Something that is *illegible*, or unreadable, cannot be *deciphered*. **Object/Action**

89. VIOLENT : AGGRESSIVE :: (*a.* brutal, *b.* **passive**, *c.* packaged, *d.* inferential) : SUBMISSIVE
(**b**) A *violent* person or animal is *aggressive*. A *passive* person or animal is *submissive*. **Synonym**

90. VOSTOK : RUSSIA :: (*a.* Fundy, *b.* Carpenter, *c.* **Mercury**, *d.* Florida) : UNITED STATES
(**c**) The *Vostok* spacecraft carried the first *Russian* cosmonaut. The *Mercury* spacecraft carried the first *U.S.* astronaut. **Characteristic**

91. COOK : FROBISHER :: EASTER ISLAND : (*a.* **Baffin Island**, *b.* Isle of Man, *c.* Balearic Islands, *d.* Solomon Islands)
(**a**) Englishman James *Cook* (1728–1779) was the first Western explorer to explore and map *Easter Island* in the South Pacific. In search of a Northwest Passage, English privateer Martin *Frobisher* (c.1535–1594) explored *Baffin Island* in the North Atlantic. **Object/Action**

92. ARTERY : ARTERIOLE :: VEIN : (*a.* varicose, *b.* heart valve, *c.* **venule**, *d.* vena cava)
(**c**) An *arteriole* is the tiniest of *arteries*; it connects the artery with capillaries. A *venule* is the tiniest of *veins*; it connects the vein with capillaries. **Degree**

93. *YOU CAN'T GO HOME AGAIN* : *YOU CAN'T TAKE IT WITH YOU* ::
(*a.* Fitzgerald, *b.* Hemingway, *c.* Welty, *d.* **Wolfe**) : HART/KAUFMAN
(**d**) *You Can't Go Home Again* is the last novel (posthumously published in 1940) by American novelist Thomas *Wolfe*. *You Can't Take It with You* is a 1936 play by Moss *Hart* and George *Kaufman*. **Object/Action**

94. VERTEBRATE : INVERTEBRATE :: SNAKE : (*a.* bat, *b.* shrew, *c.* **scorpion**, *d.* eft)
(**c**) A *snake* has a backbone and is thus a *vertebrate*. A *scorpion* has an outer shell rather than a backbone and is thus an *invertebrate*. **Classification**

95. *LORD JIM : LUCKY JIM* :: CONRAD : (*a.* Lardner, *b.* Perelman, *c.* Jerome, ***d.* Amis**)
(**d**) Polish-born English novelist Joseph *Conrad* published *Lord Jim* in 1900. English novelist Kingsley *Amis* published *Lucky Jim* in 1954. **Object/Action**

96. THALIA : GRACES :: CLOTHO : (***a.* Fates**, *b.* Muses, *c.* Horae, *d.* Danaids)
(**a**) *Thalia* was one of the three *Graces,* representing good cheer. (There was a Muse named Thalia as well.) *Clotho* was one of the three *Fates,* the one responsible for spinning the thread of human life. **Classification**

97. COIN : (*a.* mint, *b.* currency, *c.* financier, ***d.* numismatist**) :: STAMP : PHILATELIST
(**d**) A collector of *coins* is a *numismatist.* A collector of *stamps* is a *philatelist.* **Object/Action**

98. (*a.* clamorous, ***b.* resonant**, *c.* agreeable, *d.* reedy) : SONOROUS :: STRIDENT : SHRILL
(**b**) A sound that is deep and *resonant* is *sonorous.* A sound that is sharp and *strident* is *shrill.* **Synonym**

99. RICHARD I : THE LIONHEARTED :: ETHELRED II : (*a.* the Peaceable, *b.* the Martyr, ***c.* the Unready**, *d.* the Confessor)
(**c**) King *Richard I* was known as Richard *the Lionhearted.* King *Ethelred II* was known as Ethelred *the Unready,* because of his young age at succession (only ten) and his lack of success at stemming Scandinavian invasions. **Conversion**

100. (*a.* spinach, *b.* beet, ***c.* corn**, *d.* potato) : BEAN :: MONOCOT : DICOT
(**c**) *Corn* is a *monocot* plant; its seeds have only one section (one seed leaf, or cotyledon). All the other plants listed are *dicots;* their seeds have two sections. **Classification**

Part IV
Appendixes

Appendix A: Vocabulary

List of Words
Roots and Affixes
-ology Words
Foreign Words and Phrases

Appendix B: Literature

Writers
Literary Terms
Literary Movements
Mythology
The Bible

Appendix C: Art

Artists
Artistic Terms
Artistic Movements

Appendix D: Music

Musicians and Composers
Musical Terms
Musical Movements
Instruments of the Orchestra

Appendix E: Natural Sciences

Chemistry
Taxonomy
Parts of the Body
Rocks
Geologic Time
Animal Groups and Homes
Scientists

Appendix F: Social Sciences

Name Changes for Countries and Cities
Explorers
Kings and Queens
Geographical Terms
Geographical Extremes
Philosophical Movements
Psychological Movements

Appendix G: Mathematics and Numbers

Mathematicians
Measurements
Currencies
Roman Numerals

Appendix A
Vocabulary

There is no good way to study for a vocabulary test. There is no way to guess what words an MAT test-maker will choose to include on the test you take. The best way to expand your vocabulary is to read a lot and to gain a basic knowledge of Greek and Latin word parts and their meanings.

LIST OF WORDS

The words here are simply higher-level vocabulary words for which it is easy to come up with synonyms or antonyms (which, you'll remember, tend to be the way vocabulary is tested on the MAT). It is unlikely that you will see a word tested that you have never seen before. It is much more likely that you will see lots of words that you've seen before but have never bothered to define.

abdicate, *v.*	to relinquish power, renounce, abandon, resign
aberration, *n.*	deviation, irregularity
abrogate, *v.*	to do away with, abolish, annul
abscond, *v.*	to leave quickly, flee
abstemious, *adj.*	self-disciplined, temperate, moderate
accede, *v.*	to give in, agree, consent
acme, *n.*	pinnacle, summit, culmination
acrid, *adj.*	bitter, caustic, pungent
acumen, *n.*	insight, wisdom, quickness
adamant, *adj.*	unyielding, obstinate, inflexible
adjudicate, *v.*	to pass judgment, arbitrate, referee
advent, *n.*	arrival, beginning, initiation
aegis, *n.*	protection, guidance, tutelage
affinity, *n.*	attraction, sympathy, resemblance
aggrandize, *v.*	to exaggerate, enhance, overdo
agnate, *adj.*	related on the father's side
alacrity, *n.*	enthusiasm, readiness, eagerness
albeit, *conj.*	notwithstanding, although
allege, *v.*	to contend, claim, assert
amalgamate, *v.*	to combine, merge, integrate
ambient, *adj.*	surrounding, encircling
ambulate, *v.*	to walk, saunter, stroll
ameliorate, *v.*	to improve, upgrade, enhance

amicable, *adj.*	friendly, cordial, harmonious
amphora, *n.*	jar, jug
anchorite, *n.*	recluse, hermit
anima, *n.*	soul, spirit
animus, *n.*	ill will, hostility, enmity
anneal, *v.*	to strengthen, harden
anomalous, *adj.*	abnormal, atypical, deviant
antebellum, *adj.*	prewar
antediluvian, *adj.*	ancient, prehistoric, primitive
apiculture, *n.*	beekeeping
aplomb, *n.*	self-confidence, composure, self-assurance
apoplectic, *adj.*	irate, angry, furious
apostate, *n.*	renegade, disbeliever, runaway
approbation, *n.*	approval, praise, commendation
arboreal, *adj.*	tree-dwelling
archetype, *n.*	standard, model, prototype
arduous, *adj.*	laborious, difficult, demanding
arras, *n.*	wall hanging, tapestry
artisan, *n.*	craftsperson
ascertain, *v.*	to discover, determine, ensure
aspersion, *n.*	insinuation, defamation, slur
assiduous, *adj.*	industrious, diligent, persistent
assuage, *v.*	to alleviate, allay, ease
atelier, *n.*	studio, workshop
audacious, *adj.*	bold, overconfident, reckless
august, *adj.*	grand, impressive, majestic
aureole, *n.*	halo, aura
auspicious, *adj.*	lucky, favorable, fortunate
austere, *adj.*	sober, plain, severe
avaricious, *adj.*	greedy, acquisitive, grasping
avuncular, *adj.*	like an uncle
axiom, *n.*	maxim, truth, principle
babel, *n.*	din, confusion, noise
badinage, *n.*	banter, repartee, chitchat
bagatelle, *n.*	trifle, triviality
bailiwick, *n.*	specialty, field of expertise
baleful, *adj.*	sinister, menacing, malevolent
banal, *adj.*	clichéd, trite, hackneyed
bane, *n.*	blight, curse, injury
bastion, *n.*	mainstay, stronghold
bazaar, *n.*	open-air market, flea market

beatific, *adj.*	saintly, blessed, venerable
beguile, *v.*	to entice, charm, captivate
behest, *n.*	command, request, order
belay, *v.*	to secure, make fast
beleaguer, *v.*	to harass, bother, pester
belie, *v.*	to contradict, misrepresent, disprove
bellicose, *adj.*	warlike, aggressive, contentious
belligerent, *adj.*	hostile, quarrelsome, argumentative
beneficent, *adj.*	kind, charitable, of assistance
benign, *adj.*	caring, kind, gentle
berate, *v.*	to scold, reproach, criticize
berserk, *adj.*	frenzied, crazy, uncontrollable
beseech *v.*	to beg, plead, implore
bibliophile *n.*	book collector
bifurcate, *v.*	to divide, branch, fork
bilk, *v.*	to cheat, swindle, defraud
blandish, *v.*	to cajole, wheedle, sweet-talk
blight, *v.*	to damage, ruin, disfigure
bludgeon, *v.*	to club, beat, bash
boisterous, *adj.*	rowdy, noisy, unruly
bolster, *v.*	to prop up, support, encourage
bombast, *n.*	bluster, pomposity, bravado
boycott, *v.*	to reject, abstain from
brackish, *adj.*	salty, briny
brusque, *adj.*	curt, abrupt, brisk
bulwark, *n.*	fortification, rampart, embankment
burgeon, *v.*	to sprout, proliferate, multiply
cabal, *n.*	faction, conspiracy, plot
cache, *n.*	hiding place, hoard, store
cacophonous, *adj.*	inharmonious, dissonant, jarring
cadence, *n.*	rhythm, pace, lilt
cajole, *v.*	to coax, persuade, entice
calumny, *n.*	slander, defamation, slur
canon, *n.*	rule, law, tenet
capacious, *adj.*	roomy, voluminous, sizable
capitulate, *v.*	to yield, surrender, submit
capricious, *adj.*	impulsive, whimsical, variable
cathartic, *adj.*	invigorating, therapeutic, liberating
caustic, *adj.*	corrosive, biting, acerbic
caveat, *n.*	caution, warning, stipulation
celerity, *n.*	swiftness, speed, haste

chagrin, *n.*	embarrassment, mortification, disappointment
charisma, *n.*	charm, magnetism, appeal
chary, *adj.*	wary, cautious, suspicious
chicanery, *n.*	trickery, deception, fraud
chide, *v.*	to scold, rebuke, reprimand
chivalrous, *adj.*	gallant, well-mannered, courteous
choleric, *adj.*	bad-tempered, irritable, belligerent
churlish, *adj.*	rude, coarse, boorish
cicatrix, *n.*	scar
circumscribe, *v.*	to restrict, limit, encircle
clamor, *v*	to demand, exclaim, shout
cleave, *v.*	to split, slice, chop
clemency, *n.*	mercy, leniency, compassion
cloying, *adj.*	syrupy, sugary, nauseating
coagulate, *v.*	to clot, congeal, solidify
cogent, *adj.*	logical, convincing, coherent
collier, *n.*	coal miner
collusion, *n.*	conspiracy, scheme, complicity
comestible, *adj.*	edible, safe to eat
commensurate, *adj.*	proportionate, corresponding, matching
commiserate, *v.*	to empathize, sympathize, show compassion
commodious, *adj.*	ample, spacious, roomy
compendium, *n.*	summary, abstract, list
complacent, *adj.*	contented, self-satisfied, unconcerned
compunction, *n.*	regret, qualm, uneasiness
conciliate, *v.*	to pacify, appease, mollify
condone, *v.*	to pardon, overlook, forgive
conflagration, *n.*	fire, inferno, blaze
conjecture, *n.*	guess, speculation, theory
construe, *v.*	to interpret, analyze, decipher
contentious, *adj.*	controversial, argumentative, debatable
contiguous, *adj.*	adjacent, abutting, bordering
contrition, *n.*	repentance, penitence, remorse
conundrum, *n.*	riddle, puzzle, mystery
convivial, *adj.*	hospitable, cordial, sociable
coquette, *n.*	flirt, tease
corporeal, *adj.*	bodily, physical
corpulent, *adj.*	fleshy, overweight, fat
cosmopolitan, *adj.*	sophisticated, international, multiethnic
cotillion, *n.*	ball, dance, prom
countenance, *n.*	appearance, face, expression

covenant, *n.*	agreement, pledge, contract
credible, *adj.*	believable, plausible, probable
cryptic, *adj.*	puzzling, mysterious, secret
cudgel, *n.*	club, stick, truncheon
culvert, *n.*	drain, sewer, channel
curate, *n.*	clergyman, cleric
cursory, *adj.*	superficial, hasty, perfunctory
dander, *n.*	ire, temper, anger
daub, *v.*	to smear, spread, paint
debonair, *adj.*	refined, suave, elegant
deferential, *adj.*	obsequious, respectful, reverent
deleterious, *adj.*	harmful, injurious, damaging
deliquesce, *v.*	to melt, liquefy
demeanor, *n.*	bearing, behavior, conduct
demur, *v.*	to object, protest, balk
denigrate, *v.*	to belittle, vilify, disparage
denizen, *n.*	resident, citizen, native
deprecate, *v.*	to condemn, denounce, criticize
dereliction, *n.*	abandonment, neglect, desertion
despoil, *v.*	to ruin, plunder, damage
desultory, *adj.*	haphazard, aimless, random
detritus, *n.*	debris, remains, fragments
devolve, *v.*	to delegate, entrust, transfer
diaphanous, *adj.*	sheer, filmy, translucent
diatribe, *n.*	invective, tirade, rant
didactic, *adj.*	informative, educational, instructive
diffident, *adj.*	shy, reticent, timid
dilatory, *adj.*	lagging, slow, sluggish
discomfit, *v.*	to embarrass, mortify, disconcert
disparage, *v.*	to belittle, mock, criticize
dissemble, *v.*	to evade, feign, disguise
dissonance, *n.*	discord, conflict, noise
doctrinaire, *adj.*	inflexible, dogmatic, strict
dogmatic, *adj.*	rigid, unbending, stubborn
dolor, *n.*	sorrow, grief, misery
dour, *adj.*	grim, gloomy, forbidding
dragoon, *v.*	to force, coerce, intimidate
drivel, *n.*	idiocy, foolishness, nonsense
duplicity, *n.*	deception, betrayal, treachery
ebullient, *adj.*	enthusiastic, merry, jovial
echelon, *n.*	rank, level, division

eclectic, *adj.*	mixed, varied, diverse
edification, *n.*	enlightenment, learning, instruction
efficacious, *adj.*	effective, successful, efficient
effrontery, *n.*	boldness, impudence, impertinence
empirical, *adj.*	experiential, verifiable, observed
emulate, *v.*	to imitate, copy, replicate
encomium, *n.*	praise, tribute, accolade
enervate, *v.*	to weaken, debilitate, enfeeble
enigma, *n.*	puzzle, mystery, riddle
ennui, *n.*	boredom, world-weariness, tedium
entreaty, *n.*	plea, appeal, supplication
ephemeral, *adj.*	transient, fleeting, short-lived
epigram, *n.*	saying, witticism, axiom
epistle, *n.*	letter, communiqué, dispatch
equivocal, *adj.*	ambiguous, unclear, indefinite
eremite, *n.*	hermit, recluse, ascetic
ersatz, *adj.*	phony, fake, artificial
escarp, *n.*	cliff, slope, precipice
ethos, *n.*	culture, character, philosophy
eulogize, *v.*	to praise, extol, honor
euphoric, *adj.*	ecstatic, joyous, elated
evanesce, *v.*	to dissipate, vaporize, disappear
evocative, *adj.*	reminiscent, suggestive, extracting
exacerbate, *v.*	to worsen, aggravate, inflame
excoriate, *v.*	to rebuke, attack, censure
exculpate, *v.*	to clear, absolve, exonerate
execrable, *adj.*	deplorable, disgusting, hateful
exegesis, *n.*	interpretation, analysis, construal
exhort, *v.*	to encourage, urge, insist
exonerate, *v.*	to acquit, pardon, vindicate
extirpate, *v.*	to pull up, uproot, abolish
extricate, *v.*	to disentangle, free, rescue
exuberant, *adj.*	enthusiastic, fervent, high-spirited
fabricate, *v.*	to manufacture, construct, concoct
fabulist, *n.*	liar, impostor, fraud
facetious, *adj.*	flippant, humorous, playful
facile, *adj.*	superficial, effortless, simplistic
factotum, *n.*	aide, assistant, subordinate
fastidious, *adj.*	painstaking, finicky, fussy
fatuous, *adj.*	inane, foolish, idiotic
fealty, *n.*	allegiance, loyalty, faithfulness

febrile, *adj.*	feverish, flushed
fecund, *adj.*	fruitful, productive, fertile
felicitous, *adj.*	lucky, fortuitous, apt
fervid, *adj.*	zealous, passionate, ardent
filial, *adj.*	relating to a son or daughter
fissure, *n.*	cleft, crack, crevice
flaccid, *adj.*	sagging, limp, lifeless
flagrant, *adj.*	blatant, brazen, overt
flippant, *adj.*	facetious, glib, offhand
flout, *v.*	to disobey, defy, contravene
foment, *v.*	to provoke, incite, agitate
founder, *v.*	to sink, fail, collapse
fracas, *n.*	disturbance, brawl, quarrel
fractious, *adj.*	peevish, irritable, ill-tempered
fraternal, *adj.*	relating to a brother
fraught, *adj.*	burdened, laden, full
fulsome, *adj.*	flattering, overgenerous, unctuous
furtive, *adj.*	sly, secretive, stealthy
gaffe, *n.*	error, blunder, faux pas
gallantry, *n.*	courtliness, chivalry, heroism
galvanize, *v.*	to rouse, stimulate, incite
gamut, *n.*	range, extent, scope
garrulous, *adj.*	talkative, voluble, chatty
gelid, *adj.*	frozen, cold, icy
gesticulate, *v.*	to gesture, signal
gird, *v.*	to encircle, surround, enclose
glib, *adj.*	smooth, persuasive, offhand
gradient, *n.*	slope, incline, hill
grandiose, *adj.*	pompous, ostentatious, flamboyant
grandiloquent, *adj.*	pretentious, pompous, overbearing
gratuitous, *adj.*	free, unnecessary, superfluous
guile, *n.*	deception, trickery, cunning
gullible, *adj.*	naive, trusting, credulous
hackneyed, *adj.*	overused, trite, clichéd
halcyon, *adj.*	peaceful, tranquil, quiet
hapless, *adj.*	unlucky, unfortunate, wretched
harangue, *n.*	tirade, rant, lecture
harbinger, *n.*	omen, forerunner, portent
hauteur, *n.*	arrogance, self-importance, haughtiness
heinous, *adj.*	odious, shocking, monstrous
heresy, *n.*	unorthodoxy, sacrilege, deviation

hiatus, *n.*	break, pause, interval
hirsute, *adj.*	hairy, bristly, shaggy
homage, *n.*	deference, worship, respect
hovel, *n.*	hut, slum, shack
hubris, *n.*	pride, arrogance, audacity
humbug, *n.*	hypocrisy, duplicity, insincerity
iconoclast, *n.*	dissident, rebel, radical
idyllic, *adj.*	tranquil, relaxing, carefree
ignoble, *adj.*	reprehensible, dastardly, shameful
ignominy, *n.*	disgrace, humiliation, shame
illicit, *adj.*	illegal, illegitimate, criminal
imbroglio, *n.*	entanglement, embarrassment, fix
immaterial, *adj.*	irrelevant, unimportant, insignificant
impecunious, *adj.*	destitute, poor, penniless
impervious, *adj.*	impermeable, resilient, impenetrable
implacable, *adj.*	ruthless, relentless, merciless
importune, *v.*	to beg, beset, pester
imprecate, *v.*	to curse, hex
impugn, *v.*	to accuse, challenge, attack
inchoate, *adj.*	unformed, undeveloped, incomplete
incontrovertible, *adj.*	unquestionable, indisputable, irrefutable
inculcate, *v.*	to instill, indoctrinate, instruct
indigent, *adj.*	poor, impoverished, needy
indomitable, *adj.*	unconquerable, invincible, strong
ineffable, *adj.*	inexpressible, indescribable, indefinable
infamy, *n.*	disgrace, notoriety, disrepute
ingenuous, *adj.*	unsophisticated, naive, candid
inimical, *adj.*	detrimental, injurious, unfavorable
iniquity, *n.*	wickedness, evil, injustice
innocuous, *adj.*	harmless, unobjectionable, inoffensive
inscrutable, *adj.*	impenetrable, enigmatic, mysterious
insipid, *adj.*	trite, dull, colorless
intrepid, *adj.*	bold, resolute, valiant
invidious, *adj.*	offensive, unpleasant, undesirable
irascible, *adj.*	short-tempered, irritable, cranky
jaded, *adj.*	world-weary, cynical, blasé
jejune, *adj.*	immature, unsophisticated, sophomoric
jettison, *v.*	to throw away, discard, dump
juggernaut, *n.*	force, deity
keen, *v.*	to lament, bemoan, wail
ken, *n.*	knowledge, understanding, comprehension

knave, *n.*	villain, criminal, scoundrel
kowtow, *v.*	to conform, fawn, grovel
lachrymose, *adj.*	tearful, weepy, sentimental
lackey, *n.*	minion, assistant, servant
laggard, *n.*	straggler, idler, slacker
lambaste, *v.*	to beat, berate, scold
languid, *adj.*	leisurely, lethargic, unhurried
latent, *adj.*	dormant, underlying, potential
laud, *v.*	to praise, glorify, acclaim
lethargic, *adj.*	weary, sluggish, inactive
levity, *n.*	frivolity, wit, flippancy
lithe, *adj.*	supple, lissome, graceful
loquacious, *adj.*	talkative, garrulous, wordy
lugubrious, *adj.*	mournful, doleful, melancholy
lurid, *adj.*	shocking, explicit, vivid
lyrical, *adj.*	expressive, poetic, emotional
macabre, *adj.*	gruesome, ghoulish, horrid
macerate, *v.*	to soak, steep, pulp
machinate, *v.*	to plot, conspire, scheme
maelstrom, *n.*	whirlpool, vortex, turbulence
maladroit, *adj.*	gawky, awkward, inept
malaise, *n.*	dissatisfaction, discomfort, unease
malefactor, *n.*	scoundrel, criminal, evildoer
malice, *n.*	spite, hatred, wickedness
malign, *v.*	to smear, slander, disparage
malleable, *adj.*	yielding, dutiful, adaptable
manumit, *v.*	to free, emancipate, liberate
martinet, *n.*	despot, disciplinarian, tyrant
masticate, *v.*	to chew, munch, chomp
melee, *n.*	fracas, brawl, skirmish
mellifluous, *adj.*	smooth, sweet, honeyed
mendacity, *n.*	deceit, dishonesty, untruthfulness
mendicant, *n.*	beggar, almsman, pauper
mentor, *n.*	counselor, tutor, adviser
mercenary, *adj.*	money-oriented, acquisitive, grasping
mere, *n.*	pond, lake, marsh
meretricious, *adj.*	vulgar, gaudy, specious
meticulous. *adj.*	painstaking, careful, thorough
mettle, *n.*	courage, fortitude, pluck
mien, *n.*	bearing, appearance, demeanor
misanthropic, *adj.*	mistrustful, skeptical, scornful

mitigate, *v.*	to moderate, alleviate, ease
modulate, *v.*	to adjust, modify, vary
mollify, *v.*	to pacify, calm, soothe
moribund, *adj.*	dying, declining, failing
mundane, *adj.*	commonplace, ordinary, dull
munificent, *adj.*	generous, charitable, benevolent
mutable, *adj.*	alterable, changeable, variable
nabob, *n.*	ruler, noble, aristocrat
nadir, *n.*	low point, depths, bottom
naiveté, *n.*	innocence, ingenuousness, artlessness
narcissism, *n.*	self-love, conceit, vanity
nascent, *adj.*	blossoming, budding, emerging
nebulous, *adj.*	cloudy, hazy, imprecise
nemesis, *n.*	archenemy, rival, retribution
nettle, *v.*	to irritate, vex, annoy
nicety, *n.*	detail, subtlety, fastidiousness
niggardly, *adj.*	grasping, parsimonious, stingy
noisome, *adj.*	offensive, foul, rank
nonchalant, *adj.*	unconcerned, indifferent, cool
nostrum, *n.*	remedy, potion, panacea
noxious, *adj.*	harmful, lethal, toxic
nugatory, *adj.*	trifling, invalid, unimportant
numismatist, *n.*	coin collector
obdurate, *adj.*	stubborn, obstinate, unyielding
obese, *adj.*	fat, stout, corpulent
obfuscate, *v.*	to complicate, confuse, obscure
obsequious, *adj.*	sycophantic, flattering, fawning
obsolete, *adj.*	outdated, passé, archaic
obstreperous, *adj.*	defiant, confrontational, aggressive
obtrusive, *adj.*	blatant, prominent, brash
obviate, *v.*	to preclude, avert, hinder
occlusion, *n.*	obstruction, blockage, obstacle
odious, *adj.*	abhorrent, hateful, vile
oeuvre, *n.*	composition, masterwork, lifework
officious, *adj.*	self-important, bureaucratic, overbearing
oligarchy, *n.*	government by the few
omnipotent, *adj.*	all-powerful, invincible, almighty
onerous, *adj.*	burdensome, oppressive, troublesome
opaque, *adj.*	dense, obscure, unclear
opprobrium, *n.*	disgrace, ignominy, dishonor
oracle, *n.*	seer, soothsayer, visionary

oratory, *n.*	speechifying, rhetoric, eloquence
oscillate, *v.*	to swing, vacillate, sway
osculate, *v.*	to kiss, buss, contact
ossify, *v.*	to harden, solidify, set
ostentatious, *adj.*	showy, flamboyant, pretentious
palaver, *n.*	chatter, gossip, chitchat
palisade, *n.*	picket, fence, fortification
palliative, *adj.*	soothing, relieving, easing
palpable, *adj.*	tangible, obvious, physical
paltry, *adj.*	trivial, trifling, unimportant
panacea, *n.*	remedy, cure-all, solution
panache, *n.*	flair, élan, style
panegyric, *n.*	tribute, encomium, compliment
paradigm, *n.*	model, example, archetype
paramount, *adj.*	dominant, supreme, principal
pariah, *n.*	outcast, exile, untouchable
paroxysm, *n.*	outburst, convulsion, spasm
parsimony, *n.*	stinginess, frugality, economy
pathos, *n.*	pity, sympathy, sorrow
patois, *n.*	dialect, regionalism, vernacular
paucity, *n.*	scarceness, lack, rarity
peccadillo, *n.*	offense, transgression, sin
pecuniary, *adj.*	monetary, financial, economic
pedagogy, *n.*	teaching, education, instruction
pedantic, *adj.*	dull, doctrinaire, obscure
penitence, *n.*	atonement, repentance, regret
pensive, *adj.*	thoughtful, brooding, meditative
penumbra, *n.*	shadow, obscurity, shade
penurious, *adj.*	indigent, destitute, stingy
peon, *n.*	laborer, farm worker, drudge
perambulate, *v.*	to roam, stroll, amble
perfidy, *n.*	betrayal, treachery, disloyalty
perfunctory, *adj.*	mechanical, unthinking, indifferent
peripatetic, *adj.*	wandering, roving, itinerant
permeable, *adj.*	porous, leaky, penetrable
pernicious, *adj.*	deadly, destructive, harmful
persiflage, *n.*	banter, chat, repartee
perspicacious, *adj.*	astute, insightful, shrewd
petulant, *adj.*	irritable, peevish, bad-tempered
phalanx, *n.*	formation, configuration, arrangement
phantasm, *n.*	apparition, specter, ghost

pharisee, *n.*	hypocrite, goody-goody
philanthropic, *adj.*	benevolent, altruistic, charitable
philatelist, *n.*	stamp collector
philistine, *n.*	boor, barbarian, lout
phlegmatic, *adj.*	placid, undemonstrative, apathetic
picayune, *adj.*	trivial, paltry, worthless
piebald, *adj.*	spotted, mottled, multicolored
piety, *n.*	devotion, faithfulness, reverence
pilfer, *v.*	to steal, embezzle, filch
pinion, *v.*	to shackle, immobilize, bind
placate, *v.*	to calm, pacify, appease
platitude, *n.*	cliché, banality, truism
plaudit, *n.*	acclaim, recognition, approval
plethora, *n.*	excess, overabundance, surplus
polemic, *n.*	argument, controversy, refutation
politic, *adj.*	artful, shrewd, diplomatic
portentous, *adj.*	ominous, significant, pompous
portico, *n.*	entry, walkway, porch
postulate, *v.*	to hypothesize, assert, assume
potable, *adj.*	drinkable, clean
pragmatic, *adj.*	practical, sensible, down-to-earth
prate, *v.*	to chatter, jabber, babble
precipitant, *adj.*	headlong, rash, impulsive
precocious, *adj.*	advanced, gifted, premature
predilection, *n.*	partiality, tendency, preference
preponderant, *adj.*	prevalent, predominant, influential
prerogative, *n.*	right, privilege, sanction
prescient, *adj.*	clairvoyant, psychic, perceptive
prevaricate, *v.*	to lie, evade, hedge
probity, *n.*	integrity, honesty, morality
proclivity, *n.*	penchant, tendency, liking
prodigal, *adj.*	profligate, wasteful, dissolute
prodigious, *adj.*	extraordinary, phenomenal, immense
profligate, *adj.*	dissolute, decadent, extravagant
prognosticate, *v.*	to predict, forecast, portend
proliferate, *v.*	to multiply, breed, reproduce
prolix, *adj.*	verbose, wordy, long-winded
promulgate, *v.*	to broadcast, publicize, disseminate
propinquity, *n.*	closeness, proximity, relationship
propitious, *adj.*	favorable, auspicious, promising
prosaic, *adj.*	straightforward, matter-of-fact, pedestrian

proscribe, *v.*	to forbid, ban, prohibit
provisional, *adj.*	temporary, interim, short term
prowess, *n.*	skill, competence, expertise
prurient, *adj.*	lascivious, salacious, lecherous
puerile, *adj.*	juvenile, childish, immature
pugnacious, *adj.*	combative, belligerent, argumentative
pulverize, *v.*	to crush, macerate, mash
purloin, *v.*	to steal, pilfer, rob
pusillanimous, *adj.*	cowardly, timid, spineless
putative, *adj.*	supposed, alleged, presumed
putrefy, *v.*	to decay, rot, molder
quaff, *v.*	to drink, imbibe, guzzle
quagmire, *n.*	predicament, quandary, dilemma
quash, *v.*	to defeat, suppress, nullify
quay, *n.*	wharf, dock, jetty
querulous, *adj.*	petulant, complaining, whiny
quiescent, *adj.*	latent, inert, dormant
quintessential, *adj.*	exemplary, prototypical, classic
quixotic, *adj.*	idealistic, romantic, impulsive
quotidian, *adj.*	everyday, commonplace, usual
rabid, *adj.*	zealous, fanatical, fervent
raffish, *adj.*	carefree, breezy, jaunty
raillery, *n.*	teasing, banter, ridicule
rambunctious, *adj.*	boisterous, unruly, disorderly
rampant, *adj.*	unrestrained, widespread, extensive
rapport, *n.*	affinity, bond, relationship
rarefied, *adj.*	esoteric, obscure, highbrow
ratiocinate, *v.*	to reason, calculate, deduce
ravenous, *adj.*	starving, famished, voracious
recalcitrant, *adj.*	unmanageable, unruly, defiant
recant, *v.*	to disavow, retract, renounce
reciprocate, *v.*	to interchange, return, counter
recondite, *adj.*	abstruse, ambiguous, complex
recreant, *adj.*	faithless, disloyal, craven
rectitude, *n.*	decency, morality, virtue
redolent, *adj.*	aromatic, fragrant, reminiscent
redress, *v.*	to rectify, equalize, remedy
redundant, *adj.*	unnecessary, superfluous, excessive
refractory, *adj.*	disobedient, willful, resistant
refute, *v.*	to contest, disprove, rebut
reiterate, *v.*	to repeat, restate, reaffirm

reliquary, *n.*	receptacle, shrine, coffer
remiss, *adj.*	negligent, careless, slipshod
remonstrate, *v.*	to argue, dispute, protest
reparation, *n.*	amends, compensation, reimbursement
replete, *adj.*	full, sated, stuffed
reprobate, *n.*	degenerate, rascal, troublemaker
resilient, *adj.*	flexible, hardy, durable
resolute, *adj.*	determined, steadfast, unyielding
respite, *n.*	reprieve, break, rest
revile, *v.*	to censure, berate, abuse
rhapsodize, *v.*	to enthuse, rave, gush
rhetoric, *n.*	discourse, oratory, expression
ribald, *adj.*	bawdy, lewd, vulgar
rift, *n.*	fissure, crevice, schism
rigorous, *adj.*	demanding, laborious, meticulous
risible, *adj.*	laughable, humorous, ludicrous
rostrum, *n.*	pulpit, dais, podium
rout, *n.*	defeat, disorder, retreat
rubicund, *adj.*	rosy, ruddy, red
rue, *v.*	to regret, lament, repent
ruminate, *v.*	to ponder, mull over, reflect
saccharine, *adj.*	sugary, cloying, syrupy
sacrilege, *n.*	irreverence, blasphemy, profanation
sacrosanct, *adj.*	sacred, inviolable, hallowed
salacious, *adj.*	immoral, indecent, lascivious
salubrious, *adj.*	healthful, wholesome, beneficial
salutary, *adj.*	constructive, remedial, wholesome
sanction, *v.*	to permit, authorize, endorse
sanguine, *adj.*	upbeat, confident, optimistic
sapient, *adj.*	wise, astute, discerning
sardonic, *adj.*	sarcastic, derisive, mocking
satrap, *n.*	ruler, sovereign, emperor
schism, *n.*	division, rift, rupture
scintilla, *n.*	iota, bit, speck
screed, *n.*	sermon, harangue, lecture
scrupulous, *adj.*	painstaking, conscientious, thorough
scurrilous, *adj.*	defamatory, scandalous, abusive
sectarian, *adj.*	partisan, parochial
secular, *adj.*	worldly, lay, humanistic
sedition, *n.*	treason, subversion, rebellion

segue, *n.*	transition, conversion
seminal, *adj.*	influential, decisive, creative
senescent, *adj.*	aging, maturing
sententious, *adj.*	moralizing, pompous, didactic
sepulcher, *n.*	tomb, crypt, mausoleum
serendipity, *n.*	chance, destiny, accident
servile, *adj.*	submissive, docile, subservient
simulate, *v.*	to imitate, replicate, model
slue, *v.*	to pivot, rotate, veer
sluice, *n.*	channel, valve, floodgate
soigné, *adj.*	elegant, sophisticated, fashionable
solace, *n.*	consolation, comfort, succor
solicitous, *adj.*	concerned, anxious, caring
somnolent, *adj.*	sleepy, drowsy, lethargic
sonorous, *adj.*	resonant, echoing, loud
soporific, *adj.*	monotonous, hypnotic, sleep-inducing
sordid, *adj.*	foul, repugnant, squalid
sororal, *adj.*	relating to a sister
spectral, *adj.*	ghostly, ethereal, vaporous
splenetic, *adj.*	irritable, ill-humored, surly
spurious, *adj.*	bogus, inauthentic, illegitimate
spurn, *v.*	to reject, scorn, disdain
stalwart, *adj.*	valiant, sturdy, steadfast
static, *adj.*	fixed, unmoving, stationary
staunch, *adj.*	faithful, loyal, dependable
stentorian, *adj.*	loud, booming, thunderous
stigma, *n.*	disgrace, shame, ignominy
stipulate, *v.*	to specify, require, demand
stodgy, *adj.*	dull, stuffy, unimaginative
stoic, *adj.*	indifferent, unresponsive, apathetic
strident, *adj.*	shrill, discordant, clamorous
stultify, *v.*	to cripple, deaden, hamper
stupefy, *v.*	to daze, bewilder, stun
suave, *adj.*	smooth, debonair, urbane
subjugate, *v.*	to overpower, conquer, defeat
sublime, *adj.*	impressive, majestic, supreme
subtle, *adj.*	elusive, abstruse, indefinable
succor, *n.*	assistance, help, aid
succulent, *adj.*	juicy, luscious, delectable
supercilious, *adj.*	disdainful, patronizing, haughty

supersede, *v.*	to replace, supplant, succeed
surmise, *v.*	to infer, deduce, conclude
surreptitious, *adj.*	sneaky, stealthy, clandestine
sybaritic, *adj.*	sensuous, luxurious, pleasurable
sycophant, *n.*	flatterer, toady, yes-man
symposium, *n.*	meeting, conference, convention
synchronous, *adj.*	simultaneous, contemporary, concurrent
synthesize, *v.*	to integrate, amalgamate, manufacture
tacit, *adj.*	unspoken, implied, inferred
taciturn, *adj.*	reserved, reticent, silent
tangible, *adj.*	palpable, corporeal, substantial
tawdry, *adj.*	crude, gaudy, cheap
temerity, *n.*	recklessness, gall, audacity
temperance, *n.*	self-restraint, moderation, abstinence
tenable, *adj.*	plausible, defensible, justifiable
tenacity, *n.*	persistence, obstinacy, doggedness
tendentious, *adj.*	partisan, biased, opinionated
tenebrous, *adj.*	shady, gloomy, murky
tenet, *n.*	belief, precept, doctrine
tenuous, *adj.*	unconvincing, fragile, weak
tepid, *adj.*	lukewarm, unenthusiastic, apathetic
thespian, *adj.*	dramatic, theatrical, staged
timorous, *adj.*	timid, fearful, anxious
torpor, *n.*	lethargy, languor, inactivity
torrid, *adj.*	sweltering, hot, sizzling
tortuous, *adj.*	winding, circuitous, meandering
tractable, *adj.*	obedient, dutiful, governable
transitory, *adj.*	short-lived, impermanent, fleeting
transverse, *adj.*	crosswise, oblique, slanted
tremulous, *adj.*	quivering, shaky, wavering
trenchant, *adj.*	forceful, effective, incisive
trepidation, *n.*	apprehension, foreboding, dread
trite, *adj.*	stale, hackneyed, pedestrian
truculent, *adj.*	quarrelsome, argumentative, defiant
truism, *n.*	cliché, platitude, maxim
tumult, *n.*	clamor, commotion, hubbub
turbid, *adj.*	murky, cloudy, muddled
ubiquitous, *adj.*	omnipresent, everywhere
ululate, *v.*	to lament, wail, howl
umbrage *n.*	offense, resentment, indignation

unctuous, *adj.*	oily, ingratiating, obsequious
undulate, *v.*	to ripple, surge, heave
upbraid, *v.*	to scold, berate, chastise
urbane, *adj.*	suave, refined, elegant
usurp, *v.*	to appropriate, commandeer, seize
uxorial, *adj.*	relating to a wife
vacillate, *v.*	to fluctuate, hesitate, waver
vacuous, *adj.*	empty, inane, vacant
validate, *v.*	to sanction, confirm, corroborate
vapid, *adj.*	bland, lifeless, insipid
vaunt, *v.*	to boast, brag, crow
vehement, *adj.*	forceful, fervid, passionate
venal, *adj.*	mercenary, corruptible
venerable, *adj.*	esteemed, respected, honored
verbose, *adj.*	wordy, garrulous, loquacious
verdant, *adj.*	green, grassy, fertile
verisimilitude, *n.*	truth, reality, authenticity
vernacular, *n.*	dialect, idiom, argot
vertiginous, *adj.*	dizzy, giddy, reeling
vicarious, *adj.*	secondhand, delegated
vicissitude, *n.*	variation, mutation, complication
vilify, *v.*	to malign, disparage, defame
virtuosity, *n.*	genius, talent, skill
vitriol, *n.*	wrath, ire, spleen
vociferous, *adj.*	voluble, noisy, raucous
voracious, *adj.*	ravenous, greedy, insatiable
vouchsafe, *v.*	to grant, deign, bestow
wanton, *adj.*	immodest, unchaste, lewd
wastrel, *n.*	spendthrift, squanderer, profligate
wheedle, *v.*	to cajole, inveigle, coax
whet, *v.*	to sharpen, hone, stimulate
wily, *adj.*	sly, cunning, devious
winnow, *v.*	to sift, separate, extract
wizened, *adj.*	shriveled, wrinkled, withered
wrangle, *v.*	to quarrel, bicker, argue
xeric, *adj.*	dry, sere, desert
yaw, *v.*	to swerve, veer, weave
zenith, *n.*	summit, apex, pinnacle
zephyr, *n.*	breeze, gust, waft

ROOTS AND AFFIXES

Although the specific meaning of affixes are tested only once or twice on the MAT, an overall knowledge of Greek and Latin roots and affixes can help you enormously as you deal with unfamiliar vocabulary words. This table presents some common roots and affixes, their meanings, and some examples of words that contain them.

Prefix	Meaning	Examples
a-, ac-, ad-, af-, ag-, al-, an-, ap-, as-, at-	to, toward, in addition to, according to	ahead, accompany, adhere, affix, aggravate, alarm, appall, assent, attempt
a-, an-	without	amoral, analgesic
ab-, abs-	away from	abdicate, absence
ante-	before	antebellum, anterior
anti-	against	antiwar, antipathy
auto-	self	automobile, autobiography
bi-	two	biannual, bicycle
circum-	around	circumnavigate, circumvent
co-, cog-, col-, com-, con-, cor-	with, together, mutually	coherent, cognizant, collapse, companion, concur, correspond
contra-	against, opposite	contradict, contravene
de-	to do the opposite of	decriminalize, degenerate
dis-	not, opposite of	disagree, disfavor
e-, ex-	out of, away from	egress, extension
em-, en-	to put into, to cause to be	embody, endear
epi-	upon, over	epidermis, epitaph
extra-	outside, beyond	extracurricular, extraordinary
il-, im-, in-, ir-	not	illicit, impossible, incorrect, irresponsible
inter-	between, among	intercom, international
intro-	into	introduce, introvert
mal-	bad	maladjusted, malformed
mis-	wrong	misnomer, misunderstood

Prefix	Meaning	Examples
mono-	one	monotone, monogamy
multi-	many	multifaceted, multimillion
non-	no, not	nonentity, nonsensical
ob-, oc-, of-, op-	toward, against	object, occlude, offend, opposite
over-	above, more than	overachieve, overcharge
para-	beside	paradigm, paragraph
per-	through, throughout	perambulate
peri-	around, about	peripatetic, periodic
post-	after	postdate, posthumous
pre-	before	prediction, preexist
pro-	for, supporting	procreate, promotion
re-	back, again	recall, recapture
retro-	backward	retrofit, retrospective
semi-	half	semicircle, semiconscious
sub-, suc-, suf-, sup-, sus-	below, under	subarctic, succumb, suffer, suppress, suspend
super-	over, above	superfluous, superscript
sur-	over, above	surpass, surrealism
sym-, syn-	together	sympathetic, synthesize
trans-	across	transatlantic, transmission
tri-	three	tricycle, trilogy
un-	not, opposite of	unlikely, unravel
uni-	one	uniform, unisex

Suffix	Function and Meaning	Examples
-able, -ible	adjective-forming; capable of, worthy of	laudable, flexible
-acy, -cy	noun-forming; state, quality	literacy, bankruptcy
-age	noun-forming; action	breakage, blockage

Suffix	Function and Meaning	Examples
-al	adjective-forming; state, quality	communal, supplemental
-an, -ian	noun-forming; one who	artisan, librarian
-ance, -ence	noun-forming; action, state, quality	performance, adherence
-ancy, -ency	noun-forming; state, quality	buoyancy, fluency
-ant, -ent	noun-forming; one who	deodorant, antecedent
-ant, -ent, -ient	adjective forming; indicating	compliant, dependent, lenient
-ar, -ary	adjective-forming; related to	solar, imaginary
-ate	verb-forming; cause to be	percolate, graduate
-ation	noun-forming; action	hibernation, strangulation
-dom	noun-forming; place, condition	kingdom, freedom
-en	adjective-forming; made of	flaxen, wooden
-en	verb-forming; cause to be	cheapen, dampen
-er, -or	noun-forming; one who	painter, sailor
-fold	adverb-forming; divided or multiplied by	threefold, hundredfold
-ful	adjective-forming; full of	joyful, playful
-ful	noun-forming; amount	cupful, bucketful
-fy, -ify	verb-forming; cause to be	liquefy, justify
-ia	noun-forming; disease	inertia, anemia
-iatry	noun-forming; medical treatment	psychiatry, podiatry
-ic	adjective-forming; having the qualities of	futuristic, academic
-ician	noun-forming; one who	physician, mortician
-ics	noun-forming; science of	athletics, physics
-ion	noun-forming; action	completion, dilution
-ish	adjective-forming; having the quality of	foolish, boyish
-ism	noun-forming; doctrine	pacifism, jingoism
-ist	noun-forming; person who	jurist, polemicist
-ity, -ty	noun-forming; state, quality	reality, cruelty
-ive, -ative, -itive	adjective-forming; having the quality of	supportive, talkative, definitive

Suffix	Function and Meaning	Examples
-ize	verb-forming; cause to be	demonize, dramatize
-less	without	careless, hopeless
-ly	adverb-forming; in the manner of	loudly, suddenly
-ment	noun-forming; action	argument, statement
-ness	noun-forming; state, quality	kindness, abruptness
-ous, -eous, -ose, -ious	adjective-forming; having the quality of	porous, gaseous, jocose, bilious
-ship	noun-forming; condition	scholarship, friendship
-ure	noun-forming; action, condition	erasure, portraiture
-ward	adverb-forming; in the direction of	forward, windward
-wise	adverb-forming; in the manner of	otherwise, clockwise
-y	adjective-forming; having the quality of	chilly, crazy
-y	noun-forming; state, condition	jealousy, custody

Root	Meaning	Examples
ami, amo	to love	amiable, amorous
aud, audit, aur	to hear	audible, auditory, aural
bene, ben	good	benevolent, benign
bio	life	biography, biology
biblio	book	bibliography, bibliophile
brev	short	abbreviate, brevity
chron	time	chronology, synchronize
cogn, gnos	to know	cognitive, agnostic
corp	body	corpulent, corporation
cred	to believe	credible, incredulous
dict	to say	indictment, dictation
doc, doct	to teach	docile, indoctrinate
duc, duct	to lead	conducive, induction
fac, fact	to make, to do	efface, factory

Root	Meaning	Examples
fid	belief	confide, fidelity
fluct, flux	to flow	fluctuation, influx
form	shape	format, cuneiform
fract, frag	to break	infraction, fragment
gen	to produce	generation, congenital
geo	earth	geographer, geology
grad, gress	to step, to move	graduate, ingress
graph	to write	photograph, graphics
ject	to throw	project, rejection
junct	to join	conjunction, adjunct
lect	to choose, to gather	select, collection
loc	place	locale, locomotion
log	to say	logical, analog
luc, lum, lust	light	lucid, luminous, illustrate
man	to make, to do	manager, manufacture
mem	to recall	remember, memorable
mit, miss	to send	remit, admission
mob, mov, mot	to move	mobile, remove, motion
nasc, nat	to be born	nascent, prenatal
nom, nym	name	nominal, homonym
nov	new	renovate, novice
oper	to work	operate, inoperable
path	feeling	empathy, sympathetic
ped, pod	foot	pedal, podiatrist
pel, puls	to push	repel, impulse
pend	to hang	pendant, impending
phil	love	philosophy, necrophilia
phon	sound	phonograph, telephone

Root	Meaning	Examples
pict	to paint	picture, depict
port	to carry	export, portage
psych	mind	psychology, psychic
quer, quest	to ask	query, request
rupt	to break	interrupt, rupture
scrib, scrip	to write	inscribe, script
sens, sent	to feel	sensation, sentient
sequ	to follow	sequence, consequential
soci	companion	society, associate
sol	alone	solo, solitude
solu, solut, solv	to loosen, to release	soluble, solution, solve
spec, spect	to look	speculate, inspection
spir	to breathe	spirit, respiration
stab, stat	to stand	stability, statue
tact	to touch	tactile, contact
tain, tent	to hold	maintain, contents
tele	far	telescope, teleport
tend, tens	to stretch	extend, tensile
term	end	terminal, exterminate
terr	earth	territory, subterranean
therm	heat	thermal, thermometer
tors, tort	to twist	torsion, contort
tract	to pull	contract, tractable
uni	one	universe, unicycle
vac	empty	vacuous, evacuate
ven, vent	to come	convene, venture
ver	true	verify, verisimilitude
verb	word	verbal, adverbial

Root	Meaning	Examples
vers, vert	to turn	reverse, convert
vid, vis	to see	video, invisible
vit, viv	to live	vital, convivial
voc, voke	to call	vocal, invoke
vol, volt, volv	to roll	convoluted, revolt, volvox

-OLOGY WORDS

There is one suffix that tends to appear over and over on the MAT. The suffix *-ology*, meaning "the study of," is used to test your knowledge of specific branches of learning. Note that certain *-ology* words do not refer to branches of learning but rather to types of writing or speech. *Anthology* and *tautology* are two such words. Following are just a handful of *-ology* words that you might well meet on the MAT. Note that "the study of" is understood.

agrology: agriculture

anthropology: humans

arachnology: spiders

archaeology: ancient civilizations

bacteriology: bacteria

biology: living things

bryology: bryophytes (mosses, lichens)

cardiology: the heart

cetology: marine mammals

climatology: climates

cosmology: the cosmos

criminology: crime

cryology: subfreezing temperatures

cryptology: codes

cytology: cells

dendrology: trees

dermatology: the skin

ecology: the environment

embryology: embryos

endocrinology: glands and hormones

entomology: insects

epidemiology: epidemics

epistemology: knowledge

eschatology: the end of the world

ethnology: race and culture

ethology: animal behavior

etiology: the causes of disease

etymology: word history

exobiology: life on other planets

gastroenterology: the stomach and intestines

gemology: gemstones

genealogy: family trees

geology: the Earth

gerontology: aging

graphology: handwriting

gynecology: women

heliology: the sun

hematology: blood

hepatology: the liver

herpetology: reptiles and amphibians

histology: tissues

horology: timepieces

hydrology: water

ichnology: fossil tracks and burrows

ichthyology: fish

immunology: the immune system

kinesiology: movement

kymatology: waves

malacology: mollusks

mammalogy: mammals

meteorology: weather

metrology: measurement

microbiology: microbes

mineralogy: minerals

morphology: grammatical forms

musicology: music

mycology: fungi

myrmecology: ants

mythology: myths

nanotechnology: microscopic machines

neonatalogy: newborns

nephology: clouds

nephrology: the kidneys

neurology: the nerves

odontology: the teeth

oncology: cancer

ontology: existence

oology: eggs

ophthalmology: the eyes

ornithology: birds

orology: mountains

osteology: bones

otology: the ears

paleontology: fossils

parasitology: parasites

pathology: disease

pedology: soil

petrology: rocks

pharmacology: drugs

phonology: phonics

phrenology: the skull's shape

physiology: bodies

phytology: plants

pneumology: the lungs

primatology: primates

psychology: mental function

pyrology: heat or fever

radiology: radiation

rheology: flow

rheumatology: rheumatic diseases

rhinology: the nose

seismology: earthquakes

selenology: the moon

semiology: signs and symbols

serology: blood serum

sinology: China

sociobiology: the effect of evolution on behavior

sociology: society

speleology: caves

stomatology: the mouth

symptomatology: symptoms

synecology: communal relationships

teleology: purposes and ends

teratology: monsters

theology: God

topology: geometric connections

toxicology: poisons

traumatology: injuries

typology: classification

urology: the urogenital tract

virology: viruses

vulcanology: volcanoes

xenobiology: extraterrestrials

xylology: wood

zoology: animals

zymology: fermentation

FOREIGN WORDS AND PHRASES

The MAT test-makers do not expect you to be fluent in any language other than English. However, they do expect you to recognize certain words and phrases from other languages that have worked their way into the English language. Some of those words and phrases appear below.

Word or Phrase	Derivation	Meaning
ad hoc	Latin	for the specific purpose
ad hominem	Latin	"to the man"—appealing to the personal rather than the logical
ad infinitum	Latin	to infinity
ad nauseum	Latin	to the point of nausea
à la carte	French	each item (on a menu) available separately
à la mode	French	fashionable; with ice cream
alma mater	Latin	one's college or university
angst	German	anxiety, apprehension

Word or Phrase	Derivation	Meaning
anno domini	Latin	year of our Lord (A.D.)
a priori	Latin	deductive, determined through logic alone
avant garde	French	cutting edge, advanced
bête noire	French	"black beast"—something to be avoided
bona fide	Latin	"in good faith"—genuine, authentic
carpe diem	Latin	"seize the day"
carte blanche	French	free rein
coup d'état	French	governmental takeover by force
cul-de-sac	French	dead end
cum laude	Latin	with honor
de facto	Latin	in reality
déjà vu	French	"already seen"—lived through previously
de jure	Latin	in law
ésprit de corps	French	morale
ex post facto	Latin	after the fact
fait accompli	French	accomplished, irreversible fact
faux pas	French	gaffe, misstep
gestalt	German	unity, perceived whole
idée fixe	French	obsession
in absentia	Latin	in the absence of
in loco parentis	Latin	in the place of a parent
in medias res	Latin	in the middle of a plot

Word or Phrase	Derivation	Meaning
ipso facto	Latin	by that very fact
joie de vivre	French	"joy of living"
lingua franca	Latin	common language
magnum opus	Latin	masterwork
mano a mano	Spanish	"hand to hand"—face to face confrontation
mirabile dictu	Latin	"wonderful to say"
modus operandi	Latin	way of working
ne plus ultra	Latin	"no more beyond"—pinnacle, acme
noli-me-tangere	Latin	"touch me not"—do not interfere
nom de plume	French	penname
non sequitur	Latin	"not following"—off the topic
nota bene	Latin	pay attention
per se	Latin	in and of itself
persona non grata	Latin	unwelcome
prima facie	Latin	"at first view"—self-evident
pro bono	Latin	"for the good"—for free
pro forma	Latin	for form's sake, done as a formality
pro rata	Latin	in proportion
raison d'être	French	reason for being, justification
rara avis	Latin	"rare bird"—rarity
realpolitik	German	expansionist nationalism
savoir-faire	French	know-how, savvy, tact

Word or Phrase	Derivation	Meaning
schadenfreude	German	pleasure derived from others' misfortunes
sine qua non	Latin	essential condition
sui generis	Latin	"of its own kind"—unique
tabula rasa	Latin	"blank slate"—unformed opinion
vis-à-vis	French	"face to face"—in connection to
weltschmerz	German	romantic pessimism
zeitgeist	German	spirit of the times

Appendix B
Literature

Obviously, English majors and comparative literature majors have a slight advantage over other test-takers on literature questions. However, the MAT does not tend toward the obscure. Most of the authors chosen for analogies will be ones you know, the so-called dead white men of cultural literacy. They will primarily be writers of classics in American, British, and European literature. The following table lists some frequently named authors and their major works.

Author	Country of Origin	Major Genre(s)	Representative Works
Agee, James	U.S.	novel, nonfiction	*A Death in the Family*, *Let Us Now Praise Famous Men*
Andersen, Hans Christian	Denmark	fairy tale	"The Ugly Duckling," "The Tinder Box," "The Little Mermaid"
Anderson, Sherwood	U.S.	short story, novel	*Winesburg, Ohio*
Angelou, Maya	U.S.	poetry, autobiography	*I Know Why the Caged Bird Sings*
Arnold, Matthew	England	poetry	"Dover Beach"
Auden, W. H.	England	poetry	"Musée des Beaux Arts"
Austen, Jane	England	novel	*Sense and Sensibility*, *Pride and Prejudice*, *Mansfield Park*, *Emma*
Balzac, Honoré de	France	novel	*Le Père Goriot*, *Eugénie Grandet*
Barrie, J. M.	England	drama, novel	*Peter Pan*, *The Admirable Crichton*
Baudelaire, Charles	France	poetry	*Les Fleurs de Mal*

Author	Country of Origin	Major Genre(s)	Representative Works
Beckett, Samuel	Ireland/ France	drama	*Waiting for Godot, Endgame*
Bellow, Saul	Canada/ U.S.	novel	*The Adventures of Augie March, Humboldt's Gift*
Bradbury, Ray	U.S.	science fiction	*The Martian Chronicles*
Brecht, Bertolt	Germany	drama	*The Threepenny Opera, Mother Courage and Her Children*
Brontë, Charlotte	England	novel	*Jane Eyre*
Brontë, Emily	England	novel	*Wuthering Heights*
Browning, Elizabeth Barrett	England	poetry	*Sonnets from the Portuguese*
Browning, Robert	England	poetry	"Pippa Passes," "My Last Duchess"
Buck, Pearl S.	U.S.	novel	*The Good Earth*
Byron, George Gordon	England	poetry	*Childe Harold's Pilgrimage, Don Juan*
Camus, Albert	Algeria/ France	novel	*The Plague, The Stranger, The Rebel*
Carroll, Lewis	England	children's literature	*Alice's Adventures in Wonderland, Through the Looking Glass*
Cather, Willa	U.S.	novel	*O Pioneers!, Death Comes for the Archbishop*
Cervantes, Miguel de	Spain	novel	*Don Quixote*
Chaucer, Geoffrey	England	poetry	*Canterbury Tales*
Chekhov, Anton	Russia	short story, drama	*Uncle Vanya, The Cherry Orchard, The Seagull, The Three Sisters*
Coleridge, Samuel Taylor	England	poetry	"The Rime of the Ancient Mariner," "Kublai Khan"
Conrad, Joseph	Poland/ England	novel	*Lord Jim, Heart of Darkness*
Cooper, James Fenimore	U.S.	novel	*The Last of the Mohicans, The Deerslayer*

Author	Country of Origin	Major Genre(s)	Representative Works
Corneille, Pierre	France	drama	*Médée, Le Cid*
Crane, Stephen	U.S.	novel, poetry, short story	*The Red Badge of Courage,* *The Black Riders,* "The Open Boat"
Cummings, E. E.	U.S.	poetry	"anyone lived in a pretty how town," "my father moved through dooms of love"
Dante Alighieri	Italy	poetry	*The Divine Comedy*
Defoe, Daniel	England	novel	*Moll Flanders, Robinson Crusoe*
Dickens, Charles	England	novel	*Oliver Twist, David Copperfield,* *Bleak House, A Tale of Two Cities,* *Great Expectations*
Dickinson, Emily	U.S.	poetry	"A Bird came down the Walk," "Because I could not stop for Death"
Donne, John	England	poetry, meditations	"Death Be Not Proud," *Devotions Upon Emergent Occasions*
Dos Passos, John	U.S.	novel	*Manhattan Transfer, U.S.A.*
Dostoevsky, Fyodor	Russia	novel	*Notes from Underground,* *Crime and Punishment, The Idiot,* *The Brothers Karamazov*
Dreiser, Theodore	U.S.	novel	*Sister Carrie, An American Tragedy*
Dryden, John	England	poetry, essay	"A Song for St. Cecilia's Day," *Absalom and Achitophel*
Dumas, Alexandre	France	novel	*The Count of Monte Cristo,* *The Three Musketeers*
Eliot, George	England	novel	*The Mill on the Floss,* *Silas Marner, Middlemarch*
Eliot, T. S.	U.S./ England	poetry	"The Love Song of J. Alfred Prufrock," *The Waste Land, Four Quartets*
Emerson, Ralph Waldo	U.S.	poetry, essay	"Concord Hymn," "Brahma," "Self-Reliance"
Euripedes	Greece	drama	*Medea, The Trojan Women*
Faulkner, William	U.S.	novel, short story	*Sartoris, The Sound and the Fury,* *Absalom, Absalom!,* "The Bear"

Author	Country of Origin	Major Genre(s)	Representative Works
Fitzgerald, F. Scott	U.S.	novel, short story	*The Great Gatsby, Tales of the Jazz Age, Tender Is the Night*
Flaubert, Gustave	France	novel	*Madame Bovary, L'Education Sentimentale*
Forster, E. M.	England	novel	*A Room with a View, A Passage to India*
Frost, Robert	U.S.	poetry	"Mending Wall," "The Road Not Taken," "Stopping by Woods on a Snowy Evening"
García Lorca, Federico	Spain	drama, poetry	*The House of Bernarda Alba, Blood Wedding*
García Márquez, Gabriel	Colombia	novel	*One Hundred Years of Solitude, The Autumn of the Patriarch*
Gide, André	France	novel	*The Immoralist, The Counterfeiters*
Ginsberg, Allen	U.S.	poetry	"Howl," "Kaddish"
Goethe, Johann	Germany	drama, novel	*Faust, The Sorrows of Young Werther*
Gogol, Nikolai	Russia	novel, drama, short story	*Dead Souls, The Inspector General,* "The Overcoat"
Gorky, Maxim	Russia	drama	*The Lower Depths*
Gray, Thomas	England	poetry	"Elegy Written in a Country Churchyard"
Hardy, Thomas	England	novel	*The Mayor of Casterbridge, Tess of the D'Urbervilles, Jude the Obscure*
Harte, Bret	U.S.	short story	"The Outcasts of Poker Flats," "The Luck of Roaring Camp"
Hawthorne, Nathaniel	U.S.	novel, short story	*The Scarlet Letter, The House of the Seven Gables, Tanglewood Tales*
Hemingway, Ernest	U.S.	novel, short story	*The Sun Also Rises, A Farewell to Arms, The Old Man and the Sea*
Hesse, Hermann	Germany	novel	*Siddhartha, Steppenwolf*
Homer	Ionia	epic	*The Iliad, The Odyssey*
Howells, William Dean	U.S.	novel	*The Rise of Silas Lapham, A Hazard of New Fortunes*

Author	Country of Origin	Major Genre(s)	Representative Works
Hughes, Langston	U.S.	poetry	"Harlem," "The Negro Speaks of Rivers"
Hugo, Victor	France	novel	*The Hunchback of Notre Dame, Les Misérables*
Huxley, Aldous	England	essay, novel	"The Doors of Perception," *Brave New World*
Ibsen, Henrik	Norway	drama	*A Doll's House, The Wild Duck, Hedda Gable*
Ionesco, Eugène	Romania/ France	drama	*The Bald Soprano, Rhinoceros*
Irving, Washington	U.S.	short story	"Rip Van Winkle," "The Legend of Sleepy Hollow"
James, Henry	U.S.	novel	*Daisy Miller, The Turn of the Screw, The Wings of the Dove, The Golden Bowl*
Jonson, Ben	England	drama	*Volpone, The Alchemist*
Joyce, James	Ireland	novel, short story	*A Portrait of the Artist as a Young Man, Ulysses, Dubliners, Finnegans Wake*
Kafka, Franz	Austria	novel	*The Metamorphosis, The Trial*
Keats, John	England	poetry	*Endymion,* "The Eve of St. Agnes," "Ode on a Grecian Urn"
Kerouac, Jack	U.S.	novel	*On the Road, The Dharma Bums*
Kipling, Rudyard	India/ England	poetry, short story, novel	"Gunga Din," *Just-So Stories, The Jungle Book, Kim*
Lawrence, D. H.	England	novel, short story, poetry	*Women in Love, Lady Chatterley's Lover,* "The Rocking-Horse Winner"
Lewis, Sinclair	U.S.	novel	*Main Street, Elmer Gantry, Babbitt*
London, Jack	U.S.	novel	*The Call of the Wild, White Fang*
Longfellow, Henry Wadsworth	U.S.	poetry	"The Children's Hour," "The Village Blacksmith," *Evangeline, Hiawatha*
Machiavelli, Niccolò	Florence	essay	*The Prince*
Mann, Thomas	Germany	novel	*Buddenbrooks, Death in Venice, The Magic Mountain*

Author	Country of Origin	Major Genre(s)	Representative Works
Marlowe, Christopher	England	drama	*The Tragical History of Dr. Faustus, The Jew of Malta*
Marvell, Andrew	England	poetry	"To His Coy Mistress"
Masters, Edgar Lee	U.S.	poetry	*Spoon River Anthology*
Maugham, W. Somerset	England	novel	*Of Human Bondage, Cakes and Ale, The Razor's Edge*
Maupassant, Guy de	France	short story	"The Necklace," "The Umbrella"
Melville, Herman	U.S.	novel, short story	*Typee, Omoo, Moby-Dick, Billy Budd,* "Bartleby the Scrivener"
Millay, Edna St. Vincent	U.S.	poetry	*The Harp Weaver and Other Poems*
Miller, Arthur	U.S.	drama	*Death of a Salesman, The Crucible*
Milton, John	England	poetry	"Lycidas," *Paradise Lost, Samson Agonistes*
Molière	France	drama	*Le Misanthrope, School for Wives, Tartuffe*
Morrison, Toni	U.S.	novel	*Tar Baby, Beloved*
Nabokov, Vladimir	Russia/U.S.	novel	*Lolita, Ada, Pale Fire*
O'Casey, Sean	Ireland	drama	*Juno and the Paycock*
O'Connor, Flannery	U.S.	novel, short story	*Wise Blood, Everything That Rises Must Converge*
Odets, Clifford	U.S.	drama	*Waiting for Lefty, Awake and Sing*
O'Neill, Eugene	U.S.	drama	*Anna Christie, Mourning Becomes Electra, The Iceman Cometh, Long Day's Journey into Night, Moon for the Misbegotten*
Paine, Thomas	England/ U.S.	essay	"Common Sense," "The Rights of Man," "The Age of Reason"
Pinter, Harold	England	drama	*The Birthday Party, Old Times*
Pirandello, Luigi	Italy	drama	*Six Characters in Search of an Author*
Plath, Sylvia	U.S.	poetry, novel	*Ariel, The Bell Jar*
Poe, Edgar Allan	U.S.	poetry, short story	*Annabel Lee,* "The Raven," "The Tell-Tale Heart"

Author	Country of Origin	Major Genre(s)	Representative Works
Pope, Alexander	England	poetry, essay	"The Rape of the Lock," *The Dunciad*, "An Essay on Man"
Porter, Katherine Anne	U.S.	short story, novel	*Pale Horse, Pale Rider; Ship of Fools*
Pound, Ezra	U.S.	poetry	*Personae, Cantos*
Proust, Marcel	France	novel	*Remembrance of Things Past*
Pushkin, Aleksandr	Russia	poetry, drama	*Eugene Onegin, Boris Godunov*
Rabelais, François	France	satire	*Gargantua and Pantagruel*
Racine, Jean	France	drama	*Andromaque, Phèdre*
Richardson, Samuel	England	novel	*Pamela, or Virtue Rewarded; Clarissa Harlowe*
Rilke, Rainer Maria	Germany	poetry	*The Duino Elegies, The Sonnets to Orpheus*
Rimbaud, Arthur	France	poetry	*A Season in Hell*
Robinson, Edwin Arlington	U.S.	poetry	"Richard Corey," "Miniver Cheevy"
Salinger, J. D.	U.S.	novel, short story	*The Catcher in the Rye, Franny and Zooey*, "A Perfect Day for Bananafish"
Sandburg, Carl	U.S.	poetry	"Chicago," "Grass"
Saroyan, William	U.S.	drama, novel	*The Time of Your Life, The Human Comedy*
Sartre, Jean-Paul	France	novel, essay, drama	*Nausea, Being and Nothingness, No Exit*
Schiller, Friedrich von	Germany	drama	*Don Carlos, The Maid of Orleans, Wilhelm Tell*
Scott, Walter	Scotland	novel	*Rob Roy, Ivanhoe, Kenilworth*
Shakespeare, William	England	poetry	*Sonnets*, see dramas below
Shaw, George Bernard	Ireland	drama	*Arms and the Man, Major Barbara, Pygmalion, St. Joan*
Shelley, Percy Bysshe	England	poetry	"Ozymandias," "To a Skylark," "Ode to the West Wind"

Author	Country of Origin	Major Genre(s)	Representative Works
Sheridan, Richard	England	drama	*The Rivals, The School for Scandal*
Sidney, Philip	England	poetry	*Astrophel and Stella*
Smollett, Tobias	Scotland/ England	novel	*The Adventures of Roderick Random, The Expedition of Humphrey Clinker*
Solzhenitsyn, Aleksandr	Russia	novel	*One Day in the Life of Ivan Denisovich, The Gulag Archipelago*
Sophocles	Athens	drama	*Oedipus at Colonus, Antigone, Electra*
Spenser, Edmund	England	poetry	*The Faerie Queene,* "Astrophel"
Stein, Gertrude	U.S.	poetry, autobiography	*Tender Buttons, The Autobiography of Alice B. Toklas*
Steinbeck, John	U.S.	novel	*Of Mice and Men, The Grapes of Wrath, Cannery Row*
Sterne, Laurence	England	novel	*Tristram Shandy, A Sentimental Journey*
Stevens, Wallace	U.S.	poetry	"Sunday Morning," "The Emperor of Ice Cream"
Stevenson, Robert Louis	Scotland	novel	*The Strange Case of Dr. Jekyll and Mr. Hyde, Kidnapped*
Stowe, Harriet Beecher	U.S.	novel	*Uncle Tom's Cabin*
Strindberg, August	Sweden	drama	*The Dance of Death, Miss Julie*
Swift, Jonathan	England	satire	*The Tale of a Tub, Gulliver's Travels,* "A Modest Proposal"
Synge, John Millington	Ireland	drama	*Riders to the Sea, Playboy of the Western World*
Tennyson, Alfred	England	poetry	"Idylls of the King," "Charge of the Light Brigade," "Crossing the Bar"
Thackeray, William Makepeace	England	novel	*Vanity Fair, The Memoirs of Barry Lyndon*
Thomas, Dylan	Wales	poetry	"Do not go gentle into that good night"
Thoreau, Henry David	U.S.	essay	"Civil Disobedience," "Walden"
Tolstoy, Leo	Russia	novel	*War and Peace, Anna Karenina*

Author	Country of Origin	Major Genre(s)	Representative Works
Turgenev, Ivan	Russia	novel	*Fathers and Sons*
Twain, Mark	U.S.	novel	*Life on the Mississippi, The Adventures of Tom Sawyer, The Adventures of Huckleberry Finn*
Verlaine, Paul	France	poetry	"Chanson d'automne"
Verne, Jules	France	science fiction	*Twenty Thousand Leagues Under the Sea, Around the World in Eighty Days*
Virgil	Rome	epic	*The Aeneid*
Voltaire	France	satire	*Candide*
Wells, H. G.	England	science fiction	*The Time Machine, The War of the Worlds*
Wharton, Edith	U.S.	novel	*Ethan Frome, The Age of Innocence*
Whitman, Walt	U.S.	poetry	*Leaves of Grass,* "O Captain! My Captain!"
Whittier, John Greenleaf	U.S.	poetry	"The Barefoot Boy," "Barbara Frietchie"
Wilde, Oscar	England	poetry, drama, novel	"The Ballad of Reading Jail," *Lady Windermere's Fan, The Importance of Being Earnest, The Picture of Dorian Gray*
Williams, Tennessee	U.S.	drama	*The Glass Menagerie, A Streetcar Named Desire, Cat on a Hot Tin Roof*
Williams, William Carlos	U.S.	poetry	*Paterson,* "The Red Wheelbarrow"
Wolfe, Thomas	U.S.	novel	*Look Homeward, Angel; You Can't Go Home Again*
Woolf, Virginia	England	novel	*Mrs. Dalloway, A Room of One's Own, To the Lighthouse*
Wordsworth, William	England	poetry	"I Wandered Lonely as a Cloud," "The Daffodils," "Ode: Intimations of Immortality"
Yeats, William Butler	Ireland	poetry	"Sailing to Byzantium," "Easter 1916"
Zola, Émile	France	novel	*Germinal, Nana*

Arguably, the most important of the "dead white men" of cultural literacy is William Shakespeare. The MAT may test your knowledge of his work by checking to see whether you know which plays fit into each of three categories: tragedy, comedy, and history.

Shakespearean Tragedies	Shakespearean Comedies and Romances	Shakespearean Histories
Titus Andronicus	*The Comedy of Errors*	*Henry VI, parts 1, 2, and 3*
Romeo and Juliet	*The Taming of the Shrew*	*Richard III*
Julius Caesar	*Two Gentlemen of Verona*	*King John*
Hamlet	*Love's Labour's Lost*	*Richard II*
Othello	*A Midsummer Night's Dream*	*Henry IV, parts 1 and 2*
King Lear	*The Merchant of Venice*	*Henry V*
Macbeth	*Much Ado About Nothing*	*Henry VIII*
Antony and Cleopatra	*As You Like It*	
Coriolanus	*Twelfth Night*	
Timon of Athens	*Troilus and Cressida*	
	All's Well That Ends Well	
	Measure for Measure	
	Pericles, Prince of Tyre	
	Cymbeline	
	The Winter's Tale	
	The Tempest	

LITERARY TERMS

The occasional literary term may appear in an analogy on the MAT. It is in your best interest to know the difference between onomatopoeia and alliteration, or between assonance and consonance. Here are a few literary terms you may encounter.

allegory: a narrative that carries a moral meaning along with the surface meaning. EXAMPLE: John Bunyan's *Pilgrim's Progress*

alliteration: the repetition of initial consonant sounds. EXAMPLE: "As I pondered, <u>w</u>eak and <u>w</u>eary . . ." (Poe)

anagram: a word resulting from the transposition of letters. EXAMPLE: *now/won.*

anapest: a metrical foot made of two unstressed syllables followed by one stressed syllable. EXAMPLE: "The As<u>syr</u>ian came <u>down</u> like a <u>wolf</u> on the <u>fold</u>." (Byron)

anaphora: the repetition of a word or phrase. EXAMPLE: "We cannot dedicate, we cannot consecrate, we cannot hallow this ground . . ." (Lincoln)

antagonist: the major villain or character opposed to the protagonist

assonance: the repetition of vowel sounds. EXAMPLE: "I met a traveler from an antique land . . ." (Shelley)

caesura: a natural pause in a line of verse. EXAMPLE: "I see before me now/a traveling army halting . . ." (Whitman)

consonance: the repetition of consonant sounds that do not fall at the beginning of words. EXAMPLE: "The curfew tolls the knell of parting day . . ." (Gray)

dactyl: a metrical foot made of one stressed syllable followed by two unstressed syllables. EXAMPLE: "Here where the reaper was at work of late . . ." (Arnold)

denouement: the events following the climax of a plot

elegy: a poem lamenting a death. EXAMPLE: John Milton's "Lycidas"

epic: a long narrative poem with a heroic theme. EXAMPLE: Homer's *Iliad*

epistolary novel: a narrative in letter form. EXAMPLE: Samuel Richardson's *Pamela*

flashback: a scene that reveals events that happened earlier

foreshadowing: a plot device that hints at events to come later

haiku: a Japanese poem of seventeen syllables

iamb: a metrical foot made of an unstressed syllable followed by a stressed syllable. EXAMPLE: "I wandered lonely as a cloud . . ." (Wordsworth)

idyll: a short lyrical poem celebrating the pastoral life. EXAMPLE: William Wordsworth's "The Solitary Reaper"

onomatopoeia: a word whose sound expresses its meaning. EXAMPLES: ding, arf, pow

picaresque novel: a narrative featuring the adventures of a rogue. EXAMPLE: Tobias Smollett's *The Adventures of Roderick Random*

protagonist: the hero of a novel or drama. EXAMPLE: Hamlet is the protagonist of the play by that name; Claudius may be seen as the antagonist.

soliloquy: a monologue in which a character expresses his or her thoughts. EXAMPLE: Hamlet's "To be or not to be"

stream of consciousness: depiction of the random feelings and thoughts of a character in prose. EXAMPLE: Virginia Woolf's *To the Lighthouse*

trochee: a metrical foot made of a stressed syllable followed by an unstressed syllable. EXAMPLE: "Where the bee sucks, there suck I" (Shakespeare)

LITERARY MOVEMENTS

You will occasionally be called upon to match a writer to his or her particular group or movement, or to compare and contrast movements based on their principles. This chart reviews some literary movements with their chief tenets and proponents.

Movement	Key Belief	Some Key Followers
aestheticism	art for art's sake	Poe, Emerson, Keats
beat generation	alienation from society; spiritual quest	Kerouac, Ginsberg
Bloomsbury group	appreciation of art as the rational goal of human action	Woolf, Forster
expressionism	expression of the inner self	Strindberg, Brecht
imagism	precision of description	Pound, Williams, Lawrence
impressionism	accurate rendition of personal experience	Mann, Proust, Wilde
naturalism	objective view of reality	Zola, Hardy, Dreiser
neoclassicism	form over content	Racine, Swift, Dryden
realism	portrayal of life as it is	Ibsen, Flaubert, James
romanticism	belief in the goodness of people in their natural state	Wordsworth, Keats, Shelley, Byron, Cooper, Thoreau, Longfellow
surrealism	search for a reality beyond surface reality	Cummings, Thomas
symbolism	meaning conveyed through patterns of images	Baudelaire, Rimbaud, Verlaine
transcendentalism	divine nature of the individual; natural phenomena reveal spiritual truth	Emerson, Thoreau

MYTHOLOGY

Although there is a surprising amount of mythology incorporated into analogies on the MAT, it is probably not worth your reviewing all of Bulfinch's *Mythology*. The questions asked usually require matching Greek and Roman names or matching a god to his or her specialty. The following table provides some of those correlations.

Greek Name	Roman Name	Specialty
Aphrodite	Venus	love, beauty
Ares	Mars	war
Artemis	Diana	hunting, moon
Athena	Minerva	wisdom
Demeter	Ceres	harvest
Dionysus	Bacchus	wine
Eos	Aurora	dawn
Eros	Cupid	love
Fates		Clotho—weaver Lachesis—measurer Atropos—cutter
Graces	Charites	Aglaia—splendor Thalia—flowering Euphrosyne—rejoicing
Hades	Pluto	underworld
Hephestus	Vulcan	fire
Hera	Juno	queen of the gods
Hermes	Mercury	messenger, commerce
Hestia	Vesta	hearth
Kronos, Cronus	Saturn	agriculture
Muses		Calliope—epic poetry Clio—history Erato—love poetry Euterpe—music Melpomene—tragedy Polyhymnia—sacred poetry Terpsichore—song, dance Thalia—comedy Urania—astronomy
Nike	Victoria	victory
Pan	Faunus	sheep
Persephone	Proserpina	underworld, spring
Poseidon	Neptune	sea
Selene	Luna	moon
Zeus	Jupiter	king of the gods

THE BIBLE

The Bible is a key component of our cultural literacy, and on the MAT you can expect to find one or two questions relating to your acquaintance with significant characters, events, or books. As usual, the most perfunctory knowledge is all you need. Review these lists to get an idea about what may be tested. The Old Testament books listed are from the Hebrew Bible. Order and content vary from religion to religion.

BOOKS OF THE OLD TESTAMENT

Torah/Pentateuch: Genesis, Exodus, Leviticus, Numbers, Deuteronomy

First Prophets: Joshua, Judges, Samuel, Kings

Latter Prophets: Isaiah, Jeremiah, Ezekiel

Minor Prophets: Hosea, Joel, Amos, Obadiah, Jonah, Micah, Nahum, Habbakkuk, Zephaniah, Haggai, Zechariah, Malachi

Hagiographa: Psalms, Proverbs, Job, Song of Songs, Ruth, Lamentations, Ecclesiastes, Esther, Daniel, Ezra, Chronicles

BOOKS OF THE NEW TESTAMENT

Gospels: Matthew, Mark, Luke, John

History: Acts

Letters/Epistles of Paul: Romans, 1 Corinthians, 2 Corinthians, Galatians, Ephesians, Phillipians, Colossians, 1 Thessalonians, 2 Thessalonians, 1 Timothy, 2 Timothy, Titus, Philemon

General Letters/Epistles: Hebrews, James, 1 Peter, 2 Peter, 1 John, 2 John, 3 John, Jude

Prophecy: Revelation (of St. John the Divine)

A FEW IMPORTANT BIBLICAL CHARACTERS (AND SOME KEY PLACES)

Abraham and Isaac: Isaac was Abraham's son by Sarah. Jehovah commanded Abraham to sacrifice Isaac, his son by Sarah. Abraham obeyed, but an angel stopped him, and Jehovah reaffirmed the covenant between God and man.

Adam and Eve: the first man and woman, who ate the forbidden fruit in the Garden of Eden.

Apostles: the twelve disciples of Jesus—Andrew, Bartholomew, James the Lesser, James the Greater, John, Judas Iscariot (see below), Jude, Matthew, Peter, Philip, Simon, and Thomas.

Barabbas: a robber and rebel released by Pilate from prison in lieu of Jesus.

Cain and Abel: brothers; sons of Adam and Eve. Cain killed Abel in a fit of jealousy when Jehovah preferred the sacrifice of Abel's lambs to Cain's sacrifice of the fruits of the earth.

Daniel: a hero who was cast into a den of lions for praying to his own God and irking the Babylonians; he was saved and went on to interpret the handwriting on the wall.

David: the shepherd-king who challenged Goliath, loved Bathsheba, and wept over the rebellion of his son Absalom.

Esther: the queen who revealed Haman's plot to kill all the Jews; the feast of Purim celebrates her deed.

Golgotha: a hill near Jerusalem where Jesus was crucified.

Good Samaritan: a philanthropist who assisted a man robbed and assaulted by thieves.

Herod: the king of Judea at the time of the birth of Jesus; ordered the Massacre of the Innocents.

Jacob and Esau: brothers; sons of Isaac. Jacob bought the birthright of his brother for a "mess of pottage" and thus illegitimately obtained the blessing of his blind father. His 12 sons founded the 12 tribes of Israel.

Jezebel: the wife of Ahab; she tried unsuccessfully to revert her people to the worship of false gods (specifically, Baal).

Job: a devoted servant of the Lord who was tested by Satan and remained faithful.

John the Baptist: a prophet; considered a precursor of Jesus.

Jonah: a prophet; when Jehovah asked him to preach to the evil people of Nineveh, he refused, his ship was wracked by storms, and he was cast into the sea, to be swallowed by a big fish (whale). He repented and was saved.

Judas Iscariot: the disciple who betrayed Jesus to the Romans for 30 pieces of silver.

Lazarus: the brother of Martha and Mary; Jesus raised him from the dead.

Moses: the leader of the Israelites out of Egypt to the Promised Land; the recipient of the Ten Commandments.

Noah: a virtuous man spared with his family and the earth's animals from the great flood that covered the earth.

Pilate: the Roman governor of Judea during the time of Jesus; he handed Jesus over to the mob, literally "washing his hands" of the problem.

Prodigal Son: a profligate sinner who repented and was forgiven by his father.

Rachel and Leah: sisters; wives of Jacob. Jacob fell in love with Rachel and worked for her father for seven years but then was tricked into marrying her sister Leah and forced to work another seven years to win the woman he wanted.

Samson and Delilah: he was a judge known for his strength; she was the woman with whom he was obsessed. She cut his hair, removing the source of his strength.

Sodom and Gomorrah: cities that were struck down because of their wickedness. Lot and his family were spared from Sodom, but as they left, his wife looked back and was turned into a pillar of salt.

Solomon: a son of David and Bathsheba; the wisest of the kings of Israel.

Tower of Babel: erected by the descendents of Noah, who wanted it to reach to heaven. Jehovah, angered by their audacity, forced them to speak in diverse languages and scattered them to the ends of the earth.

Quickly, think of the names of five famous artists. The odds are pretty good that those will be the ones whose names appear on the MAT. Once again, the test-makers tend to focus not on the little known but rather on the familiar. Some of those artists are named here, along with a few of their masterworks.

Artist	Country of Origin	Major Medium	Representative Works
Adams, Ansel	U.S.	photography	*Aspens, New Mexico*
Arp, Jean	France	painting, sculpture	*Configuration, Oriforme*
Bacon, Francis	Ireland/ England	painting	*Crucifixion*
Bartholdi, Frédéric	France	sculpture	*Liberty Enlightening the World*
Benton, Thomas Hart	U.S.	painting	*July Hay, Indiana Murals*
Bosch, Hieronymus	Flanders	painting	*Garden of Earthly Delights*
Botticelli, Sandro	Florence	painting	*Birth of Venus, Nativity*
Bourke-White, Margaret	U.S.	photography	*You Have Seen Their Faces*
Bracque, Georges	France	painting, sculpture	*Nude, The Table*
Brady, Mathew	U.S.	photography	*The Dead of Antietam*
Brancusi, Constantin	Romania	sculpture	*Sleeping Muse*
Breuer, Marcel	Hungary/ U.S.	architecture	Whitney Museum
Breughel, Peter the Elder	Flanders	painting	*The Harvesters, Peasant Wedding*
Calder, Alexander	U.S.	sculpture	*Red Mobile, Man*
Caravaggio, Michelangelo	Italy	painting	*Supper at Emmaus, Flagellation of Christ*

Artist	Country of Origin	Major Medium	Representative Works
Cartier-Bresson, Henri	France	photography	*Sunday on the Banks of the Marne*
Cassatt, Mary	U.S.	painting	*Mother and Child, Young Mother Sewing*
Cézanne, Paul	France	painting	*The Kitchen Table, Vase of Flowers*
Chagall, Marc	Russia/ France	painting	*I and the Village, Birthday*
Constable, John	England	painting	*The Hay Wain, Weymouth Bay*
Courbet, Gustave	France	painting	*Stonebreakers, Bathers*
Cranach, Lucas	Germany	painting, engraving	*Adam and Eve, Stag Hunt*
Dalí, Salvador	Spain	painting	*Persistence of Memory*
Daumier, Honoré	France	lithography, painting	*Third-Class Carriage*
David, Jacques-Louis	France	painting	*Death of Socrates, The Death of Marat*
da Vinci, Leonardo	Italy	painting, sculpture, architecture	*The Last Supper, Mona Lisa*
Degas, Edgar	France	painting, sculpture	*The Rehearsal, The Dance Lesson*
Delacroix, Eugène	France	painting	*Women of Algiers, Liberty Leading the People*
Donatello	Florence	sculpture	*St. Mark, Magdalen*
Doré, Gustave	France	engraving	illustrations for *Paradise Lost, The Divine Comedy*
Dubuffet, Jean	France	painting, sculpture	*Smiling Face, Woman Grinding Coffee*
Duchamp, Marcel	France	painting	*Nude Descending a Staircase*
Dufy, Raoul	France	painting	*The Palm, Window at Nice*
Dürer, Albrecht	Germany	painting, engraving	*A Young Hare, Melancholia*

Artist	Country of Origin	Major Medium	Representative Works
Eakins, Thomas	U.S.	painting	*The Chess Players, The Thinker: Portrait of Louis N. Kenton*
Eisenstaedt, Alfred	Prussia/ U.S.	photography	*VJ Day, Premiere at La Scala, Milan*
Ernst, Max	Germany	painting	*Two Children Are Threatened by a Nightingale*
Escher, M. C.	Holland	lithography, engraving	*Drawing Hands, Ascending and Descending*
Evans, Walker	U.S.	photography	*Let Us Now Praise Famous Men*
Fragonard, Jean-Honoré	France	painting	*Love's Vow, The Music Lesson*
Fuller, Buckminster	U.S.	architecture	*Geodesic Dome*
Gainsborough, Thomas	England	painting	*The Blue Boy, Portrait of Mrs. Graham*
Gaudí, Antoni	Spain	architecture	Casa Milà, Sagrada Família
Gauguin, Paul	France	painting	*Night Café at Arles, By the Sea*
Gehry, Frank	Canada/ U.S.	architecture	Guggenheim Museum Bilbao
Giacometti, Alberto	Switzerland	sculpture, painting	*Man Walking, The Artist's Mother*
Giotto (di Bondone)	Florence	painting	*St. John the Baptist, Madonna in Glory*
Goya, Francisco	Spain	painting	*The Nude Maja, The Third of May 1808*
El Greco	Greece/ Spain	painting	*Baptism, View of Toledo*
Hals, Frans	Belgium/ Holland	painting	*The Merry Drinker, The Smoker*
Hogarth, William	England	painting, engraving	*The Rake's Progress*
Holbein, Hans the Younger	Germany	painting	*Madonna of the Burgomaster Meyer*
Homer, Winslow	U.S.	painting	*Breaking Storm, Mending the Nets*

Artist	Country of Origin	Major Medium	Representative Works
Hopper, Edward	U.S.	painting	*Early Sunday Morning, Nighthawks*
Johns, Jasper	U.S.	painting	*White Flag, Flag*
Johnson, Philip	U.S.	architecture	Glass House
Jones, Inigo	England	architecture	The Queen's House
Kahlo, Frida	Mexico	painting	*Self-Portrait with Monkey*
Kandinsky, Wassily	Russia	painting	*The Blue Rider, On White II*
Klee, Paul	Switzerland	painting	*Twittering Machine, Ad Parnassum*
Klimt, Gustav	Austria	painting	*Judith I, Salome*
Lange, Dorothea	U.S.	photography	*Migrant Mother, Executive Order 9066*
Le Corbusier	Switzerland/ France	architecture	Villa Savoye, Chapelle Notre Dame du Haut
Magritte, René	Belgium	painting	*La Condition Humaine, Le Fils de l'Homme*
Manet, Édouard	France	painting	*Le Déjeuner sur l'Herbe*
Matisse, Henri	France	painting, collage	*The Blue Nude, Jazz*
Michelangelo (Buonarotti)	Florence	painting, sculpture	ceiling of the Sistine Chapel, *David, Pietà*
Miës van der Rohe, Ludwig	Germany/ U.S.	architecture	Seagram Building
Millet, Jean-François	France	painting	*The Gleaners, The Sower*
Miró, Joan	Spain	painting	*Dog Barking at the Moon, The Birth of the World*
Modigliani, Amedeo	Italy	painting, sculpture	*Madam Pompadour, Head of a Woman*
Mondrian, Piet	Holland	painting	*Composition with Red, Blue, and Yellow*
Monet, Claude	France	painting	*Wheatstacks, Water Lilies*
Moore, Henry	England	sculpture	*Reclining Figure, Recumbent Figure*

Artist	Country of Origin	Major Medium	Representative Works
Munch, Edvard	Norway	painting	*The Scream, Vampire*
Nevelson, Louise	U.S.	sculpture	*Sky Garden, Night Tree*
O'Keeffe, Georgia	U.S.	painting	*Cow's Skull; Red, White, and Blue*
Oldenberg, Claes	Sweden/U.S.	sculptor	*Lipstick, Soft Pay-Telephone*
Olmsted, Frederick Law	U.S.	landscape architecture	Central Park, Audubon Park, Prospect Park
Orozco, José Clemente	Mexico	painting	*Mankind's Struggle*
Parks, Gordon	U.S.	photography	*Ella Watson*
Picasso, Pablo	Spain	painting	*Blue Boy, Les Demoiselles d'Avignon, Guernica*
Pissarro, Camille	France	painting	*Bather in the Woods, The Beet Harvest*
Pollock, Jackson	U.S.	painting	*Silver over Black, Autumn Rhythm*
Raphael	Italy	painting	*School of Athens, Madonna and Child*
Rauschenberg, Robert	U.S.	painting, collage	*Bed, Satellite*
Ray, Man	U.S.	photography, painting	*Lips, Tears*
Rembrandt (Harmenszoon van Rijn)	Holland	painting	*Aristotle Contemplating the Bust of Homer, The Jewish Bride*
Renoir, Pierre-Auguste	France	painting	*Le Bal au Moulin de la Gallette, The Luncheon of the Boating Party*
Rivera, Diego	Mexico	painting	*Fruits of Labor, Allegory of California*
Rockwell, Norman	U.S.	painting	*The Four Freedoms*
Rodin, Auguste	France	sculpture	*The Thinker, The Burghers of Calais*
Rothko, Mark	U.S.	painting	*No. 13 (White, Red, on Yellow)*
Rouault, Georges	France	painting	*Clown, Three Judges*
Rousseau, Henri	France	painting	*The Snake Charmer, Sleeping Gypsy*

Artist	Country of Origin	Major Medium	Representative Works
Rubens, Peter Paul	Flanders	painting	*Three Graces, Venus and Adonis*
Saarinen, Eero	Finland/ U.S.	architecture	Gateway Arch, TWA terminal
Sargent, John Singer	Italy/U.S.	painting	*Portrait of Madame X*
Schiele, Egon	Austria	painting	*Seated Woman, Embrace*
Seurat, Georges	France	painting	*A Sunday Afternoon on the Island of La Grande Jatte*
Steichen, Edward	U.S.	photography	*The Flatiron*
Sullivan, Louis	U.S.	architecture	Wainwright Building
Tintoretto	Venice	painting	*Miracle of the Loaves and Fishes*
Titian	Venice	painting	*Salomé with the Head of John the Baptist*
Toulouse-Lautrec, Henri de	France	painting	*At the Moulin Rouge, The Toilette*
Turner, J. M. W.	England	painting	*Sun Rising through Vapor; Rain, Steam, and Speed*
Utrillo, Maurice	France	painting	*Lapin Agile, Les Trois Moulin de Montmartre*
van Eyck, Jan	Flanders	painting	*The Arnolfini Portrait*
van Gogh, Vincent	Holland	painting	*Sunflowers, The Starry Night*
Vasarely, Victor	Hungary/ France	painting	*Vega-Kontosh, Zebegen*
Vermeer, Johannes	Holland	painting	*The Milkmaid, Woman with a Pearl Necklace*
Warhol, Andy	U.S.	painting, silkscreen	*Campbell's Soup 1, Marilyn Monroe*
Watteau, Jean-Antoine	France	painting	*Pierrot, Love in the French Theatre*
Weston, Edward	U.S.	photography	*Pepper No. 30, Nude*
Whistler, James Abbott McNeil	U.S.	painting	*Arrangement in Gray and Black, No. 1*
White, Stanford	U.S.	architecture	Washington Square Arch

Artist	Country of Origin	Major Medium	Representative Works
Wood, Grant	U.S.	painting	*American Gothic*
Wren, Christopher	England	architecture	St. Paul's Cathedral
Wright, Frank Lloyd	U.S.	architecture	Fallingwater, Guggenheim Museum
Wyeth, Andrew	U.S.	painting	*Christina's World*

ARTISTIC TERMS

Even if you don't know a thing about art, be sure that you can define these terms, which may appear within an analogy on the MAT.

annunciation: the depiction of the announcement by the angel Gabriel to Mary of Jesus' impending birth

aquatint: an etching technique that deals with tone rather than line

assumption: the depiction of Mary rising to heaven at the end of her earthly life

chiaroscuro: the use of contrasts between light and dark

collage: a low-relief artwork made by pasting scraps of paper, fabric, or other materials onto a surface

complementary colors: colors that lie opposite each other on the color wheel; for example, red and green, yellow and violet, orange and blue

engraving: a printing process in which lines to be printed are cut into a metal plate

etching: a printing process in which a metal plate is coated with acid-resistant resin or wax and is then drawn on with a sharp tool

fresco: the art of painting on plaster

gesso: a plaster and glue mixture used as a surface for painting

hatching: a shading technique using thin parallel lines

impasto: paint applied thickly to create texture

intaglio: a printing process created from an incised design; engraving and etching are intaglio processes

lithography: a printing process involving drawing on a surface with an oily substance that resists ink

mezzotint: a printing process in which a metal plate is roughened, and a design is scraped into the rough surface

monochrome: an artwork that uses tints and shades of a single color

opaque: not allowing light to pass through

pietà: a depiction of Mary mourning her dead son

primary colors: blue, red, yellow; the colors from which other colors are made

relief: printing process in which an image is drawn on a plate and then the plate is cut around the image so that the recessed areas print white; the opposite of intaglio

secondary colors: violet, orange, green; the colors made from equal parts of two primary colors

shade: a change in the value of a color made by adding black

stippling: a shading technique using dots

tesserae: small pieces of glass, tile, or other materials that make up a mosaic

tint: a change in the value of a color made by adding white

triptych: a painting made of three panels

warp: fibers stretched vertically on a loom

weft: fibers woven from side to side on a loom

ARTISTIC MOVEMENTS

Matching people with their cliques is one way the MAT test-makers test your cultural literacy. The following table presents just a few popular artistic movements and their proponents.

Movement	Characteristic	Some Key Followers
abstract expressionism	nonrepresentational, bold colors and brushstrokes, spattered or poured paint	Pollock, Rothko
art nouveau	curving lines, asymmetry, natural forms	Klimt
baroque	grandeur, richness, dramatic themes	Rembrandt, Caravaggio, Vermeer
Bauhaus	geometric, spare, functional	Miës van der Rohe
cubism	basic geometric forms, objects viewed from all sides at once	Picasso, Braque

Movement	Characteristic	Some Key Followers
Dada	absurdism, randomness, incongruity	Arp, Duchamp, Ray
expressionism	expression of emotion through color and brushstroke	Gauguin, Munch
fauvism	vivid colors, simple forms	Matisse, Rouault
impressionism	variations in light and color, short brushstrokes	Manet, Monet, Renoir, Cézanne
op art	optical illusions that suggest movement	Vasarely
photographic realism	exact replication of forms from real life	Wyeth
pointillism	tiny dots of color rather than brushstrokes	Pissarro, Seurat
pop art	subject matter and style derived from popular culture	Oldenberg, Warhol
primitivism	bold, childlike strokes; bright colors	Klee
realism	accurate, detailed representation of everyday life	Courbet, Millet
rococo	airiness, delicacy, elaborate curves, natural forms	Fragonard, Watteau
romanticism	emotion and picturesque expression	Millet, Delacroix
surrealism	emphasis on the subconscious and dreams, fantastic imagery	Dalí, Magritte
symbolism	expression of ideas indirectly through symbols	Gauguin, Munch

Appendix D
Music

In general, the MAT requires you to know very little about the modern world. Most of the composers that appear on the test have been dead for centuries. As with literature and art, you should be familiar with a few key people from the canon of cultural literacy, which is to say European and American composers and musicians whom you might study in Music Appreciation 101. The following table names some of them, along with a few of their major works.

Musician	Country of Origin	Forte	Representative Works
Armstrong, Louis	U.S.	jazz trumpet	
Bach, Johann Sebastian	Germany	composition	*Brandenburg* concertos, *St. Matthew Passion, Well-Tempered Clavier*
Bartók, Béla	Hungary	composition	*Duke Bluebeard's Castle,* Improvisation on Hungarian Peasant Songs
Basie, William "Count"	U.S.	jazz piano, composition	"One O'Clock Jump"
Beethoven, Ludwig van	Germany	composition	*Moonlight* and *Kreutzer* sonatas; "Für Elise"; *Eroica, Pastoral, Choral* symphonies
Berlin, Irving	U.S.	composition	"God Bless America," "White Christmas"
Bernstein, Leonard	U.S.	composition	*Fancy Free, West Side Story*
Bizet, George	France	composition	*Carmen*
Brahms, Johannes	Germany	composition	*A German Requiem,* Hungarian Dances

Musician	Country of Origin	Forte	Representative Works
Britten, Benjamin	England	composition	*Bully Budd, Peter Grimes*
Callas, Maria	Greece/U.S.	soprano	
Caruso, Enrico	Italy	tenor	
Casals, Pablo	Spain	cello	
Chopin, Frédéric	Poland/France	piano, composition	*Études, Les Sylphides*
Copland, Aaron	U.S.	composition	*Rodeo, Appalachian Spring*
Davis, Miles	U.S.	jazz trumpet	
Debussy, Claude	France	composition	*Prelude to the Afternoon of a Faun, Noctures: La Mer,* "Clair de Lune"
Delibes, Léo	France	composition	*Coppélia*
Dvořàk, Antonin	Bohemia	composition	Slavonic Dances, *New World* symphony
Elgar, Edward	England	composition	"Pomp and Circumstance," *The Dream of Gerontius*
Ellington, Edward Kennedy "Duke"	U.S.	composition, bandleader	"Take the 'A' Train," "Satin Doll"
Foster, Stephen	U.S.	composition	"My Old Kentucky Home," "Camptown Races"
Gershwin, George	U.S.	composition	*Rhapsody in Blue, Porgy and Bess*
Goodman, Benny	U.S.	jazz clarinet, bandleader	
Gould, Glenn	U.S.	piano	
Grieg, Edvard	Norway	composition	*Peer Gynt, Holberg Suite*
Handel, George Frideric	Germany/England	composition	*Messiah, Water Music*
Haydn, Franz Joseph	Austria	composition	*Surprise* and *Clock* symphonies
Heifetz, Jascha	Russia/U.S.	violin	
Holiday, Billie	U.S.	jazz/blues vocalist	
Horowitz, Vladimir	Russia/U.S.	piano	

Musician	Country of Origin	Forte	Representative Works
Humperdinck, Engelbert	Germany	composition	*Hansel and Gretel*
Ives, Charles	U.S.	composition	*Three Places in New England*
Joplin, Scott	U.S.	jazz piano, composition	"The Entertainer," "Maple Leaf Rag"
Lehár, Franz	Hungary	composition	*The Merry Widow*
Lind, Jenny	Sweden	soprano	
Liszt, Franz	Hungary	composition	Hungarian Rhapsodies, "Liebestraum"
Mahler, Gustav	Austria	composition	*Resurrection* symphony, *The Song of the Earth*
Massenet, Jules	France	composition	*Manon*
Mendelssohn, Felix	Germany	composition	*A Midsummer Night's Dream, The Hebrides*
Menotti, Gian-Carlo	Italy/U.S.	composition	*Amahl and the Night Visitors*
Menuhin, Yehudi	U.S.	violin	
Miller, Glenn	U.S.	bandleader	"In the Mood," "Moonlight Serenade"
Monk, Thelonius	U.S.	jazz piano	
Mozart, Wolfgang Amadeus	Austria	composition	*The Magic Flute, The Marriage of Figaro, Don Giovanni, Jupiter* symphony
Mussorgsky, Modest	Russia	composition	*Pictures at an Exhibition, Night on Bald Mountain, Boris Godunov*
Offenbach, Jacques	Germany/France	composition	*Orpheus in the Underworld, The Tales of Hoffman*
Orff, Carl	Germany	composition	*Carmina Burana*
Paderewski, Ignacy	Poland	piano	
Paganini, Niccoló	Italy	violin	
Parker, Charlie "Bird"	U.S.	jazz saxophone	
Pavarotti, Luciano	Italy	tenor	

Musician	Country of Origin	Forte	Representative Works
Porter, Cole	U.S.	composition	*Kiss Me Kate, High Society*
Prokofiev, Sergei	Russia	composition	*Romeo and Juliet, Cinderella*
Puccini, Giacomo	Italy	composition	*Manon Lescaut, La Bohème, Tosca, Madame Butterfly, Turandot*
Purcell, Henry	England	composition	*Dido and Aeneas, The Fairy Queen*
Rachmaninov, Sergei	Russia	piano, composition	*The Bells,* Rhapsody on a Theme of Paganini
Ravel, Maurice	France	composition	*Daphnis et Chloé, Boléro*
Rimsky-Korsakov, Nicolai	Russia	composition	*Sheherazade*
Rossini, Gioacchino	Italy	composition	*The Barber of Seville, William Tell*
Saint-Saëns, Camille	France	composition	*Carnival of the Animals, Danse Macabre*
Schoenberg, Arnold	Austria/U.S.	composition	*Gurre-Lieder, Pierrot Lunaire*
Schubert, Franz	Austria	composition	*Lieder,* "Unfinished" symphony, "Ave Maria"
Segovia, Andrés	Spain	guitar	
Shostakovich, Dmitri	Russia	composition	*Leningrad* symphony
Sibelius, Jean	Finland	composition	*Valse Triste, Finlandia*
Smith, Bessie	U.S.	jazz vocalist	
Sousa, John Philip	U.S.	composition	"The Stars and Stripes Forever"
Strauss, Johann	Austria	composition	*Die Fledermaus,* "The Blue Danube"
Strauss, Richard	Germany	composition	*Thus Spake Zarathustra, Der Rosenkavalier, Ariadne auf Naxos*
Stravinsky, Igor	Russia/U.S.	composition	*The Firebird, The Rite of Spring*
Sullivan, Arthur	England	composition	*The Pirates of Penzance, The Mikado*

Musician	Country of Origin	Forte	Representative Works
Sutherland, Joan	Australia	soprano	
Tchaikovsky, Peter Ilich	Russia	composition	*Romeo and Juliet, Swan Lake, The Sleeping Beauty, The Nutcracker*
Toscanini, Arturo	Italy	conductor	
Verdi, Giuseppe	Italy	composition	*La Traviata, Il Trovatore, Aida*
Vivaldi, Antonio	Italy	composition	*The Four Seasons*
Wagner, Richard	Germany	composition	*Der Ring des Nibelungen, Tristan und Isolde, Parsifal*

MUSICAL TERMS

Most musical terms derive from Italian. Since Italian is a Latinate language, a little knowledge of Latin roots can help you decipher unfamiliar musical terms. Here are a few terms you might want to remember.

accelerando: speed up tempo

adagio: slow tempo

allegretto: not quite so fast as allegro tempo

allegro: fairly fast tempo

andante: leisurely tempo

coda: music added to the end of a piece

crescendo: gradually louder

diminuendo: gradually softer

forte: loud

fortissimo: very loud

grave: solemn and slow

intermezzo: music played between scenes of an opera

largo: slow and stately

legato: flowing without a break

ostinato: repeated over and over

pianissimo: very soft

piano: soft

pizzicato: with plucked strings (rather than bowed)

prestissimo: very fast

presto: fast

sforzando: with force or emphasis

sostenuto: smoothly

staccato: quick and detached

tutti: for full orchestra

vivace: lively

MUSICAL MOVEMENTS

Matching composers to their times and movements is part of cultural literacy. You should know the difference between classical and baroque or between romanticism and realism.

Movement	Characteristic	Some Key Followers
baroque	harmonic complexity	Bach, Vivaldi
classical	clarity, balance, and order; form rather than emotion	Beethoven, Haydn, Mozart
expressionism	atonality or harmonic distortion for expressive effect	Schoenberg
impressionism	focus on moods and emotions	Debussy, Ravel
nationalism	incorporation of national elements such as folk songs or folk dances	Grieg, Bartók, Dvořàk, Copland
neoclassical	return to classic forms	Stravinsky
realism	portrayal of life as it is (in opera form)	Bizet, Puccini
romanticism	emotion and picturesque expression over form and structure	Mendelssohn, Liszt, Chopin

INSTRUMENTS OF THE ORCHESTRA

When it comes to knowing about instruments, the most you will be asked for on the MAT is to differentiate between woodwinds and brass or between percussion and strings. The following table names the four families of instruments and then lists those members you would be likely to find in a modern orchestra.

Strings	Woodwinds	Brass	Percussion
violin	flute	French horn	timpani
viola	piccolo	trumpet	drum
cello	oboe	trombone	glockenspiel
double bass	cor anglais	tuba	xylophone
	clarinet		triangle
	bassoon		cymbals
			tambourine
			bells

Appendix E
Natural Sciences

CHEMISTRY

Chemistry is represented on the MAT in the form of elements and their atomic numbers; elements and their abbreviations; and elements that share qualities or are somehow related. The best way to review these details is to skim the periodic table. On the table, elements are listed with their atomic numbers and abbreviations (symbols). They are grouped according to qualities they share.

A FEW KEY ATOMIC SYMBOLS

Ag = Silver

Ar = Argon

As = Arsenic

Au = Gold

C = Carbon

Ca = Calcium

Cl = Chlorine

Co = Cobalt

Cr = Chromium

Cu = Copper

Fe = Iron

H = Hydrogen

He = Helium

I = Iodine

K = Potassium

Mg = Magnesium

Mn = Manganese

N = Nitrogen

Na = Sodium

Ne = Neon

Ni = Nickel

O = Oxygen

P = Phosphorus

Pb = Lead

Ra = Radium

S = Sulfur

Sn = Tin

U = Uranium

Zn = Zinc

PERIODIC TABLE OF THE ELEMENTS

1 H																	2 He
3 Li	4 Be											5 B	6 C	7 N	8 O	9 F	10 Ne
11 Na	12 Mg											13 Al	14 Si	15 P	16 S	17 Cl	18 Ar
19 K	20 Ca	21 Sc	22 Ti	23 V	24 Cr	25 Mn	26 Fe	27 Co	28 Ni	29 Cu	30 Zn	31 Ga	32 Ge	33 As	34 Se	35 Br	36 Kr
37 Rb	38 Sr	39 Y	40 Z	41 Nb	42 Mo	43 Tc	44 Ru	45 Rh	46 Pd	47 Ag	48 Cd	49 In	50 Sn	51 Sb	52 Te	53 I	54 Xe
55 Cs	56 Ba	see below	72 Hf	73 Ta	74 W	75 Re	76 Os	77 Ir	78 Pt	79 Au	80 Hg	81 Tl	82 Pb	83 Bi	84 Po	85 At	86 Rn
87 Fr	88 Ra	see below	104 Rf	105 Db	106 Sg	107 Bh	108 Hs	109 Mt	110 Ds	111 Rg	112 Uub	113 Uut	114 Uuq	115 Uup	116 Uuh	117 Uus	118 Uuo

■ = Alkali Metals   ■ = Halogens   ■ = Noble Gases

RARE EARTH ELEMENTS

Lanthanides	57 La	58 Ce	59 Pr	60 Nd	61 Pm	62 Sm	63 Eu	64 Gd	65 Tb	66 Dy	67 Ho	68 Er	69 Tm	70 Yb	71 Lu
Actinides	89 Ac	90 Th	91 Pa	92 U	93 Np	94 Pu	95 Am	96 Cm	97 Bk	98 Cf	99 Es	100 Fm	101 Md	102 No	103 Lr

SOME COMMON ALLOYS

brass = copper + zinc

bronze = copper + zinc + tin

pewter = tin + lead

steel = iron + carbon

stainless steel = iron + nickel + chromium

TAXONOMY

For years, scientists classified life forms using a system called *Linnaean taxonomy*. This is a hierarchy composed of the levels shown below in **boldface**, along with subcategories. Today two additional kingdoms are usually included within taxonomic classification: Monera, which contains bacteria and blue-green algae, and Fungi, which includes yeast, mold, mushrooms, and their relatives.

On the following chart, three living things are presented as examples: humans, red oak trees, and amoebas. Their classifications, from kingdom to species, are listed below each.

	Human	**Red oak tree**	**Amoeba**
Kingdom	Animalia	Plantae	Protista
Phylum	Chordata	Tracheophyta	Plasmodroma
Class	Mammalia	Angiospermae	Sarcodina
Order	Primata	Fagales	Amoebida
Family	Homindae	Fagaceae	Amoebidae
Genus	*Homo*	*Quercus*	Amoeba
Species	*Homo sapiens*	*Quercus rubra*	*Amoeba proteus*

PARTS OF THE BODY

You do not need arcane medical knowledge to succeed on the Miller Analogies Test, but be aware that occasional bones and body parts appear within MAT analogies. This list defines a few you should know.

adrenal glands: glands near the kidneys that regulate salt and water balance and the use of carbohydrates and proteins; producers of the "fight or flight" hormone, adrenaline

aorta: largest artery; carries oxygenated blood from the heart to the body

atrium: one of two upper chambers of the heart

cerebellum: the brain part in back of skull responsible for coordination of muscle movements

cerebrum: the upper and largest part of the brain; responsible for voluntary motor and mental functions

clavicle: the collarbone

cortex: the area of the brain covering the cerebrum; responsible for most higher-level thinking

femur: the thighbone; the longest bone in the body

fibula: the outer calf bone extending from knee to ankle

hippocampus: the area of the brain below the cortex responsible for learning and memory

humerus: the upper arm bone

hypothalamus gland: the gland located in the brain that controls sleep, appetite, and body temperature

ilium: part of the hip bone

mandible: the jawbone

medulla oblongata: the part of the brain stem that regulates breathing and blood flow

metatarsals: foot bones located between ankle and toes

patella: the knee bone (kneecap)

phalanx: a finger or toe bone

pituitary gland: the master gland located at the base of the brain; regulates growth and reproduction

radius: the outer bone of the forearm

scapula: the shoulder blade

septum: a wall of tissue separating the two sides of the heart

sternum: the breastbone

thyroid gland: the gland at the base of the neck that controls metabolic rate

tibia: the inner bone of the lower leg; shin bone

ulna: the inner bone of the forearm

vena cava: a large vein that carries blood to the heart

ventricle: one of two lower chambers in the heart

ROCKS

Knowing the differences among the three types of rocks and being able to identify some examples of each will help you solve the occasional analogy that refers to rocks.

Type of Rock	Qualities	Examples
sedimentary	created when pieces of rock are cemented together through weathering processes	sandstone, limestone, shale
igneous	formed by the cooling of magma inside or on the surface of the earth	basalt, granite, obsidian
metamorphic	formed under great pressure and high temperature within the upper crust or mantle of the earth	slate, quartzite, marble

GEOLOGIC TIME

Geologic time is another area of geology that is easy to test in an analogy. You should know the comparative size of the different units, from eon to age, and you should be able to match each era to the rise of life forms on earth. The following diagram, although incomplete, should help.

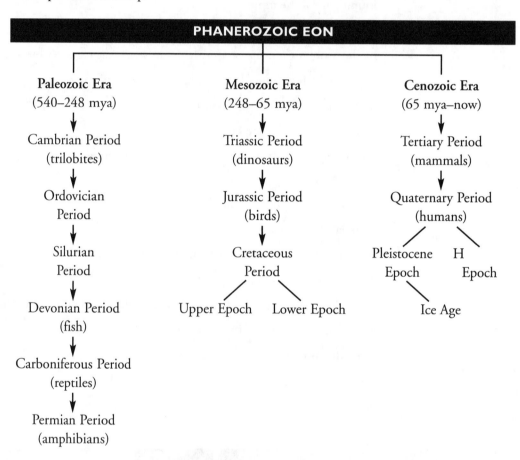

ANIMAL GROUPS AND HOMES

MAT test-makers love unusual vocabulary words, and, for that reason, they enjoy stumping you with odd nouns that name groups of animals or animal homes. This chart shows some of the less obscure groups and homes, any of which you might find on the MAT.

Animal	Young	Group	Home
ants		army, colony	nest, anthill, formicary
badgers	cubs, kits	sett, cete, colony	sett
bears	cubs	sloth, sleuth	den

Animal	Young	Group	Home
bees		hive, swarm	apiary, hive
birds	chicks, hatchlings	flock, congregation	nest, aviary
cattle	calves	herd, drove	barn, byre
chickens	chicks, pullets	flock, brood, peep	coop, run
crows	chicks	murder, hover	nest, rookery
deer	fawns	herd, parcel	
doves	squabs, chicks	bevy, flight, dule	dovecote
eagles	eaglets, fledglings	convocation, flock	aerie
elephants	calves	herd	
fish	fry, fingerlings	school, shoal	aquarium, fishpond
foxes	kits, cubs	skulk, leash	earth, den, lair
frogs	tadpoles, polliwogs	army, colony	froggery, ranarium
geese	goslings	gaggle, skein, wedge	nest
goats	kids	herd, drove, tribe, trip	pen
horses	foals, colts, fillies	herd, troop, team	stable, stall, paddock, mews
larks	chicks	ascension, exaltation	nest
leopards	cubs	leap	
lions	cubs	pride, troop	den, lair
monkeys	infants	tribe, troop	nest
owls	owlets	parliament	nest, owlery
oxen	calves	drove, herd, team, yoke	barn, byre
pigs	piglets	herd, litter, , farrow	sty, pen
quail	chicks	bevy, covey	nest
rabbits	nestlings, kittens, bunnies	colony, leash, trace, nest	warren, burrow, hutch
seals	pups, calves, cubs	harem, herd, pod	rookery
sheep	lambs, cossets	flock, drove	fold, pen, cote
swans	cygnets	bevy, wedge	nest, swannery
whales	calves	pod, herd, gam, school	

SCIENTISTS

As you know from skimming the literature, art, and music appendixes, you are often expected to match important people to their contributions to the culture. The same is true in the sciences. The following table lists some key scientists and their most important discoveries or inventions.

Scientist	Country of Origin	Field	Discovery, Invention, and/or Specialty
Agassiz, Louis	Switzerland/ U.S.	paleontology	ichthyology, ice age, glacier theory
Ampère, André	France	physics	electrodynamics, wave theory of heat
Ängström, Anders	Sweden	physics	measurement of spectral wavelength
Audubon, John James	Haiti/U.S.	biology	ornithology
Becquerel, Henri	France	physics	radioactivity in uranium
Bell, Alexander Graham	Scotland/U.S.	engineering	telephone
Benz, Karl	Germany	engineering	motor car
Bohr, Niels	Denmark	physics	quantum mechanics
Brahe, Tycho	Denmark	astronomy	astronomical measurements
Celsius, Anders	Sweden	physics	temperature scale
Colt, Samuel	U.S.	engineering	revolver
Copernicus, Nicolaus	Poland	astronomy	heliocentric model of solar system
Crick, Francis	England	genetics	model of DNA
Curie, Marie	Poland/ France	chemistry	radioactivity in polonium and radium
Daimler, Gottlieb	Germany	engineering	automobile, motorcycle
Darwin, Charles	England	biology	natural selection, theory of evolution
Diesel, Rudolf	France	engineering	diesel engine
Eastman, George	U.S.	engineering	photographic film
Edison, Thomas	U.S.	engineering	phonograph, electric light bulb

Scientist	Country of Origin	Field	Discovery, Invention, and/or Specialty
Einstein, Albert	Germany/ U.S.	physics	relativity, photoelectric effect (quantum mechanics)
Fahrenheit, Daniel	Germany/ Holland	physics	alcohol and mercury thermometers
Faraday, Michael	England	chemistry	dynamo, second law of electrolysis
Fermi, Enrico	Italy/U.S.	physics	nuclear chain reaction
Fleming, Alexander	Scotland	medicine	penicillin
Fokker, Anthony	Holland/U.S.	engineering	aircraft
Fossey, Dian	U.S.	biology	gorilla behavior
Fulton, Robert	U.S.	engineering	steamboat
Galen	Greece	medicine	anatomy, medical experimentation
Galileo Galilei	Italy	astronomy	motion of bodies, telescope, craters on moon, sunspots
Gatling, Richard	U.S.	engineering	machine gun
Goddard, Robert	U.S.	engineering	liquid-fueled rocket
Goodall, Jane	England	biology	tool use in chimpanzees
Halley, Edmond	England	astronomy	Halley's comet, diving bell
Harvey, William	England	medicine	blood circulation
Hertz, Heinrich	Germany	physics	electromagnetic waves, oscillator
Hippocrates	Greece	medicine	observation, diagnosis, prognosis
Howe, Elias	U.S.	engineering	lock-stitch sewing machine
Jenner, Edward	England	medicine	smallpox vaccine
Joule, James	England	physics	heat produced by motion, Joule's law
Kepler, Johannes	Austria	astronomy	Kepler's laws of planetary motion
Lamarck, Jean	France	biology	evolutionary theory of acquired characteristics, classification of invertebrates
Land, Edwin	U.S.	engineering	instant photography

Scientist	Country of Origin	Field	Discovery, Invention, and/or Specialty
Lavoisier, Antoine	France	chemistry	chemical nomenclature, conservation of mass
Linnaeus, Carolus	Sweden	biology	botany, taxonomy
Lister, Joseph	England	medicine	antiseptic surgery
Marconi, Guglielmo	Italy	engineering	radio
Maxwell, James	Scotland	physics	electromagnetic field, kinetic theory of gases
McCormick, Cyrus	U.S.	engineering	mechanical reaper
Mendel, Gregor	Austria	genetics	dominant and recessive traits
Mitchell, Maria	U.S.	astronomy	comet C/1847 T1
Morse, Samuel	U.S.	engineering	telegraph, Morse code
Newcomen, Thomas	England	engineering	steam engine
Newton, Isaac	England	physics	Newton's laws of motion, calculus, light spectrum, experimental methodology
Nobel, Alfred	Sweden	engineering	dynamite
Oersted, Hans	Denmark	physics	electromagnetism
Otis, Elisha	U.S.	engineering	elevator brake, passenger elevator
Pasteur, Louis	France	chemistry	pasteurization, germ theory
Pauling, Linus	U.S.	chemistry	protein structure, chemical bonding
Planck, Max	Germany	physics	quantum theory
Priestly, Joseph	England	chemistry	oxygen
Ptolemy	Rome	astronomy	geocentric theory of the solar system, star catalog
Röntgen, Wilhelm	Germany	physics	X-rays
Rutherford, Ernest	New Zealand/ England	physics	alpha, beta, gamma rays; half-life; neutrons
Sabin, Albert	Poland/U.S.	microbiology	oral polio vaccine
Salk, Jonas	U.S.	microbiology	polio vaccine

Scientist	Country of Origin	Field	Discovery, Invention, and/or Specialty
Sikorsky, Igor	Ukraine/U.S.	engineering	helicopter
Singer, Isaac	U.S.	engineering	mass production of sewing machines
Szilard, Leo	Hungary/U.S.	physics	nuclear reaction, atomic bomb
Teller, Edward	Hungary/U.S.	physics	hydrogen bomb
Tesla, Nikola	Serbia/U.S.	engineering	system of generating alternating current
Tull, Jethro	England	engineering	seed drill
van Leeuwenhoek, Anton	Holland	microbiology	microscope
Volta, Alessandro	Italy	physics	battery
Watson, James	U.S.	biochemistry	model of DNA
Watt, James	Scotland	engineering	steam engine
Whitney, Eli	U.S.	engineering	cotton gin
Wright, Wilbur and Orville	U.S.	engineering	airplane

Appendix F
Social Sciences

Because it makes for interesting analogies, the fact that some countries' names have changed over the years is a routine part of the Miller Analogies Test. Although you are not likely to see more than one question related to country name changes, that one question does equal 1 percent of the test. For that reason, it's in your best interest to skim the name changes shown below.

CURRENT AND FORMER NAMES OF COUNTRIES

Current Name	Former Name
Armenia, Azerbaijan, Belarus, Estonia, Georgia, Kazakhstan, Kyrgyzstan, Latvia, Lithuania, Russia, Tajikstan, Turkmenistan, Ukraine, Uzbekistan	Soviet Union (U.S.S.R.)
Bahrain	Dilmun
Bangladesh	East Pakistan
Belize	British Honduras
Benin	Dahomey
Bosnia and Herzegovina, Croatia, Macedonia, Serbia and Montenegro, Slovenia	Yugoslavia
Botswana	Bechuanaland
Burkina Faso	Upper Volta
Cambodia	Kampuchea, Khmer Republic
Canary Islands	Fortunate Islands
Central African Republic	Ubangi-Shari
Cook Islands	Harvey Islands
Czech Republic and Slovakia	Czechoslovakia, Bohemia and Moravia

Current Name	Former Name
Democratic Republic of the Congo	Zaire
Djibouti	French Somaliland
Egypt and Syria	United Arab Republic
Equatorial Guinea	Spanish Guinea
Ethiopia	Abyssinia
French Guiana	Inini
Germany and Poland	Prussia
Ghana	Gold Coast and Togoland
Guadaloupe and Martinique	French West Indies
Guyana	British Guiana
Indonesia	Dutch East Indies
Iran	Persia
Iraq	Babylonia
Israel and West Bank	Galilee and Judea, Palestine
Jordan	Transjordan
Korea	Choson
Kyrgyzstan	Turkestan
Lesotho	Basutoland
Liberia	Grain Coast
Madagascar	Malagasy Republic
Malawi	Nyasaland
Malaysia	Malay States
Mali	French Sudan
Mozambique	Portuguese East Africa
Myanmar	Burma (we still call it "Burma")
Namibia	South-West Africa
Oman	Muscat and Oman
Romania and Moldova	Moldavia and Transylvania

Current Name	Former Name
Somalia	Benadir
Sri Lanka	Ceylon
Suriname	Dutch Guiana
Switzerland	Helvetia
Taiwan	Formosa
Tanzania	Tanganyika and Zanzibar
Thailand	Siam
Tonga	Friendly Islands
Tuvalu	Ellice Islands
United Arab Emirates	Trucial Coast
Vanuatu	New Hebrides
Vietnam, Cambodia, Laos	Indochina
Zambia	Northern Rhodesia
Zimbabwe	Southern Rhodesia

CURRENT AND FORMER NAMES OF CITIES

Following are cities whose names have changed.

Current Name	Former Name
Brno	Brünn
Gdansk	Danzig
Istanbul	Constantinople
Kinshasa	Leopoldville
Mumbai	Bombay
St. Petersburg	Leningrad
Volgograd	Stalingrad, Tsaritsyn

EXPLORERS

If you were raised in the United States and think back over your elementary education, you will realize that an enormous part of your social studies instruction was dedicated to the exploration of the New World. The following table names some of the major explorers, their countries of origin, and what they discovered.

Explorer	Country of Origin	Discovery or Region Traveled
Amundsen, Roald	Norway	South Pole
Balboa, Vasco Núñez de	Spain	Isthmus of Panama, eastern shore of Pacific Ocean
Cabot, John	Italy/England	Grand Banks, parts of eastern Canada
Cabrillo, Juan Rodriguez	Portugal/Spain	Guatemala, California coast
Cadillac, Antoine de	France	Detroit, Great Lakes area
Cartier, Jacques	France	St. Lawrence River, Montreal
Champlain, Samuel de	France	Quebec, Lake Champlain
Columbus, Christopher	Italy/Spain	West Indies, coastal Central and South America
Cook, James	England	New Zealand, Australia, Hawaii, Pacific Northwest
Coronado, Francisco Vasquez de	Spain	northwestern Mexico, southwestern U.S.
Cortes, Hernando de	Spain	Veracruz, Aztec Empire (Mexico)
da Gama, Vasco	Portugal	around Africa to India
de Soto, Hernando	Spain	southern U.S., Mississippi River
de Vaca, Alberto Núñez Cabeza	Spain	northwest Mexico, Paraguay
Dias, Bartolomeu	Portugal	Cape of Good Hope
Drake, Francis	England	second voyage around the world
Erikson, Leif	Norway	Newfoundland
Frobisher, Martin	England	Baffin Bay, north Atlantic
Hudson, Henry	England	Hudson River

Explorer	Country of Origin	Discovery or Region Traveled
Joliet, Louis	France	upper Mississippi, Illinois, Wisconsin
La Salle, Sieur de	France	Mississippi River to Gulf of Mexico, Louisiana
Magellan, Ferdinand	Portugal	first voyage around the world, Strait of Magellan
Marquette, Jacques	France	upper Mississippi, Illinois, Wisconsin
Peary, Robert	U.S.	North Pole
Pizarro, Francisco	Spain	Lima, Incan Empire (Peru)
Ponce de Leon, Juan	Spain	Florida, Puerto Rico
Raleigh, Walter	England	Roanoke Island
Vancouver, George	England	Puget Sound, Vancouver Island, Mount Rainier
Verrazzano, Giovanni da	Portugal	east coast of North America
Vespucci, Amerigo	Italy/Spain	coastal Venezuela and Brazil

KINGS AND QUEENS

It's not a crucial part of American cultural literacy, but a little familiarity with British and French kings and queens will help you with the occasional question on the subject on the MAT.

DYNASTIES OF ENGLAND

Some Saxon Kings (before 1066)	Normans/Blois (1066–1154)	House of Plantagenet (1154–1399)
Ethelred I	William I ("the Conqueror")	Matilda
Alfred ("the Great")	William II	Henry II
Edgar ("the Peaceful")	Henry I	Richard I ("Lionheart")
Edward II ("the Martyr")	Stephen	
Ethelred II ("the Unready")		
Edward III ("the Confessor")		

House of Lancaster (1399–1461)	House of York (1461–1485)	House of Tudor (1485–1603)
Henry IV	Edward IV	Henry VII
Henry V	Edward V	Henry VIII
Henry VI	Richard III	Edward VI
		Lady Jane Grey
		Mary I
		Elizabeth I

House of Stuart (1603–1714)	House of Hanover (1714–1901)	House of Saxe-Coburg-Gotha/House of Windsor (1901–present)
James I	George I	Victoria
Charles I	George II	Edward VII
(Oliver and Richard Cromwell)	George III	George V
	George IV	Edward VIII
Charles II	William IV	George VI
James II	Victoria	Elizabeth II
Mary II		
William III		
Anne		

DYNASTIES OF FRANCE

Carolingians ➔ Capetians ➔ Valois ➔ Bourbons ➔ First Republic ➔ First Empire ➔ Second Republic ➔ Second Empire

DYNASTIES OF RUSSIA

Some Czars of the House of Rurik (864–1613)	Some Czars of the House of Romanov (1613–1917)
Ivan IV ("the Terrible")	Peter I ("the Great")
Boris Godunov	Catherine II ("the Great")
	Alexander I
	Nicholas I
	Alexander II
	Alexander III
	Nicholas II

GEOGRAPHICAL TERMS

Knowing the following geographical terms and how they relate to one another may help you with an analogy or two.

archipelago: a chain of islands

arroyo: a deep, dry, water-carved gully

atoll: a coral reef that encircles a lagoon

bay: an inlet of a sea or lake, larger than a *cove*, smaller than a *gulf*

butte: a flat-topped, steep hill, smaller than a *mesa*

caldera: a bowl-shaped hollow in the peak of a volcano

canyon: a narrow, deep valley with steep sides

cape: a pointed piece of land that sticks out to form a bay

cove: a small inlet of a sea or lake

delta: a fan-shaped alluvial deposit at the mouth of a river

desert: an area of scant precipitation and little vegetation

estuary: the salty end of a river where it meets the sea

fjord: a glacier-produced coastal valley filled with seawater

gulf: a large inlet of a sea

hurricane: a high-wind tropical storm in the Atlantic (called *typhoon* in the Pacific)

isthmus: a narrow strip of land with water on both sides

lagoon: a shallow body of water between a reef and shore or within an atoll

loess: a fine deposit of silt, sand, and clay

marsh: a fresh or salt wetland found near ponds, lakes, rivers, or seacoasts

mesa: a flat-topped, steep hill

moraine: an accumulation of glacial deposits

oasis: a fertile area in a desert

peninsula: a mass of land surrounded by water on three sides

plain: flat, usually grassy land

plateau: a large, elevated, flat area of land

prairie: a wide, flat grassland

range: a chain of mountains

sound: a long inlet usually separating the shoreline from an island

strait: a narrow body of water that connects two larger bodies of water

swamp: a freshwater wetland

tundra: a cold, treeless region

watershed: an area drained by a river and its tributaries

GEOGRAPHICAL EXTREMES

You don't need to memorize the name of every mountain range in Asia, but it would be wise to know some of these highest/longest/largest facts about world geography.

Highest peak (world): Mount Everest, Nepal

Highest peak (U.S.): Mount McKinley, Alaska

Largest lake (salt): Caspian Sea, Central Asia

Largest lake (fresh): Lake Superior, United States

Deepest lake (world): Lake Baikal, Russia

Largest ocean: Pacific Ocean

Longest river (world): Nile River, Africa

Longest river (U.S.): Mississippi-Missouri River

Largest river system (with tributaries): Amazon River, South America

Highest waterfall: Angel Falls, Venezuela

PHILOSOPHICAL MOVEMENTS

Just as you should be able to identify well-known authors and their works, so should you be able to identify famous philosophers and the movements with which they are affiliated.

Branch of Philosophy	Key Focus
aesthetics	study of art
epistemology	study of knowledge
ethics	study of behavior
metaphysics	study of existence
politics	study of society

Movement	Key Belief	Some Key Followers
anarchy	government is evil	Zeno, William Godwin, Emma Goldman
causality	all actions have specific reactions	Aristotle
collectivism	humans are just a subset of society	Karl Marx, Friedrich Engels
communism	collective ownership of the means of production	Karl Marx, Friedrich Engels
conservatism	individualism and minimal intervention of government	Edmund Burke, Thomas Hobbes, Leo Strauss
Cynicism	people are evil	Antisthenes, Diogenes, Zeno
democracy	rule by the people	EXAMPLE: ancient Athens
determinism	all events are predetermined	Jonathan Edwards, John Calvin
egalitarianism	all people are created equal	Jean-Jacques Rousseau
empiricism	experience is the only source of knowledge	John Locke, David Hume
Epicureanism	value is measured by happiness	Epicurus
existentialism	it is up to the individual to determine his or her own meaning and purpose	Søren Kierkegaard, Jean-Paul Sartre, Martin Heidigger
fatalism	all events are determined by fate	Oswald Spengler, Arthur Schopenhauer
free will	humans have the power to make choices	most Christian sects, with the exception of Calvinists
hedonism	value is measured by pleasure	Aristippus, Epicurus
idealism	value is measured by mind over matter	Immanuel Kant, Georg Wilhelm Friedrich Hegel
individualism	society is essentially the sum of its individuals	Thomas Jefferson, Thomas Paine
liberalism	defense of individual freedom is the purpose of government	John Locke, Jean-Jacques Rousseau, John Stuart Mill, John Dewey
libertarianism	the right to freedom from restraint trumps all other rights	Herbert Marcuse

Movement	Key Belief	Some Key Followers
materialism	value is measured by material goods and matter	Democritus, Thomas Hobbes
meritocracy	government by those with the greatest ability	EXAMPLE: Mongol Empire
nihilism	value and meaning do not exist	Mikhail Bakunin
oligarchy	government by the few	EXAMPLE: South Africa under apartheid
plutocracy	government by the wealthy	EXAMPLE: ancient Venice
positivism	scientific observation is the only source of knowledge	Auguste Comte, Rudolf Carnap
pragmatism	value is measured by whatever works	William James, John Dewey
rationalism	deductive reasoning is the only source of knowledge	René Descartes, Benedict Spinoza
realism	reality consists of universals that humans see imperfectly as specifics	Plato, Pierre Abélard
relativism	all points of view are equally valid; truth is subjective	Friedrich Nietzsche, Ludwig Wittgenstein
skepticism	all knowledge should be viewed with doubt	Pyrrho, Arcesilaus
Stoicism	only through indifference to pleasure and pain can people know how to act	Zeno, Epictetus
theocracy	government by the religious order	EXAMPLE: Islamic Republic of Iran
transcendentalism	spiritual feelings and the process of thought are the only source of knowledge	Ralph Waldo Emerson, Henry David Thoreau, Bronson Alcott
utilitarianism	value is measured by usefulness for the group	Jeremy Bentham, John Stuart Mill

PSYCHOLOGICAL MOVEMENTS

Developments in psychology are almost as likely to turn up on the MAT as are movements in philosophy. Here are some major nineteenth- and twentieth-century movements and facts you should know about each.

Movement	Characteristic	Some Key Followers
behaviorism	investigation of external behavior rather than internal processes	John B. Watson, B. F. Skinner, Ivan Pavlov
cognitive psychology	scientific study of mental processes	Jerome Bruner, Alfred Binet, Jean Piaget
functionalism	focus on the purpose of behavior	William James, John Dewey, Edward Thorndike
gestalt	notion that perception is structured according to natural patterns; focus on the whole rather than separate elements	Max Wertheimer, Wolfgang Köhler
humanistic psychology	qualitative research on subjective experience	Fritz Perls, Carl Rodgers
phenomenology	study of experience as it reveals itself to the consciousness	Edmund Husserl
psychoanalysis	study of the subconscious and sense of self through free association	Sigmund Freud, Anna Freud, Carl Jung, Erich Fromm, Alfred Adler, Erik Erikson
structuralism	search for the components of the consciousness through controlled introspection	Wilhelm Wundt

Appendix G
Mathematics and Numbers

The MAT does not test your computational ability; it tests your cultural literacy. In the area of mathematics, as in science, art, music, and literature, you are expected to know a few famous people and their contributions to the culture. Names of mathematicians you may see on the test appear on the table below. As usual, most MAT references will be to people who lived 100 or more years ago.

Mathematician	Country of Origin	Discovery, Invention, and/or Specialty
Archimedes	Greece	pi, the lever, the screw, formulas for the areas of various plane and solid figures
Babbage, Charles	England	difference engine, analytical engine (early calculator/computer)
Descartes, René	France	analytic geometry, x and y axes
Diophantus	Greece	algebra
Euclid	Greece	euclidean geometry
Euler, Leonhard	Switzerland	differential calculus, algebraic notation
Fermat, Pierre de	France	number theory, probability theory
Fibonacci	Italy	Fibonacci's sequence: 1, 1, 2, 3, 5, 8, 13, 21 . . . (each number is the sum of the two previous numbers)
Hipparchus	Rhodes	trigonometry, mapping
Leibniz, Gottfried	Germany	calculus, symbolic logic
Lovelace, Augusta Ada King	England	analytical engine
Möbius, Auguste Ferdinand	Switzerland	topology, Möbius strip
Napier, John	Scotland	logarithms, calculating machine

Mathematician	Country of Origin	Discovery, Invention, and/or Specialty
Newton, Isaac	England	gravitation, integral and differential calculus
Pascal, Blaise	France	calculating machine, barometer, Pascal's triangle
Pythagoras	Greece	irrational numbers, Pythagorean theorem, prime vs. composite numbers
Russell, Bertrand	England	formal logic

MEASUREMENTS

If you recall that mathematical analogies can be thought of as ratios, you will understand why MAT test-makers like to use measurements in some analogies. You should know simple conversions and recognize the meaning of Latin prefixes in metric measurements.

ENGLISH MEASUREMENTS

Length/Distance
1 inch = 1/12 foot = 1/36 yard
1 foot = 1/3 yard
1 mile = 1,760 yards = 5,280 feet
1 fathom = 6 feet
1 square mile = 640 acres

Capacity
1 cup = 1/2 pint = 1/4 quart = 8 fluid ounces
1 pint = 1/2 quart = 1/8 gallon = 16 fluid ounces
1 quart = 1/4 gallon = 32 fluid ounces
1 teaspoon = 1/3 tablespoon = 1/6 fluid ounce

Mass
1 ounce = 1/16 pound
1 pound = 1/2000 ton

METRIC MEASUREMENTS

Length/Distance
1 millimeter = 1/1000 meter
1 centimeter = 1/100 meter
1 decimeter = 1/10 meter
1 dekameter = 10 meters

1 hectometer = 100 meters
1 kilometer = 1,000 meters

Capacity
1 milliliter = 1/1000 liter
1 centiliter = 1/100 liter
1 deciliter = 1/10 liter
1 dekaliter = 10 liters
1 hectoliter = 100 liters
1 kiloliter = 1,000 liters

Mass
1 milligram = 1/1,000 gram
1 centigram = 1/100 gram
1 decigram = 1/10 gram
1 dekagram = 10 grams
1 hectogram = 100 grams
1 kilogram = 1,000 grams
Other units of mass include grain, troy ounce, avoirdupois pound, and apothecaries' dram.

CURRENCIES

You might wonder why it's important to know that Algeria uses dinars while Aruba uses guilders. The answer is that it's easy to create an analogy comparing the currencies of two countries. Here is a quick list that does not include every country in the world but does include many. Notice that the original currency of the country's occupiers has much to do with the current monetary system of that country. In other words, knowing a little history and a little geography can help you infer a lot about world currencies.

Country	Currency	Country	Currency
Afghanistan	100 puls = 1 afghani	Bermuda	100 cents = 1 dollar
Algeria	100 centimes = 1 dinar	Bolivia	100 centavos = 1 boliviano
Antigua	100 cents = 1 dollar	Botswana	100 thebe = 1 pula
Argentina	100 centavos = 1 peso	Brazil	100 centavos = 1 real
Armenia	100 luma = 1 dram	Bulgaria	100 stotinki = 1 lev
Aruba	100 cents = 1 guilder	Cambodia	100 sen = 1 riel
Australia	100 cents = 1 dollar	Canada	100 cents = 1 dollar
Bahamas	100 cents = 1 dollar	Chad	100 centimes = 1 franc
Bahrain	100 fils = 1 dinar	Chile	100 centavos = 1 peso
Bangladesh	100 paisa = 1 taka	China	100 fen = 1 yuan
Barbados	100 cents = 1 dollar	Colombia	100 centavos = 1 peso
Belize	100 cents = 1 dollar	Congo	100 centimes = 1 franc
Benin	100 centimes = 1 franc	Costa Rica	100 centimos = 1 colon

Country	Currency	Country	Currency
Cuba	100 centavos = 1 peso	Nigeria	100 kobo = 1 naira
Czech Republic	100 haleru = 1 koruna	Oman	1,000 baiza = 1 rial
Denmark	100 ore = 1 krone	Pakistan	100 paisa = 1 rupee
Djibouti	100 centimes = 1 franc	Panama	100 centesimos = 1 balboa
Ecuador	100 centavos = 1 sucre	Paraguay	100 centimos = 1 guarani
Egypt	100 piastres = 1 pound	Peru	100 centimos = 1 sol
El Salvador	100 centavos = 1 colon	Philippines	100 centavos = 1 peso
Ethiopia	100 cents = 1 birr	Poland	100 groszy = 1 zloty
European Union	100 cents = 1 euro	Puerto Rico	100 cents = 1 dollar
Gabon	100 centimes = 1 franc	Qatar	100 dirhams = 1 riyal
Gambia	100 bututs = 1 dalasi	Romania	100 bani = 1 leu
Ghana	100 pesewas = 1 cedi	Russia	100 kopecks = 1 ruble
Guatemala	100 centavos = 1 quetzal	Saudi Arabia	100 halala = 1 riyal
Haiti	100 centimes = 1 gourde	Senegal	100 centimes = 1 franc
Honduras	100 centavos = 1 lempira	Somalia	100 centesimi = 1 shilling
Hong Kong	100 cents = 1 dollar	South Africa	100 cents = 1 rand
Hungary	100 filler = 1 forint	Sri Lanka	100 cents = 1 rupee
Iceland	100 aurar = 1 krona	Sweden	100 ören = 1 krona
India	100 paise = 1 rupee	Switzerland	100 centimes = 1 franc
Indonesia	100 sen = 1 rupiah	Syria	100 piastres = 1 pound
Iran	100 dinars = 1 rial	Taiwan	100 cents = 1 dollar
Iraq	1,000 fils = 1 dinar	Tanzania	100 cents = 1 shilling
Israel	100 agorot = 1 shekel	Thailand	100 satang = 1 baht
Japan	100 sen = 1 yen	Tunisia	1,000 millimes = 1 dinar
Jordan	1,000 fils = 1 dinar	Turkey	100 kurus = 1 lira
Kenya	100 cents = 1 shilling	Uganda	100 cents = 1 shilling
Korea (North and South)	100 chon = 1 won	Ukraine	100 kopiykas = 1 hryvnia
		United Arab Emirates	100 fils = 1 dirham
Kuwait	1,000 fils = 1 dinar	United Kingdom	100 pence = 1 pound
Latvia	100 santimi = 1 lats	Uruguay	100 centésimos = 1 peso
Lebanon	100 piastres = 1 pound	Venezuela	100 centimos = 1 bolivar
Libya	1,000 dirhams = 1 dinar	Yemen	100 fils = 1 rial
Malaysia	100 sen = 1 ringgit	Zambia	100 ngwee = 1 kwacha
Mali	100 centimes = 1 franc	Zimbabwe	100 cents = 1 dollar
Mexico	100 centavos = 1 peso		
Mongolia	100 mongo = 1 tugrik		
Morocco	100 centimes = 1 dirham		
Myanmar	100 pyas = 1 kyat		
Namibia	100 cents = 1 dollar		
Nepal	100 paisa = 1 rupee		
New Zealand	100 cents = 1 dollar		
Nicaragua	100 centavos = 1 cordoba		
Niger	100 centimes = 1 franc		

ROMAN NUMERALS

If you haven't used Roman numerals since grade school, it's time to brush up on them. Because it is easy to create an analogy that deals with equivalence of Roman (I, II, III, IV . . .) and Arabic (1, 2, 3, 4 . . .) numerals, it is very likely that you may find such an analogy on the MAT.

I = 1

V = 5

X = 10

L = 50

C = 100

D = 500

M = 1,000

Placing a small number after a larger number denotes addition.

VI = 6   XV = 15   CL = 150   MD = 1,500

Placing a small number before a larger number denotes subtraction.

IV = 4   IX = 9   XL = 40   CD = 400

Try deciphering these examples.

XXIV   CCLI   MCMV   DLXII

Did you get these answers?

24   251   1,905   562

About the Author

Kathy A. Zahler has more than 25 years' experience writing and editing textbooks and testing materials for students from kindergarten through college. In addition, she is the author of several bestselling quiz books and parenting books for adults. She has a degree in English and history from Cornell University and a degree in education from the University of Chicago. She now lives in Freeville, New York, where she owns and operates Midline Editorial.